Part One

In the Shadow of the Giant:

1945–1963

One

Brave New World

Canadians were jubilant on 7 May 1945, as the morning headlines screamed the long-awaited news: victory in Europe had been achieved; the barbaric National Socialist regime of Adolf Hitler in Germany had been crushed by the Allies. While rioters in Halifax looted stores and vandalized buildings, most of the spontaneous celebrations across the country were more controlled. After almost six years of war, a semblance of normal life could resume.[1] The war with Japan continued but, shorn of its German ally, Japan seemed a marginal threat. When that country was forced to surrender in August after nuclear bombs were dropped over Hiroshima and Nagasaki, most Canadians were so relieved that the war was over, they never gave much thought to the justice or even the necessity of killing 130,000 civilians to stop a war. Canada had lost 42,024 members of its armed forces in the war. While this may have seemed a small

VE celebrations in Toronto, May 8, 1945. NAC RD-885.

Personnel from HMCS Prince Robert visit former prisoners of war at Sham Sui Po Barracks, Hong Kong, September 1945. NAC PA-116808.

number in a war that is estimated to have caused the deaths of 50 million people, Canadians believed they had made many sacrifices in the cause of defeating the expansion-minded, brutal dictators of the Axis. More than 1 million Canadians from a population of only 11 million had worn the uniforms of the Army, Navy, or Air Force.

Canada had changed during the war and most Canadians were determined that it not revert to what it had been when war was declared in September 1939. At that time Canada had endured a ten-year depression. Though economists claimed that the country was gradually pulling itself out of the long period of recession followed by stagnation, almost ten percent of non-farm households required social assistance. Such assistance was available only to those with no means whatsoever to support a subsistence living. That figure might well have been higher if, in the two years that preceded the war, the rebuilding of European armed might had not increased the demand for Canadian metals and other exports. Recruiters had little difficulty finding young Canadians willing to risk their lives to fight in the second major European war in twenty-five years. "Now we eat!" yelled the hopeful recruits waiting in line in Montreal. Indeed, wartime planning achieved what politicians and businessmen completely failed to produce during the Great Depression: work at decent wages for most of those who wanted it and an end to relief lines and streets filled with starving, shivering children.

Canadians had fought the authorities in the 1930s for better treatment of the unemployed and for job creation programs. Large demonstrations by the unemployed against meagre social allowances and regimentation by municipal councils often forced municipal leaders to relent. The "On-to-Ottawa" Trek, in 1935, which sought to bring single, unemployed men working in remote work camps to the nation's capital, gathered momentum as it moved from Vancouver eastward, only to be violently dispersed by the RCMP in Regina on orders from the multi-millionaire Prime Minister R.B. Bennett. The small but disciplined Communist Party of Canada (CPC) played a key role in the relief strikes and a variety of union organization drives and strikes during the Depression decade. Somewhat more popular with the electorate was the Co-operative Commonwealth Federation (CCF), the result of a 1932 merger of a variety of socialist, labour, and farmer political organizations behind a democratic socialist program embodied in the Regina Manifesto of 1933. Neither the CPC nor the CCF, however, rivalled the traditional bourgeois parties, the Liberals and the Conservatives, in elections during the 1930s. While many Canadians were prepared to resist oppressive treatment, they were not easily won over by parties that promised to replace the existing capitalist economic system with a new socialist order. In Alberta, a majority of electors were swayed by the charismatic radio preacher William Aberhart, who promised to preserve the economic order, and to eliminate poverty by giving adults social dividends of twenty five dollars per month to be created by monetary inflation. This Social Credit movement, or the "funny money" party as its opponents called it, governed Alberta without interruption from 1935 to 1971. Insulated by the Canadian constitution's reservation of currency and credit matters for the federal government, it never had to demonstrate how its monetary policies could work.

For many historians, however, the post-war strength of the CCF in Saskatchewan, Social Credit in Alberta and Maurice Duplessis' Union Nationale in Quebec, demonstrate the durability of political parties formed under Depression circumstances but tell us little about Canadians' lives in the post-war period. The image of Canada that emerges in the standard post-war textbook, *Canada Since 1945: Power, Politics, and Provincialism* is one of a country where almost-uniform prosperity is brought into being by a dynamic capitalism and a wise federal bureaucracy presided over by a progressive Liberal party with intelligent leaders. These forces also contributed to a larger Canadian role in the world. This chapter begins a questioning of such claims. Post-war Canada was indeed prosperous, but the prosperity was unequally shared by Canadians. The federal government did implement some progressive programs, but their fear of offending investors by initiating a full welfare state and the steep taxation needed to finance it restricted their willingness to move too far in the direction of social reform. As for Canada's increased involvement in the world, it often seemed to be an echo of the Americans whose economic power within Canada, already great before the war, increased during the period of economic expansion. We look now, in outline form, at Canada and Canadians in the period from the end of the war to the end of the Diefenbaker government in 1963. This was the period of the greatest economic expansion witnessed to that time (1945–57), followed by a fairly minor recession that nonetheless raised doubts about whether the Keynesian policies prescribed after the war had fundamentally reformed capitalism or simply delayed the inevitable return of boom–bust economic cycles. The gradual restoration of prosperity in 1963 marked a new beginning of hope for a future of plenty.

The Promise of Prosperity

During the war, many Canadians began to believe that it was insufficient to resist only occasionally the system's worst manifestations of callousness. If wartime planning and national enterprise — the latter evident in the twenty-eight Crown corporations started during the war to make everything from plastics to wartime housing — could lead to economic stability and a fairer distribution of wealth, why not continue such planning and public ownership into peacetime? Wartime surveys indicated that at least four in ten Canadians wanted extensive public ownership[2] while twice that number wanted the federal government to institute a comprehensive national medical insurance plan covering all Canadians.[3] Fully thirty-nine percent of Canadians were prepared to support government ownership over private management in November 1943 when the choices put to them by the Gallup organization were quite stark. "Do you think workers would be better off if all the industries in Canada were owned and run by the Dominion government after the war, or do you think that workers would be better off if these industries were left under private management?"[4] Forty-seven percent of the Gallup sample supported private management in answer to the pollsters' question while fourteen percent were undecided.

Polling in Canada had only begun in a serious manner as the war began, so it is difficult to be certain if such views were as widely held before the war. In any case, support for the CCF, the more respectable of the two parties that advocated widespread social ownership and comprehensive social security programs, jumped from a mere 8.5 percent nationally in the 1940 federal election to twenty-nine percent in the Gallup Poll in September 1943. The socialists were briefly ahead of both the Liberals and the Conservatives in the polls. They had almost formed the government of Ontario in the 1943 provincial election and they did form the government of Saskatchewan in a provincial election the following year. In both British Columbia and Manitoba, the old parties felt compelled to unite electorally to prevent a CCF victory. Even the Communists, whose importance in the union movement was never matched by widespread voting strength, managed to win two seats in the Ontario provincial election of 1943, and a federal by-election in a working-class riding in Montreal. They held on to their provincial seat in Manitoba in 1945, and continued to hold city council seats in both Toronto and Winnipeg.

Both the Liberals and the Conservatives, wishing to stem the growth in support for socialism, began to advocate extensive programs of social insurance, labour rights, and job creation. During the federal election of June 1945, it was difficult to find voices that favoured a return to the *laissez-faire* practices that had produced the Great Depression, but had completely failed to solve it. A managed capitalism in which the state would play a major role became the new ideal. For a time even much of big business supported this goal, if only to hold the socialists in check. N.R. Crump, president of the CPR, was one of the businessmen who had an enlightened view of how state intervention and private profit could complement one another. Though the Canadian Chamber of Commerce had turned against new social spending programs soon after the end of the war, Crump maintained in 1958 before that organization that the post-war welfare state in Canada — which groups outside the business community considered too modest — had proved essential to business success and vice versa. He claimed that the market economy was "self-adjusting if allowed to work" but that the "process of adjustment can be somewhat painful."

Crump's congratulatory view of both business and government success in the post-war period nicely encapsulates the views that have become conventional in summarizing the two decades or so that followed the war.

> A brief glance backward over the last decade must convince even the most skeptical that for Canada the Fifties have been truly fabulous years. The measure of our achievement lies in the magnitude of our resource development, in the explosive growth of our cities and towns, in the revolutionary progress in transportation, in the expansion of industry and the dynamic changes in farm technology. It lies, too, in our social progress. High among the accomplishments of Canadians in the decade now drawing to a close is the evolution of a social security system based on the wealth-generating capacity of private enterprise — a system which, while far from perfect, has nevertheless alleviated the misery of unemployment and mitigated the economic hardships of illness and old age of millions of our fellow-citizens.
>
> ... Indeed, social legislation has removed the only valid criticism of free enterprise — namely the exposure of individuals to the occasional hardships of the ebb and flow of the market economy.[5]

Today's environmentalists and feminists might wince at the suggestion that problems associated with the business cycle provide "the only valid criticism of free enterprise." Certainly, in the 1950s, critics of the capitalist system focussed on distribution of wealth to the exclusion of issues associated with the environment or of economic democracy. But how correct was Crump on his own terms? Many of the post-war economic indicators seem to confirm his triumphal view of the progress of corporate capitalism and its partner, the liberal state. In the first decade after the war ended, output increased on average by 5.3 percent a year, and even during the slump of 1957–61, output was increasing by 2.9 percent per year. Gross national product in constant dollars almost quadrupled from 1945 to 1960 (see Table One) and GNP per capita doubled. The population had grown from 11,506,655 in the 1941 census to 18,238,247 twenty years later. Both job prospects and wages grew faster than the population in the post-war decade and the official unemployment rate from 1945 to 1956 averaged 2.5 percent, a negligible rate when placed against the double-digit levels of unemployment during the Depression. That rate had almost tripled in 1958 and stayed above five percent until 1964.

Table One GNP (in 1971 dollars)	
1945	3,182,000,000
1950	7,042,000,000
1955	9,678,000,000
1960	11,790,000,000

Source: F.H. Leacey, ed., *Historical Statistics of Canada, 2nd ed., Series F 1–13.*

On the surface, all was well. Consumption was increasing, new inventions were being announced every day, and doomsayers who claimed to see a new Depression on the horizon were proven wrong. Each year the Big Three automakers in the United States announced a new look and new technological features for their expanding product lines, and a growing middle class put their deposits down for a new sedan or station wagon, buying a new status symbol "on time." For the large section of the population that felt immune to the threat of unemployment, it made sense to buy homes, furniture, cars, and appliances on the instalment plan. Retailers expanded the availability of credit and the acquisition of refrigerators, washing machines, ad later, television sets, increased apace. Inflation, which was fairly high in the early post-war years after wartime price controls were quickly lifted, was negligible in the 1950s, though wage increases for unionized workers during this decade were respectable, if somewhat modest relative to the increases in corporate profits.

All the popular images of the 1950s and early 1960s reveal a population innocently pursuing consumerism, attempting to erase the memories of the Depression and war. But prosperity was less well distributed than the clichés of the period, repeated by Crump, suggested. A Statistics Canada study of non-farm families in 1961 revealed that the combination of a booming post-war economy and social programs designed to compensate for marketplace adjustment had by no means lifted all Canadians out of poverty. The study defined families as "low income" if seventy percent of their income was required to meet the basic costs of food, clothing, and shelter, leaving them little room for choice in acquiring these necessities and little spare income for other needs and wants. Using this definition, twenty-seven percent of non-farm Canadians, including 1.7 million children under age eighteen, were poor. If sixty percent of income required for bare necessities replaced seventy percent in the equation,

forty-one percent of Canadians were living well outside the stereotypes of prosperity commonly applied to the post-war boom period.[6]
The exclusion of farm families reduced the reportage of the total
incidence of poverty. While a small percentage of farmers increased
their landholdings and used newer machinery to improve their yields
and incomes, most farmers became relatively poorer as prices for
farm products failed to keep up with increases in national income.

CPR president Crump was partly right when he suggested that
state intervention had provided a floor of earnings for most Canadians. Why then, sixteen years after the war had ended, were so many
Canadians poor or almost poor?

In part, it was because industrial prosperity was unevenly distributed within the country. Most regions in the Atlantic provinces, the
Gaspé and northern Quebec, eastern Ontario, Manitoba, Saskatchewan, and northern Alberta shared but little in the new prosperity.
Industry concentrated in southern Ontario's "Golden Horseshoe" and
in the Montreal region, though mining and lumbering also created
dramatic economic growth in British Columbia, northern Ontario,
and, to a lesser extent, northern Manitoba and northern Saskatchewan. Wealth disparities were also produced by structural divisions
within the labour force. While organized labour doubled its membership in Canada during World War II, only about a quarter of the
labour force belonged to recognized trade unions in 1945, a figure
that rose to about a third by 1961. Though unions in this period won
respectable wage increases for their members, and sometimes important improvements in working conditions, two of every three workers
were unable to share in these gains. Some, of course, were administrative and professional employees who won substantially better
improvements in pay and working conditions than unionized workers. Most, however, were "unskilled" workers or workers in small
shops susceptible to employer interference in union drives (such
interference was illegal, but provincial labour relations boards did
little to stop it). In particular, women, people of colour, and immigrants who were not of British descent suffered discrimination. So
did francophones, even in Quebec, at least before the Quiet Revolution that began in 1960. A study of income-earners in Quebec, using
1961 census data, conducted for the Royal Commission on Bilingualism and Biculturalism, revealed that only Québécois of Native and
Italian descent earned less on average than francophones in the province. Employers largely reserved jobs labelled as "unskilled" for the
non-anglophone elements of the labour force, and their wages were

more likely to be determined by the minimum wage set by the provincial governments (and by the federal government for workers covered by federal legislation such as federal civil servants, bank and railway workers) than by collective bargaining. The minimum wage in all provinces was a bare subsistence wage which could not support a family or, for that matter, keep an individual with no family responsibilities out of poverty. Popular stereotypes and, to a degree, union collaboration maintained the discrimination of hiring on the basis of gender, race, and country of origin.

Popular opinion, for example, still held that a woman's calling was tending a home for a husband and children. While she was single, she was to concentrate on making herself attractive to potential husbands and when married, she was expected to help her daughters perform the same role. Popular journals and newspapers assumed this role unquestioningly. A 1947 *Star Weekly* article, for example, showed a picture of a young girl with the caption: "The proud mother of this lovely little girl is teaching her daughter early the importance of a proper care of the hair. A 'debby' of 1960, the little lady gets in training now by pinning posies in her shining locks."[7]

From this point of view, a single woman was a mother-in-waiting, who could work to augment her parents' income but did not require a "living wage." Once she married, it was her husband's obligation to procure a living wage which would maintain her as well as their children. In a departure from the pre-war tradition that women left the work force after they married, it became common for women to work until their first child was born. Gradually, as the clerical and sales jobs, which became women's "job ghettoes," expanded, it also became acceptable for women with older children to be in the work force. But, just as single women were seen as dependent on their parents and therefore doing little more than bringing an income supplement into the home, married women who worked were viewed as earning "pin money." The notion that a woman did not have the right to an income that could support her, never mind a family, was all-pervasive and gave pause to many women whose marriages were loveless or even abusive and who might otherwise consider leaving their husbands. Women who never married, divorcees, and deserted wives had little choice but to work for a living. The wages available to most of them were miserable since the labour force was structured around principles that failed to account for their existence.

Employers discriminated against visible minorities and, for that matter, "audible" minorities — francophones and Europeans who had thick accents that betrayed their origins. Such discrimination, though, could not be as blatant as it had been before the war. In 1945 Saskatchewan and Ontario became the first Canadian provinces to legislate against discrimination in hiring and accommodation on the basis of race and religion. Courts in the post-war period were increasingly willing to disregard real estate covenants that restricted home ownership and rental accommodation in certain neighbourhoods to white Christians of particular ethnic backgrounds. Laws, like those in Nova Scotia, which forced African-Canadians to sit in the back of theatres, were quietly dropped. But informal racism could hardly be kept in check without legal enforcement. African-Canadians, Natives, and Asian-Canadians found that good jobs — sometimes all jobs — were closed to them and certain neighbourhoods were off limits to them, even if they did earn a decent income. A 1955 report for the National Council of Women of Canada on the status of women in Nova Scotia concluded that most employers were unwilling to hire African-Canadian men for any position and were mainly interested in African-Canadian women as maids. Noted the report writers:

> We have learned that when a Negro girl has completed her course in secretarial training, she frequently applies at a regular business office before she makes application for a Government position. She is invariably refused by a business no matter what her qualifications, as soon as they know she is coloured. Often the employer makes the excuse that his other employees would object to the coloured applicant.[8]

A campaign led by Pearline Oliver, a founding member of the Nova Scotia Association for the Advancement of Coloured People, convinced some hospitals in the late forties to allow African-Canadian students into their nurse training programs for the first time. A few years later, Ontario hospitals also relented, but in Quebec, African-Canadian women had to wait until the 1960s to be admitted to nurse training. In any case, before the sixties, the numbers of African-Canadian women, like the number of Native women admitted to nursing programs, were quite modest.[9]

Native organizations complained bitterly that, apart from seasonal farm jobs which were not even covered by the minimum wage, Native people were almost completely shut out of the labour force. For those who had left overcrowded reserves to move to cities, this

A Native family visits the Hudson's Bay Company store at Read Island, British Columbia, 1950. NAC PA-164744.

meant lives of hopelessness on social assistance. While prejudice against Natives was nothing new, First Nations people had been integrated into the labour force in British Columbia during the boom in that province that preceded the 1930s Depression. Afterwards, they were the last to be hired for wage work though many continued to earn a good living as fishers in competition with European-origin fishers.

To the conservatives of the post-war period, it seemed irrelevant that inequalities within the population, whether along class, race, or gender lines, were not disappearing. Economic growth, they argued, was making the pie bigger and life at the bottom was less unpleasant than it had been a generation earlier.

In 1941, only 12 percent of farm homes were not forced to get their water from wells whereas in 1961, three in five had inside running water. There had been a similar fivefold increase in the number of farms with flush toilets while fridges, available at the earlier date to fewer than one in twenty-five farm wives, were in four of every five farm homes in 1961.[10] But it is important to keep in mind that prevailing community standards usually determine our view of poverty rather than simply comparisons with other nations or with other periods in our history where most people appear to have been worse off than they are now.

Educators argued, not without reason but not without self-interest either, that there was a clear correlation between education and levels of income. Though no one bothered to say so at the time, gender had to be factored out completely to make this argument since even university-educated women in the work force — for example, social workers and some nurses and school teachers — earned less money on average than men with less than nine years of education. The public certainly believed that improved education at all levels was the key to Canada maintaining its position as an industrial nation and to upward mobility. Politicians promised, and generally kept their promises, to spend tax dollars to build schools, increase the numbers of teachers, and make more places available for study in Canadian universities. Fewer than one percent of Canadians in their late teens could expect to enter a university before World War II. By the early 1960s, it was ten percent and a large number of new universities were on the drawing-boards. Despite the rhetoric that suggested that the universities would act as levellers of economic inequality, most of the new students were from solid middle-class backgrounds. Many working-class children, however, did benefit from the new community colleges that emphasized technical training.

Spending on education indicated the high priority that the public and government alike placed on creating greater equality of opportunity for Canadians. That less social mobility than might be expected would result from such spending was foreseen by few. In any case, for the political and economic elites, the pay-off from education was less in social mobility than in economic growth, though again the link between the two is perhaps less clear than it was thought to be at the time. It was economic growth, above all, that was supposed to deal with the problem of poverty. In this context, public spending on education, like spending on highways, hydroelectricity, and other infrastructure that attracted new industrial and commercial investments, was seen as a means of indirectly dealing with the problems of low-income individuals and families. What then of a more direct redistribution of wealth? We look now at the limited character of the welfare state that emerged in Canada from the end of the war until the Pearson years began in 1963, and ushered in the major — and, for this century, the last — wave of social reform.

Dampening Wartime Radicalism: A Weak Welfare State Emerges

No national medical care insurance program had been implemented by the early 1960s. Public demand for such a program was overwhelming. The major labour federations, the Canadian Council of Agriculture, and the Canadian Welfare Council had all supported a comprehensive national medical insurance scheme during the war, the latter with support from many major Canadian industrialists. Even more encouraging for proponents of socialized medicine was the endorsation of the Canadian Medical Association in 1943 of a national program, though the doctors insisted that only average and low-income Canadians should be forced into a national program. Citizens above a certain income should have the right to choose either state or private medicine. Nonetheless, reflecting wartime concern that the post-war world not mark a return to the inequalities of the Depression, the doctors called for a program that would include not only doctors' visits and hospital care, but also dental care, prescription medicine, and even housing for the poor and playgrounds for children.

The doctors were haunted by memories of starving families unable to pay their medical bills while the corporate executives were haunted by the accusations during the Depression that it was the capitalist system that had created so much misery. Aghast at the rise of the CCF and as pessimistic as anyone else about the possibility of a post-war depression, normally conservative groups were prepared to make concessions to the masses to buy social peace. But, as the war wound down, the economy did not collapse, and CCF support began to drop, many conservatives began to feel that they had been too hasty in endorsing costly concessions to the less well off. Perhaps, they argued, it would be best to focus on tax breaks for the wealthy so that rates of private investment would remain high and provide the engine for post-war growth. Perhaps private medical insurance carriers could step into the breach and make a state program redundant.[11]

Prime Minister William Lyon Mackenzie King was one of those whose thinking had shifted in this manner. Assuming the party leadership in 1919, King committed the Liberals to a broad program of social reform, but ignored all of his promises when in office from 1921 to 1930. Nevertheless, in return for support from the two Labour MPs when his government lacked a majority, he introduced a modest dominion-provincial shared-cost program of means-tested pensions for destitute, elderly people. He proved little more reformist when returned to power in 1935, though he made an important concession when he introduced unemployment insurance (UI) in 1940. The timing however was interesting. Introduced during wartime, UI initially served as a program of forced savings that helped to fund the war effort (the lack of unemployment during the war meant that there was little draw on the funds collected, so these were temporarily available to the government for purposes other than aid to the unemployed).[12] The clamour for reforms during the war and the rise of the CCF convinced King that he had to act to save his government from defeat by the Left. In 1941 his government appointed a Committee on Reconstruction, headed by McGill University president Cyril James. The committee issued a number of reports calling for new social programs. The housing sub-committee report called for a national social housing program; the committee on the post-war problems of women recommended a national program of morning nursery schools. But the best-publicized and most comprehensive report to emerge from the committee was the *Report on Social Security for Canada*, prepared in 1943 by the committee's research director, Leonard Marsh. Marsh proposed a comprehensive national program of social insurance covering medical treatment, pensions, and retraining for labour force participation. While Marsh aimed at greater equality among households and full employment for males, feminists have noted that his report, like most of the reform documents of his period, assumed the continuation of the pre-war model of a "traditional family" in which women were relegated to the home and dependent upon men's wages.[13]

Marsh's report went too far for King, though he did not say so publicly. A fiscal conservative, King was never comfortable with proposals for wholesale reform though he was prepared to go as far as he must to keep the Liberals in power. With the Conservatives having adopted a program embracing social security proposals and protection of the right of collective bargaining in 1942 and renaming themselves the Progressive Conservatives to boot, King was hardly prepared to let the reform mantle fall upon his political enemies. But he used the war as an excuse to stall the introduction of new programs, insisting that most programs would need to be cost-shared by the provinces and the federal government. That meant having a dominion-provincial conference and this, he insisted, would be inap-

Table Two Federal government total direct and indirect debt ($)	
1939	5,114,000,000
1945	18,443,000,000
1950	17,305,000,000
1955	20,044,000,000
1960	26,389,000,000

Source: F.H. Leacey, ed., *Historical Statistics of Canada, 2nd ed.,* Series H35-51.

propriate when the government's attention had to be riveted upon the defeat of the Axis powers.

King however recognized that vague promises of social security measures to come after the war would not be enough to convince the electorate of his sincerity. As an instalment on the reforms to come, his government introduced legislation in 1944 to pay family allowances to mothers of children under sixteen, beginning the next year. The allowance was set at eight dollars per month per child for the first four children, with a smaller rate for subsequent children (the differential rate for children after the fourth was dropped in 1949). The Liberals' "baby bonus" was meant to provide families with additional income and encourage the exit from the labour force of mothers, many of whom had wartime jobs, even traditional male jobs, because of labour shortages.[14]

In the June 1945 election, King and Progressive Conservative leader John Bracken vied with M.J. Coldwell, leader of the CCF, whose commitment to social security antedated the war, in promising Canadians security during illness, old age, or involuntary unemployment. Only the Social Credit party, which performed poorly outside Alberta, seemed to stand against the tide for social reform.

In the end, King won a bare majority with 125 of the 245 seats at stake. Within the much-divided opposition, the CCF had won a comparatively modest twenty-nine seats and taken only 15.6 percent of the popular vote, about half of what polls less than three years earlier had suggested they might win. Fears of a post-war recession, much like the one that followed World War I, receded as it became apparent that the established politicians, as much as the CCF, were committed to maintaining public spending to keep the economy afloat and to guarantee social security. The federal government's debt had risen from just over five billion dollars in 1939 to over eighteen billion dollars in 1945 (see Table Two) but, other than

Social Crediters who saw the conspiracy of the "money power" everywhere, politicians were not prepared to make this an issue. The writings of British economist John Maynard Keynes had influenced the politicians and, perhaps as importantly, the Department of Finance and the Bank of Canada, towards a focus on aggregate spending rather than the narrow, pre-war focus on debt. The failure of traditional economic nostrums to end the Depression, combined with the economic health of the debt-ridden wartime economy, seemed to refute the view that government debts would simply force up interest rates and dampen private investment. The "experts" at the Bank and in Finance were converted to the view that government spending on public works should be timed to coincide with the beginning of recessions in the private market. Modest deficits could be countenanced during recessions on the understanding that they were to be balanced by surpluses on current account when the economy had been revived.

But where in such an economic universe would social programs fit? The business elite, with the CCF and Communist threats fading, argued that they would be a millstone on private investment. The taxes required to pay for social spending would, in part, be taken from corporations and high-income individuals who might otherwise invest these monies. In the economists' language, social programs would transfer income from those with a "propensity to invest" towards those with a "propensity to consume." While consumption would stimulate private enterprise, the fear of taxation gradually hardened business' attitudes against state-sponsored, compulsory, social programs. If such programs had seemed attractive in the context of social unrest during the Depression and the war, they seemed unnecessary in the context of a growing economy in the post-war period in which radicalism seemed less of a threat.

Radicalism in the form of the CCF or the Communist Party might be on the wane but labour militancy was not. For big business, one of the attractions of a larger "social wage" had been the possibility of holding down wages paid by companies. But a post-war strike wave made such a hope irrelevant. Workers won major concessions and their employers, in turn, crying poverty in the face of record profit levels, argued that they could hardly be expected to pay both for increased wages and for new government social programs.

Mackenzie King, though he pretended otherwise publicly, was gradually won over by such arguments. The premiers of Quebec and Ontario, Maurice Duplessis and George Drew, were both conservatives opposed to universal social programs. So, somewhat less vocally perhaps, were Alberta Premier Ernest Manning and Nova Scotia Premier Angus L. Macdonald. King called together the premiers in August 1945 and presented them and the Canadian public with a "Green Book" of proposals, aimed at giving Canadians advanced social welfare legislation and a clear federal commitment to job creation. Universal pensions at age sixty-five, a comprehensive medical insurance proposal including coverage for dental and pharmacy bills, doctors' visits and hospital stays, federal relief payments to employables ineligible for unemployment insurance, and federal contributions towards provincial public works were part of the sweeping package. The tradeoff was that the provinces would be required to give up most of their taxing power to the federal government in return for a fixed per capita grant, a continuation of a wartime practice meant to be temporary. Though few Canadians knew it at the time, the entire proposal was a charade meant to make the provinces appear to be the cause of a planned federal retreat from wartime promises.

Predictably, some provinces were unhappy with any suggestion that they would have few tax fields of their own and would be dependent on federal goodwill to fulfil voters' increasing demands for more schools, better roads, and other things clearly under provincial jurisdiction. Premiers Drew and Duplessis were particularly obstreperous. The premiers did not, for the most part, accept that the federal government's ability to proceed with Green Book promises depended on a tax deal with the provinces. But the Department of Finance and the Bank of Canada were insistent that investors would be deterred from investing in Canada if there was an unpredictable tax environment. The federal government would have to collect a large amount of money to fund its promised social programs and this would inevitably mean a rise in both personal and corporate income taxes. It was necessary, therefore, that provinces not be in a position to levy these types of taxes as well. Inevitably, the provinces and federal government could find no early agreement and the dominion-provincial conference of August 1945 resulted only in consultation committees and agreements to have further conferences to discuss the federal proposals.

King quickly recognized that the federal position was unrealistic and indeed unfair. The provinces would be faced with huge outlays in the early post-war years; how could they afford them if they had no large sources of income to tap at will? But, as he confessed in his diaries, King thought the programs promised in the Green Book would result in increased taxation and the risk of intolerable debt for the federal government. Little convinced by the Department of Finance Keynesians that monetary and fiscal policy could prevent recessions, King expected that by the end of the forties or the beginning of the fifties, the economic cycle would produce another "inevitable economic collapse." So he allowed the federal-provincial talks to collapse without making a single concession to provincial views with which he sympathized, only to turn around afterwards and blame the premiers for the failure of the Green Book promises to materialize for Canadians. Privately, he took the self-serving view that many Canadians, including members of his own government, had simply misunderstood his promises in the 1945 election. He told the Cabinet that family allowances should have marked the end of major new programs "until the end of another four or five years" because of the huge expenditures involved. Keeping taxation down for individuals and corporations was to be the government's focus and this conflicted with introducing a plethora of social programs. As for medical insurance, he wrote in his diary:

> I had never dreamt of a health programme and the like to be a matter of a year or so but that it would take years to work out an agreement with the provinces which would help to establish a national minimum. All of this is very true but the way in which the thing has been misrepresented in the public mind is deplorable. We have gotten in far too deeply in the matter of possible outlays.[15]

The federal government did provide health grants to the provinces and cost-sharing for a variety of infrastructure programs in the late forties and early fifties. But it made little effort to revive the Green Book promises, always pleading that provincial unwillingness to co-operate made it impossible to implement new universal social programs. The exception was the implementation in 1951 of a nation-wide old-age pension of forty dollars a month for Canadians over age seventy, replacing the means-tested old-age pension. Supporters of universally available pensions were well organized and had successfully delegitimized older societal notions that it was the responsibility of children and other relatives, not the state, to look after older people.[16] The ten provinces agreed to an amendment to the constitution, only the second successful amendment in Canadian history — the first established a national program of unemployment insurance in 1940 — that gave the federal government the power to implement this program. Pension campaigners were dismayed however that pensions were not available to Canadians until age seventy. They had called for pensions at age sixty-five for men and sixty for women and had expected more generous provisions for seniors. In most Canadian cities by the early fifties, forty dollars a month was the cost of a modest rent. An unattached senior with no income other than the pension would only be able to eat if she or he took a sub-standard accommodation and made no other expenditures.

But Louis St. Laurent, who had replaced King as Liberal leader and prime minister after a party convention in 1948, was, if anything, more conservative than his predecessor. While King might be criticized for being overly zealous to protect the interests of corporate capital, he was not part of the economic elite. He owed much of his income as prime minister and Liberal leader to a trust fund established for him by the heir to the Salada Tea fortune and his party was dependent on the funds it raised from corporation owners and managers. St. Laurent, by contrast, was himself a member of the economic elite. Before joining Mackenzie King's Cabinet as Minister of Justice and later Minister of External Affairs, St. Laurent was a corporate lawyer in Quebec City who sat on the board of a dozen leading Canadian firms. St. Laurent's concerns for his corporate friends, as well as his unwillingness to step on the toes of Quebec's nationalist Premier Duplessis, caused him to resist most proposals for social spending. He did agree to provide federal aid to universities in 1951 only to be denounced by Duplessis, who nonetheless initially accepted the grants. Bowing to nationalist pressures, Duplessis rescinded that decision in 1953, forbidding Quebec universities from accepting their share of the federal grant. Education, after all, was a jurisdiction reserved to the provinces and, though the initial federal grants came without strings attached, they could be seen as the thin edge of the wedge that would have Ottawa dictating what could and could not happen within Quebec's universities.[17]

St. Laurent did not relish this fight with the premier of his province, a province whose federal seats had gone almost entirely to the Liberals in most elections since the time of Laurier. He was therefore cool to calls within his own party and from several provinces, particularly Saskatchewan, under CCF premier Tommy Douglas, to establish a national medical insurance program. By the late forties, the Canadian Medical Association had withdrawn its support for

In 1944, Tommy Douglas (centre) led the CCF to victory in Saskatchewan. SA R-B2895.

medicare and the Canadian Chamber of Commerce and other business organizations were equally opposed. Both groups supported private insurance programs; the main programs were operated by physicians' organizations themselves. This allowed doctors to set whatever rates for medical care the market might bear. The physicians, however, unlike the corporate elite and particularly the insurance industry, were not opposed to public hospital insurance. Saskatchewan had implemented Canada's first provincial hospital insurance program in 1946 and British Columbia followed six years later. Ontario was considering such a program, but preferred to have the federal government take the lead. St. Laurent was reticent but finally gave in to provincial pressures, abetted by reformists in his own Cabinet like Paul Martin, the Minister of National Health and Welfare. In 1957, a federal-provincial cost-shared plan was passed by Parliament.[18]

St. Laurent's conservatism in the social welfare area hurt his government in the 1957 federal election. The Liberal government, having allowed inflation to erode the value of the federal pension for many years, finally introduced an increase from forty dollars to forty-six dollars in 1957. The meagre increase won the derision of the new leader of the Conservative Opposition, John Diefenbaker, a theatrical Prince Albert lawyer who had been a member of the House since 1940. The Tory attack on the Liberals' social welfare record, though largely limited to the pension, demonstrated how far the Liberals had retreated from their Green Book days. While they were still conscious of public opinion polls and willing to make some moves that appeased popular demands, as the hospital insurance bill suggested, they were not reformers at heart. Many supporters of social reform emphasized the responsibilities of a national government towards its citizens and suggested that redistribution of wealth helped to maintain consumer power and thus to keep the economy running smoothly. But this presupposed a degree of economic nationalism. The Liberals did not share such a view. They were free enterprisers and continentalists.

The American Colossus: Economic Domination

Canada's economic and political elite had been converted to a moderate Keynesianism. Economist Harold Chorney observes that, within both the Bank of Canada and the Department of Finance, there was no real echo of the "sound finance" ideas that dominated during the Depression. They would recover their former prominence in the mid-seventies under the new name of "monetarism." The real rate of interest, the differential between the rate of interest charged and the rate of inflation, was kept low. Indeed, it was negative from 1946 to 1952, and averaged only 1.2 percent for the entire decade of the 1950s. Bank of Canada Governor Graham Towers, appearing before the House of Commons Committee on Banking and Finance in 1954, explained that the Bank had rejected the traditional notion of using high interest rates to fight inflation and potential inflation because they would have slowed down the rate of post-war economic recovery and raised unemployment to unacceptable levels. The fall in the rate of inflation despite low interest rates seemed to demonstrate that there was no necessary relationship between low rates and inflation.[19]

But the Liberal government had made it clear in its White Paper on post-war reconstruction in April 1945 that its conversion away from "sound money" policies and its acceptance of the need for some government social programs did not change its basic views on the efficacy of the private enterprise system. Under the leadership of C.D. Howe, the Minister for Reconstruction, and with the support of the nation's business elite, the Liberals steered the country further along a road that it had been travelling with increasing speed from the time of Confederation: that of greater economic integration with the United States. The size, wealth, and proximity of the American market had made it seemingly natural that the United States would become Canada's largest trading partner even while the high tariffs of John A. Macdonald's National Policy were in force. To the extent that that policy created challenges for American manufacturers with Canadian competitors, it also invited these manufacturers to establish Canadian branch plants so that they could scale the Canadian tariff wall. Preferential tariffs within the British Empire in the 1930s made such investments even more profitable because they meant scaling not only the wall into Canada but into the entire British Empire.

There were certainly concerns within Canada about the impact of close Canadian-American economic ties on the country's political future and on its cultural development. Although a few anti-continentalists of the inter-war period, such as CCF leader J.S. Woodsworth, were concerned that Canada develop a true political and economic independence, many Anglo-Canadian nationalists were British imperialists. They wanted the "white dominions" to join with Britain in working out a united foreign policy and trade strategy. But such a "nationalism" seemed unrealistic in the inter-war years as Britain's international economic position slipped considerably. After the war, with Britain a minor player in both the political and economic spheres, it made only sentimental sense and it had no political significance.

Canada's close co-operation with the United States during the war was both military and economic. When Britain seemed vulnerable to Axis defeat after the capitulation of France in June 1940, Prime Minister King approached American President Franklin Delano Roosevelt for talks on common defence planning. The result was the creation in August 1940 of the Permanent Joint Board on Defence. Roosevelt declared publicly that the Americans, though they remained non-combatants in the war until December 1941, would not countenance any attack on Canada.

In April 1941, the Hyde Park Declaration created reciprocity in the defence production industries of the two countries. For the next four years, production of armoured vehicles, which constituted a major part of Canada's war production, occurred mainly in the branch plants of American automobile plants. By the end of the war, Canadian imports from the United States had tripled while imports from Britain remained static. Though Britain remained the major overseas market for Canadian grain, American demand for Canadian lumber and minerals made the United States Canada's major export

C. D. Howe was responsible for the Canadian economy in King's government during WWII. NAC C-472.

market. The American share of non-resident investment in Canada reached seventy percent.

Not only were American goods popular in Canada but so was the United States itself. Wartime and early post-war surveys suggested a sizeable minority of Canadians would welcome Canada's absorption into the United States. Not surprisingly, the free enterprisers in the government believed that close economic relations with the Americans remained the country's best guarantee for prosperity in the post-war period. C.D. Howe, the man most responsible for making economic policy, had little time for the views of Canadians who wanted a huge public sector, whatever the polls might say about their numbers. He could ignore both the CCF and members of the Cabinet, such as Labour Minister Humphrey Mitchell,[20] who believed Crown corporations offered the best way to develop the economy. Most of the Crown corporations established during the war were sold off at what critics regarded as fire-sale prices to private, mainly American, interests. The government made clear its view that American investment was welcomed without reservation.

By 1947 however, it was clear that the two-way trade of the two countries favoured the United States more than Canada. Canada faced a currency crisis because post-war shoppers were snapping up

Edmonton, 1951. Advertisers found increasing receptivity among newly-prosperous middle class. PAABL-1890-3.

American goods in quantities so much greater than Canada's exports, mainly resources, to the United States, that Canada was forced to export gold to make up the difference. The imbalance of imports over exports might have been less of a problem if Canada's traditional European markets, particularly Britain, were importing Canadian grain and goods at rates that made up for the American imports, but these countries were simply too poor in the immediate post-war period to import more than they absolutely had to. Canada imposed temporary restrictions on American goods while trade officials tried to determine a solution to this financial impasse. The solution they favoured was a reciprocity agreement that would create a common market within North America and peg the Canadian dollar to its American counterpart. Mackenzie King, cognizant of the humiliation his Liberal predecessor, Sir Wilfrid Laurier, had suffered at the hands of the electors in 1911 when he proposed a reciprocity agreement, balked at this suggestion. In the end, it became unnecessary when the Americans agreed that Marshall Plan aid money for economic recovery to European countries could be used to purchase Canadian as well as American products. In 1947, also the year of the Marshall Plan, Canada joined the General Agreement on Tariffs and Trade, whose signees agreed to significantly lower tariff and non-tariff trade barriers to each other's goods. The tariff would cease to be an issue in Canadian politics for many years after 1947. When it re-emerged in the context of the Free Trade Agreement with the United States in the 1988 federal election, it covered only a small portion of the goods traded between the two countries.

As the Cold War between the United States and the Soviet Union began, Canada benefited from American plans to stockpile resources needed to maintain American military and industrial might. Public opinion generally favoured the increased integration of the two North American economies with surveys suggesting few Canadians feared the impact on Canadian independence. Indeed many accepted the steady diet of business propaganda that suggested Canada required American capital to fuel economic growth and improve the Canadian standard of living. Only much later would economists such as Kari Levitt, Melville Watkins, and Abe Rotstein as well as prominent politicians such as Walter Gordon and Tommy Douglas challenge the received wisdom of the fifties that Canadians could choose between greater economic independence and a robust economy but that they could not have both. Levitt, in her important work, *Silent Surrender*, in 1970, and Watkins, in his detailed task force study on foreign ownership for the federal government in 1968, pointed out that most of the supposed foreign investment in Canada was being financed by Canadians themselves. In Levitt's estimate, seventy-eight percent of foreign investment in the 1960s was simply retained earnings of firms already in the country, and seventeen percent of this investment was in the form of loans from Canadian banks. In other words, only five percent of foreign investment in Canada was new investment. That five percent was a small figure compared to the large amounts of dividends that were drained annually out of the Canadian economy to pay American residents who owned the branch plants that had come to dominate many sectors of the Canadian economy.[21]

There were prominent Canadians in the fifties who suggested that Canada's trade and investment policies made the country little more than a subsidiary of the American colossus. Harold Adams Innis, the economist whose "staples theory" had marked the beginnings of a distinctly Canadian school of economic history, was perhaps the most outspoken. Though he was a conservative — perhaps because, unlike others who styled themselves with that word, he really did wish to conserve historical differences that made nations unique — Innis was critical of the world's leading free-enterprise nation. He

Harold A. Innis's highly original works in economics and communications continue to influence scholars today. NAC C-003407.

believed that the Americans were too self-righteous and too willing to impose their views and their investments on countries with dubious benefits to the hosts. In *The Bias of Communications*, Innis warned that huge media empires were subverting local traditions by propagating consumerist values as if they were completely natural and universally applicable. Innis' student, Marshall McLuhan, would, in the 1960s, became a celebrity by turning this observation into a positive message: a "global village" was emerging in which all citizens of the world wanted the same things and could communicate with one another beyond the national blinders that had caused warfare and misunderstanding since time immemorial. Innis, unlike McLuhan, saw the diffusion of American culture as a new form of cultural impeiialism. Where McLuhan saw an amalgam of national and local cultures fusing to create new social values and cultural forms, Innis saw the imposition of American norms on other peoples.

Historian Donald Creighton, an arch-imperialist, regarded Canada's close relations with the United States as subservience to a new imperial master that lacked the sophistication and the willingness to consider the views of the white dominions that Britain had exhibited. Most of Canada's academic community, however, was unwilling to tweak the trunk of the American elephant during the Cold War. It was surprising, therefore, when Arthur Lower complained of American control of Canada's economy. Lower's forties text, *Colony to Nation*, made use of Frederick Jackson Turner's frontier theory. Lower's work contradicted the long-held views, still in vogue at the time in Creighton's competing text, *Dominion of the North*, that Canadian political developments were best understood in terms of the evolution in "metropolitan" (that is, British) political ideas. Suddenly, hotheads such as William Lyon Mackenzie, Joseph Papineau, and other leaders of the failed rebellions of 1837 were presented as within the mainstream of Canadian thinking for their times. The United States, viewed in traditional histories as an example of mob rule, was recognized as an important source of ideas for reform-minded Canadian politicians. Like other frontier theorists, however, Lower was leery of threats to the liberal tradition and did, like Innis and Creighton, see dangerous tendencies inherent in the American rise to global power. Of its impact on Canada, he wrote in 1952:

Canada in fact could hardly be more completely subject to American industrial imperialism than she is at the moment. Her business world accepts the maximum of American leadership and shows no originality of conception; it is completely imbued with the branch plant, colonial mentality. As a result, Canada does not enjoy all her own wealth. She is an exploited area in a more intense sense than India ever was.[22]

But in most of his writings in the fifties, Lower adopted the conventionally sanguine views that the extent of American investment and trade in Canada and the close intertwining of their defence and foreign policies did not mean subservience on Canada's part. The demands of the Cold War made such conclusions seem necessary. Any other conclusion in the bipolar world that the Cold War attempted to create might be viewed as a concession to Communism.

The Cold War

The Cold War pitted the democratic West against the Communist East. At least that was the image presented in the United States and Canada. Within the Communist bloc of nations, a different image was provided: the capitalist West was making war on socialist nations and on liberation movements that wanted to free peoples of the Third World — nations that were neither part of the industrialized West nor of the Communist bloc — in order to ensure that their resources and markets were freely available to Western-based capitalists. There was some truth to both versions of the Cold War and a great deal that was false in both. The governments of the "democratic West" were not committed to democracy *per se* and, as the Soviets suggested, were opposed to social equality in the Third World. Not only did the Americans and their allies stand steadfastly against popular Communist movements such as in Vietnam, they were unprepared to countenance non-Communist reformist regimes who used legislation to protect their markets for national capitalists rather than to allow American and European capital to dominate their trade and investment. The West, particularly the Americans, assisted in the overthrow of a wide variety of governments, sometimes leaving millions dead in the wake of the overthrow, as in Indonesia in 1965. Among elected governments overthrown with American aid from 1945 to 1980 were administrations in Guatemala, Iran, Brazil, the Dominican Republic, Cuba, Chile, Greece, Ecuador, Uruguay, and Argentina.

The Communist regimes, though not as monolithic as the Americans believed or pretended to believe, were quite vicious, for the most part, their particular brand of socialism deeply authoritarian, hierarchical, and bureaucratic. Stalin's long reign of terror in the Soviet Union created an ossified hierarchy of cranky old patriarchs quite prepared to shoot or jail all who breathed the mildest criticism of government policy or Communist philosophy. Even without the propaganda machine working overtime to blacken Communism's name, there was little to attract most Westerners to the Communist side.

Still, the Soviet Union had done most of the fighting and dying during World War II, and as the war ended, Canadians and their government hoped that good relations might be established with the wartime Communist ally.

Within the Department of External Affairs, the American view of the Soviets as expansion-minded warmongers was taken with a huge grain of salt. The more common view among those in the know in Canada was that Stalin, as brutal as he was, was mainly concerned with rebuilding the war-shattered economy of the Soviet Union, which had lost almost twenty percent of its population during the war. While they did not trust Stalin, they believed that deliberate attempts to isolate the Soviets could only create tensions that would work against the goal of creating post-war peace and an effective United Nations that might be able to defuse regional tensions. Secretary of State for External Affairs Louis St. Laurent, in a newspaper interview in February 1947, indicated his "definite conclusion" that Russia was too poor to risk war. Dana Wilgress, Canadian representative in the Soviet Union from 1942 to 1946, concurred. Yet, when President Truman, seeking congressional approval for economic and military aid to Turkey and Greece in March 1947, made a tough speech that suggested the Soviets were behind left-wing and nationalist struggles everywhere, Wilgress indicated candidly to Lester Pearson, Under-Secretary of State for External Affairs, that Canada had little choice but to fall into line behind American policy. Otherwise Canada would find itself without influence in the country that was about to impose a Pax Americana on the world similar to the Pax Britannica that characterized the nineteenth century.

Historians Jack Granatstein and R.D. Cuff, examining the documentary evidence of this period, note that Canadian politicians and officials believed it was in Canada's interest to provide support for their American counterparts who favoured trade liberalization and a United States that took an active interest in world affairs. The Canadians hoped to discourage elements in Congress that wanted a reversion to pre-war isolationism and protectionism.

> In the context of Washington politics Canadian negotiators found a natural affinity with those who favoured lower tariffs rather than protectionism, with those who sought generous funds for off-shore purchasing rather than adherence to the Buy American principle, and with those who lobbied against political isolationism on behalf of European reconstruction. In the most general terms of all, Ottawa found itself lined up with an aggressive president against his Congressional critics. Given the importance of Washington's politics to Canada's economic future, a public declaration of a cautious, balanced

assessment of Russian policy, such as that offered by Wilgress, would not in fact have served the Canadian interest.[23]

This rather jaded view of how Canada regarded its responsibilities
to maintain world peace contrasts with the conventional viewpoint
that the Cold War was a titanic struggle between good and evil and
Canada had aligned itself with the good guys. The 1983 Canadian
survey text co-written by Granatstein, *Twentieth Century Canada,*
reverts to the conventional view that "the West had to organize itself
to resist Soviet Communism and, above all, the United States had to
be dragged out of its self-satisfied isolationism and made aware of
its responsibilities to the rest of the world."[24] So Canada had gone
from irresponsibly refusing to stand up to American extremism because it might hurt its trading possibilities, to a position where it was
forced to convince the Americans that the Soviet threat needed to be
met head-on.

In Granatstein's new version of the events of the Cold War,
Canada was no bit player. A section entitled "Canada on the World
Stage" provides a grandiose view of Canada's role in precipitating
the Cold War. After Igor Gouzenko, a Soviet embassy employee in
Ottawa, defected to Canada in late 1945, the story of how Soviet
spies were attempting to unearth all manner of secret information,
particularly regarding nuclear experimentation, apparently alarmed
both the Canadian and American authorities. "Carrying with him
documents that irrefutably demonstrated that the Soviet Union had
been operating major spy rings in Canada throughout the war,
Gouzenko's flight might be said to have launched the Cold War."[25]
This is a judgment which no American historian of the Cold War
seems to share. The Gouzenko affair rarely even rates a footnote in
American histories of foreign policy for this period.

The Cold War at Home

Whatever the government may have thought of the real threat which
the Soviet Union posed, it was determined to prevent Communism
from becoming an important influence in Canadian life. From the
early post-war years, Liberal governments began a systematic effort
to suppress dissenters in influential positions within Canadian society, including the civil service, universities, science-based industries,
and trade unions.[26]

Igor Gouzenko, 1945. NAC PA-129625.

Several civil servants had been implicated by Gouzenko in Soviet spying efforts and the government began surveillance of its employees to ensure that no one with sympathies for the Soviets was in any position to betray secrets to them. Most government jobs, even low-level jobs in departments with no strategic importance, required a security clearance. If government snoops had reason to believe that an individual or her/his relations were involved in activities which also involved Communists, she/he was blacklisted from government employment. Rulings by the government's Security Panel on an individual's suitability for obtaining or continuing to hold a government job were not subject to appeal as they were in the United States, making the likelihood of arbitrary decisions even greater. Aspirant government contractors and nuclear plant employees were also subject to inspection and blacklisting. The RCMP collaborated with the FBI and CIA in the United States to exchange information on "subversive" individuals to ensure that these people were not employed in supposedly sensitive positions.[27]

Not only left-leaning individuals were ruled ineligible to hold government jobs. Homosexuals were hounded out of their jobs on the grounds that they had "defects in their character which may lead to indiscretion or dishonesty, or may make them likely subjects of blackmail." But talk in security circles, especially within the RCMP, about homosexual "pollution" of the civil service suggested a rather more entrenched prejudice against homosexuals as violators of the accepted sexual code within Canadian society. If the numbers of suspected homosexuals interrogated by the RCMP in connection with government employment and those later fired by the state authorities are compared with the numbers for suspected Communists, it would appear that the sexual threat to state security was viewed as greater than the threat from the Left. The government of John Diefenbaker, which prided itself on the Bill of Rights it introduced in 1960 guaranteeing basic human freedoms for citizens, refused to stop the witchhunt against homosexuals. Indeed in 1963 it approved a proposal that allowed the RCMP to use what insiders in the police force called a "fruit machine" to ferret out gays and lesbians. Prospective employees for certain positions would be shown erotic poses of both men and women while tied to an apparatus that would measure their sexual arousal. The "fruit machine" was not long-lived, but only because its accuracy was soon in doubt; the principle of delving into people's minds to determine if they had correct sexual thoughts was itself not rejected.[28]

Just as homosexuals were seen as threats to the traditional Canadian nuclear family, working wives were frowned upon and the federal policy was not to hire married women though it did not fire women already employed in the civil service when they married as several provincial governments did.

Cold War concerns about Communists and homosexuals also pervaded post-war immigration policy. As the country gradually opened its doors again to immigrants in the post-war years after keeping the gate fairly firmly shut during Depression and war, security checks of prospective immigrants began in 1946.[29] Nazis and fascists unsurprisingly were not wanted at the time. As for Communists, a firm decision was made in 1947: "The Cabinet, after discussion, agreed that where, as a result of security investigation, it was demonstrated that a prospective immigrant was a Communist, admission should be refused by the Immigration Branch without reason assigned for such action."[30] Again there was collaboration with foreign authorities, particularly the United States and Britain, to determine who might be a Communist or a radical. In 1952 homosexuals were added to the list of undesirables and remained there until 1976.[31] Homosexuality remained illegal in Canada, and the government's immigration policy reflected its desire to ensure sexual conformity as well as ideological conformity. White skin was also generally a prerequisite for immigrants before the 1960s.

A Canadian Seamens' Union demonstration against the Seafarers' International Union, 1949. NAC PA-128759.

The Cold War was used as a pretext for state intervention in struggles between labour and capital. In 1950 the federal government ordered 130,000 striking railway workers back on the job, claiming their job action interfered with Canada's obligations in Korea.[32] Whether because of a fear of Communism or simply because it wanted to help employers forced to deal with a militant union, the Canadian government also helped to smash the Canadian Seamen's Union, the democratic organization of sailors on the Great Lakes in 1949. The CSU's leaders were Communist Party members and when the union closed down shipping in eastern Canada that year, the government charged that the leaders' goal was to prevent goods purchased by western European nations under the Marshall Plan from reaching their destination. It ignored the issue of wage cuts raised by the workers and imposed a gangster union on the seamen, the Seafarers' International Union. The union was led by a notorious American felon, Hal Banks, who was not eligible to enter Canada because he had a criminal record. The government waived the eligibility rules so that this paragon of democratic unionism could enter Canada and save the seafarers from the union leaders whom they had democratically elected and refused to eject despite a government

Hal Banks, controversial leader of the Canadian District of the Seafarers'
International Union. NAC PA-152496.

anti-Communist campaign.[33] Banks blacklisted about 2000 seamen
who remained loyal to the CSU.

Not all union organizers from the United States were to be treated
with the same cordiality as this gentleman. Reid Robinson, an organizer for the International Union of Mine, Mill, and Smelter Workers,
had been booted out of the country in 1948 because Minister of
Mines and Resources J.A. Glen, reflecting the views of the mine
owners, believed he was a trouble-maker. The policy under which
Robinson was ejectèd while Banks was welcomed was worked out
by Cabinet in 1948. It directed the ministers of Mines and Resources
and Labour to "compile a confidential list of approved United States
labour organizers with a view to having Immigration Officers instructed that only such individuals as were on the list (and such others
as were cleared on specific reference to Ottawa) were to be admitted
to Canada as labour organizers; others seeking entry as such were to
be refused."[34]

Sleuthing by the RCMP (albeit mainly through the files provided
by potential immigrants' countries of origin) and the careful screening of a Security Panel established to consider RCMP rulings of
ineligibility of immigrants worked to keep the country free of new

Communists and other leftists. For example, until 1959, all members of the Socialist Party of Italy were excluded from consideration for immigration to Canada. Members of Italy's neo-fascist party, by contrast, were eligible to come to Canada until that year. Indeed from 1950 onwards the federal government began quickly to reverse its policy of excluding Nazis and fascists. That year, under pressure from Ukrainian nationalist organizations, it rescinded a decision made in 1949 not to accept 8000 Ukrainians detained in Britain for having served willingly in the German army during the war. It also removed restrictions on entry to Canada for those who had been members of the Nazi party or served in the German army but did not hold high office in either. Within a few years restrictions on most Nazi officials evaporated. By January 1953, William Kelly, the RCMP officer in charge of security screening of prospective European immigrants, was protesting that the government was allowing war criminals into the country, reclassifying them by dubious means as "minor offenders."[35]

While Communists were seen as representatives of the enemy, and potential trouble-makers among Canadian workers, ex- and not-so-ex Nazis and fascists were seen as willing workers unlikely to disturb the Canadian status quo and more than likely to make difficulties for Canada's Left. Certainly the threats made by newly arrived Ukrainian nationalists with a Nazi past against pro-Communist Ukrainians caused some of the latter to pull away from left-wing ethnic organizations. On one occasion a bomb caused extensive damage to a Communist bookstore.

The Canadian state systematically infiltrated Communist organizations, trade unions, and other progressive organizations to gather information on their activities, to gather names for the government's hiring blacklist, and to cause divisions within these movements. McCarthyism — the paranoid identification of individuals as Communists and Soviet spies on the basis of irrelevant or unreliable information, and the creation of mass hysteria about Soviet infiltration — was paler in Canada than in its American home. Still, it had a palpable presence in the lives of Canadians in the early post-war period.[36] To be a Communist was to support the other side in the Cold War. Thus, to tolerate Communists was to concede merit to the "enemy's" viewpoint. And, of course, to make more than mild empirical criticism of Canada's economic or political system was letting down the side and abetting the "commies."

Most Canadians were unwilling to stand up to such intolerance. The 1950s in Canada, as in the United States, became a period of conformism. Radicals were kept out of the media, the universities, and the civil service.

Unions purged Communists from leadership positions and often from membership (and therefore the right to work in the trade or company covered by that union). Often, fairly undemocratic regimes emerged within unions in the name of extirpating undemocratic Communism. The Communists often owed their election to union positions to their organizing skills and manipulative tactics, but they usually observed democratic norms and kept themselves in office by dedicated work that led members who did not vote Communist in political elections to re-elect them as individuals. The new union leaders, in the name of resisting Communism, often suspended democratic norms, insisting that Communists would seize control if open, democratic unionism were practised.[37] Many unionists grumbled that their leaders had become as much part of the establishment as the corporate leaders unions once had fought.

Cold War thinking debased political thought and reduced political options. Cold Warriors labelled their opponents and their opponents' ideas as Communist and therefore outside the pale of proper politics, rather than dealing with their substance. For example, Cold Warriors attached the Communist label to campaigns for publicly subsidized quality childcare organized both by committed feminists and socialists, as well as working mothers who needed childcare so that they could work outside of the home for wages to support their families. Communists certainly played an important role in the struggle for daycare and opponents of daycare therefore found it easier to deal with the presence of Communists in the struggle rather than the issues raised by the struggle. In 1951, for example, Toronto city councillors attacked a broad coalition of pro-daycare groups as Reds.[38] The president of the upper-class women's organization, the National Council of Women of Canada, joined business leaders in confounding working women's demands for good, affordable childcare facilities with state socialization of young children.[39] In a setting where debate was posed in so simplistic a framework, it is unsurprising that little progress was made in the daycare struggle.

Conclusion

Government policies in the early post-war period were shaped by conflicting pressures. On the one hand, the public's demand for social reforms argued for new forms of state intervention. On the other, the demands of the business community and international capital suggested that such intervention must have clear limits even if it meant that a high rate of poverty would have to be tolerated in a period of unprecedented economic growth. The political elite tried to accommodate both sets of demands. More money was spent on social programs but not so much that business people could not make handsome profits. While fiscal and monetary politicies were implemented to regulate the level of business activity, the government left private enterprise to make the daily decisions affecting the economy and did not distinguish between foreign and national investors. Recognizing the close economic linkages between Canada and the United States, Canadian governments tread warily in the area of foreign policy, accepting the broad outlines of American external policies.

Two

A Home Fit for Heroes

The contradictory images of post-war Canada discussed in Chapter One, one emphasizing prosperity, the other inequality, are nowhere clearer than in housing and in the neighbourhoods where houses were clustered. Increasingly the two Canadas that existed within most urban areas were well segregated. This was the period of suburbanization, with state policy and presumably consumer choice favouring single-family detached homes with picket fences marking off property boundaries. In everything from school readers to television shows to all forms of advertising, the white, suburban, middle-class, two-parent family with its shiny new home was presented as both ideal and typical. Meanwhile, the equally large numbers of working-class people who lived in the core areas of cities often faced decaying housing and municipal services. The authorities sometimes dealt with the problem of the mean streets with dilapidated housing by sending in wrecking crews and following policies of "urban redevelopment." The result was often simply to create a greater housing shortage since social housing appeared only sporadically before the late sixties. This chapter explores the ways in which state policies helped to create both of the Canadas that the suburban/urban-core divide only partly captures. It also explores resistance to the social values that underlay the post-war society: working-class resistance to perceived injustices and middle-class rumblings about the dull conformity of their lives. The emphasis here is on housing, immigration, "Indian Affairs," and labour policies. Finally, we will explore the environmental understanding of the period and the ecological impact of this model of social development.

Housing and Housing Policy

The wartime Advisory Committee on Reconstruction appointed a Housing and Community Planning subcommittee, headed by Queen's University economist C.A. Curtis, to report on Canada's

East end cabins in the 1960s, Vancouver. NAC PA-154626.

housing conditions and make recommendations on how they could be improved. The Curtis committee, reporting in 1944, concluded that a large minority of Canadians were poorly housed. Ten percent of all dwellings needed to be replaced while another twenty-five percent needed major repairs. Using a modest definition of space needs, the committee suggested that one in five households was overcrowded. To deal with both overcrowding and replacement of homes beyond repair, Canada would need an increase in housing supply of about one-third. Yet, even with rents controlled, one-third of urban residents were unable to pay an "economic rent" — a rent that provided a landlord with a sufficient rate of return that she/he could both maintain the dwelling and make a modest profit. Indeed, among the poorest third of the population, nine in ten were paying more for accommodation than economists thought wise if the other basic needs of food and clothing were to be paid for.

Since two-thirds of urban Canadians were tenants, Curtis concluded that the differences between household incomes and market costs for the purchase and rental of homes meant that a large proportion of the population would remain inadequately sheltered if market forces alone were allowed to deal with the housing problem. His committee called for a long-term program of building social housing units targeted at low-income renters and for a continuation of war-time rental controls.[1] After the war, this approach won the endorsation of the Canadian Congress of Labour, tenants' organizations, city planners, the Canadian Federation of Mayors and Municipalities, the Canadian Legion, the CCF, and, to a lesser extent, the National Council of Women of Canada and local councils of women. It also had the support of urban coalitions that had formed around housing issues such as the Vancouver Housing Association and Toronto's Citizens' Housing Association.[2] But it was opposed by the construction industry, and by industry generally, as socialist. Industry had the ears of the government and particularly the deputy minister of Finance, W.C. Clark.

Clark was opposed to social housing and to programs geared to renters. His department urged the government to build upon pre-war policies that promoted home ownership. In the summer of 1945, circumstances militated against Clark's approach. Depression poverty, followed by wartime mobilization of the economy with civilian housing low on the priority list, had resulted in a severe housing shortage. Many families had rented space in private dwellings during the war, sheltered from the worst effects of market pressures by rent control. With the war over, the owners of these homes moved in large numbers either to take over the whole home or to evict tenants paying controlled rents in favour of more prosperous new tenants. Owners anticipated the lifting of rent controls and hoped to charge these new tenants higher rents. Veterans, finding themselves without homes, joined social housing activists in demanding government action, often using noisy demonstrations to make their point to a government terrified at the possibility of post-war unrest. In July 1945 the federal government suspended the right of homeowners to evict current, well-behaved tenants. It also committed to a target of 10,000 Wartime Housing units per year. Wartime Housing had been devised during the war as a means of dealing with at least some of the congestion that urban areas were experiencing. It involved the construction of serviceable, prefabricated homes made available at low, and often subsidized rent. Some government buildings were also converted into temporary shelters.[3]

But the federal government's long-term aim remained to make Canada mainly a nation of homeowners. Veterans received low-interest loans for the purchase of homes and land. The Canada Mortgage and Housing Corporation was established in 1944 to make second-mortgage loans to middle-class Canadians. As building ma-

Modern Canadian living room, 1956. NAC PA-111484.

terials, set aside in wartime for military purposes, were freed again for house-building, the government ended its construction of Wartime Housing units and placed many of the existing housing units on the private market. By 1949, it was clear that social housing advocates had lost the battle with the state. Homes fit for heroes would be single detached homes built by private developers with state subsidies.

In 1954, aware that the private mortgage lenders remained conservative in their mortgage approvals, CMHC guaranteed the entire mortgage for approved lenders who were buying new homes. The banks collected commissions for handling CMHC mortgages but took no risks on these loans. Meanwhile, rent controls were relaxed and by the early fifties had disappeared. Though provision was made under CMHC legislation in 1949 for federal support for publicly-provided low-income housing, the clause was quite restrictive and led to few projects.[4] Campaigns on the part of supporters of social housing and state-regulated rents continued but fell on deaf ears in Ottawa. During the 1950s, only one percent of dwellings built were social housing units. The biggest success story was Toronto's Regent Park. Thanks to a campaign by the Citizens' Housing Association, the voters of Toronto elected in a plebiscite in 1947 to build a large public housing development in one of the city's most run-down areas

Switchboard operator, Royal Victoria Hospital, Montreal, 1953. NAC PA-133210.

even though initially neither the province nor the federal government offered to help (eventually the province did provide a substantial portion of the financing). In 1951, when the first stage of the development was completed, 1062 units of social housing were available for low-income Torontonians. A study in 1958 by Albert Rose, a social worker who had played a leading role in the campaign for Regent Park, suggested that Regent Park's combination of decent housing with rents geared to income, and good community and playground facilities had created a successful community. The social problems of poor areas, such as juvenile delinquency, were far less evident in Regent Park than in unrehabilitated slums.[5]

But with few Regent Parks available, most families had to choose between renting in a tight housing market that allowed landlords to gouge tenants and get away with poor maintenance, and buying a home. For those whose incomes were very low, this was no choice at all, they had to rent. Modest-income earners often made the plunge to home ownership even if they did not qualify for CMHC mortgage guarantees. Different family strategies were employed. A common one was to have both parents in a two-parent family in the work force despite the prevailing philosophy of the period that mothers should stay home with the kids and despite inadequate childcare facilities. Taking in boarders was another common strategy. "Moonlighting" by men was yet another way of boosting family income in a market where jobs did not always pay well, but where labour shortages were common. Many immigrant families, notably in the Italian community, doubled or tripled up so as to set aside the monies required for the large down payments on homes that would reduce the size of mortgages. Some new home-owners simply resigned themselves to "house poverty": they would realize the North American dream of a privately owned home but at the expense of not having enough money to meet any but the most basic needs of food and clothing.

Supporters of the Clark approach claimed that they were vindicated by the rapid pace of construction of new homes in the 1950s. With the support of government at all levels, developers were buying up land on the periphery of cities and developing new suburbs. The Ontario government, which dealt with 100 proposals for subdivision planning in 1945, dealt with 1200 in 1953. North York's population, for example, exploded by 914 percent from 1945 to 1962.[6] The burgeoning post-war middle class flocked to the suburbs. In the early years, residents complained about the lack of nearby shopping and entertainment. Public transportation was often unavailable or inconvenient in these areas, and having two cars in a household became an important status symbol. For many middle-class housewives, the second car seemed more a necessity than a status symbol. Without cars, they were unable to shop or take their children to doctors and dentists, music lessons, or organized kids' sporting events.

Suburbs during the day were largely populated by women whose husbands were off at work downtown or in an industrial area, and whose kids were off at school. Though many women were knee-deep in housework and many were bored and depressed, others created community groups that both provided them with a social life, and gave some community spirit to what were otherwise clusters of housing with no central focus. Community centres, playgrounds, playschools for pre-schoolers, and a variety of entertainments were organized and largely operated by suburban women. Their husbands might be asked to coach the local hockey or baseball team, but most other community work was undertaken by women. Women also became volunteers in the local schools, hospitals, and seniors' centres. While this unpaid work was largely an extension of women's traditional housekeeping and "caring" roles, it provided many mothers with confidence in their abilities and gave many the courage to take advantage of the paid jobs available for women when their kids were all in school.[7]

Though suburban living supposedly meant privacy and a degree of freedom of action for both women and men, the moral code of the 1940s and 1950s remained as censorious as it had been in the pre-war period. Indeed there was something of a moral panic as editorialists, preachers, social work professionals, doctors, and the courts bemoaned a supposed loosening of sexual and social norms during the war. Working mothers and single women working in blue-collar jobs side-by-side with men were said to be responsible for increasing rates of sex outside marriage. The claimed, but largely undocumented, increase in juvenile delinquency was attributed to working mothers. After the war, the social pillars were constantly harping on the need for sex to remain solely within marriage and for monogamous wives to become stay-at-home mothers. The much-publicized Kinsey reports in the United States revealed that adultery and homosexuality were both more common than the opinion leaders might like to think. This did not lead to many changes in this period. Abortions remained illegal and deaths from back-room abortions were not uncommon; birth control devices, while more generally available, were never on open display in pharmacies and were unavailable to teenagers; homosexuality remained illegal. Gays and lesbians had their own meeting places that existed in the shadow of the law. Working-class lesbians, for example, met in tough bars also frequented by prostitutes, places which middle-class lesbians refused to patronize. A suburban woman, if she was to retain the respect of her neighbours, could not frequent taverns, have male friends other than her husband, or be unaware of where her children were at any time. Her daughters would have to walk a straight line sexually as well to avoid developing a bad reputation. Her sons, though, could do pretty much as they wished, as long as they were heterosexual, since it was generally viewed as all right if young men "sowed their wild oats."[8]

The privacy that many regarded as the main advantage of suburban living meant that an effort had to be made to be sociable. In the

urban core, women tended to encounter their relatives and neighbours on the street and in local shops. They did not have to make the
effort to join clubs and volunteer groups as suburban women did, an
effort that required considerable time for busy homemakers as well
as an outgoing personality. Children also tended to make friends on
the street in crowded neighbourhoods, whereas in suburbs of white
picket fences, many found it less easy to get together with other
children outside school hours. Psychologists and social workers,
soon joined by feminists such as American author Betty Friedan,
began to catalogue a variety of problems that women and children
in suburbs were confronting. Many women felt trapped by a round
of activities that seemed to subordinate their own needs to others'
and which gave them far less scope than their employed husbands to
make use of skills and knowledge acquired during their years of
education. Still, the suburban ideal was a magnet to those who lived
in the inner cities, many of whom were new immigrants.

Just Off the Boat

From 1946 to 1962, a total of 1,761,505 documented immigrants
arrived in Canada. We have already seen in Chapter One that the
federal government excluded Communists and homosexuals as undesirables. It also excluded most non-whites and put some restrictions on Jews and Italians as well. Keeping Canada white had been
a goal of immigration policy since Confederation and attitudes in the
early post-war period showed that little had changed. The legislation
that had banned all immigration from China from 1923 to 1947 was
repealed because it was an embarrassment to Canada as a member
of the United Nations but Mackenzie King's government ensured
that administrative practices achieved the same ends as the Chinese
Exclusion Act. The St. Laurent government in the early fifties imposed quotas on each Asian country that ensured that only a trickle
of immigrants would arrive from countries where non-whites predominated. There were no comparable quotas on European countries.[9]

Department of Immigration policies, rather than formal legislation, had always been the means used to keep blacks out of Canada.
In the 1950s, because upper-class Canadians complained of a shortage of housemaids, a small number of Caribbean women received
permission to enter Canada after signing employment contracts.
Though many of these women had professional training, they were

War brides and their children in Halifax, 1946. PANS, 31.2.1, N-082.

restricted to work as housemaids.[10] Other people of African origin aspiring to come to Canada soon learned that the colour bar excluded their presence. Indeed only four percent of the new Canadians from 1946 to 1962 came from Africa and Asia and the bulk of the immigrants from these continents were whites from South Africa, Rhodesia, and Israel.

Many Anglo-Canadians had fretted in the 1890s as the government, anxious to provide the country with a sufficiently large labour and agricultural force to maintain a fast pace of economic growth, opened the gates to central, eastern, and southern Europeans. There had been a temporary closing of the door to immigrants from these areas after World War I and again during the Depression. But the post-war labour shortage meant that little thought was given after World War II to limiting immigration largely to those of "Anglo-Saxon stock," to use the phrase that Ontario's Premier George Drew used to describe the immigrants he preferred. British immigrants were wooed by the United States, Australia, and New Zealand, in addition to Canada, and Canada could realistically expect that only a portion of its labour needs would be met by the old Mother Country. So it turned to other countries of western Europe and to the "DP" camps — displaced persons camps — that included many eastern Europeans.

The destination of immigrants changed dramatically after 1945 from the pattern that had been established from the late 1890s to the late 1920s. Before the Depression, most non-Anglo immigrants were headed towards Prairie and British Columbia farms, railway camps, mines, and cities. While northern Ontario mines and logging camps also became home to many immigrants from central and southern Europe and Cape Breton's coal mines also received workers from these regions, southern Ontario and the Atlantic region remained overwhelmingly areas populated by people of British descent. Immigrants also came to Montreal, and Quebec nationalists noted with some concern that ninety percent of them chose to learn English, the language spoken by the economically powerful, rather than French, the language of the majority. But French-Canadian birth rates, while they fell substantially in each generation, remained high enough that the influx of immigrants unwilling to learn French had little impact on the prevalence of French speakers in the province. In the post-war period, immigrants were usually directed towards the Golden Horseshoe and Montreal, the areas where industrial and service jobs were rapidly expanding. This created a degree of hostility on the part of many Anglo-Ontarians who viewed their province as an outpost of the British Empire, and fear on the part of many Franco-Québécois who worried about their province's declining birth rate and the continuing tendency of newcomers to adhere to the language of the province's most powerful minority. Regions which experienced slow economic growth during the era of economic expansion unsurprisingly saw fewer of the new immigrants. The Atlantic region's ethnic composition changed little and Quebec outside Montreal remained largely the preserve of the descendents of the pre-1760 French colonists though small anglophone communities and Native reserves persisted. Saskatchewan experienced out-migration while Manitoba had little population growth, though Winnipeg continued to be a host to many new arrivals from central and eastern Europe. Alberta and British Columbia, by contrast, enjoyed soaring economies and became home to more polyglot populations than they had known before the war.

Not everyone was equally welcome. Jews had been largely prevented from immigrating to Canada in the inter-war period by the racist policies of the director of immigration, F.C. Blair, supported by a significant section of popular and government thinking. After the Holocaust, a greater degree of toleration towards Jews became evident. But there were still attempts to limit their numbers among immigrants. Senior immigration officials cynically used security concerns in a racist attempt to keep both Jews and Italians out of the country. One leading official boasted to another:

> We were faced at one time with an increasing volume of applications filed in several of our offices in Europe largely by two national groups — Jews and Italians. In the absence of any legal basis for refusing to deal with such applications, I thought that any stall would be helpful, that is the institution of a residence rule ... the two year residence rule boils down to an immigration device which was at the same time helpful to the RCMP which gave us the cover of "security requirements" for instituting that rule.[11]

By the early 1960s however restrictions against both of these groups on grounds other than security had largely evaporated. Though governments remained unprepared to accept more than a trickle of visible minority people into the country, they became increasingly tolerant of all groups of Europeans, or at least their non-Communist, non-homosexual members, in their pursuit of an ample labour force to meet industry's demands.

Like earlier waves of immigration into Canada, the post-war immigrants from non-anglophone, non-francophone environments often found their new home was not as ideal as they might have supposed. Exploitive employers, hostile Anglo-Canadians, and a state apparatus that did little to help newcomers adjust forced them to fall back on their own means for survival. Mutual aid within the group had long been the response of ethnic groups to a lack of support from outside. Among the Italians of post-war Toronto, for example, families shared rented homes until they could afford to build or buy their own. Single men co-operated to establish boarding houses that would provide reasonable rent and a convivial home environment for men without families in the country. First informal and then formal networks were created to help newcomers to the community find work and learn enough English to get by. A rich community life soon blossomed to include soccer clubs that competed in the Italian-Canadian Soccer League, social clubs, a trade school, and the Italian Immigrant Aid Society.[12]

Greek and Italian immigrants making television consoles in early post-war Montreal. NAC PA-127037.

Though the small Italian-Canadian business class was perhaps most influential within the community's associational life and espoused conservative social values, the vast majority of Italian-Canadian immigrants were peasants from southern Italy who worked in industrial jobs, usually at low-wage employments that were labelled semi-skilled or unskilled. Italian men were in demand for the most physically demanding and dangerous jobs in construction as well as for assembly-line and custodial jobs. The dangers facing the construction workers, whose jobs paid better than most factory jobs, were exemplified by the Hogg's Hollow tunnel disaster of March 1960. Five Italian-Canadian workers who were helping to install a water main perished after being trapped in the tunnel by a fire. Among other problems with the construction site was the employer's inadequate equipment for fire-fighting.

The Italian workers were hardly silent victims. Both in 1960 and 1961 they conducted huge strikes in the house construction industry in an attempt to win union recognition and improve their pay and working conditions. The height of their solidarity in this period was a rally of 17,000 immigrants in June 1961 at the Canadian National Exhibition stadium to demand more just treatment of Italian-Canadian workers by the construction industry. The 1961 strike, which lasted seven weeks, won the workers wage increases though only a

Westclox clock assembly, c. 1930. PCMA 79-016.

minority of the construction firms agreed to recognize the workers' union as a collective bargaining agent and to deduct union dues from their workers' paycheques.[13]

Italian-Canadian women were also well-represented in the work force. While the dominant view in Canadian society at the time was that married women ought not to work, family strategies for survival among immigrant groups argued for more flexibility. With minimal public daycare available, married women who chose to work depended upon relatives, often their own mothers, and friends to mind children during the workday. They then came home to face a second work day. The language barrier limited the choices of jobs available to immigrant women. While women's jobs were ghettoized and paid far less than jobs largely reserved for men, the better-paid women's jobs were, in turn, largely reserved for Anglo-Canadians. Few Italian-Canadian women in this period were nurses, school teachers, or secretaries. Most worked either in the poorest-paying manufacturing sectors — the labour-intensive sectors such as clothing, food, and textiles — or in the service sector as cleaning ladies, and laundry and dry-cleaning employees. Giuseppina Mazoli described her life as a 19-year-old, full-time steampress operator who also looked after her son, her husband, her father-in-law, and two brothers-in-law.

Oh poor me, fulltime work ... wash, clean, cook, I did all that!
I was really just a girl, 19 years old and thin, thin like a stick.

> I had four men, a baby. I was with no washing machine. I
> would go down to the laundry tub to do it. Then I had to cook
> and I had to work. And it was not only me.[14]

In many cases, Italian families were separated for a period as young
men attempted to establish themselves in Canada and earn enough
to afford the cost of passage to Canada for their wives, children, and
parents. Such separation was enforced by the state upon the approxi-
mately one hundred thousand immigrant men and women who came
into the country from the d.p. camps under the sponsored labour
program of the federal Department of Labour. The program was
designed to find cheap but hard-working labour for industries that
were having a particularly difficult time in finding workers in the
late forties: mining, lumbering, textiles, and domestic service. Immigrants signed a contract with a particular employer that bound them
to that employer at set wages for one or two years. Married women
were usually excluded altogether while married men could only bring
families after they had saved enough money to assure the Department
that they could care for their dependents. Usually that meant a wait
of several years since their wages were so low. The conservative
Toronto *Globe and Mail* was appalled by the plan's lack of a hu-
manitarian approach to immigration and commented: "Instead of a
bold, imaginative, large-scale plan for bringing them in, the Government offers paltry schemes allowing employers to recruit labour on
a plan of semi-servitude utterly at variance with Canadian notions of
human rights and freedom."[15] Political scientist Gerald Dirks, however, points out that though the plan was motivated by demands for
cheap labour, "from the standpoint of the displaced persons themselves, it provided a means by which they might leave the unsuitable
conditions prevailing in the European camps and resettle with some
hope of building a stable new life."[16]

Many immigrants, of course, were very happy in their adopted
homeland. Even ignoring the disruptions and tragedies that World
War II had imposed upon their lives, many had never been anything
but poor in Europe. While they might be classified as low-income or
poor Canadians by Statistics Canada and by middle-class Canadians
born in the country, they were often content with their new level of
material well-being. Their apartments or rented rooms in others'
homes might be cramped by Canadian (or even their own) standards,
but they usually had such amenities as running water and, by the late
fifties, refrigerators and television sets. Most were making payments

on a family car. Some descriptions of their lives help to place the poverty versus wealth debate in perspective.

Historian Franca Iacovetta describes her early days in the 1950s and 1960s "in a crowded southern Italian immigrant household in an ethnic neighbourhood in downtown Toronto." She and her five siblings were cared for by her grandmother while her parents worked, her father as a bricklayer and her mother in an industrial laundry. Her father worked late hours. Writes Iacovetta:

> I shared my bedroom — the main-floor living room — with two younger brothers and the family TV set. My parents slept in the dining room, and two older brothers occupied a third-floor attic room. At night, I would listen in on my parents' conversations. I can still hear the adults gathered around the kitchen table, endlessly discussing how to get jobs, the daily grind at work, and the struggle to get ahead.[17]

My own experience was not dissimilar, and since my family's income was usually at or slightly below the margin of what Statistics Canada classified as low income, it may be instructive about what was present and what was lacking from the homes of the almost-poor of the 1950s and the early 1960s. We were a family of six children born between 1947 and 1964. My father was a pre-war Jewish immigrant from the Polish-controlled zone of what is now Ukraine and my mother arrived in Canada in 1930 from Soviet Ukraine. From their marriage in 1945 until they bought their own home in late 1958, they rented a suite in my grandmother's North Winnipeg home. "Baba" also rented out another suite in the home. Like Iacovetta, I slept in the living room, sharing this "bedroom" with a brother, a sister, and the television set. My mother worked as a secretary until 1947 when my older brother was born, and though nominally she did not return to the paid labour force until 1966, she was frequently part of the army of largely undocumented home-workers who typed labels at home for direct-mailers without any protection from labour laws. This earned little income and my father usually held two and sometimes three jobs to make ends meet. From 1956 onwards, his principal job was at the CPR, initially as a carman's apprentice. To avoid a layoff during the recession that began in 1957, he took a labourer's designation and a cut in pay in 1958, though he emerged as a carman once the economy picked up again in the early sixties. A full-time cab driver after he was laid off from an electrician's job

in 1954, he continued to drive cab on weekends and during the CPR shop shutdown for four weeks in summer, for which only very senior workers received vacation pay for all four weeks.

When my parents bought a rundown two-storey home in December 1958, they were only able to make mortgage payments when the upstairs of the house was rented. On at least one occasion, we required help from a better-off uncle to avoid foreclosure. Until the mortgage was paid off in 1967 (after which our economic situation improved markedly), we lived in four rooms. This time, there was a living room but it was a room added on after the house had been built and often registered below-zero temperatures during the winter. For much of the year we bathed in a metal tub pulled out of the basement into the kitchen. As I was growing up, we had only three vacations, each of them lasting one week and involving rental of a modest cottage at nearby Winnipeg Beach. We ate royally but we never ate out. Still, poverty is relative. I felt poor when I was in the company of many of the children who were fellow evening pupils at I.L. Peretz Folk School, a Jewish parochial school, though most came from families with modest incomes. I suspected that everyone knew I was a charity case whose parents paid a fraction of the regular fee for pupils and could only envy these kids as they spoke about material acquisitions and outings that were out of the question for myself and my siblings.

By contrast, most of the kids I went to school with, when I attended David Livingstone School on Flora Avenue, were much worse off than me. The school board provided free milk for the poorest children in first grade. But it was obvious to the rest of us that many of these kids had little to eat at home. One friend lived with his parents and a large brood of siblings in a tumbledown one-room shack next to the school. Of course, it was precisely dwellings of that kind that urban planners argued should be torn down in favour of high rises. But the families who lived so shabbily were almost certain to be unable to afford to live in modern apartments. "Urban redevelopment" removed them from unsuitable accommodations only to force them to search for accommodations at the same rent elsewhere in town. What they found was usually as abysmal as what they had left, but their community roots were often weakened in the process as they were separated from the people they had once called neighbours.

Africville, a poor African-Canadian community in Halifax from the mid-nineteenth century, serves as an example. Halifax City

Council decided in 1961 to tear down this "slum," which the city had never provided with most municipal services, rather than to give its residents the sewer connections and garbage pick-up that white Haligonians enjoyed. It would be replaced by an industrial district. Africville's citizens organized a sustained, though ultimately unsuccessful, protest, focussing on the cultural richness of the community, centred around its church, of which the town councillors, because of racial prejudice or a narrow focus on poor material conditions, seemed ignorant. The businessmen who led the campaigns in Halifax and other cities for "urban redevelopment" were largely uninterested in the possibilities of letting core-area residents themselves determine ways of improving their areas. From their point of view, the public good and commercial interests happily coincided. The general manager of the Halifax Board of Trade summed up this view neatly as he addressed the Canadian Chamber of Commerce annual meeting in 1958:

> Halifax is presently in the midst of a very substantial redevelopment program ... supported by civic authorities and the business community. Wretched disease infested slums are being levelled to be replaced with new low cost housing, to give today's children a chance to grow into useful productive citizens. Relocating many of these families in already zoned residential areas is opening up new land for commercial development.[18]

First Nations in Post-war Canada

What was easily evident at David Livingstone School was that the poorest of the poor were not the immigrants but the children with the deepest roots in Canada: the Native children. Poorly dressed and often malnourished and lethargic, they were streamed into the "low grade" classes even when they were good academic performers. This official segregation was matched by social segregation in the schoolyard. Most Native kids were happy to play with white children but most of the white kids were warned by parents to avoid "Indian" children, as if their poverty were contagious. The "cowboys and Indians" movies also often served to make non-Native children fear, despite all evidence to the contrary, that Native kids were violent and anti-white. They would have little to fear from them after junior high. Almost all of the Native children had dropped out of school before

reaching high school. I do not remember a single Native boy or girl attending St. John's High School during my high school years (1963–6) and Sisler, the other North End high school with a large Native population nearby, was similarly lily white.

The large presence of Native children in Winnipeg's North End schools by the mid-fifties reflected a post-war movement of First Nations peoples in western Canada off reserves and into cities. Racial discrimination dogged their every step. Employers and landlords did not want them; whites complained when Natives moved into their neighbourhoods; the social welfare authorities accused them of laziness. Yet, for many, a move to the cities from crowded reserves made sense. As Europeans encroached on their reserve lands, subsistence as hunters, trappers, and fishers became more difficult. Yet there were few opportunities to seek wage work on or close to reserves. The Department of Indian Affairs ruled their lives on reserves, often imposed its will on them in the selection of leaders, and seemed more concerned with building its Ottawa bureaucracy than in providing services on reserves. Though it paid Native health costs, doctors' visits to reserves were few and far between. In the city, hospitals were close by and though the Department of Indian Affairs was inconsistent in its willingness to cover the health costs of Natives who left reserves, few hospitals turned away "indigent" patients. Education in the cities, however poorly it addressed the culture of First Nations, was at public schools close to home. The children were not separated from their parents. On the reserve, there was Department pressure to send children to off-reserve residential schools where they could receive indoctrination about the need to assimilate into white society without their parents serving as a counter-weight at home. Here they were told that their parents' ways were obsolete, if not immoral, by the women and men of the cloth who ran the residential schools. Native children were often embarrassed by their people's ways when they got home. Limited contact with their kin caused estrangement for many and left them without parenting models when they began to have families of their own. Many of these children experienced violence at th hands of the preacher-teachers. They were beaten for speaking their home languages or for infringing other rules of the school and were told that it was for their own good because the school was out to "civilize" them. Many became sexual prey to pedophiles who, safe behind the mystique that society bestowed upon clerics, exploited small children and created psychological damage that would last a lifetime. Others encountered kinder

Mohawk Private Huron Eldon Brant receives Medal of Courage from General Bernard Montgomery. NAC PA-130065.

teachers and some enjoyed their education. But most keenly felt the separation from their families during their formative years.[19]

Federal education policies for Natives did begin to change in the 1950s after the report of the Special Joint Committee of the Senate and the House of Commons that sat in 1947 and 1948 was prepared. The committee had heard testimony from Native peoples from across the country, but it heard them through the prism of European understandings. First Nations peoples provided the committee with graphic evidence of the poverty of their reserves and the poor medical treatment available in their communities. They blamed the Indian Act which gave control over their lives to government bureaucrats and they blamed the government and private interests who ignored the spirit and sometimes the letter of treaties. Native lands were signed away by government officials without Native consent and industrial developments were established on their land without their participation and without thought given to the impact on wildlife upon which Native hunters depended. The First Nations people wanted their rights respected and control over their own communities.

But the senators and MPs had their own view of what was good for Native people. Rejecting Native calls for respect for traditional Native lifestyles and beliefs, the Joint Committee focussed on assimilation of First Nations people into the larger Canadian population. This was the philosophy that had guided government policy since the Indian Act was first proclaimed in 1876: Native people's separate existence within Canadian society was doomed in the long term and government policy must look to their gradual integration into the larger society. Rather than calling for the Department of Indian Affairs to be disbanded or to have its powers reduced, the committee wanted its powers strengthened so that Natives need deal with only one branch of government. The committee recognized, however, that governments had not treated Native people magnanimously and did recommend a greater infusion of cash into Native housing, education, and social welfare. During the 1950s, the Department began to construct schools on reserves to replace the residential schools. But control over the schools rested with the Department rather than the communities.

The federal government's notion of what was good for Natives often led to decisions to close down existing reserves and relocate them. There was usually little consultation with the Natives, but promises of new housing and better medical care led some younger Natives to greet such relocations more optimistically than the older people who feared a further erosion of Native independence. Such a division was noticeable, for example, on the Grassy Narrows reserve near Kenora, Ontario, which was relocated in 1963 despite resistance from most reserve residents. The old reserve had been remote enough to keep the forces of the state away most of the time. That changed after the move. As a former chief would later recall:

> You have to remember that just twenty years ago our people saw no social workers, no welfare administrators. No police force was stationed on our reserve; no teachers lived on our reserve. The first white doctors started flying in to treat tuberculosis cases only in the 1950s, just before the Mennonites came.
>
> Suddenly, after we moved to this new reserve, we saw government people all the time. They came to tell us how we should build our houses and where we should build them. They came to tell us how we should run our Chief and Council. They told us about local government, and they told us we

Inuit children return to the North in 1960, after hospitalization for tuberculosis. NAC
PA-193047.

had to have a band administration to take care of the money
and the programs that were going to come from the government.
Within a few years of the move to the new reserve, we had
social workers taking our children away to foster homes.[20]

For the Inuit, like the Indians, government bureaucrats envisaged
greater self-reliance but also greater integration into Canadian life.
"Instead of reservations they wanted 'northern suburbs,'"[21] write the
authors of a study of Inuit relocation in the eastern Arctic. By the
mid-sixties, most Inuit had been removed from their traditional hunting and trapping camps to live in sedentary communities where social
workers, teachers, and administrators from the south tried to reshape
their social values. Like other First Nations, they resisted the
changes: "Inuit struggled to preserve hunting and trapping practices,
language, artistic forms of expression, cosmologies, and collective
social and economic organization."[22] Interestingly, while many Natives were moved to settlements that were less remote, the better to
"civilize" them, some Inuit were moved into the high Arctic as part
of a Canadian effort to assert sovereignty over the region. In their
new homes, which were often shacks rather than the modern-comfort
homes promised by the bureaucrats, they often went hungry because
they were far from the caribou that were their traditional food source
and suffered periodic epidemics of tuberculosis.

Class, Gender, and Post-war Society

Apart from race, social class was the main determinant of whether one shared in the good life of the early post-war years. Vacations, new cars, visits to beauty salons, cottages at the lake, golf club memberships, electric toys for kids, and an array of electric appliances were available to women and men of the middle class and to a broadening group of blue-collar workers. Indeed, both rising prosperity and Cold War ideology caused a rethinking during the 1950s and 1960s of the concept, "working class." Karl Marx had called upon workers of the world to arise in the 1840s, telling them "You have nothing to lose but your chains." In part, Marx was calling upon workers to rise up against an economic system which gave profit-minded employers the right to determine how work was organized rather than allowing workers themselves to shape their work-day and the priorities of their workplace. In this regard, the capitalist system had changed little since Marx's day. But Marx had also condemned capitalism because it deprived workers of the products of their own labour. Such an analysis seemed less appropriate for the years of the post-war boom than it may have seemed before the war. Windsor and Oshawa autoworkers were able to buy new cars; lumber workers in British Columbia were able to build comfortable homes; Canadian General Electric workers in Peterborough bought new appliances. If a quarter of Canadian society was excluded in whole or in part from the orgy of 1950s buying, many others were doing quite well financially.

Among the poor, the elderly loomed large. Their situation reflected several factors. Elderly men had passed their most productive years in the labour force in a period when wages were low and it was difficult to save for years beyond retirement. (Indeed, compulsory retirement at age sixty-five or seventy had not been as prevalent before the war as it would become afterwards and many old men worked until they were dead or too old to work.) Elderly single women were even less likely than men to have savings to rely upon when they could no longer work since women's wages were so much lower than men's. Widows were the most vulnerable and the most numerous group among the aged. Out of the work force since their marriages, they were unlikely to be able to find paid work if they were over forty. If their husbands had left no insurance — and the majority would have carried no life insurance — they were destitute and reliant upon state and private charity unless they had living children willing to pay for their upkeep.

Poverty among the elderly also reflected the insufficiency of Canada's old-age pensions. Even after they were raised from forty-six dollars to fifty-five dollars per month by the Diefenbaker government in 1957, that was barely enough to rent an apartment. In several wealthy provinces, led by Alberta, there was a modest top-up of the senior's pension by the province. This helped, but would still not provide enough income to allow a pensioner to eat, clothe herself, and pay her medical and transportation bills, much less have money to spare for entertainment. Some lived with their grown children but many had no grown children living nearby. There was, in any case, less willingness on the part of families in the post-war period to have three-generations living under the same roof. Instead, families exerted pressure on the state authorities to care for the indigent or sick elderly. In the social discourse of the period, elderly people had a right to live on their own if at all possible and to receive institutional care if necessary. They were viewed as having made their contribution to Canada during their working years and to be entitled to consideration by its governments in their declining years. Unlike working-age people, particularly men and single women, they were not regarded as parasitical if they were on social assistance.[23] Governments responded to this changing view of the state's responsibility to the aged by subsidizing community and church groups that undertook to build seniors' lodges. There were few such projects in the fifties but a fairly large number were constructed in the sixties and afterwards.

In Newfoundland, the law required a son or daughter, grandchild, step-child, or foster child to take responsibility for a dependent parent. The province had a provincial Home for the Aged and Infirm, a Salvation Army Sunset Lodge, as well as licensed boarding-houses and approved private homes for old people. Residents of the Home for the Aged and Infirm were charged thirty-five dollars of their forty dollars monthly Old Age Security cheque for room and board. In Prince Edward Island destitute old people were cared for at public expense at the provincial infirmary, along with "the infirm, feeble minded, crippled, and helpless." Nova Scotia, like Prince Edward Island, had no government-financed homes for the aged and placed its elderly poor in county homes or poor houses, operated by municipalities under the terms of the Provincial Relief Act. New Brunswick's system paralleled Nova Scotia's.[24] The poor house, as its name implied, was a dumping-ground for those too poor to pay for their own accommodations and food. Only after federal monies aided the provinces, beginning in 1956, to provide direct assistance to the poor were the Atlantic poorhouses gradually shut down.

Men of working age in the 1950s could hope for a better time in their twilight years. Men enjoyed a limited mobility within the social structure. Though most sons of blue-collar workers and farmers also took on blue-collar work or remained on farms, some were able to take advantage of a growing number of opportunities for salesmen, supervisors of various kinds, and other white-collar jobs in an expanding economy. Education helped in the search for employment and some entered the professions that benefited from the growing prosperity of the period such as engineering, medicine, and dentistry. But most of the men who took advantage of university education continued to come from advantaged backgrounds, from families either with money or with high educational attainments, often both.

Whether they were professionals, business people, white-collar or blue-collar workers, men who were "breadwinners" in the late forties and the fifties worked long hours to make a living for their families. Armed forces personnel, truck drivers, train crews, and airplane pilots, among other groups, spent days or weeks at a time away from their families. Workers in industry and salesmen often worked shifts, and long, irregular hours. Many, nonetheless, spent a great deal of time with their children either at home or in organized community activities such as sports and Scouts. Because the home was regarded as the locus of women's work, most men did no cooking or cleaning, doing only yard work and chores requiring brawn. A large cohort of the family men of this period indeed spent little time at home. Work kept them away, they argued, and because of their long hours of work, they had a right to spend their free hours with buddies in the tavern or pool hall rather than with their wives and children. Men interviewed for oral histories of the period almost universally expressed regret for not having spent more time with their kids when they were growing up.[25] In some cases, at least, it seems likely that their rationalization of this failure in terms of necessary working hours owes more to collective mythology than to a reasonable assessment of what their choices were at the time. Just as most suburban women in oral histories deny that they ever fit Betty Friedan's categories of depressed housewives, most working men of the postwar period deny that they had any choice but to make home life a small part of their day. In fairness, the structure of many jobs meant that many indeed had no choice.

Women enjoyed less social mobility and their class position was generally determined by whom they married rather than by what work, if any, they performed outside the household economy. The position of women in any social class could be precarious. Violent husbands who beat wives and children existed in all social classes, and social conventions made it difficult for women of any social class to lay charges against their husbands or even to let friends and relatives know about the abuse they were suffering. While divorces increased dramatically from the mid-forties onwards, they had started from a rather low base and remained uncommon throughout the 1950s and early 1960s. In 1960, there were only about 7000 divorces for a population of 18 million. Divorces were expensive and grounds for divorce were restricted to adultery, except in Nova Scotia where cruelty could also be invoked. Limited opportunities for employment gave many women pause before considering a divorce. Courts were often stingy about divorce settlements and were notoriously uninterested in enforcing maintenance agreements and child support payments.

The gender ideal of this period was quite clear: men were to go out and work for income, while women were supposed to have babies and take care of the home. This had also been the pre-war ideal, but it had been somewhat shaken by the extent of wartime employment for women, though jobs remained sex segregated in almost all industries even during the war.[26] Many women, for personal and/or financial reasons, wanted to continue to combine motherhood with paid work after the war. But the choice was often not provided. Industrial employers fired women from production jobs that were traditionally a male preserve, leaving only the stereotyped clerical and sales jobs available for women. Married women were fired in preference for single women who were presumed less likely to leave work within a short time to have a baby; pregnant women were denied leave from work to have their babies: few employers were willing to hire mothers of babies or small children. Government policies also attempted to discourage working wives and mothers: federal funds for daycare, never more than token, were withdrawn along with tax concessions for employed wives; mothers who left the work force to have babies were automatically denied unemployment insurance.[27]

Trade unions often worked with employers to ensure that such gender discrimination was practised. Though women within the trade

Claude Jodoin (standing), first president of the CLC. NAC PA-116448.

union movement attempted to convince their union brothers that women should have equal rights with men to secure employment and the opportunity to pursue the same range of jobs, the notion that men should earn "family wages" was paramount with male trade unionists. The trade union movement did go on record as favouring "equal pay for equal work," that is, parity across gender and age lines for the same job, but this was largely motivated by concerns that employers would hire women and children to do "men's work" if pay equity were not in place to remove this incentive. The unions themselves were almost exclusively run by men and gave little consideration to issues that were important to women's participation in the labour force. The subject of daycare, for example, received no consideration from either of the two major labour federations, the Congress of Canadian Labour (CCL) and the Trades and Labour Congress (TLC), that merged to form the Canadian Labour Congress (CLC) in 1956. Daycare never made the agenda of any national convention of the CLC before the seventies.

Even progressive trade unions such as the Communist-led United Electrical, Radio, and Machine Workers of Canada (UE) did little to promote either employment of women or women's activities inside the union. The UE called upon women to take a more active role in the union but ignored the structural reasons why working mothers, in particular, were unable to do so. Insisting that gender and race should not be used to divide workers as a class, the UE acted as if women and non-whites did not have specific issues to deal with that might require them to make cross-class alliances. Men and women within the union, for example, came to opposite conclusions on the campaign to have the federal Department of Labour establish a Women's Bureau. The men regarded this as "playing into the hands" of class enemies who wanted to divide and weaken workers, while the women saw this as a recognition of the special problems confronting working women.[28]

Popular periodicals of the time condemned mothers who went out to work as a disgrace to their sex. They were blamed for a host of real and imagined social problems such as increased juvenile delinquency and a supposed emasculation of men that was occurring with the transition from farming and blue-collar work to white-collar employment. The "organization man," lamented psychologists with reference to the growing army of supervisory employees, accountants, salesmen, and advertising executives, had little opportunity to express his masculinity within the confines of work that was highly structured by the organization and its efforts to maximize profits and services to clients. Idealizing the lives of men of earlier generations, these supposed experts on human behaviour, themselves the product of a society of greater specialization of work and expertise, suggested that earlier generations, in their struggle for survival, had required men to demonstrate their physical prowess on a daily basis. Now men were becoming soft and unsure of their masculinity. The last thing they needed, worried the male psychologists, was to have women usurp from them their last shred of masculinity: their exclusive role as breadwinner.[29] This social construction of eternal masculine and feminine social roles, which people transgressed (it was claimed) with the risk of destroying the social fabric, was abetted by Cold War rhetoric which placed the blame for all challenges to social rules at the door of foreign-influenced Communists. In Quebec, the notion of a rigid separation of sex roles was particularly touted by the Roman Catholic Church, whose influence throughout Quebec society was omni-present before the 1960s. The Church hierarchy, Catholic-oriented newspapers such as *Le Devoir*, and the Catholic trade union federation, the Confédération des travailleurs catholiques et canadiens, all joined in promoting a maternalist ideology, denouncing paid work for women and rejecting publicly sponsored daycare as encouraging women to abandon their motherly duties.

Advice columns about raising children assumed that mothers alone were responsible for their children. So, for example, a registered nurse, writing in *The Star Weekly* in 1947 about buying toys for children, addressed all her comments to "Mommy," and advised that "a wise mother will study the educational value of toys."[30] The same issue of the popular magazine carried ads that made clear that when mother was not playing Mommy, she was to focus on her looks.

Polls suggested that there was little support for working mothers. In 1960, a Gallup poll reported that ninety-three percent of all Canadians, with little difference among men and women, believed that married women should "concentrate on looking after the home when they have young children" rather than combining childcare with paid work. Indeed polls suggested that most Canadians favoured discrimination against *any* woman, married or unmarried, in the awarding of jobs, though significantly this prejudice declined markedly when rates of unemployment were low. The message was clear however: Canadians believed that men were the natural providers for a home and that women should resign themselves to either motherhood without paid work or paid work in a narrow band of low-paying jobs which most men did not consider fit jobs for their sex.

But feminists made their point of view known. Freda F. Waldon, in a letter to *Saturday Night* in May 1945, described herself as a feminist from the twenties, and applauded the writer of an earlier letter who opposed the idea of women's economic dependence on men. She predicted that many young working women, once the war was over, would react as she and many of her friends did "after the last war." "Jobs were plentiful: we didn't worry about getting a job, but about getting an interesting one; and having settled into an interesting career, we asked why we should give it up if we happened to marry?" The Depression, she noted, had resulted in a setback for the cause of women's work but she trusted that gains made in the twenties would be retained and extended after World War II.[31]

After an initial steep decline in female employment in the post-war period, the numbers of women working began to creep up. So did the percentage of married women among them, including married women with children. Only 4.1 percent of married women had been in the work force in 1941; the corresponding figure for 1951 was ten percent and, for 1963, 22.9 percent. Some of these women actively defied the social convention that labelled them selfish people who were depriving men of jobs and their children of mothering. Most of them probably accepted this convention but felt they had no choice but to work because they were sole providers for their households, or because their husbands earned insufficient or fluctuating incomes.

Some were not dirt poor but they were caught in the contradictions that the post-war picture of gender roles embodied. If they were to live the lives that American television shows and Canadian government advertising campaigns extolled, they were supposed to be raising their children in single-family homes with at least some of the material advantages that post-war prosperity promised. They were also supposed to be setting aside money so that their children might later enjoy the benefits of higher education, which remained prohibitively expensive for a majority of families. But the "family wage" ideal, while it reflected the gender stereotype that the state as well as popular perceptions endorsed, was at odds with the workings of a marketplace economy. Though the government gave mothers family allowances, these were quite small, particularly since governments, conscious of trying to keep taxes down in the 1950s, had failed to raise the allowances to match increases in the cost of living. So, working families in which the "breadwinner" received a small wage could only share in post-war prosperity or, at a minimum, raise themselves above the poverty level by having both adults in a household work.[32]

With editorialists and public officials continuously berating the working mother, working mothers tended to be defensive about their decision to seek work outside the home. Few were persuaded to join campaigns to make a public issue out of what governments pretended was a private issue: daycare for children of working mothers. As we saw in Chapter One, the authorities branded such campaigns as Communist attempts to undermine the Canadian family. Working mothers defensively told researchers that their children were well cared for while they went out to work, but studies of private childcare disputed such claims. Two Edmonton studies in the late 1950s were typical. One, by the Edmonton Council of Community Services in 1956, revealed that children as young as one month were "being left at 6 a.m. and being picked up at 7 p.m. in places which cared for twenty-five or thirty children with one adult in charge." The University Women's Club two years later, after investigating fifty-four private facilities that advertised preschool childcare, advised the provincial government that the condition of the facilities (usually private homes), the child–supervisor ratio, and the lack of programming in these daycare centres all pointed out the need for provincial supervision of childcare for working mothers. But nothing was done. Social service agencies, especially those dominated by women, having attempted unsuccessfully in most provinces — Ontario and British Columbia were partial exceptions — to convince governments to regulate childcare operations, began information campaigns to let the public know how many women were working, and how precarious their childcare arrangements were. The hope was that there would be a groundswell of support for public involvement in making high-quality, affordable daycare available to working families.[33]

The jobs available to women were restricted. Nursing, teaching, and social work were the professions dominated by women, and women in these fields earned significantly more money than the majority of working women who were concentrated in secretarial, clerical, and cashiering jobs. But they faced "pink ceilings" since most jobs for hospital administrators, school principals and social agency managers went to men. Women were employed as salespersons by department stores in women's clothing, but the better-paying sales jobs in the economy, selling cars, appliances, and real estate, were still largely seen as men's preserves. Most men and women preferred to buy from a commission salesman rather than a saleswoman because they did not, as the discourse of the time would have it, "want to deprive a married man of money for his family."

Just how well many married men were able to bring home a "family wage" was often the result of union struggles. Though the image of the period suggests quiescence, the truth is that the working class's ability to share, at least in part, in post-war prosperity was the result of a great deal of militancy.

Trade Union Struggles

Trade union membership had doubled during World War II and at the end of the war, workers were determined to win wage increases that wartime wage controls had denied them. In 1946 and 1947 there were over 400 strikes involving about 175,000 workers and embracing "logging and lumbering, metal, asbestos and coal mining, steel, textiles, transportation, meat packing, and automobile and rubber production."[34] The strikers had the upper hand. With companies anxious to cash in on consumers' wartime savings — even if earnings were often modest, the priority placed on war effort production ensured that they had little to spend them upon while the war raged — few industries could afford to starve the workers into submission. Worker militancy made it apparent in most cases that workers would remain out for a long time unless companies made significant concessions. For example, ten thousand striking Ford autoworkers in

1945 kept maintenance men and police out of Ford's powerhouse by parking their locked cars in front of the plant and going home. The blockading automobiles occupied about twenty city blocks. About 35,000 British Columbia loggers, striking in 1946, used marches on the provincial capital and "tag days" in Vancouver to raise money for the strikers, to win sympathy for strikers' demands for a forty-hour week, a wage increase, and industry recognition of the International Woodworkers of America.

Corporations were anxious to settle strikes and even willing to concede wage increases in order to get production rolling. But they were determined, in many cases, to resist having to recognize unions, fearing that an independent and democratically chosen set of workers' representatives might demand a voice in running businesses. Governments attempted to allay their fears while still conceding the right of workers to bargain collectively through unions of their choosing. First the federal government and then the provinces established legislation that recognized the right of workers to join unions and then limited the powers of these unions so that the rights of property remained vastly superior to the powers of labour. The federal Cabinet responded to wartime labour radicalism, as well as the growing strength of the CCF among working people, by passing Privy Council Order 1003 in February 1944. Using its wartime emergency powers over labour relations, the government declared that workers had a right, by majority vote, to declare their adhesion to a trade union and to have that union certified by government as their bargaining agent. Management was then required to bargain collectively with the union and the contracts arrived at in such negotiations would have the force of law behind them.

Such legal recognition of unions was hailed as a victory by many labour leaders who had been frustrated for years by a legal regime in which employers were not required to negotiate with unions under any circumstances. Since only a minority of employers had chosen to work with the unions, workers had been forced to resort to extra-legal methods to compel employers to bargain collectively with their labour force. But this only rarely resulted in victories because the state almost invariably came to the protection of capital in its battles with labour. Communists and other radicals however questioned the new framework for "labour-capital harmony" which PC 1003 envisioned. The order-in-council restricted areas of bargaining to wages and a small set of working conditions, mainly hours of labour. Once a contract was negotiated between management and workers, the union was held legally responsible for ensuring that no strikes or other industrial action would occur over any issue, including flagrant violation of the agreement by the company, until the contract had expired. Whereas, previously, workers might lay down tools in solidarity with an employee unjustly treated by management or to protest speed-ups or unsafe working conditions, now they would have to resort to a third-party grievance arbitration process. Legalisms rather than class conflict would determine the outcome of workers' grievances. Critics of these provisions suggested that the government was incorporating unions into the state apparatus. In future, unions, instead of being the expression of workers' autonomous wishes, would be agents of the state and employers in forcing workers to limit their weapons for dealing with employer malfeasance.

After the war, as labour relations outside of jurisdictions controlled by the federal government, such as railways and banks, returned to the provinces, legislation modelled on PC 1003 was passed by the various provinces as well as by the federal government. But, while left-wing critics of the new labour regime worried that it weakened labour autonomy, many employers remained determined to limit union incursions into their workplaces. During the Ford strike in 1946, for example, the employer held out against the union's demand for a "closed shop," that is, the inclusion in a certified bargaining unit of all workers in the designated company or production group, whether or not they had been part of the majority who voted to have the union represent the workers. With organized labour across the country holding demonstrations in favour of the Ford workers, the Ontario government appointed Supreme Court Justice Ivan Rand as an arbitrator with power to deal with the thorny closed-shop issue. The "Rand formula" for ending the impasse was to allow workers the right to remain outside the union but to require all workers to pay union dues since they would all benefit from the union's successes in collective bargaining.

While radicals may have lamented that the price for union recognition was the agreement by labour leaders to collaborate with management in preventing workers from "wildcatting" to rectify an injustice, many workers were pleased with the results of the new labour regime in Canada. The strike wave of 1946–7 led to major wage gains for workers, including workers in non-unionized firms whose employers hoped to use wage concessions to prevent unionization and strikes. Average wages increased from 69.4 cents per hour in 1945 to 91.3 cents per hour in 1948, while the average work week

Policing the asbestos strike, 1949. The strike was a turning point in Quebec and helped form the basis of the Quiet Revolution. NAC PA-130356.

fell from 44.3 to forty-two hours, the latter partly the result of labour's success in getting legislatures to require employers to pay overtime pay for most workers who logged in over forty hours per week.

Unionization was uneven across the labour force. Large manufacturers in southern Ontario and resource industrialists in British Columbia and northern Ontario proved least able to resist the union drive. Smaller employers, even in manufacturing, could use intimidation to prevent their workers from organizing and provincially appointed labour boards proved largely unwilling to investigate union claims that employers threatened workers who supported union drives with dismissal or the removal of the firm to another city. The expanding service sector, however, proved largely resistant to organized labour's attempts to enrol workers.

Beginning in the late 1940s, the Retail Wholesale and Department Store Union (RWDSU), aided by the CCL, made a concerted attempt to organize the T. Eaton Company in Toronto as a prelude to a major effort to organize the retail sector across the country. While the RWDSU signed up thousands of women, it could not overcome a massive campaign by the company against unionism that included everything from Red-baiting to threats to reduce the number of part-time employees if the unionization drive succeeded. The company also used some carrots: wage increases and an employee pension fund materialized close to the time of the certification vote for the union. A majority of Eaton's workers voted not to unionize but the strike drive left them a short-term legacy of better wages.

CCL leaders, tied to breadwinner notions, argued that the strike demonstrated that women, who formed the overwhelming majority of Eaton's employees, were uninterested in unions. They put little effort afterwards into trying to organize firms where women workers predominated. The sexist stereotype however, had little basis in fact. In Montreal the workers at Dupuis Frères, a department store, which, like Eaton's, had a mainly female labour force, not only joined the Confédération des travailleurs catholiques et canadiens (CTCC), but struck the store in a successful bid to win wage concessions and improved working conditions. The CTCC, formed in 1921 by the Catholic church in an effort to counter the "godless" unions that had organized Quebec workers to that point, had begun with the philosophy that workers' and owners' rights were harmonious and that strikes resulted because unions applied man's rules of violence rather than God's rules of co-operation and humility. They quickly learned that the Catholic workers who joined their federation had no interest in the Church hierarchy's views of unionism as such. They wanted results, and to deliver, the Catholic unions had to behave much like other unions, resorting to strikes when necessary to pressure recalcitrant employers and to prevent workers from leaving the CTCC and joining the Trades and Labour Congress (TLC) or the CCL.

The Dupuis Frères workers' achievement was particularly remarkable because Quebec's labour code was the most pro-employer in the country and the provincial government of Maurice Duplessis the most ham-fisted in dealing with workers' grievances. In Quebec, the Padlock Law of 1937, which forbade Communist gatherings, remained on the lawbooks until the Supreme Court ruled the law unconstitutional in 1957. Duplessis used the law and restrictive labour legislation to outlaw Communist unions, jail labour activists, and make liberal use of the provincial police to limit the ability of striking workers to picket and to keep scabs from taking their jobs. A turning-point for Quebec's labour movement came in 1949 during a five-month strike of asbestos workers in the company town of Asbestos in the Eastern Townships. The workers had been organized by the CTCC and, aware of the large gap between their wages and those of Ontario miners, called for a large wage increase. They also wanted asbestos dust in the mine cleared up and the imposition of the Rand formula on Canadian Johns-Manville, the subsidiary of the American company which owned the mines.

Supported by the Duplessis government, which sent in provincial police to protect strikebreakers, the company refused to negotiate with the union. The workers, supported by most townspeople, took control of the town. But Duplessis, screaming about Communist plots, had hundreds of workers arrested. The company, which owned the workers' homes, evicted strikers and used the scabs and provincial police to break the strike. Quebec society was polarized by the strike. Many workers questioned the sincerity of Duplessis' rhetorical nationalism when, once again, he proved to be virtually a puppet of English-speaking capitalists. The Roman Catholic Church was unable to paper over the cracks in its own organization; though the hierarchy was deeply enmeshed with Premier Duplessis because of his firm support of continued church authority over social services and education, many priests, particularly in the Eastern Townships, had taken the strikers' side. They were joined by Archbishop Joseph Charbonneau of Montreal. The hierarchy transferred Charbonneau to Victoria but it could do little to stem the tide of disaffection for church conservatism among workers. The CTCC moved further and further away from the church and in 1960 renamed itself the Confédération des syndicats nationaux, breaking all ties with its confessional past. The change had great symbolic importance because it reflected both the growing secularism of Quebec society and the weakening links in the province between nationalist ideology and Catholic ideology. Before the war, the two had seemed inseparable.

More defeats were in store for Quebec workers after the Asbestos strike. Textile workers striking in Valleyfield and Louiseville were defeated by state intervention that included the arrests of the strike leaders. In 1957, a long and bloody strike by the United Steelworkers of America at Murdochville had the feel of a rerun of Asbestos: provincial police and company thugs working together to knock strikers senseless and protect scabs; nonsensical statements from Duplessis about Communists; but also collaboration between the international unions and the Catholic unions in trying to deal with a ruthless employer aided by a compliant, pseudo-nationalist provincial government. The death of a steelworker and the injuries experienced by many others demonstrated the ruthlessness of both the provincial government and the employer. The election of the Liberals in 1960, which ushered in the so-called "Quiet Revolution," marked another turning point. The Liberals brought Quebec labour law in line with that of Ontario, and unions in the province proved better able than ever to win wage and working condition concessions for their members.

Labour relations in the 1950s were rocky in more places than Quebec. Alberta's labour law was almost as reactionary as Quebec's and Alberta Social Credit Premier Ernest Manning firmly believed that unions formed part of an international Communist conspiracy to undermine capitalism and democracy. While Saskatchewan's labour laws made unionism relatively easy to achieve, Alberta established a variety of roadblocks that made it difficult to organize workers and even more difficult to lauch successful strikes. In Newfoundland, where Premier Joey Smallwood prided himself on his past experiences as a labour organizer, it became clear that this particular worm had turned. Smallwood sided with the employers in a strike led by the International Woodworkers of America, used state violence that led to three deaths to break the strike, and then declared the IWA illegal, imposing a company union on the workers, that is, a union that was not independent of the companies with which it had to bargain.

For all the apparent militancy of some unions, most would have been quite happy had governments simply lived up to the spirit of PC 1003. Though employers and governments pretended otherwise, the trade union movement of the 1950s was far from revolutionary. It was better characterized by the outstretched hand than the mailed fist. While labour did support the extension of the welfare state to include prepaid medical insurance, generous universal pensions, and the like, it accepted the capitalist system. It was largely uninterested in nationalization of private industry and even less interested in any ideas favouring workers' control over industries rather than control by managers answerable to shareholders mainly interested in profits. Gordon Cushing, general secretary of the TLC, told the Canadian Chamber of Commerce delegates at their annual convention in 1955 that the worker "doesn't want to be or to share management." As for unions, "we in organized labour do not want to interfere with management. We do not want any part of the management of the enterprise."

Workplace democracy, then, had no role in the union agenda. All that workers asked for, if their unions were to be believed, was for their share of the growing economic pie of the 1950s. They did not quite succeed in getting it, although many did not do badly. Manufacturing employees experienced a thirty-seven percent increase in their standard of living during the fifties. This did not quite match the forty-eight percent increase in output of manufacturing firms in Canada, and provides part of the explanation for the recession that began in 1957, that is, a lack of purchasing power relative to inventories. Still, for the workers who experienced a marked increase in living standards, the system seemed to work. Why, conservative editorialists asked, were socialists still harping on the need for redistribution of the existing economic pie when the capitalist system provided incentives to individuals to increase the size of that pie? Trade unions indeed seemed more interested in ensuring that workers received their share of the increased pie rather than in the overall distribution of wealth in Canadian society. Still, one can easily overstate the conservatism of Canadians in the age of prosperity. Opinion polls in the late fifties and early sixties suggested that four Canadians in ten with an opinion on the matter would like to see extensive nationalization of industry.[35] Why these people chose, for the most part, not to vote for the CCF is unclear though, in practice, even that party was soft-pedalling its support for nationalization by that time. Many people who had doubts about the durability of the prosperity of the post-war period had mixed feelings about the debate between capitalism and socialism. That debate was largely one regarding the best ways to encourage both economic growth and a better living for those at the bottom of the economic ladder. While everyone debated ways of making the economic pie grow and how that pie should be redistributed, almost no one with a public forum seemed to worry abou the impact on the human and global environments of the relentless pursuit of growth.

Economic Growth and the Environment

Throughout the early post-war period, there was little public concern about the ecological impact of the pace and character of economic development. The omnipresence of the privately owned vehicle meant the need for burning seemingly unlimited quantities of fossil fuels to produce and then operate this symbol of individual freedom. Vast oil discoveries in Alberta, added to increased supplies of petroleum from the Middle East, caused complacency about supply. Oil prices were so low that Alberta required a federal subsidy to encourage the major energy companies to explore and produce in the province rather than simply import foreign petroleum. While people complained about the smell of gasoline and there was a vague awareness that the lead it contained might be harmful to people, such complaints were usually set aside with an "oh well, that's the price of progress." That price also seemed to include a denuding of Canada's forests. Forest companies argued that they were tenants and could not be expected to worry about reforestation. The provincial governments that leased the land to these wealthy tenants, meanwhile, spent only 2.5 cents on each dollar they received in 1950 in taxes and stumpage fees from these companies on reforestation.[36] In British Columbia in the 1950s, only one tree was planted for every eight that were cut down.

On the Prairies, a long-term process of soil erosion continued unabated and much-advertised fertilizers had dangerous side effects on the health of both the soil and the farmers. The influence of a few multi-national seed companies led to a focus on planting a few highly productive seed hybrids, resulting in less plant biodiversity and the danger that a blight that struck a few seeds could lead to international catastrophe.[37]

Water diversions, carried out throughout northern Canada to satisfy southern Canada's insatiable demands for more hydroelectricity in the era of prosperity, were hailed as examples of the wonders of modern engineering in the service of humanity, or at least of consumerism. But for northern Natives they meant a serious disruption in millennia-old lifestyles as ecological change affected animal and plant populations, making subsistence outside the industrial capitalist economy ever more elusive.

The public's short-term memory regarding environmental disasters is evident in many local histories. Oka, the small Quebec municipality that only became known to most Canadians when Natives and the town leaders came into open conflict in July 1990, serves as an example. Deforestation of the area surrounding the village in the eighteenth and nineteenth centuries removed wind breaks and led to huge sand slides on the town by the end of the nineteenth century. A pioneer reforestation program begun by Oka village priest Joseph-Daniel Lefebvre, from 1886 to 1897, was the opening salvo in an ecological campaign to save the town and the surrounding area. The Mohawk of the Kanawake and Kanesatake reserves then planted a hemlock forest west of the pine plantation under Lefebvre's direction. The tree-planting saved the area. The sandy soils remained in the forest rather than spilling out onto the town and both tree branches catching falling rain and pine needles on the ground helped to stop soil erosion. In 1947, the townspeople, anxious to prevent a recurrence of the ecological disasters of an earlier generation, expropriated local forest lands to protect their town. The municipal council banned all development in the forested area except for a golf course in the eastern half of the expropriated area. Ten years later, however, they allowed a housing development on the western half of the forest and before long, developments were being permitted with little thought given to either the forest's protection of the town or the impact of developments on the local Natives.[38]

Some of the post-war unconcern about the environment was shattered in 1962 when the American scientist Rachel Carson produced a hard-hitting environmental picture of North America in her best-seller *Silent Spring*. While the rest of North America was celebrating the ingenuity that had created such prosperity after the war, no matter its distribution, Carson painted a picture of a deteriorating environment in which fertilizers were ruining the soil and poisoning wildlife, rivers and lakes were dying, and both animal and plant species were disappearing because of humans' anthropocentric thinking. DDT had been portrayed by *Maclean's* in 1945 as an "orchard guardian" and killer of the spruce budworm, with no effect on mammals except where there were "very heavy concentrations." Birds, honeybees, and most fish, frogs, snakes, and toads were admitted to suffer from its effects.[39] Carson provided evidence that DDT, in fact, had a devastating impact on the natural environment.

While many people read Carson, there was no significant broad-based environmental movement in Canada in the early sixties. The closest thing was the anti-nuclear movement which opposed nuclear deterrence, the centrepiece of Cold War diplomacy, as madness that threatened the continued existence of life on earth. There were also groups who took no position on the use of nuclear weapons in warfare as such, but who opposed nuclear tests because of the dangers for human health that the release of large amounts of radioactivity into the air posed.

Conclusion

A snapshot of Canada in the fifties would certainly include the suburban nuclear family with Dad at work in an office and Mom tending children and making purchases for the surburban home from an expanded array of stores. But it would be a distorted picture if it excluded the working mother, the blue-collar worker on strike for a decent wage, the children without lunches, and the homeless old people. Veterans had been promised homes fit for heroes, and veterans were relatively well treated by the Canadian state. But, though media images might like to capture only the suburban families familiar to viewers of television "sitcoms," the real portrait of Canada at the time is far more complicated.

Three

The Regions and the Provinces

The general trends of poverty in the midst of plenty mentioned in the first two chapters were observable throughout Canada. But there were important regional variations in terms of economic development, political developments and the degree of social change. This chapter explores developments within the various regions and sub-regions of the country.

Quebec: Towards the Quiet Revolution

In September 1959, Maurice Duplessis, "le Chef," who had ruled the province from 1936 to 1939 and then from 1944 to 1959, died. His replacement, Paul Sauvé, appeared more liberal and less venal than the long-time Union Nationale leader, and the promise of evolution of government programs in much the same direction as in the rest of Canada seemed strong. But Sauvé died after only four months in office and his replacement, Antonio Barrette, a long-time Labour Minister in the Duplessis years, led a divided party with little clear direction.[1]

The result was that there was an opening for the Quebec Liberals, who had been unable to penetrate rural Quebec during the years of Duplessis' politics of rewarding constituencies that voted for the government and punishing those that did not. As in other provincial legislatures, rural Quebec was over-represented in the Quebec National Assembly in proportion to its percentage of the Quebec population. The francophone districts of working-class Montreal, in any event, also gave significant support to the Chef, accepting, to some degree, his propaganda that he was standing up for the rights of Québécois against a federal government in which francophones, inevitably, could only play a minority role. With Duplessis gone and a lacklustre premier leading the Union Nationale in the 1960 election, the Liberals won a small majority on a platform whose key slogan was: *"C'est le temps que ça change."* Within a few years the Liberals

Maurice Duplessis and his Union Nationale governed Quebec in the early post-war years. NAC C-9338.

changed dramatically the direction of government in Quebec. *Time* magazine talked about a "Quiet Revolution" to describe the increasing secularization of education and social services, and the new involvement of the state in the Quebec economy. But, while Liberal Premier Jean Lesage and his *équipe de tonnerre* accomplished much, their legislation reinforced as much as it redirected tendencies evident in Quebec society from World War II onwards. English Canada generally regarded Quebec as a quaint society little changed since the time of the Conquest and largely in the thrall of its priests. But the Quebec reality was very different.

Gratien Gélinas, a key founder of contemporary theatre in Quebec, and his puppet, 1945. NAC A-122724.

Quebec was still a church-going society. As late as 1960, over sixty percent of nominal Roman Catholics in Montreal, which included most of the francophone population as well as many non-francophone immigrants, attended church on Sunday and rates of attendance were even higher in rural areas.[2] As they had since before Confederation, the churches ran the educational system at all levels, the hospitals, and most of the social services, though state funds

Montreal slums, 1949. NAC P-151688.

played an ever-increasing role. Services in these areas were segregated between Catholics and Protestants. But control in these areas did not automatically give the Roman Catholic Church political power. While outsiders to Quebec might believe that Maurice Duplessis worked hand in glove with the Church hierarchy, there was in fact a fair bit of friction between the two, with the Church more willing to modernize its view of Quebec society than the premier. Duplessis, not the Church, controlled the lion's share of funds for education, social services, and health, and he dispensed state monies quite cynically. A local priest or someone higher in the hierarchy who openly criticized government policies or supported initiatives undertaken by the Opposition might find that his area's school board had its provincial education grant cut, or that his bid for a new hospital for his area had been set aside in favour of the request from a neighbouring region where the clergy had been wise enough to show deference to its Union Nationale masters.[3]

Many members of the clergy, as well as professionals and government officials at all levels, were concerned that Quebec lagged far behind Ontario in its industrial development and general prosperity. In a province where out-migration had taken a toll of about seven hundred thousand francophones in the nineteenth century and several hundred thousand more in the 1920s, there were fears that a return to prosperity would result in yet another period of heavy emigration of francophones to areas where there were more and better job opportunities. There were concerns as well that the Quebec economy was dominated by anglophone firms with anglophone managers. While the exclusion of Catholics from positions of authority within industry was partly the result of the workings of the anglophone old boys' club in the province, the limited educational attainments of most francophones contributed to their being passed over for important positions in industry. Though the clergy had, at one time, opposed compulsory education of children and extensive state funding of the church-run schools because of the likelihood that this would lead to greater state control over the content of education, they had recognized by the 1940s that both were necessary if Quebec francophone Catholic children were to match the educational achievements of their anglophone counterparts.

Though elements of both the Church and small business opposed wartime Liberal Premier Adelard Godbout's decision to make education compulsory, Godbout made the move only after ascertaining that important sections of both these interest groups were behind him. The legislation requiring all children to attend school from ages six to fourteen also required school boards to hire attendance officers charged with determining whether children were legitimately absent from school or simply playing hooky. Though some rural Catholic boards complied reluctantly, hiring few officers relative to the number of children to be monitored and paying them poorly, others, particularly in urban settings with a higher property-tax base, made provision for a good level of staffing and paid their attendance officers a good salary. A working arrangement developed between some Quebec officials and the family allowance bureaucracy in Ottawa which enforced the law requiring school attendance for a family to receive family allowance. Though Duplessis wanted no co-operation with Ottawa and its plans for using family allowances for social engineering, the education officials in the province, anxious to promote school attendance, worked quietly with Ottawa, hopeful that parents threatened with an end to cheques from Ottawa would think twice about letting their children drop out of school. Child welfare officials and reformist priests similarly collaborated with Ottawa in what they believed were the interests of the children.

Duplessis, while espousing a rhetorical commitment to parental choice on the issue of how much education children needed and of what type, contributed to improvements in the province's education system if only because his extensive patronage in rural areas that voted for his party made it easier for many school boards to erect buildings, hire teachers, and provide free schoolbooks.

The extent of this educational improvement should not be overstated. In 1961, only half of Quebec's young people between the ages of fifteen and nineteen were attending school, a figure significantly below the rest of Canada.[4] For francophones, the figure was considerably lower than for anglophones in the province. Continued poverty forced many families to pull their children out of school at age fourteen and have them seek low-wage work to supplement the family income. The province required fourteen and fifteen-year-olds to seek a special permit to work, but these were issued freely. Poor parents used illness or distance to school to disguise the fact that a child had dropped out of school while employers and parents faked younger children's ages to get permits. There were few apprenticeships for the young workers that might get them into better-paying work as adults. Those who began work young increasingly faced the indifference of a society that inisisted on a more educated work force, yet did not always provide the conditions that would allow young people to receive the education that was demanded by employers for all but the most menial jobs.

Education for girls was still less valued than education for boys in Quebec in this period. Though more parents were demanding a classical college education for their girls and for their boys, the Church promoted an expansion of the *instituts familiaux*, segregated girls' schools that focussed more on domestic training than academic subjects.[5] The Church's rigid patriarchal views on appropriate roles for the sexes had changed little with time. For the Church, socially constructed limitations on women's participation within society were treated as if they were, in fact, divinely ordained. The hierarchy, along with the media and the Catholic unions, had vociferously opposed the federal government's policy of aiding the establishment of daycares during the war so that married women with children could seek work and alleviate the labour shortage. The Quebec government therefore set up few childcare centres and closed them all as soon as the war was over, a contrast with Ontario where women's organizations and socialist parties in Toronto successfully joined forces with mothers of children in daycare to persuade the Conservative provincial government to spare the daycares already in operation.[6]

Still, Quebec women were quietly transforming their position in society in defiance of Church notions of gender roles. While the Church still extolled large families, Quebec women, usually using the rhythm method as their form of birth control since this was the only contraception not denounced by the Church, were bringing the size of their families closer in line with the Canadian average. Increasing numbers of mothers of young children were in the part-time or full-time labour force. Only eight percent of working women in 1941 were married but that figure rose to seventeen percent in 1951. Study circles of women in which women's common problems could be discussed bloomed within both Church and government-sponsored organizations. Most farm women, generally regarded as more conservative than their urban sisters, resisted a Church demand that they leave the state-sponsored *cercles fermières*, organizations that largely dealt with farm women's roles as mothers and housekeepers, to join Church-sponsored equivalents. The farm women demanded to know why the hierarchy wanted them to leave organizations that they deemed helpful and when told that the Church did not have to supply reasons, they largely chose to disobey the Church. The Church had censored Simone de Beauvoir's *The Second Sex*, the major feminist work published in French after the war (it was published in 1949 but only made generally available in Quebec in 1962),[7] though some women had obtained copies outside the province. On television and radio, a number of Quebec personalities, including Solange Chaput-Rolland, Thérèse Casgrain, Jeanne Sauvé, and Judith Jasmin, challenged traditional gender roles.[8]

While most of the women's resistance to conventional Catholic teachings and *duplessiste* rhetoric was individual and quiet, there were more and more voices being raised against the notion that an increasingly urban and industrialized Quebec should cling to traditionalist values rather than embrace the consumer-oriented society that the rest of North America and Europe appeared to embody. The trade unions, as we have seen, increasingly rejected the view that workers should accept whatever working conditions and wages employers were willing to bestow upon them. The Catholic trade union federation, increasingly outside of the Church hierarchy's control after the war, made a clean break from the Church in 1960, renaming itself the Confédération des syndicats nationaux (Confederation of National Trade Unions). Like the trade unionists, many Québécois began to identify more with a "Quebec nation" built around a francophone identity rather than with Roman Catholicism. But the break with Catholic ideology should not be overstated. The CSN, in its early years, like its CTCC predecessor in the post-war years, owed much of its ideological perspective to the French Catholic Left.[9]

Quebec intellectuals, though less influential than they would become during the Quiet Revolution, were at odds with the Duplessis government and traditional Roman Catholicism during the 1950s. It was the intellectuals who tried to synthesize the complaints that were being made by growing elements of the Quebec population and to propose new directions for Quebec society.

> ... the group that took on the task of conceptualizing and explicitly formulating this program for change was made up of intellectuals, writers, journalists, university professors and social scientists, many of whom had been educated outside Quebec and were influenced by the new ideological currents circulating in postwar Europe and America. They belonged to the rising new elites that wanted to shape Quebec society according to their own values and interests.[10]

While the English-language network of the Canadian Broadcasting Corporation was fairly staid in this period, the French-language network, operating out of Montreal, provided a forum for opposition thinkers and, as a federal institution, was beyond the power of Duplessis to control. Some of the opponents of traditionalism in Quebec were liberals who regarded Quebec nationalism, like *pur et dur* Roman Catholicism, as a danger to individual freedom and to Quebec's development as a dynamic society open to outside influences. Pierre Trudeau, editor of the influential, if modestly circulated, journal *Cité Libre*, a merciless opponent of the Duplessis regime, embodied this trend. But, more commonly, Quebec intellectuals wanted Quebec to make a break with traditional values without losing its

M. Duplessis (centre), premier and attorney general of Quebec, 1935–59 and 1944–59. NAC PA-115820

sense as a distinct entity within North America with a proud past. If Québécois were no longer to constitute a "folk" society, they could nonetheless draw collective strength from identifying themselves as a distinct people for whom their provincial government ought increasingly to act as a national government.

Some nationalist historians began to interpret Quebec's past in a manner that reflected this vision of the Quebec future. Maurice Séguin, Michel Brunet, and Guy Frégault, among others, hotly disputed the long-established Church version of the province's history in which otherworldly Roman Catholicism, veneration of the land and rural living, and opposition to entrepreneurialism constituted the essence of Quebec's history from the time of Champlain to the time of Duplessis. They accused Quebec's historians of reading history backwards. Pre-Conquest Quebec, they claimed, had been dynamic, its bourgeoisie at least as influential as the Church. The British Conquest limited the opportunities available to the conquered francophones and gradually the Quebec majority were marginalized in Quebec's economic life, argued the "decapitation" school of Quebec historians, who suggested that the entrepreneurial elements of New France, cut off from their links with French merchants, returned to France. The people who remained in the colony made a virtue out of necessity and created the quaint "folk" society that both the Church and the anglophones liked to pretend had always been there.[11] The message of the new nationalist historians was clear: Quebec's francophone majority had to rid themselves of post-Conquest mythologies, reassert a national identity that was forward-looking, and assume control of an economy that foreigners had been colonizing for two hundred years.

Ontario: Wealth and Want

Ontario was the envy of the rest of Canada during the post-war boom. About fifty percent of all industrial production in Canada occurred in that province, mostly within a 400-kilometre radius of Toronto. This left even Quebec, with thirty percent, in the dust. Toronto, strengthened in the inter-war period as the financial and industrial centre for an expanding Northern Ontario mineral industry, pulled ahead of Montreal as a financial centre in the post-war period, and matched Montreal, once far more populous, as a megalopolis of two million people in the census of 1961. The automobile industry was the key to Ontario's success. Almost all of the automobile assembly that occurred in this country was centred in southern Ontario. To the extent that the post-war boom in North America was propelled by the automobile, Ontario was poised to reap the richest rewards of any province in Canada. The Ontario rubber, glass, plastics, automobile parts, and steel industries all owed their health to the province's robust automobile industry. Most of these industries were American branch plants employing few design experts or research scientists. But they employed a large variety of unionized skilled and assembly workers whom they could afford to pay well because of the high productivity of workers in machine-intensive companies. Indeed, because of the high cost of letting machinery go idle, the companies had a strong incentive to settle with unions at the bargaining table and not risk a strike. While unemployment remained low, there was little realistic chance of keeping factories operating during a strike. What some now call "Fordism" was thus marked by high-paid workers, usually with high school education or less, earning good wages at unionized jobs with a virtual lifetime guarantee of employment. Cities such as Oshawa, Windsor, and St. Catharines owed their new neighbourhoods with large family homes on good-sized properties to the large companies that located in their midst, and to the unions that foughtfor decent contracts from the employers.

It is important to note however, that in the rest of the country, there was little "Fordism." Jobs were plentiful in the late 1940s and throughout most of the 1950s before the recession struck. But most workers did not work in machine-intensive factories with unions, high wages, and little chance of layoff. Workers moved from job to job, and in the early sixties there was a great deal of concern about such job mobility because pensions tended not to move with the worker, leaving many workers without savings towards old age. Even in Ontario, "Fordist" jobs were by no means there for everyone. Most workers in the province's mass-production industries were men, and people of British descent were still heavily favoured for skilled jobs and even more favoured when time came to appoint foremen or supervisors. Small manufacturers usually employed immigrant men and women, and were fairly vigilant about keeping out the unions. They paid their workers few of the fringe benefits, such as medical plans and pension plans, that became common as a result of union contracts in the major companies.

Still, relative to the rest of the country, Ontarians were well off. The province's farmers, even if most were not wealthy, were far more likely to live in homes with modern plumbing and electricity, as well as electrical appliances, than their counterparts in otber provinces. Its women, like women in other provinces, were victims of patriarchy and the mythology of the family wage. But they were more likely to have a job than women in other provinces because the province's prosperity generated more of the pink-collar and poorer-paying blue-collar jobs that were usually reserved for women. In 1939, only one married Ontario woman in twenty worked for wages. That figure rose to one in ten by 1951 and doubled again to one in five by 1961. As a result, the participation rate of women in the Ontario labour force far exceeded that in other provinces.[12] Immigrant women appeared as eager as Canadian-born women to find paid work to help make ends meet in homes where there was no male "breadwinner" or where he existed but earned wages too modest to support the household. But they were less likely to get white-collar work and usually took jobs as cleaning ladies, assembly line workers, seamstresses, and machine operators.[13]

Ontario could be a mean-spirited place for those unlucky enough not to be part of either the traditional middle class or the new stratum of well-paid workers found in mass-production industries and other unionized sectors such as mining and industrial construction. Though the province could afford to look after its poor far better than other provinces, it largely chose not to do so. Mothers' allowances, once given only to widows and long-deserted wives, were now given to other single mothers. But the size of the allowance was well below the poverty levels calculated in a careful study by the Toronto Welfare Council. Nor was the granting of an allowance to a single mother by any means automatic. The provincial Department of Social Services had a network of largely unpaid spies across the province whose job was to determine whether recipients of mothers' allowances remained chaste. If there was a man in the house from time to time, it was assumed that he could or should support the mother in question and her children, rather than have the state provide support. There was a not-so-subtle supposition here that a woman who slept with a man must be receiving money for her sexual services. The government did not think that it had to prove the woman was receiving income; she was guilty purely because she was not celibate outside marriage. The large group of men and women willing to report on neighbours to the welfare authorities, particularly in towns and smaller cities, attests to the widespread acceptance of the government's prurient views on the sexual needs or rights of single mothers.[14]

Social welfare for single people and couples without children, as well as the aged, was also minimal despite campaigns by social service councils in the metropolitan areas as well as by the poor themselves for better consideration. Only unemployables qualified, with those between jobs expected to rely on unemployment insurance. Only in 1958 did those whose benefits had been exhausted or who never qualified for unemployment insurance become eligible for social welfare thanks to the Unemployment Assistance Act which provided for a sharing of the costs between the federal government and the provinces.

Though daycare centres opened during World War II were not closed down, as in Quebec, no new daycare centres were opened and the existing ones had their fees raised to a point in the early fifties where they were of little use to most working-class women.[15] Little money was spent on mental health care, and both the mentally ill and the old and feeble often found themselves living in Dickensian conditions in institutions subsidized by the state. In general, the provincial government, though by no means short of cash, was unwilling to treat with kindness those who were unable to make a go of things in the booming economic environment of the post-war period. Immigrant groups, as suggested in Chapter Two, often helped each other, and private charities tried to deal with lost souls who had neither a local community nor a government program that could help them out. But many people simply fell through the cracks.

Neither the provincial government nor the province's leading businessmen wanted to hear about the poor of Ontario. The Toronto Welfare Council's study *The Cost of Living*, published in 1939 and updated in 1944, was suppressed in 1947 by businessmen-charity fundraisers who were able to overrule the social workers within the Council. The document had been used by unionists in their campaigns for better wages, to the outrage of businessmen like Edgar Burton, president of Simpsons department stores and chairman of Toronto's Community Chest, the fundraising arm of the Toronto Welfare Council. The study was eventually revised and released in the spring of 1949 as *A Guide to Family Spending in Toronto*, the title reflecting the change from a document indicating what wages workers might need to live decently to one which placed the onus on individual consumers to make wise choices with whatever dollars their employer might deign to give them.[16]

Faced with such pressures from business, Ontario social workers were divided on strategies for helping the poor. Social work was regarded as a "woman's profession," that is, an extension of nurturing in the home and, therefore, barely a profession at all. Some social workers, anxious to put the profession on a firmer footing, wanted to avoid radicalism and focus on reforming individuals who were not conforming to the demands of the existing social structure. A growing number of social workers, however, including leading figures such as Bessie Touzel, long-time executive director of the Toronto Welfare Council, believed that social workers must join with labour and other progressive forces to pressure governments for structural changes. But, as social work historian Gale Wills observes: "The woman in social work became dependent on her male supervisor, on a male-dominated financial federation for her livelihood, and on male colleagues for her access to the power structures of society."[17]

Examining the province's programs for the poor in the early post-war period and the 1950s, historian James Struthers writes:

> The willingness of governments to allow the gains achieved by universal social entitlements such as family allowances and old age security to be eaten up by grossly inadequate or unaltered shelter, heating, and clothing allowances not only eroded the value of these initiatives for the fight against poverty, but also nullified the marginal gains achieved after 1944 by the provision of nutritionally adequate food allowances. Quite simply, in postwar Ontario the poor went hungry to pay the rent.[18]

The Atlantic Revolution

Far more people per capita fell through the cracks in Atlantic Canada. The economy of the Atlantic region had been in decline relative to the rest of the country since at least the 1880s. Out-migration exceeded in-migration, with only the birth rate accounting for modest increases in population over time. World War I had revived a sagging ship-building industry and stimulated industrial production in the region more generally, but much of that industry shut down when the war was over. With the fisheries also in trouble, the Atlantic economies were depressed even before the Great Depression came along to make things worse. There was another economic revival during World War II, and provincial governments were determined not to let the economy simply slip back into depression at the war's end. Regional pressures forced the federal government to accept the idea of "equalization," that is, the transfer of some of the taxes collected in wealthier provinces to the poorer provinces so that these provinces could provide services to citizens similar to those in the better-off provinces. Similar pressures from the Atlantic premiers caused all political parties to accept the idea of using federal monies along with provincial monies to attract industrial development to the region. This recognition of the right of the Atlantic region both to social services similar to services in the rest of the country and to state aid for economic development constitutes what some scholars call the "Atlantic Revolution."[19]

The shift towards an activist state in the Atlantic provinces, aided by an activist federal government, did not always yield the desired results. The difficulties faced by politicians attempting to stimulate a marginalized economy are exemplified in the case of the New Brunswick mineral industry in the 1950s. Though the province's forestry industry remained healthy, the manufacturing sector was weak and unemployment in the province in the early 1950s was twice the national average. New Brunswick's per capita income had fallen from 72.4 percent of the national average in 1945 to 64.5 percent in 1952, and its political leaders were determined to prevent further economic erosion. In 1953, just one year after the Paley report in the United States called on President Truman, for Cold War reasons, to institute stockpiling of twenty-two strategic resources, base metal discoveries on New Brunswick's North Shore attracted several American mining companies. They wanted tax incentives and provision of free infrastructure, and Premier Hugh John Flemming's Conservative government believed these were the price of good mining jobs for the province. Ottawa and the province's municipalities cooperated.

Such generosity on the part of three levels of government did create a large number of jobs for miners in the short term. But by 1957 there was an oversupply of lead and zinc in North America and the American government put quotas on lead-zinc imports. Several key companies that had established New Brunswick operations now abandoned them. The provincial government rejected greater state intervention as a solution.[20]

In the 1940s, 93,000 people left the Atlantic region, and in the 1950s another 82,000 went "down the road." Those who remained were more likely to find work in government than in the resource sectors that had once been the mainstay of the regional economy. In 1961, there were over 140,000 Atlantic Canadians on public payrolls, including over 40,000 defence employees, who between them accounted for more jobs than forestry and mining combined provided.[21] There were fewer manufacturing jobs than there had been a decade earlier.

Newfoundland was the newest Canadian province in the Atlantic region and the poorest. It had joined Confederation in 1949 after a close vote in a referendum. The island colony had been self-governing until 1934 when, bankrupt, it had agreed to allow a British-ap-

Joseph Robert Smallwood, premier of Newfoundland from 1949–72, signing agreement admitting Newfoundland to Confederation, Ottawa, 11 December 1948. NAC PA-128080.

pointed commission to govern. After the war, with democracy restored, islanders had to decide whether independence or union with Canada was the colony's best option. Their narrow vote to join Canada was fuelled in part by generous financial promises on Canada's part. Canada's more generous social insurance schemes — particularly unemployment insurance — were also attractive in a province with chronically high rates of unemployment and poverty. Canada was motivated in part by a desire to make the country truly reach "from sea to sea," but also by pressure from within NATO to have this strategic island within the orbit of a trusted NATO member. Joining Confederation did little for Newfoundland's long-troubled fisheries or indeed for any of its productive sectors, but it did provide the promised social insurance programs, the transfer grants that created a great deal of government employment, and public services. The federal government came through with somewhat less in the way of cash grants than Newfoundland had been led to expect but, in economic terms, Newfoundland had certainly gained by its decision to join with Canada. Pressure from Newfoundland fishers resulted in all of Canada's once-excluded fishers being included in the unemployment insurance scheme as of 1 April 1957.[22]

The new bureaucrats in Saint John's were as wedded to ideas of modernizing their province's economy as their counterparts in the

Maritime provinces were. Regarding many of the province's outports as backwaters with no economic future, they embarked on a program to remove the population from some of these outports and move them to places where there was supposedly a better economic future. Many outport families objected to the destruction of long-established communities and only moved because government officials insisted they move and promised them a new world of steady employment and middle-class living. But this new world did not emerge for most of the relocated outporters.

A Tale of Two Wests

The economic situation of the Western provinces demonstrated far less homogeneity than the Atlantic provinces. British Columbia and Alberta witnessed staggering resource-led growth, while the remaining two western provinces, Saskatchewan and Manitoba, largely stagnated. Politically, these provinces also represented a mixed bag, ranging from the left-wing CCF government of Saskatchewan to the avowedly right-wing Social Credit regimes of Alberta and British Columbia, with Manitoba's old-party regimes somewhere in the middle.

British Columbia's new-found prosperity was largely the result of exploitation of the province's vast natural resources. Booming American markets revived a forestry industry that had lacked markets during the Depression, while the combination of federal, provincial, and municipal giveaways to corporations, which had yielded little in the long term in New Brunswick, proved a success in British Columbia. With a long-established metal mining sector and a diversity of mineral products, British Columbia was well poised to meet industrial and military demands for a steady diet of minerals in the post-war period. Premier W.A.C. Bennett, in an attempt to promote a fast pace of mineral development, imposed a tax in 1957 on undeveloped iron reserves controlled by mining companies. Demand also increased for the fruits of the Okanagan. The increased mobility of North Americans and Europeans in a prosperous period gave rise to a large tourist industry in a province blessed with the beautiful scenery of an ocean, mountain ranges, and lush greenery.[23]

The accumulation of new wealth in British Columbia did not quell the class divisions that had long characterized the Pacific province. Miners, woodworkers, and pulp and paper workers, earned good wages relative to Canadian workers as a whole. But the work was dangerous, the work environment often unhealthy, and the compa-

Tommy Douglas pioneered medicare as premier of Saskatchewan (1944–6), before becoming leader of the national NDP (1961–71). NAC C-36219.

nies that they worked for were generally large firms making large profits. Unions in these industries won important concessions from the companies in the form of wages, fringe benefits, and working conditions. But these were the fruit of drawn-out negotiations and frequent strikes. The result was a continuing political polarization in British Columbia. The CCF had won about a third of the vote in the first election it contested in the province in 1933, and retained a similar share of the popular vote in the 1950s. The Conservatives and Liberals in the province had formed a coalition government in the forties to block the socialist advance, but disputes regarding the division of patronage had split the coalition government asunder by the early fifties. In 1952, in a four-party race, Social Credit, second in the popular vote to the CCF, formed a minority government. Unlike Alberta's "funny money" Social Credit party, the British Columbia Social Credit party, by the time it formed the government, had little connection with the movement's roots. It had become simply a vehicle for dissident Conservatives such as W.A.C. Bennett who were able to win the votes of British Columbians tired of the corruption of the coalition government, but afraid of the CCF. Within

The Keep Our Doctors Committee protests the introduction of Saskatchewan medicare. SA R-B3980-1.

a year, Bennett called another election and successfully convinced most of the electorate that uniting behind his party was the only way to keep the "socialist hordes" from taking the reins of power in British Columbia. The CCF and its successor, the NDP, would have to wait until 1972 before they could interrupt Social Credit's reign.[24]

Alberta's Social Credit party defeated its CCF rival decisively in a provincial election in 1944 and afterwards, basking in oil riches, faced no serious electoral opposition for a generation. The Alberta oil boom, which had once been confined to the modest petroleum fields of the Turner Valley, took off with a huge find at Leduc in 1947. In the 1930s, Alberta was still one of three agricultural provinces that together made up the Prairie region, and with seven hundred thousand people, the smallest of the three. Its two big cities each had fewer than one hundred thousand people and existed mainly to service the surrounding agricultural areas. The province carried a huge debt load from its pioneer investments in railways and other infrastructure. By 1961, the Alberta economy was dominated by the energy industry, with Calgary serving as Canadian headquarters of the giant multinational companies that dominated the industry. Edmonton had become the centre of petroleum refineries, the petroleum-equipment industry, and an expanding provincial government bureaucracy. Both major cities had tripled in size over twenty years and the provincial population had almost doubled, making Alberta the largest of the three Prairie provinces. With petroleum royalties filling the provincial treasury, it was also far and away the richest, and a debt-free government boasted huge annual surpluses despite large expenditures on health, education, and roads.

Though it was not a penny-pinching government, the Social Credit regime opposed universal social programs, claiming that they robbed the individual of choice. The government continued to impose a "co-insurance" fee on hospital patients even after the federal government's hospitalization insurance plan was established and required provinces to provide free access to hospitals. The province preferred to pay a financial penalty rather than to give in to the federal government's "socialist" requirement. When poor people wrote the premier about the hardships hospital fees had imposed upon them, the premier responded with homilies about the virtues of self-reliance. Premier Ernest Manning regarded the trade union movement as an enemy of such self-reliance and his government imposed rules that made it difficult for unions to form or to strike. An evangelist who had left his Saskatchewan farm to study in "Bible Bill" Aberhart's Prophetic Bible School, Manning followed Aberhart not only to the premier's chair but also to the pulpit of the "Back to the Bible Radio Hour," which was recorded weekly. Manning emphasized the individual's need to find salvation. He regarded the state as a potential enemy of religion to the extent that it provided for individuals and left them without the need to seek God's help to find salvation on their own.[25]

Saskatchewan followed a very different political direction. In 1944, the CCF, led by T.C. Douglas, formed the government. While Douglas was a former Baptist minister, his religious views were in the tradition of the "social gospel," which foresaw the creation of the Kingdom of Heaven on earth. Each individual was part of God's plan and individuals could work together for salvation rather than focus solely on a personal relationship with God. The democratic state, from the CCF point of view, could redistribute wealth and provide services for all without violating the tenets of Christianity. Douglas' government established public automobile insurance, the first public hospital insurance program in North America in 1947, and the first public medical insurance program in North America in 1962. The latter was instituted only after a doctors' ·strike. The government is often given credit for standing firm with the doctors, but in fact it altered its initial plans to deal with physicians' fears that they would lose their hard-fought "expert" control over medicine. While the popular movement for medicare in Saskatchewan had fought for community clinics with popular participation and an emphasis on all aspects of health promotion, the doctors opposed any sharing of their power with other groups of health workers or with community members. They also convinced the government to set aside any notion of putting doctors on salary and to accept a fee-for-service scheme. Still, for a small and quite poor province, Saskatchewan's achievements in the area of public services, particularly in health, were remarkable. In the early post-war period however, the province remained dependent upon the price of wheat and this depended, in turn, upon fluctuating international markets over which Canadians had little control. The costs of farm machinery and consumer goods were rising more rapidly than grain prices. Only the farmers who bought out other farmers so that they had a large number of acres under plow could make a livig from farming. Most farm families by 1961 had at least one member of the family working off-farm for all or part of the year to bolster the household income. Thousands of farmers left the land and indeed the province to find urban jobs in a period of job opportunities. By 1961, Saskatchewan, the most populous of the three Prairie provinces twenty years earlier, was the least populous, its population having stabilized at about nine hundred thousand, a figure quite close to the 1941 figure.[26] Efforts to develop potash and oil in the province had yielded little result in the 1940s and 1950s. In its first term of office, the CCF government had planned to use Crown corporations to develop the province's resources. But the province lacked capital and private companies proved hostile to making purchases from Crown-owned firms. In the 1950s, Saskatchewan followed a model similar to New Brunswick, providing long-term leases and generous royalty concessions to companies willing to put capital into the development of the province's resources.

Manitoba fared marginally better than Saskatchewan before the sixties. Its rural economy, more diversified than Saskatchewan's, was somewhat less dependent on grain prices. Winnipeg, which had developed as a railway and wholesaling centre for the Prairie region during the early part of the century, expanded its manufacturing base. But the city began to lose its pride of place in the region. The railway became less important as a means of transportation as the trucking industry began to haul more of the region's freight. There were some mining developments in northern Manitoba, but the province's Native people were largely frozen out of the jobs that these created. Many left poverty- and disease-stricken reserves for the slums of

North Winnipeg, only to find that employers in the "big city" were generally uninterested in hiring them.[27]

Until 1958, Manitoba was governed by the Liberal-Progressive alliance which had governed the province in one form or another since 1922. It was neither liberal nor progressive. Dominated by rural constituencies, the government focussed on keeping taxes low and the province out of debt, a combination that could only be achieved by providing minimal services. Duff Roblin's Conservatives formed a minority government in 1958 and then a majority government in 1959 by promising to modernize Manitoba's schools and roads and otherwise to make Manitoba an attractive place for industry to locate. His efforts in the latter regard, however, like those of the Atlantic premiers, would yield only a modest return.

But, as we shall see in Part Two, Manitoba and the other have-not provinces would prove desperate for development in the 1960s and 1970s and would throw away millions of dollars in often fruitless efforts to diversify their economies.

Four

The Politics of a "Middle Power"

There were two Canadas living side by side in the post-war period, one that fit the image, however imperfectly, of an affluent, consumer society, the other the Canada of the poor. It was the former Canada which state officials tried to advertise to the rest of the world as the nation sought out immigrants, markets, and trade deals. There were similarly two Canadas on view in the area of foreign policy. One, the Canada that the Department of External Affairs tried to project, was a "middle power," a "helpful fixer" whose role was to keep the peace in trouble spots. But the other Canada that the Communist countries and much of the Third World claimed to find was an echo or a puppet of America. Indeed, Canadian officials worked overtime to try to influence the course of world events without stepping on the Americans' toes. The Canada that scholars have depicted in discussions of foreign policy often depends on the extent to which they have focussed on the efforts at influence and the extent to which they have looked at the substance of Canada's intervention.[1] Few suggest that Canada, in the end, had a great influence on world events.

The Nuclear Debate

Canada stepped lightly, for example, in the early post-war debates in the United Nations on how to control nuclear weapons. Canada had been a junior partner in the wartime American-British-Canadian co-operative effort to unleash the destructive potential of the atom. The three countries had chosen to exclude their wartime Soviet ally from their atomic planning. Canada's nationalized uranium refinery in Port Hope shipped its entire production to the Americans and in 1944, Canada began to construct a heavy-water pile at Chalk River, Ontario, to transform uranium into plutonium. Though the King government decided in December 1945 that Canada would not join the nuclear club, Canada countinued to supply plutonium and uranium to the Americans.[2]

Canada's role in the nuclear industry won it a position on the Atomic Energy Commission (AEC) established by the United Nations in 1946 to deal with the international control of nuclear weapons. Bernard N. Baruch proposed the American plan for nuclear limitation: an international authority answerable to the UN Assembly would have the responsibility of preventing research or development of non-peaceful uses of the atom. It would have the power to inspect nations to insure compliance. The Soviet counter-proposal would have seen the immediate destruction of existing nuclear weapons — the Americans claimed they would only destroy their bombs after the Baruch Plan was implemented and demonstrated to be effective — and weaker inspection than the Americans wanted. They wanted the authority to answer to the Security Council where they had a veto rather than to the Assembly where they did not. Both sides, as General A.G.L. McNaughton, Canada's representative on the AEC, recognized, were playing games. McNaughton considered the Baruch Plan a "one-sided proposition" and "insincerity from beginning to end" because it inhibited Soviet nuclear research, granting permanent status to the Americans' technological superiority in the area of nuclear weapons. McNaughton was able to convince the Soviets to make several concessions because they were desperate to get an agreement that would stop nuclear weapons production and testing without stopping them from doing the basic research required to learn what the Americans already knew about nuclear weapons.[3] But the Americans proved unwilling to consider any changes to the Baruch Plan. Forced by the Americans' intransigence to vote yes or no for a proposal they considered insincere, Canada voted yes.[4]

To some External Affairs officials, the Soviet fears appeared absurd. For Lester Pearson, for example, it was inconceivable that the United States, a democracy, would launch a war of conquest with nuclear weapons. Only dictatorships such as the Soviet Union were capable of such behaviour in his mind.[5]

Canadian support for the North Atlantic Treaty Organization first proposed by Britain and formed in 1949 had rested on a hope that the United States, inclined to act alone and yet to presume to speak for all of the non-Communist world or "free world" (though the concept seemed to include fascist dictatorships supported by the American government and military), could be forced to consult its major allies. This proved a largely vain hope because the American

Lester B. Pearson (centre-front) led Canada's delegation to NATO in 1953. He won a Nobel prize for his work in peacekeeping. NAC C-70449.

Congress and military continued to mistrust foreign critics of American policy, however sympathetic their aims, and to regard the United States, with its heavy military expenditures, as the real defender of freedom, or at least capitalism.[6] The growing "military-industrial complex," which President Eisenhower warned about in his farewell speech as president in January 1961, had a vested interest in maintaining tensions between East and West because growth of the military and of military spending were predicated on the intense global rivalry between the Americans and the Soviets.

Canada supported NATO's decision in 1954 to back American Secretary of State John Foster Dulles' plan to make the nuclear deterrent the major feature of Western defences. Rather than respond in kind to Soviet increases in conventional armed forces, the West would increase its nuclear arsenals and threaten the Communists with massive retaliation if they intervened in areas where the West felt its strategic interests were threatened. The Americans had already threatened to use nuclear weapons against North Korea on several occasions as well as against China, and over the next decade, such threats were made on several occasions to both the Soviets and Chinese.[7] While the leaders of the armed forces saw such threats as more than bluff, President Eisenhower recognized that the bombers of this period could be shot down by the Soviets, who, he feared, might also invade western Europe as a retaliation for any attack on Soviet territory.[8] By the beginning of the sixties, the growing Soviet nuclear might, while it did not match the Americans', was great enough to give America pause before considering nuclear attacks.

The 1954 NATO meeting that backed Dulles' philosophy also approved the production of "tactical" nuclear weapons alongside the strategic nuclear weapons already in American arsenals. While the latter were long-range weapons intended for a full-scale nuclear war, the former were intermediate-range weapons designed for a regional confrontation.[9] Anti-nuclear activists, then and now, regarded the distinction between strategic and tactical nuclear weapons as an illusion. A nuclear war once begun would be difficult to contain within one region since neither side could be certain that the other would limit its retaliation to the region in question rather than jump the gun to be the first to use strategic weapons. But, while Western nuclear arms stocks exceeded their Soviet equivalent, the tough-talking deterrent policy seemed an appropriate way to frighten the Soviets away from adventurism while allowing the capitalist countries to maintain smaller conventional forces than the Soviets.

During the 1950s, Canada integrated its air defences with those of the Americans. Three Arctic lines for monitoring the North were jointly constructed from 1951 to 1955 — the Pinetree, Mid-Canada, and Distant Early Warning (DEW) — to screen incoming Soviet bombers. In 1957, the North American Air Defence Treaty created NORAD, a unified air command for North America. NATO and NORAD decisions of the fifties with which Canada acquiesced would cause a great deal of controversy during the stormy prime ministership of John Diefenbaker, as we shall see.

The Korean War (1950–1953)

The Korean War provided a test of Canada's "middle power" role. Canadian authors suggest that Canada played an important role as a mediator in the dispute. If American and British authors are to be believed, Canada played a role unworthy of mention, whereas India and its Prime Minister, Jawaharlal Nehru, played the key role in conciliating the two sides.[10] The Canadian authors insist that Canada achieved a great deal through "quiet diplomacy" while never publicly criticizing the Americans.[11] Nehru, it should be noted, was able to play a conciliatory role despite and perhaps because of, having pub-

René Lévesque as a journalist conducting an interview at the front during the Korean War, 1951. NAC C-79009.

licly criticized both sides at times. Unlike Canada, India seemed a truly neutral party to the dispute.

Korea was a Japanese colony until Japan's defeat in World War II when opposing forces captured its northern and southern halves. Communists gained control of the north, while forces supportive of the West controlled the south. Canada joined a UN commission on Korea in 1947, the purpose of which was supposed to be to work towards unification of the two Koreas. Canada, therefore, balked when the Americans called for elections in the south and was disturbed again when the elections appeared to be fraudulent. The Canadians feared that the Americans were determined to see Korea permanently divided. By 1950, however, the Americans appeared to have lost interest in Korea. North Korean Communist leader Kim Il Sung took American indifference to mean that there would be little response if he invaded the south. He miscalculated. The Americans called on the UN to send troops to Korea to repel the North Koreans. Normally, the Soviets would have used their veto in the Security Council to prevent such action. But the Soviets were boycotting the

Security Council because of the UN's refusal to oust the former non-Communist government of China, then in exile in Taiwan, from UN and Security Council membership even though the Communists had enjoyed clear control of the mainland since 1949. The result was that the Americans were able to retaliate in Korea under the mantle of UN protection.

In practice, the UN command was led solely by the Americans who also provided eighty-eight percent of the troops. But other countries, including Canada, did participate. Canada committed 22,000 troops and dramatically increased its defence budget. Indeed, the Korean War boosted the Canadian economy, which had begun to sag after the early years of post-war prosperity, demonstrating again the utility of war in dealing with downturns in the business cycle. Canadian scholars of the war suggest, largely on the basis of what External Affairs officials later claimed, that Canadian participation gave Canada the leverage to urge caution upon the Americans. Right-wing forces in the US, led by General Douglas MacArthur, wanted to widen the war to China and "roll back" the frontiers of Communism. Truman fired MacArthur in 1951 and both Truman and Eisenhower pursued a negotiated settlement of the Korean conflict. That settlement, in the form of a cease-fire between the two Koreas, occurred in 1953 and Canadian officials took some of the credit.[12]

The Indochina War

Canada's participation in the Korean War was protested at the time only by Communists and by a relatively dispirited peace movement. By contrast, the war in Indochina sparked lively debate, and a large anti-war movement. As a result, perhaps, there has been only a modest output of scholarly literature on Canada and Korea, all of it confirming the views favourable to Canada mentioned above. By contrast, there is a respectable literature on Canada's role in Indochina and a great deal of debate about the main lines of Canada's involvement.

Canada played no role in Indochina before the rout of French colonial forces by Communist nationalists in 1954 at Dien Bien Phu. The Communists had won control of the northern half of Vietnam. A subsequent peace conference produced the Geneva Accords, which created a three-member International Control Commission (ICC) to supervise the ceasefire between the formerly warring sides and to ensure democratic elections within two years that would precede reunification of the two Vietnams. Canada agreed to serve as the representative of the West on the commission with Poland serving as the Soviet bloc representative and India representing supposedly neutral Third World nations. Under American pressure, the French abandoned their puppet regime in the region still under their control and Ngo Dinh Diem became president of South Vietnam. Diem had been a French functionary and his strong anti-Communism endeared him to the Americans who, after 1954, bankrolled the anti-Communist movements of the region. But Diem, it soon became apparent, represented a small group of landowners and former collaborators with the French and Japanese. American efforts to create support for the regime in the south by pouring in money for infrastructure largely failed because the regime was corrupt and brutal.

The Americans were determined nonetheless to keep Diem in power for lack of another clear alternative to the Communists. Recognizing that the Communists, well-respected throughout both Vietnams because they had defeated a haughty colonizer, would win an all-Vietnam election, the Americans were determined to prevent it occurring. Both the Americans and the South Vietnamese claimed that northern incursions into the south and intimidation of individuals in both north and south would invalidate any election even if it occurred under Commission auspices.

Canada supported their protests in the ICC and it soon became apparent that there would be no election in 1956. The Americans had decided to support the permanent division of Vietnam as an alternative to letting the country go Communist.[13]

Both James Eayrs and political scientist Douglas Ross, who defends Canada's overall record in Vietnam, agree that Canada initially tried to be impartial in assessing claims by the north and south of violations of the Accords. By 1956, however, according to Eayrs, the policy had changed and the new Canadian commissioner, Bruce Williams, recognized that "thwarting Communist expansion" rather than enforcing the accords had become the commissioner's main goal. "Williams warned Ottawa that the United States was about to violate Article 16 of the Geneva Agreement for Vietnam, and expressed the view that it would be well if the Commission did not find out."[14] Ross argues that Canada became more partisan because Poland, almost from the start, was fiercely partisan and Canada felt the need to counter this Communist country's behaviour. The North Vietnamese Communist government, he suggests, had been ruthless in its implementation of its agricultural collectivization program, and had executed several thousand opponents.[15]

American historians, however, have documented the even greater brutality of the greedily corrupt South Vietnamese regime, with its relocation of peasants in soldier-"protected" *agrovilles*; its summary execution of individuals who had fought against the French or who appeared to support the Communists; and its rigged election in 1955. Though the Americans would eventually tire of Diem and his associates and arrange for Diem's assassination in 1963, they failed in their various efforts to reform the government of South Vietnam and make it acceptable to the South Vietnamese people.

Historian Victor Levant suggests that opposition to Communism rather than opposition to brutality dictated Canada's less-than-even-handed attitude to the Geneva Accords. Its willingness to pretend that the violations of the Accords were the work of only one of the Vietnams would prove inestimable to the Americans. In 1962, Canada and India co-signed a document called the *Special Report to the Co-chairmen of the Geneva Conference on Indo-China*. It outlined North Vietnamese violations of the Accords with no mention of the more numerous South Vietnamese and American violations.[16] India, which had tried to play an honest broker role, was in a vulnerable position in 1962. Facing a war with China, it sought Western support and tried to win favour with the Americans, whose fixation with the Vietnamese issue was apparent.[17] Several years later, its war with China over and a close friendship with the Soviets having been established, India would become an open opponent of American intervention in Vietnam. Yet the Indians would have to face the embarrassing fact that the Americans, trying to justify an escalating involvement in Indochina, would often brandish the one-sided Canadian-Indian report on violations of the Geneva agreement.

According to Douglas Ross, Canada's goal on the ICC was "peace promotion." It tried to convince the Americans to exercise restraint while trying to convince the North Vietnamese that they must accept the division of Vietnam. If he is correct, however, it would appear that Canada quickly abandoned the goal of implementing the Geneva Accords, the *raison d'être* of the ICC, which clearly called for unification of Vietnam. For good measure, Ross, in his defence of Canadian policy, argues that Canada had to avoid alienating the Americans by appearing too independent on the ICC if it wished to influence the Americans not to use nuclear weapons to resolve the Indochina issues.[18] But he offers no evidence that discussions over a nuclear solution ever occurred between Canadian and American officials or indeed that the Canadian government was concerned at the time that the Americans might drop "the big one" over Vietnam.

Victor Levant, by contrast, argues that Canada's goal on the ICC was to prop up the South Vietnamese regime. He suggests that Canada was not coerced by the Americans to behave in a subservient manner on the ICC; rather it chose to act in this way because of a shared set of values among the elites of both countries. Canada, like the United States, was unwilling to see yet another country remove itself from the global market economy. Levant notes that Canada's attempts to portray itself as an impartial member of the Commission, an interlocutor between the Americans and the North Vietnamese Communists, were misleading. Canada received arms contracts from the Americans that were related to Vietnam and provided foreign aid to South Vietnam but not to the north. Canadian officials tended to balk at such observations while the war raged in Vietnam. Canada, they noted, had signed the Defence Production Sharing Agreement with the Americans in 1959. This created a free market in defence contracts between Canada and the United States. Canada could hardly be asked to determine which contracts for weapons-making were related to the Vietnam conflict and which were not. This was disingenuous, but there was no doubt that continental integration of defence production demonstrated the extent to which the foreign policies of the two countries were viewed by both sides as quite compatible. It was the weaker of the two powers, however, that was expected to play ball with Big Brother. Nonetheless, for a brief period in the early sixties, it appeared that Canada wanted to challenge the rules of the game.

Should Canada Go Nuclear?

In early 1963, as Canadians headed to the polls for their second federal election within a year, there was a clear, public split between official Canadian and American attitudes regarding both the usefulness of nuclear deterrence as the foundation for Western defence strategy, and Canada's role in promoting that strategy. The split had developed gradually and proved short-lived.

When John Diefenbaker assumed the leadership of the country in 1957, there was no reason to suspect that there would be any major changes in relations between Canada and the United States. Diefenbaker, who was nostalgiac for the old close imperial ties among

In 1957, Ellen Fairclough became Canada's first female cabinet minister when she was appointed secretary of state in Diefenbaker's government. NAC PA-129249.

Canada, Britain, and the nations of the disintegrating British Empire, had talked about trying to increase trade among the nations of the British Commonwealth, the voluntary organization of Britain and its former colonies. But British politicians' eyes were on Europe and the newly formed European Economic Community, whose goal was to create free trade within western Europe. An attempt to create a tariff wall around the old Empire would alienate Britain's potential European trading partners, not to mention that it would likely violate the General Agreement on Tariffs and Trade, which, since 1947, had been reducing international trade barriers. In any case, Britain's relations with the Americans were close: both were united in supporting NATO's Cold War policies. Within Canada, these policies enjoyed support from both the Conservative and Liberal parties, though their reception was colder in the CCF.

Since 1954, as noted earlier, NATO's focus was on the nuclear deterrent. Before Diefenbaker's election, the chiefs of military staff in Canada and the United States had made the arrangements for continental integration of air defences. Diefenbaker signed the resulting NORAD agreement on the recommendation of his Minister of Defence, General George Pearkes, without consulting External Affairs, Cabinet, or Parliament. General Charles Foulkes, the chairman of the chiefs of staff of the armed forces, as he later admitted, convinced Diefenbaker and Pearkes that the St. Laurent government had already approved the NORAD plans and speed was essential.[19] While Foulkes may have misled the new prime minister about the attitude of the outgoing government, there is little doubt that the military welcomed steps leading to integration of the armed forces of Canada and the United States. The armed forces leaders had been pushing for common defence planning for the two countries since 1946 and, while the politicians were more cautious, the military had interpreted the establishment of the jointly operated northern air defence lines as a move in this direction.[20] General Pearkes, a close associate of Foulkes, had long shared such views.[21]

The contintental air defence policy led to the purchase of several expensive hardware systems, mainly Voodoo interceptors meant to monitor and counter a long-range bomber attack, and Bomarc missiles. Both were offensive systems requiring nuclear warheads to carry out their tasks effectively. Long-time External Affairs official George Ignatieff would later write in his memoirs:

> One of the inevitable side-effects of the integrated air defence command was that Canadians would have little or no say in the choice of strategy or weapons. The decision to equip our northern defences with the surface-to-air Bomarc missiles was just one in a chain of military hardware purchases made not on the basis of what's best for Canada, but rather what is for sale in the United States.[22]

Indeed, Canada decided in 1959 to scrap an expensive program begun in 1955 to develop its own military aircraft carrier, the AVRO Arrow. Relying on the continental integration that both the Defence Production Sharing Agreement and NORAD provided, the Diefenbaker government decided that the country could not afford to continue development of the Arrow. Fourteen thousand workers were tossed out of work in the middle of a recession and many scientific and technical workers headed to the United States. Supporters of continental defence have maintained ever since that the government had had little choice but to scrap an expensive albatross, and that indeed much money could have been saved had Diefenbaker not delayed his decision for a year after it became clear that the project was doomed. Nationalists have tended to take the view that the Arrow's importance went beyond its cost-efficiency; the Arrow had allowed Canada to create a scientific establishment with expertise that could be diffused to a variety of industries. Its cancellation increased the gap between American and Canadian scientific research that resulted from the almost universal tendency of American-controlled companies in Canada to conduct their research solely in the United States.[23]

In December 1957, the new Diefenbaker government indicated continuity with the former Liberal government's overall foreign policy objectives by agreeing at a meeting of NATO heads of government that tactical nuclear weapons should be the main element in the defence of western Europe. The next year, Canada agreed that its role in implementing this policy would be to carry nuclear weapons behind enemy lines. The government purchased 200 Starfighter aircraft in 1959, carriers meant to fulfil Canada's new NATO obligation, and Honest John missiles the following year. Again, Canada had acquired weapons systems that were largely irrelevant if they did not carry nuclear weapons. In 1959 Canada also accepted the storage of American nuclear weapons at Goose Bay and Harmon Air Force bases, both of which were under American control in any case.[24]

Within a few years, the various weapons systems acquired by Canada had become obsolete. Yet, even as their utility disappeared, they became the subject of a nasty spate between the Canadians and Americans that had to do with basic principles rather than the efficiency of particular weapons systems. At the same time as he was acquiring military hardware that required nuclear warheads, Diefenbaker had acquired a Minister of External Affairs who was committed to nuclear disarmament. Howard Green succeeded the conventionally minded Sidney Smith when the latter died suddenly in March 1959. The appointment was a surprise because, while Green's pacifist-minded views were well known, there is no evidence that that they were shared at the time by the prime minister. Yet within a few years, Diefenbaker was leaning towards the views of Green, Green's advisor on disarmament, Lieutenant-General E. L. Burns,[25] and some of his own anti-nuclear advisors, such as George Ignatieff.[26] This led inevitably to a confrontation with the Americans about whether Canada would keep its commitments to NATO and toe the line that NATO heads of government were all expected to toe.

It is interesting to note that Canada's foreign-policy specialists, who are generally very generous in their assessments of the high motives and basic intelligence of the Liberal foreign policy-makers,

are equally scornful of Diefenbaker. Most of these specialists are
men and they imply that Diefenbaker failed to demonstrate manly
virtues. He changed his mind; in the process, he broke his word to
the other fellows in NATO; he pretended that he had not given his
word in the first place. From this point of view, a man's word is his
bond and the same goes for the country that a man leads. Diefenbaker, then, from this point of view, embarrassed his country. Worse,
there is reason to believe that he did so capriciously, that he changed
his mind because American President John F. Kennedy, unlike Eisenhower before him, treated Diefenbaker with disdain, or because he
saw a partisan advantage to attacking American efforts to dictate to
Canada as he sought desperately, during the election of 1963, to
deflect attention from the domestic failures of his government.[27]

Diefenbaker was, no doubt, hardly a saint. This does not excuse
the historians' and political scientists' unwillingness to give any
credence to his side of the argument, or indeed, in most cases, to
relate his arguments. Once he had decided that nuclear deterrence
was madness and that Canada had a duty to pursue nuclear disarmament, Diefenbaker was indeed caught in a trap. He had, unthinkingly,
been following American policies that provoked increases in the size
of nuclear arsenals and therefore increased the dangers of a nuclear
holocaust. He wanted to reverse these policies but, like his critics,
he believed that it was wrong to renege on his word, regardless of
the reasons. So he managed to convince himself that he had been
ill-informed by the Americans and had thought that the weapons
systems Canada had acquired did not require nuclear warheads.

In a parliamentary speech on 25 January 1963, shortly before the
election that would oust him from office, Prime Minister Diefenbaker outlined the government's goals: "the abolition of nuclear
weapons, the end of nuclear weapons, the systematic control of
missiles designed to deliver nuclear weapons of mass destruction,
the designation and inspection of launching sites for missiles, the
abolition of biological and chemical weapons and the outlawing of
outer space for military purposes."[28] Though his speech was somewhat rambling, Diefenbaker made use of ideas that were common to
peace groups in the country such as Voice of Women which had
formed in 1960. He suggested that nuclear deterrence was outmoded
because it only heightened world tensions. Canada could contribute
to creating a climate for negotiations leading to nuclear disarmament
and international control of the atom for peaceful purposes by refusing to be part of policies that inevitably led to escalation in the

*Progressive women working for peace in the movement to ban the atomic bomb.
A0 447.*

production of nuclear weapons and to threats to use them to settle
various regional conflicts.

Interestingly, Lester Pearson, the leader the Liberals elected after
St. Laurent's electoral defeat, had embraced similar ideas at the time
of a national Liberal rally in early 1961. The rally passed a resolution
stipulating that a Liberal government must commit itself to keeping
Canada non-nuclear.[29] Pearson made an abrupt change in his party's
policy in January 1963. He announced that while he remained committed to making Canada non-nuclear in the longer term, he felt that
the most important issue was that Canada must maintain its international obligations. He claimed that when his party had embraced the
anti-nuclear position, he had been unaware that Diefenbaker had
promised the Americans to acquire nuclear warheads for the aircraft
systems that Canada had purchased.[30] But this was surely disingenuous for, like Diefenbaker, he was aware of NATO's nuclear policies
as well as the logic of NORAD, and aware that Canada's acquies-
cence in both meant acquisition of nuclear weapons. Indeed Diefenbaker had told the House of Commons in 1959 that "the full potential
of these defensive weapons is achieved only when they are armed
with nuclear warheads."[31]

Pearson, whose motives are less often challenged than Diefenbaker's, is perhaps the one who most deserves to be branded an

opportunist. The Liberal flip-flop occurred within a few months of the Cuban missile crisis, a standoff between the Soviets and Americans that had brought the world close to nuclear annihilation. Leftist nationalists, led by Fidel Castro, had come to power in a revolution in Cuba in 1959 that overthrew a dictatorial regime friendly to the United States. Castro's determination to nationalize some American corporations and absentee landlord landholdings led to an American embargo on trade with Cuba, a declaration by Castro that Cuba intended to have a Communist regime, a wide-ranging Soviet deal with the Cubans to save their economy, beginning with the purchase of all of Cuba's sugar crop, and in early 1961 to a clumsy attempt by Cuban exiles armed by the Americans to start a popular uprising against the new regime. Castro pressured Soviet dictator Nikita Khruschev to supply Cuba clandestinely with nuclear missiles so that Cuba could deter any future American attacks. But American military intelligence discovered the Soviet installation and President Kennedy threatened an American nuclear response if the missiles were not removed. The Soviets backed down after receiving a public assurance from the Americans that there would be no further government-backed hostilities directed against Cuba.

During the crisis, Prime Minister Diefenbaker had attempted unsuccessfully to have the superpowers let the United Nations mediate their differences.[32] Kennedy kept Canada, though not Britain, largely in the dark about events unfolding in the crisis, but the Americans expected a swift compliance to a request that Canada put its NORAD forces on alert. Diefenbaker waited three days before giving the green light, not knowing that Defence Minister Douglas Harkness had ordered the alert before Cabinet approval had been given. What he saw as Kennedy's rash behaviour during the crisis deepened Diefenbaker's misgivings about the policy of nuclear deterrence.[33]

Canadians rallied behind the young American president. Opinion polls after the crisis was settled demonstrated that a respectable majority of Canadians now believed that Canada should acquire nuclear weapons to fulfil its responsibilities to NATO and NORAD.[34] The Liberal party had never been united behind the anti-nuclear stance adopted by the 1961 Liberal rally and several Liberal frontbenchers now pressured Pearson to reverse the party's position. Pearson succumbed to both popular and party pressures. He may also have been influenced by a desire to get on good terms with the Americans as he approached the prime ministership.

While the Liberals united behind their flip-flopping leader, the Conservatives could not unite behind theirs. Defence Minister Douglas Harkness believed as passionately in NATO's tactical nuclear strategy as External Affairs Minister Green believed in nuclear disarmament. Harkness left the Cabinet once Diefenbaker, after months of waffling, announced firmly in January 1963 that Canada would not acquire nuclear warheads. The Conservative party was deeply divided not only on the nuclear issue but on the advisability of going into another election with Diefenbaker at their helm. They fought the election as a party in seeming disarray.[35]

Diefenbaker, after taking the high ground in his parliamentary speech on nuclear weapons, focussed more on American attempts to defeat him because of his stance on the nuclear question than on the stance itself. The Americans certainly had no time for the Canadian prime minister. General Laurence Norstad, the retiring NATO commander, allowed himself to get caught up in the Canadian nuclear debate in a press conference in early January 1963, by affirming that Canada had committed to equipping its Starfighters with tactical nuclear weapons. Then, on 30 January 1963, the American Secretary of State took the unprecedented step of releasing a press statement that directly contradicted the statements made by a Canadian prime minister. The statement rejected the philosophy adumbrated by Diefenbaker in the House of Commons and reasserted the American belief that nuclear weapons were needed by both NATO and NORAD to protect against Soviet aggression.[36] Diefenbaker's efforts to make this American interference an issue fell flat if only because President Kennedy was then so popular among Canadians. This focus also diverted attention away from his anti-nuclear message, reinforcing the media's claims that "the Chief" was a bombastic old man with little substance.

Media focus on the prime minister's personality and on whether he was breaking earlier promises rather than on nuclear issues resulted in a rather shallow debate on Canada's foreign policy, the country's relationship with the United States, and the efficacy and the morality of nuclear weapons. When the ballots were counted, Lester Pearson's Liberals had won and the Americans could assume that Canada would return to being a reliable supporter of American foreign policies dressed up in NATO garb.

For the peace movement in Canada, Pearson's flip-flop followed by his election represented a setback. The major peace movement until the late fifties had been the Canadian Peace Congress, formed in 1947 and simply the Communist-dominated Canadian outpost of the World Peace Congress, a supporter of Soviet views. In 1958, the Combined Universities Campaign for Nuclear Disarmament signalled the beginning of campus-based radicalism autonomous from the pro-Moscow movement. The Campaign distributed petitions across the country, mainly on campuses, denouncing any government moves to acquire nuclear weapons for Canadian bases. Just as student movements for peace were becoming common in Western countries, so too were women's peace organizations. Voice of Women, organized in 1960, joined the international movement that held that men, too involved in power politics and the search for economic advantage to search for peace, needed to be prodded by women into realizing the dangers of modern warfare. VOW organized campaigns against war toys and led demonstrations and vigils on sites for nuclear tests, chemical warfare manufacture, and nerve gas research. Its Baby Tooth campaign measured radiation from nuclear test fallout in children. In 1964, a VOW delegation attempted to march into the office of the secretary general at NATO headquarters in Brussels, Belgium, to protest an apparent escalation in NATO's policy of nuclear deterrence. VOW president Thérèse Casgrain, who had been the leading figure in the fight for votes in provincial elections for women in Quebec and later Quebec provincial leader of the CCF, was arrested for leading this demonstration.[37]

Canada and the Commonwealth

Britain emerged from World War II in poor financial shape. Deeply in debt to the Americans and Canada for wartime expenditures and facing revolts in many of its colonies, Britain was hardly in a position to dictate the course of world events. Unable to repress the rising tide of anti-colonial discontent, it granted independence to India, "the jewel in the Crown," which, at independence, became two nations: India and Pakistan. By the end of the 1950s, most of Britain's former colonies throughout the world were independent states or on their way to becoming independent states, though many had weak economies that were dominated by First World countries — sometimes Britain, though over time, more likely the United States.

Countries once politically subservient to Britain met informally as members of the British Commonwealth. The historically white dominions — Canada, Australia, New Zealand, and South Africa (which was governed undemocratically by whites but was, in fact, overwhelmingly a nation of non-whites) — had both sentimental and economic ties with Britain that they wished to maintain, while the Third World ex-colonies were interested in maintaining and extending trade and investment relations with the former colonizer. For Canada, Britain became a less and less important trading partner as the post-war years went by. But Canadian leaders recognized that for a large section of the Canadian population, maintenance of relations with the Crown was important. The monarchy was popular in Canada and royal visits were thronged along all routes. Queen Elizabeth II, who ascended to the throne upon the death of her father, George VI, in 1952, was held in high regard by most Canadians. Canadians in this period continued to call their national birthday Dominion Day in recognition of Canada's one-time colonial status and to celebrate as a national holiday the birthday of the late Queen Victoria. English-speaking Canadians waited by the radio on Christmas morning for the Queen's Christmas address.

So, while the Canadian government was more afraid of alienating the powerful Americans than the weakened United Kingdom, it found itself in a delicate position on the occasions where these two powers were at odds. After 1945, for example, Canada had great difficulty deciding what position to take on the issue of the partition of Palestine, which was administered by Britain, into two states. Many Jewish survivors of the Holocaust had headed for Palestine, joining earlier Jewish settlers in demanding the creation of an autonomous Jewish state in the region. Britain attempted to limit the number of refugees who settled there but, with news of the Holocaust so fresh, it was unwilling to use maximum force to stem the tide of illegal immigration. Jewish terrorist organizations seeking British withdrawal from the region carried on a campaign of terror against British residents and buildings. In July 1946, for example, they bombed the King David Hotel, leaving ninety-one dead.

In 1947, half of all Canadians told pollsters that they opposed any Jewish immigration to Canada, Holocaust or not. But most Canadians supported unlimited immigration of Jews to Palestine, though they were aghast at the actions of the Jewish terrorist organizations. The American government quickly took the side of the Jews in Palestine, calling both for a British pull-out from the territory and for partition. The British rejected partition, either because they wanted a pretext to remain in the region or because they correctly foresaw that partition would lead to war because of its rejection by the Arab majority of Palestine. Canada kept its head low but supported the Americans and the United Nations majority in the vote on partition in the UN Assembly in 1947. The next year however, it was joining Britain in asking for a reconsideration of partition.

No sooner had the United Nations agreed to place Palestine under trusteeship than the Jews of Palestine declared the formation of the State of Israel on 14 May 1948. While the Americans immediately recognized Israel, the British refused to follow their lead. Canada joined Britain in withholding recognition. Within days the new Israeli state faced a war with its Arab neighbours who opposed the establishment of a Jewish nation within the Arab world. Only after Israel had won its first war and Mackenzie King had been replaced by Louis St. Laurent did Canada agree to recognize the new Jewish state.[38]

Britain, in any case, soon gave up its opposition to the new Israeli state and was won over to the American argument that a country led by Western-born Jews was a better bulwark against Communism than Arab countries only recently freed from Western colonialism and perhaps susceptible to Soviet Communist wooing. The next time Canada faced a Middle Eastern dilemma, Britain and Israel were working hand in glove. In July 1956, President Gamel Abdul Nasser of Egypt nationalized the Franco-British firm that owned the Suez Canal and Egypt took direct control of the canal. Israel, France, and Britain responded to this Egyptian action and subsequent threats by Nasser to close the canal to shipments to Israel and its allies with a lightning attack in October 1956 and seizure of the canal. The Americans regarded this seizure, meant to guarantee both Israeli security and Western Europe's supplies of oil from the Middle East, as adventurism. With the Soviets threatening retaliation on behalf of their Egyptian ally if the aggressors did not pull out, the Americans wasted little time in letting their three allies know that they had behaved foolishly and must now simply admit their folly and retreat.

Canadians divided almost evenly on the issue of whether Canada should support Britain or the Americans on the 1956 Middle East crisis. While francophone Canadians tended to agree with the Americans that Britain, France, and Israel had committed naked aggression, a majority of anglophones believed, at least initially, that Canada should stand behind Britain. The government tried instead to play a "helpful fixer" role. Lester Pearson proposed to the United Nations a compromise that would allow hostilities to end in the Middle East without a clear victor or a clear loser. The three aggressors would pull back but peacekeeping troops under United Nations control would be sent into the region to ensure that the ceasefire would last. A Canadian officer, General E.L.M. Burns, was put in charge of the United Nations Emergency Force (UNEF) that was assembled following Pearson's recommendation. Canada would remain part of UNEF until 1967 when President Nasser, expecting another war with Israel, ordered UNEF to disband. Pearson won the Nobel Peace Prize in 1957 for his role in ending the Middle East war of 1956. Canada would later join other United Nations peacekeeping efforts including one in the Congo in 1960 and a lengthy emergency force presence on Cyprus, beginning in 1964. Certainly, for Canadian governments, the country's role in maintaining ceasefires in trouble spots reinforced the image they wished to project, both internally and externally, of an independent and peace-minded nation which, while clearly in the Western capitalist camp, was committed to higher goals than the containment of Communism.[39]

The loftiness of Canada's goals as well as the principles it wished the British Commonwealth to embody were tested on the issue of relations with South Africa. The white minority's undemocratic rule in this dominion had caused little concern in unabashedly racist, pre-World War II Canada. After the war, however, as anti-colonial movements tore asunder notions that Africans and Asians benefited from and appreciated white man's rule, racist ideas had to be removed or, at least, removed publicly from Canada's foreign policy. This was not always easy since Canada, one of the favourite destinations for emigrants searching a new homeland, maintained a transparently racist immigration policy. Canadian governments were also reluctant to imply any criticism of British colonial rule anywhere and were unwilling to grant recognition to liberation movements in various countries until Britain had conceded a right to independence to the colony in question, a process that stretched out over the two decades following the war.

The result was that Canada played a negligible role in supporting the forces that were trying to liberate the Third World from colonialism. One exception was Canada's lone vote among the white dominions in 1946 against South Africa's annexation of South West Africa (Namibia).[40] But Canada took no position when the National Party, dominated by Dutch-descended Afrikaners, won the South African elections in 1948. The National Party, inveighing against signs of desegregation of whites and blacks in the country and opposing even the small number of seats granted blacks in Parliament, proposed a system called "apartheid." The term meant "separate but

equal development" — equal, however, being a deliberate falsehood
since the "Nats" stood for a strict segregation of the races in which
the majority of the population would receive a tiny bit of the land
base, no voting or civil rights, and be relegated to unskilled, poorly
paid positions within the economy.

Only in 1960, when the National Party government banned the
major anti-apartheid organizations, of which the African National
Congress (ANC) was most prominent, and jailed its leaders, including Nelson Mandela, did South Africa become an issue which Canada could no longer ignore. A massacre of sixty-nine demonstrators
in Sharpeville, protesting against the "pass books" which every black
in the country had to carry to prove the right to work or live in a
particular location, mobilized the newly independent nations of the
Commonwealth to isolate South Africa. African nations in particular
demanded that South Africa either abandon apartheid or leave the
Commonwealth. John Diefenbaker, while denouncing apartheid, opposed this step, arguing unconvincingly that the Commonwealth
could better exert pressure on South Africa to modify its racist
practices if it maintained a dialogue with the country. He opposed
military or trade sanctions against the apartheid regime called for by
African countries in the United Nations and by the ANC.[41] His
Cabinet agonized about the possibility that if Canada made too great
a fuss about South African racism, it might cast an unwanted spot-
light on its own racist immigration policy. Diefenbaker told the
Cabinet: "If Commonwealth Conferences should once adopt the majority vote as a means of reaching its [sic] decisions, the non-white
majority at the next Conference would probably support free migra-
tion of peoples. Such an immigration policy was clearly unacceptable
to the Canadian people."[42]

But, after South Africa became a republic in 1961, it was required
by Commonwealth rules to seek re-entry. With most of the non-white
members of the Commonwealth hostile to South Africa's continued
membership, Diefenbaker proposed to the South Africans that they
reinstate the three black seats that had existed in the white Parliament
in the period before 1948. The South Africans were not willing to
take this modest step, which, in any case, would not likely have
mollified the Commonwealth leaders who regarded South Africa as
a pariah among nations. After South Africa withdrew its application
for membership in the Commonwealth, Diefenbaker claimed that the
organization now accepted the principle that countries that discrimi-

nated against citizens on the basis of colour, race, or religion could not be part of the Commonwealth.[43]

But the government refused to break its trade ties with South Africa, as the liberation movements in the country called upon foreign governments to do. Diefenbaker's answer to NDP member David Lewis' call for a ban on trade with South Africa was: "South Africa ... is one of the countries with which we have dealt on the friendliest terms throughout the years. Sanctions could have the effect of denying to Canadians business to the extent of perhaps $40 million or $50 million a year."[44]

As the Sixties Began

Canada's trade interests, its goal of preventing the spread of communism, its need to please the Americans yet not alienate the British, and its desire to project an image of a forceful, yet peaceful, independent presence on a world stage, all worked together to produce a foreign policy that sometimes seemed riddled with contradictions. Anxious to please the Americans regarding Vietnam, Canada lied to make the South Vietnamese government look better than it was relative to the North Vietnamese regime. Yet Canada refused to follow the American lead on Cuba in 1960, continuing trade with Castro after the Americans implemented their embargo. It also rejected a request from President Kennedy in 1961 to stop selling grain to mainland China in order to pressure its Communist government to end shipments of military equipment to North Vietnam.[45] Canadian grain sales to China boosted the western Canadian economy and such a boycott was therefore unthinkable to Prime Minister Diefenbaker.

The musical chairs that the major party leaders played in the early sixties nuclear debate demonstrated perhaps more vividly than any other issue how ambivalent Canadians were about following American initiatives. In the end, though the nuclear issue did not likely determine many votes, Canadians demonstrated by ousting Diefenbaker that they felt comfortable within the American nuclear camp and were unsure about the results if Canada decided to strike a more independent, even neutralist, position in world affairs.

Part Two

Traditions and Invented Identities:

1963–1980

Five

The Search for Political Identity

Along with the United States and Europe, Canada experienced a cultural upheaval in the 1960s and 1970s. While the generation that had grown up in the Depression had been mainly interested in achieving a degree of economic security and had posed little challenge to the values of their parents and grandparents, the "baby boomers" of the post-war period (and indeed the smaller cohort of babies born during the war) proved a restless generation. The middle class "boomers," in particular, often spoiled rotten as children, found their parents' suburban lifestyles alienating, and with the religious underpinnings to many conventional notions of respectability increasingly eroded, many young people questioned their parents' views on sexuality, sobriety, and success. Particularly after the mass availability of the contraceptive pill in 1960, pre-marital sex became common and common-law marriages and multiple sex partners, once seen as phenomena associated with the non-respectable "lower class" of society (as well as the very rich, who could always afford to flout social norms), were evident in all social classes. Marriages broke up more frequently, and after divorce laws were liberalized in 1969, the rate of divorce skyrocketed. By the end of the 1970s, one of every three people marrying for the first time could expect that the vows they exchanged to remain together with one another "'till death do us part" would be undone in a divorce court (and indeed many of them refused to accept the traditional vows at their wedding ceremonies). Gays and lesbians came out of their closets, where both the law and social opposition had shut them in, and in 1969 sex between consenting adults of the same sex was removed from the Criminal Code.

The use of soft drugs, particularly marijuana, again once associated with marginal groups in society, increased dramatically, with well-educated, middle-class young people becoming the principal users. Though efforts to remove the use of marijuana from the Criminal Code failed, enforcement of the laws against its use became inconsistent in most jurisdictions.

"Hippies" in the 1960s, social drop-outs who lived on the margins of city life and sometimes off the land, reflected the questioning of middle-class values of success, measured by material acquisition. Popular culture, mainly imported from the United States, extolled hippie values. But most middle-class kids were, at best, weekend hippies. While they might be more critical of conventional notions of success and respectability than their parents, they were, on the whole, prepared to seek formal training to take up a respectable middle-class vocation and to emulate their parents in moving into suburbs and filling up their homes with the products of a prosperous industrial society. Many working-class kids had no suburban existence to oppose and, while some aspired to the middle-class existence that the hippies opposed and a few more wished to become hippies, most simply accepted modern industrial society and their place within it. If a "post-modern" critical consciousness was slowly developing among well-educated upper and upper middle-class young folk, it had little echo within society as a whole. While there was a "generation gap," as some critics referred to the youth rebellion of middle-class kids, it was hardly the only or even the major dividing point within Canadian society. Older divisions of class, race, and gender persisted and young people did not escape such divisions. As we shall see in subsequent chapters, Canadians, including — and often led by — baby boomers, rather than identifying simply with a ubiquitous "youth culture," often defined their interests in terms of some combination of class, race, ethnicity, and gender. A Québécois middle-class feminist and separatist, a First Nations Warrior, a Nova Scotia woman factory worker, and a male engineering student in British Columbia might all be 21 years old in 1975 and all enjoy listening to the Rolling Stones and smoking marijuana. But their views of the world and of the directions in which Canada should develop would often have little in common. They would all, however, be forced, along with their elders, to make political choices about what political party or parties, federally and provincially, would represent their vision of the country's future. Part Two looks at some of the choices Canadians made from 1963 to 1980 and the consequences.

First, a few statistics that demonstrate how Canada was changing in the 1960s and 1970s. The population increased from 18,238,000 in the 1961 census to 22,993,000 in 1976. But there was a "baby bust" in the 1960s and 1970s, as dramatic as the "baby boom" that had preceded it. Canadian adults were producing children at a rate below the replacement rate (2.1 children) of the population by 1979 (the fertility rate had peaked at 3.9 children for completed families of adult women in 1959 and had fallen to 1.7 in 1981), but high rates of immigration allowed the population to grow apace and labour force requirements to be met. Because immigrants were not available in the 1960s from the traditional sources of recruitment in western Europe — those countries were in excellent financial shape and fewer citizens chose to emigrate — Canada revised its immigration rules in 1962 and 1967, removing overtly racist criteria in favour of criteria that gave preference to immigrants who matched Canada's labour needs. Though immigration rates were high, so were emigration rates, with the United States serving as the chief destination of people leaving Canada. From 1961 to 1971, there were 1,429,000 new arrivals in Canada but also 707,000 emigrants. Fewer migrated over the next ten years — once again there were 1,429,000 immigrants but this time only 566,000 emigrants. The gross national product, in constant dollars, increased from $11.8 billion in 1960 to $27.3 billion in 1976.[1]

Political Overview

On 8 April 1963 the Canadian electorate rejected the faltering government of John Diefenbaker. They were not, however, universally impressed with Lester Pearson's Liberals, especially on the Prairies, where voters remained loyal to Diefenbaker thanks to the Canadian Wheat Board's big grain sales to the Soviet Union and the People's Republic of China. Pearson had to be content with forming a Liberal minority government. For the next sixteen years, the Liberals would hold power in Canada, as a minority government from 1963 to 1968, and again from 1972 to 1974, but as a majority government under the leadership of Pierre Elliott Trudeau from 1968 to 1972, and again from 1974 to 1979.

Canadians' boredom with the choices before them on 8 April 1963 was evident not only in their unwillingness to give any party a majority, but also in their unwillingness to watch the election results on television. The Neilsen ratings suggested that as many Canadians were watching the American Academy Awards that evening as the Canadian election results and even the prime-minister-in-waiting joked with journalist Pierre Berton, as the election results poured in, that he would like to change channels and see who was winning the Oscars. But the years of Liberal minority governments would prove

Party time on University of Alberta campus, 1965. UAA 79-86-4

to be among the busiest years of reform legislation in the twentieth century in Canada. Dependent on NDP support and hoping to win more voters by appearing progressive, the ideologically flabby governing party used its minority government years from 1963 to 1968 to introduce the Canada Pension Plan, the Canada Assistance Plan, a national student loans plan for postsecondary students, and "the jewel in the crown" of social reforms, a national program of prepaid medical insurance. Complacent during the next four years of majority government, the Liberals, once again dependent on NDP support for almost two years after an indecisive election in the fall of 1972, introduced Petro-Canada and the Foreign Investment Review Agency, and hiked many social benefits. They worked closely with the provinces, attempting to produce a guaranteed annual income program. The reformist impulse dimmed again when the voters gave the Liberals a majority in August 1974. By the late seventies, the guaranteed annual income had all but disappeared from the political agenda and, though unemployment had reached levels reminiscent of the Diefenbaker era recession, the government seemed far more concerned about high levels of inflation than about the workless. Indeed, the focus on high levels of unemployment that had characterized Department of Finance deliberations from the end of the war to the mid-seventies was largely absent by the late seventies Inflation was the obsession now and, increasingly, higher levels of unemploy-

Table One Income distribution among households in Canada by quintiles		
	Percentage of total after-tax income reported in Canada	
	1951	1981
Lowest quintile	6.1 percent	6.4 percent
Second quintile	12.9	12.9
Third quintile	17.4	18.0
Fourth quintile	22.4	24.1
Fifth quintile	41.1	38.4

Note: Totals less than 100 percent due to rounding.
Source: *The Canadian Encyclopedia*, 2nd ed., Vol. 2 (Edmonton: Hurtig, 1988), 1051.

ment were seen as a partial answer to Canada's economic problems rather than a problem to be avoided.

This chapter explores the evolution of this change in economic thinking. The shift away from post-war liberalism and Keynesianism will also be important as we look in subsequent chapters at the evolution of other key movements in the 1960s and 1970s: the movement towards Quebec sovereignty; regional movements for greater independence from Ottawa; the movement in anglophone Canada towards greater assertion of national sovereignty vis-à-vis the United States; the women's movement; the trade union and poverty movements; and the First Nations movement. In the late sixties, in particular, with the economy growing by leaps and bounds, there was a widespread belief that there was no limit to the gains that could be made by well-organized groups of the oppressed pressuring the state for social justice. Poverty action groups sprang up across the country and made confident demands for guaranteed annual incomes and national programs of social housing and daycare, while a revived women's movement called for many of the same demands, as well as full equality of the sexes. By the end of the seventies, it was evident that these groups faced an uphill fight in their demands for social change.

By the end of the seventies, however, Canadians could boast a "welfare state" that provided better security than Americans enjoyed. In that country there was no universal medical or even hospital insurance, no family allowance, and no state-paid maternity benefits.

Still, when compared to European countries, Canada's provision of social and educational services appeared quite modest. While Canada spent 21.7 percent of its gross domestic product on social expenditures in 1981, every industrial power in western Europe spent more: Belgium, 38 percent; the Netherlands, 36.1 percent; Sweden, 33.5 percent; and West Germany, 31.5 percent.[2] While social spending, along with unionization of most of the labour force, had significantly reduced the income gap in many European countries, particularly in Scandinavia, Austria, and the Netherlands, the new social spending in Canada barely made a dent in income distribution (see Table One). This was because marketplace forces were redistributing wealth upwards. Social service spending countered the market's tendencies, leaving everyone in relatively the same place. Those at the very bottom, however, could count on certain state programs to provide a minimal social wage. But it was misleading to suggest, as some commentators did, that all Canadians enjoyed equal access to good health services. They all had equal rights to see a doctor or, when necessary, to be looked after in a hospital. But other contributors to good health such as proper nutrition, healthy accommodation, and a clean working environment eluded many. By the late seventies, the mental stress caused by the lack of these things was joined for many by fears of unemployment.

The Pearson Years

Denied the spoils of office in 1957 and 1958, the federal Liberals began a soul-searching that they had been able to avoid as the smug "governing party." One wing of the party, led by reformists like Walter Gordon, the millionaire accountant who had headed the Royal Commission on Canada's Economic Prospects, and Tom Kent, editor of the *Winnipeg Free Press*, wanted the Liberals to commit themselves to a progressive program. They favoured universal social programs, regional development programs, and programs for Canadianization of the economy. These views were anathema to traditional free-trade liberals.

It was the reformists, however, who proved better able to take over, indeed to remould, the party's organizational structure and to win support from rank-and-file Liberals. The Liberal Party, during its long period in office, had largely become the plaything of powerful regional Cabinet ministers. Men such as Jimmy Gardiner in western Canada and C.D. Howe in northern Ontario distributed pa-

Prime Minister Pearson lights the Centennial flame, December 31, 1966. In 1965, his government introduced the red and white national flag in use today. NAC C-26964.

tronage to supporters of the Liberal cause within their area, and patronage was the glue that held this ideologically diffuse party together. Contracts to design or build harbours and highways or to handle legal matters for the government, as well as staffing appointments for government agencies, were vetted by powerful ministers (as well as local MPs, if the riding was represented by a Liberal). With the Liberals out of office, the party could not maintain a network of regional fiefdoms based on patronage. There was, however, a sharp dispute about whether the party should be centralized or decentralized, with the centralizers winning and reformists taking charge of the central office. The Liberal Rally in 1961, organized by Kent and Gordon, committed the party to a national medical insurance program as well as a contributory pension plan.[3]

In a sense, the entire political environment of the times favoured the reformist forces. But right-wingers had hardly been banished from the Liberal party, which remained in many respects simply a magnet for opportunists of all kinds as well as genuine reformers. When the party took office in 1963, it proved to be quite divided on social welfare issues, on issues of foreign control of Canadian industry, and on foreign policy. Right-wing Liberals such as Robert Winter and Mitchell Sharp led the charge in the Cabinet against the adoption of expensive social programs whose costs could only grow with time. The right wing had the support of the business community and, on medicare, the medical profession. But the tide of public opinion was clearly in favour of social programs. As the Canadian Chamber of Commerce, which was then lobbying against both the Canada Pension Plan and medicare, learned at its 1965 annual meeting, the Canadian public was unimpressed by Chamber campaigns against social programs. J.M. Keith, vice-chairman of the executive council of the Chamber and president of the Imperial Tobacco Company of Canada, reported on an extensive survey of public attitudes commissioned by the Chamber.

> The desire for extensive programmes of social welfare are (sic) broadly and strongly rooted in the public mind. It is doubtful whether such deeply rooted feelings can be altered. On the basis of the foregoing, it would appear to be necessary for the Chamber to take stock of its position on social welfare programmes and adopt a stance that accommodates this situation; it would seem unlikely that any education programmes will succeed in changing this now fundamental desire of the majority of Canadians.[4]

Indeed, within a year, the Chamber, while still foursquare against medicare, had not only accepted the Canadian Pension Plan as a *fait accompli*, but admitted that the plan would provide inadequate or no coverage for many Canadians and called for a minimum income for the elderly, with the state providing the funds required to bring the elderly poor up to that (unspecified) level.[5]

If business had to "adopt a stance that accommodates this situation" of massive public support for social programs, the pressures upon a political party that formed a government to do so were obviously far greater. This was particularly the case for the Liberals who had campaigned on a program of social reforms in 1963, and did so again in 1965, in vain attempts to form a majority government. But there were obstacles to overcome in the establishment of some of the major proposed programs. The Canada Pension Plan (CPP) ran into rather different objections from the two largest provinces. Quebec, which was experiencing the Quiet Revolution (Chapter Six), wanted to operate its own plan and use current revenues to finance industrial expansion in the province. Ontario, with a Tory govern-

ment solicitous of the interests of the private life insurance companies headquartered in the province, was only willing to back a plan
that paid modest pensions in order to ensure that better-off individuals were not dissuaded from purchasing life insurance. The life insurance industry vigorously fought the CPP, claiming it was an
unwarranted intrusion of the state into the private sector. In the end,
the federal government conceded Ontario's point and created a plan
with modest payouts while attempting to harmonize the national
program with the program that Quebec was establishing. To assure
the co-operation of the remaining provinces, the federal government
promised them that they could use revenues in the early years of the
plan, when few Canadians would be eligible to receive a significant
pension, for infrastructure projects.

When the plan was implemented in 1966, only contributors to the
plan could collect pensions from the plan. Deductions would be made
both from employee pay packets and from employers to provide
revenues to the plan. But this gave no added revenue to existing
old-age pensioners and, until individuals had a chance to contribute
for a significant number of years, would not provide a reasonable
return to the elderly. The plan based benefits on income earned
during one's years in the paid labour force and the number of years
worked. As feminists pointed out, the plan was heavily biased towards males, since it was men who earned a greater income and spent
more years in the labour force. The government tried to placate such
complaints by introducing a means-tested Guaranteed Income Supplement (GIS) to the basic old-age security pension that all Canadians over 65 received. But the modest GIS added to an old-age
security cheque would leave an individual impoverished if she or he
had no other income coming into the household, a situation in which
many elderly women, in particular, often found themselves. Nonetheless, both the CPP and GIS contributed over time to improvements
in the lives of elderly Canadians.

Medicare, in contrast to the CPP, provided benefits for Canadians
of all ages, social classes, and genders. It was the product of a long
struggle on the part of labour, farm, and social welfare groups. As
we observed in Chapter One, state medical insurance had overwhelming public support in the late 1940s, but both federal and
provincial politicians were reluctant to implement such a program.
They worried about its eventual costs and they did not wish to offend
the Canadian Medical Association (CMA), which briefly supported
a federal scheme but had become a vociferous opponent of medicare

by the end of the decade. Hospital insurance, which the doctors did not, for the most part, oppose, was introduced in 1957, but neither St. Laurent nor Diefenbaker was keen on making universal public medical insurance the second phase of a national health insurance policy. In the wake of continuing public pressures for medicare, particularly from labour and the newly formed NDP, Diefenbaker followed the time-honoured Canadian tradition of relegating consideration of the issue to a Royal Commission. Since most of the appointees were known Conservatives, it was generally expected that the Commission would oppose a compulsory medicare scheme.

The Commission, led by Justice Emmett Hall of Saskatchewan, a lifelong Conservative, held hearings across the country. The physicians were well organized to tell their story. More and more Canadians, perhaps as many as sixty-five percent, had some form of private medical coverage. The CMA reckoned that another twenty percent could afford private coverage. That left only fifteen percent of Canadians, the country's very poor, who ought to be covered by state plans. Some of these "indigents" already had their medical bills paid for by the state. The physicians bitterly denounced Saskatchewan's universal program that had been introduced in 1962, but indicated their support for voluntary programs of medical insurance implemented by the provincial governments of Alberta, British Columbia, and Ontario. The Canadian Chamber of Commerce also supported the voluntary approach.

Though most Canadians told pollsters they preferred a national, state-controlled, compulsory plan, few individuals showed up to challenge the doctors. One Toronto woman who complained that she and her son were treated differently by an unnamed physician because she was a welfare mother was publicly denounced by the physician. Instead, the task of defending the need for a national plan was left to organized groups, principally the trade union movement and social workers, and to a lesser extent, the farm movement and the churches. The social workers told tale after tale of poor people who did not go to see doctors when they were ill because they could not afford to pay the fees charged and were ashamed to be treated as charity cases. The farmers made a similar case. As for the unions, their tales of the weaknesses of existing private plans questioned the relevance of the doctors' case that time would place all but the poorest within private health insurance schemes.[6]

Hall and his fellow commissioners did not report until 1964, when the Liberal government had replaced the Diefenbaker Conservatives.

The commissioners concluded that prepaid health insurance and an emphasis on health promotion that encouraged preventive medicine, including the alleviation of poverty, were necessary if all Canadians' health needs were to be met as effectively as possible. They supported the inclusion of visits to doctors and other health professionals, pharmaceutical costs, dental fees, the cost of eyeglasses, psychologists' fees, and the like within a comprehensive health insurance program that would guarantee Canadians prepaid access to all health services. Recognizing that the cost of a comprehensive program might be prohibitive, they suggested that the government might consider phasing in the various components.

That was indeed what the Pearson government decided to do. Medical insurance would cover visits to doctors and other health professionals, as well as laboratory tests. It was to be the second phase of the national health program that began with hospital insurance and subsequent phases would give Canadians the comprehensive plan envisaged by Hall. Indeed after the legislation of medicare in 1968, no further phase of the Commission's plan has been implemented. Hall's report made it difficult for Liberals who opposed new social programs because of their likely long-term cost, and the resultant impact on the taxes of corporations and wealthy individuals, to win their argument within the government. Pearson had promised a modest medicare program as a progressive Liberal measure and now a Tory-appointed commission was calling for a sweeping program along the lines of the National Health scheme implemented by a Labour government in Britain in the late forties. Pearson began negotiations with the provinces to introduce a national medicare scheme.

The provincial governments, except for Saskatchewan and Newfoundland, were unenthusiastic and sometimes downright hostile. Pearson's proposed scheme would split medical costs evenly between the provinces and the federal government. The wealthy provinces — Ontario, British Columbia, and Alberta — were, as usual, not especially happy to see a national program that took taxes disproportionately from taxpayers in their provinces to subsidize services for people in other provinces. But Premier Manning of Alberta, in particular, also saw compulsory programs as a form of socialism that denied people freedom of choice. Even in less wealthy provinces such as Manitoba, the Conservative government largely bought the doctors' arguments and advised the federal government not to proceed with its plans.[7]

Quebec's Liberals had intended to implement a provincial medicare scheme and were initially wary about a federal scheme. But they accepted a compromise in which each medicare scheme would be implemented by a province. If the scheme met the four goals of the federal government — universal coverage of provincial residents, coverage for a comprehensive set of medical services, government administration, and portability of coverage (coverage when residents were outside their home province) — the federal government would match provincial expenditures. In other words, while the federal government would pay half the costs and would do so only when certain principles underlay a provincial program, the program would, in each case, be a provincially administered program without direct federal involvement in management.

After the 1965 election, the progressive Finance Minister Walter Gordon was replaced by the conservative Mitchell Sharp, who, along with Robert Winter as head of the Treasury Board, was quite prepared to do as Mackenzie King had done in the forties: use provincial opposition as an excuse to kill a popular but expensive proposed social insurance program. Inflation was on the rise by the late sixties and conservatives in government, as in business, were more concerned about achieving stable prices than they were about achieving social security. The Pearson government stalled and it was only when Pierre Trudeau assumed office that the medicare scheme was pushed through.[8]

The Canada Assistance Plan (CAP), implemented in 1966, seems to have been subject to less intrigue than either the CPP or medicare. The Unemployment Assistance Plan of 1956 had extended federal aid to the provinces for unemployed unemployables for the first time. The CAP broadened such aid to include most categories of recipients of social assistance from the provinces as well as certain social services provided to these recipients, such as social worker visits. The provinces had been pressing for such aid since World War II, as the scope of their own expenditures on social assistance had broadened.[9]

With CAP, medicare, and the CPP in place, reformers moved their attention both to improved benefits within these programs and to new programs such as a national daycare program and a guaranteed annual income. But, while social reform rhetoric remained important throughout the Trudeau years, an important shift in government thinking was occurring that would eventually replace post-war liber-

Prime Minister Pearson with his Minister of Justice, Pierre Trudeau, at a constititutional conference. NAC C-25001.

alism with a conservatism that bore a great resemblance to its pre-war counterpart.

The Trudeau Years to 1975

Pierre Trudeau appealed to many baby boomers. Though he was forty-eight when he became prime minister, the suave bachelor had lived an unconventional life and was not part of the staid political establishment that many young people distrusted. The son of a multi-millionaire, the well-educated Trudeau had not had to work for his money. He had been able to travel around the world and had founded a daring magazine of public opinion called *Cité Libre* which thumbed its nose at Duplessis and other pillars of the Quebec establishment. A one-time socialist, his first foray into electoral politics had come in the federal election of 1965, when he stood as a Liberal. Lester Pearson made Trudeau Minister of Justice and he gained support from social liberals when he announced his intentions to reform the nation's laws on divorce, abortion, and homosexuality. His suggestion that the "state has no place in the bedrooms of the nation" struck a responsive chord among young people who believed Canada was

Academic quadrangle at Simon Fraser University, British Columbia. Canadian universities expanded rapidly in the 1960s and early 1970s. SFUA 87096-16.

an old-fashioned and repressive place, attempting to impose uniformity in areas where individual choice should prevail. Trudeau's reputation as a former supporter of the CCF and NDP, his one-time criticisms of American domination of Canada, and his call during the election for a "just society" suggested that he was a progressive in the area of social reform. He was vague about what legislative changes might produce this "just society." Indeed, the successful Liberal campaign of 1968 focussed on the glamorous character of the prime minister rather than on issues. The media, delighted to have a Canadian politician who seemed to excite young people at home and to draw international attention to Canada, were happy to speak of "Trudeaumania" and to let the prime minister promise Canadians rather little.[10]

Overall, in terms of social reform, the Trudeau years were stand pat years. Trudeau supported existing social programs and did implement some modest extensions in their coverage, notably to unemployment insurance. Maternity benefits, provided through unemployment insurance, were also introduced in 1971.[11] But, once he had won his majority government, Trudeau made public his concern that inflation was threatening the well-being of Canada's middle classes. He was prepared, he said in 1969, to take drastic measures in order to bring inflation down and save Canada's middle class,

A. Y. Jackson's Canadian flag proposal, 1964. NAC PA-136154.

which he did not define, from ruination. Nonetheless Trudeau was confronted with both a growing movement of the poor and a well-organized, broadly based women's movement, both of which he felt some need to appease.

When Trudeau assumed office, Canada was in the midst of a period of exceptional economic growth that lasted from 1962 to 1973. Fuelled by American government economic policies, including the military spending during the Vietnam war, the North American economy grew even faster than it had during the post-war boom that was interrupted by the recession from 1957 to 1961. But, for conservatives, there were dark clouds on the horizon. While the fifties had featured both low unemployment and good labour-capital relations as grateful workers pocketed wages their parents could only have dreamed of during the Depression, younger workers in the sixties proved less deferential. With little cause to fear unemployment, workers proved more than willing to strike to compel employers to give labour a greater share of company earnings. In the public sector, where strikes were generally illegal, they occurred anyway, especially in the post office, causing governments to give workers the right to form legal unions that governments hoped would curb wildcat strikes.[12]

With replacement workers hard to find during a period of low unemployment, companies often conceded unions' demands and then passed along the cost of their extra wage bills to consumers. Since workers were also consumers, they would take advantage of the next set of contract negotiations to demand wage increases that outstripped increases in the cost of living. Nor was the conflict between capital and labour the only cause of rising inflation. The American government, prosecuting an increasingly unpopular war in Vietnam, refused to tax its citizens more in order to pay for the enormous costs of the war. Instead it printed money, fuelling an inflation that spilled over its own borders into the economies of the United States' principal trading partners.

The Pearson government, fearful of inflation after 1965, tried to cut government expenditures to take some of the heat out of the economy. But their new social spending programs counteracted the marginal cuts they made in other areas. The Bank of Canada tried to slow growth in the money supply to dampen the economy. It proved unable to do so because the Diefenbaker government had pegged Canada's dollar to 92.5 cents American. Canada's buoyant economy made the Canadian dollar an attractive investment to currency buyers and the Bank had little choice but to keep enough new money in circulation to prevent the dollar's value from moving upwards.[13]

Trudeau resolved to be tougher than his predecessor. He made larger spending cuts than Pearson and, in May 1970, he ended the pegging of the dollar. Its value quickly rose above par with the American dollar. That made American imports cheaper to purchase in Canada than they had been for many years and, in turn, made Canadian exports less competitive. Unemployment, which had averaged 4.4 percent in 1969, averaged 5.7 percent the following year and 6.2 percent for 1971 and 1972.[14] Trudeau eased up on the attack against inflation, fearing that further rises in the unemployment rate would prove politically unacceptable. The Conservative opposition, though led by a political moderate, Robert Stanfield, former premier of Nova Scotia, attacked alleged abuse of unemployment insurance rather than policies that were leading to higher unemployment. The strategy appeared to be to blame the unemployed themselves for the increasing numbers in their ranks by suggesting that large numbers of them simply did not want to work.

While Trudeau's spending and monetary policies suggested a desire to give greater weight to capital than to labour, it was in the area of taxation that the government demonstrated its essential conservatism. The Pearson government had appointed a Royal Commission on Taxation under the guidance of Kenneth Carter, a Toronto accountant. Carter, like Emmett Hall, proved a surprise to those who had appointed him. His Commission's studies persuaded him that

Canada's taxation policies were riddled with special exemptions and distinctions between types of income, promoting unfairness. He wanted most sources of income to be treated the same because, as he argued, a larger tax base would enable existing taxpayers without access to loopholes to pay less. There would be fewer marketplace distortions if certain types of income did not receive special treatment. In particular, Carter thought Canada should copy the Americans and institute a capital gains tax rather than allowing such gains to be treated as if they were not income.[15]

Commission studies revealed that the poorest Canadians paid proportionately more taxes than well-off citizens. While 34.7 percent of all income went to taxes, the group earning under $2000 lost sixty percent of their income to taxes. The poorest were hit hardest by taxes because of the regressive impact of property tax, sales tax, excises, and social security deductions. The wealthy benefited from tax loopholes, dividend tax credits, and the exemption of capital gains and other forms of income from taxation.[16]

Carter's report was released in November 1967, but the Liberals largely ignored it until they established a Cabinet committee in April 1969 to study its recommendations. Business opposition to the Royal Commission's recommendations caused Finance Minister Edgar Benson to reduce by two-thirds the planned tax increases for mining and petroleum companies. The move away from Carter's ideas had only just begun. By the time that the tax reforms were passed by Parliament in December 1971, little of Carter's approach remained. Capital gains would be taxed but only at half the rate attached to other forms of taxation; inherited wealth, instead of being taxed at the same rate as other income, would not be subject to federal tax at all (by 1980 the provinces, except Quebec, had also abolished estate taxes); Carter's proposed taxes on expense-account living were dropped.[17]

When Trudeau went to the electorate again in the fall of 1972, his reputation as a reformer was tainted. The Liberals decided to run an upbeat campaign with the election slogan "The land is strong." With unemployment and inflation both at higher levels than they had been when Trudeau took office, many Canadians found the governing party's campaign insensitive. The NDP, led by David Lewis, attacked the government's timidity in tax reform, and denounced the "corporate welfare bums" who received huge subsidies from the state without having to provide guarantees to hire more workers or to treat their labour force well. The Conservatives, though vague about their

Plaque commemorating the sixtieth anniversary of Ukrainian settlement in Canada, Manitoba Legislative Building. PAM, Boadway Collection, N 13048.

policy differences with the Liberals, proved able to capitalize on discontent with the government's complacency. The Liberals emerged with 109 seats to 107 for the Tories, leaving 31 for the NDP, 16 for the Créditistes (Quebec Social Credit), and 1 Independent.

Dependent upon NDP support and hoping to regain his progressive credentials with the electorate, Trudeau ensured that the 1973 budget was even more expansionary than the budgets for the two previous years. The money supply was allowed to grow at a reasonable rate. In 1973 and again in 1974, the rate of unemployment fell, reaching an average of 5.3 percent in the latter year.

Though re-election, rather than inflation, now became the government's priority, the latter had become a bigger problem after the Organization of Petroleum Exporting Countries (OPEC), dominated by Arab states, decided upon a ten-fold increase in the price of their petroleum exports in the wake of the Arab-Israeli Yom Kippur War in the fall of 1973. OPEC would continue escalating prices for almost a decade before a fall in demand forced prices downwards. Trudeau encouraged labour-capital co-operation to prevent the higher costs of oil from precipitating an inflationary spiral and appointed a board under economist Beryl Plumptre whose job was to publicize apparently unjustified price increases. Plumptre could do little, however, as inflation climbed over ten percent in both 1974 and 1975.

During the 1974 election, Stanfield, still the Tory leader, called for state-enforced price and wage controls as the best way to control inflation. Trudeau warned Canadians that many prices of goods in Canada were determined outside the country; "he's going to control your wages," not prices, Trudeau predicted. Stanfield lost, but fourteen months after the election it was Trudeau who imposed the wage controls he had railed against, particularly to organized labour audiences, during the campaign.

Wage Controls and Monetarism

"Stagflation," a term designed to describe an economy with high rates of both inflation and unemployment, characterized both the American and Canadian economies for much of the seventies and early eighties. Canada's rate of unemployment had averaged 3.9 percent from 1965 to 1969, well above an OECD average of 2.3 but still indicative of an economy where jobs were not hard to find (this ignores real discrimination against Natives and married women, who often were excluded from the count when the labour force was calculated). That percentage had increased by almost one-half to 5.7 percent for the period from 1970 to 1974, and stood at 7.3 percent for 1975–9. For both periods, Canada's rate of unemployment was almost three percent greater than the average for the OECD countries. In the 1975–9 period, for example, Japan averaged unemployment of two percent, Sweden, 1.9 percent, Austria, 1.9 percent, Norway, 1.9 percent, and West Germany, 3.5 percent. All of these governments made full employment the major goal of public policy. Japan's conservative government could rely on paternalistic industrial structures to maintain high levels of employment while reducing worker wages to cope with slower growth. State policies discouraged the growth of unions, leaving employers with a great deal of power in the area of labour relations. In the other countries mentioned, the Social Democrats, with their base in the trade union movement, were the most powerful political force, and public expenditures were expanded, along with public employment, to compensate for job losses in private industry.[18]

The Trudeau government had neither the luxury of relying upon paternalistic industrial relations nor the willingness to follow social democratic Keynesian prescriptions. It began to listen to economists who were labelled "monetarists." The "monetarists" called for a shrinking of the money supply to wring inflation out of the economy. Though the focus on the money supply characterized monetarism, most monetarists, led by their guru, American economist Milton Friedman, were opposed generally to the policies of state interventionism that characterized post-war economic policy-making. They suggested, besides use of the money supply, a new set of policy instruments that included a vast reduction in state expenditure with the private sector taking up functions long assumed by the state, tax cuts for the wealthy and for business so that potential investors had more money to invest, the replacement of universal social entitlements with a minimum means-tested guaranteed annual income program, and a weakening of the power of unions so that investors had greater potential profits to anticipate. While monetarists admitted such policies would increase unemployment in the short term and permanently increase inequalities, they argued that, in the long term, the freeing of capital from the shackles of the state and the unions would produce higher and more stable rates of economic growth and thus a good employment picture as well. So-called "neo-conservatives," among whom monetarists figured prominently, claimed that the post-war welfare state had created a society of complacent individuals who took security for granted and therefore had little incentive to be entrepreneurial, or even to be hard workers. A greater dose of market discipline, including unemployment and a smaller safety net, would force individuals to work harder for their money and to ask employers for less.

Neo-conservative economists did not say, in plain English: "We want unemployment to rise so that the workers will be frightened and their unions will allow wages to fall and profits to rise." Instead, they spoke of the "NAIRU," an acronym for the "non-accelerating inflation rate of unemployment," also sometimes called the "natural rate of unemployment." This was the rate of unemployment at which wage demands would be low enough so that companies no longer rasied prices. It was an ideological construct since, of course, rates of unemployment are not a product of nature but of social construction.

Throughout the post-war boom from 1945 to 1975, Keynesians had scoffed at the monetarists, pointing out that their policies replicated the policy environment of the period before World War II that had produced the Great Depression. Their faith in the marketplace's ability to self-adjust, and therefore their call for monetary and fiscal restraint, had been tried and found disastrous. By contrast, thirty years of expansion of the state's social and economic role had produced an economic miracle in the Western world. Within Canada, Keynesians lamented the half-hearted way in which the Bank of Canada and the Department of Finance had followed Keynesian prescriptions even during the boom, but they felt that the basic Keynesian monetary and fiscal presciptions remained valid.[19] "Post-Keynesians," responding to the monetarist critique that linked Keynesian policies with stagflation, called for a continuing emphasis on state activism as the prime method of dealing with economic problems but with more attention to factors other than fiscal and monetary policy. Their focus in the 1970s was on "active labour-market policy to provide the skilled workers necessary for a growing economy, industrial strategy to assist growth sectors and encourage adjustment of uncompetitive sectors, and wage and price controls to control inflation."[20]

The Trudeau goverment decided to combine aspects of both the monetarist and post-Keynesian agendas. In October 1975, Finance Minister Donald Macdonald announced that the government, in consultation with the provinces, would impose guidelines for wage and price increases over a three-year period. An Anti-Inflation Board

(AIB) would be established to monitor compliance with the government guidelines. The government also decided to follow a tight-money policy. The money supply would be restricted so as to dampen inflationary expectations within the marketplace. Fiscal policy would also be restrictive, but the government would pursue some of the structural policies advocated by the post-Keynesians.[21]

Trudeau gave conflicting signals about the direction in which his government wanted to take the nation. In the early months of the AIB, he made speeches and gave interviews in which he suggested that the private marketplace was too much under the influence of the monopoly power of big corporations and big unions to deliver economic stability without the involvement of the state. He wanted to see a "tripartite" direction of the economy in which major corporations, unions, and government worked together to set and implement economic targets. Big business, which welcomed both the AIB and monetarism, denounced any suggestion that private enterprise required government direction (as opposed to state subsidies, which were rarely complained about) or union interference in management prerogatives. The trade union movement was split regarding the prime minister's vague suggestions, with CLC president Joe Morris intrigued with the idea of organized labour enjoying a seat at the corporate table, and other union leaders arguing that what Trudeau really envisaged was a token role for labour in corporate decision-making in return for concessions regarding wages and working conditions to increase profits.[22] Detailed suggestions for tripartism drawn up by Morris' advisors received a cold response from the government, suggesting that Trudeau did not want formal power-sharing arrangements but rather a more submissive attitude on the part of the labour movement.

Labour was angry with the government for implementing the Stanfield promise it had denounced a year earlier. Trudeau's 1974 prediction that the government would prove less able to control prices than wages proved correct. While wages over the three years of the program increased slightly less than the guidelines allowed, prices increased almost six percent more than the guidelines were supposed to allow. Workers' real earnings fell two percent, with companies not only benefiting from that loss but also taking all the benefits of continuing increases in economic growth.

The Conference Board of Canada (a research organization sponsored by large companies), concluded, without disapproval: "Controls resulted in a significant shift in income distribution in Canada away from persons and in favour of business compared to what would have occurred over the period (1975–8) in the absence of the programme."[23]

Meanwhile, unemployment continued to rise. Beginning in 1975, the government, which had posted either small surpluses or deficits under $500 million from 1970 to 1974, began to post larger deficits. In 1975 the deficit was $3.8 billion and in 1978, it reached $10.9 billion.[24] Unemployment was largely the cause of the deficit since higher unemployment meant not only fewer taxpayers, but also the need to inject more money into the unemployment insurance fund and to provide provinces with more money through the Canada Assistance Plan. The government's introduction of various "tax expenditure" programs which gave individuals and corporations exemptions from taxes if they invested their money in certain ways also limited government revenues. The Registered Retirement Savings Plan, meant to encourage retirement savings, programs to encourage individuals to purchase their own home and investors to build apartment buildings, and new programs to spare investors in resource industries from having to share much of their booty with the taxman all fell into this category.[25]

Keynesian and socialist critics of the government attacked the government's apparent obsession with inflation and its view that tight money was the answer to inflation. Many warned that tight money simply led to high unemployment and while high unemployment might indeed humble the unions and reduce wage demands, thus leading to lower inflation, this was not a humane way to deal with class conflict. It was also creating government deficits that were more the result of unemployment and high interest rates than of attempts to stimulate employment. Rentiers, not workers, seemed to be the principal beneficiaries of the government's policies.[26]

But the monetarists, including the leading figures at the Bank of Canada, argued that this was a short-term view. The high unemployment would lead to lower inflation, and this would trigger economic growth that would restore private-enterprise jobs, leaving everyone richer than before the monetarist experiment had begun. Ironically however, the central premise of monetarism, that the rate of monetization and the rate of inflation are directly related, proved to be false. Political economist Harold Chorney demonstrates that there is no clear relationship between these two variables. So, for example, in 1953, the year when the rate of monetization was highest between 1950 and 1989, the rate of inflation was minus 0.2 percent. Chorney points out that in the 1950s and 1960s the Bank of Canada held over twenty percent of the national debt, and inflation remained low. The commercial banks were required to keep relatively high proportions of total deposits on deposit with the Bank of Canada.[27] Writes Chorney:

> The Bank of Canada was converted to monetarist doctrine in 1975. The bank then accepted that growth in the stock of money and nothing else causes inflation. It focused on controlling the growth in the money stock and gave up trying to control interest rates. Because of this the bank attempted to shrink the share of the government's debt that it purchased directly. This is what led to the sharp rise in interest rates that preceded and accompanied the first big recession in the 1980s.[28]

Monetarists and neo-conservatives also suggested that the government continued to spend too much and that expenditures rather than the high interest rates generated by a tight money policy explained government's revenue shortfalls. The National Accounts indicate another story. In 1974, Canada's last year with a budget surplus, federal government spending accounted for 18.9 percent of gross domestic product. In 1979, when the budget deficit was 9.4 billion dollars, government spending had risen by only 0.2 percent. But federal government revenues had declined from 19.7 to 15.7 percent of GDP during those five years.[29]

The weak performance of the economy created considerable disillusionment with the Trudeau government, and in elections in May 1979, a minority Conservative government led by Joe Clark took office. Clark was a lacklustre Alberta politician who had succeeded Robert Stanfield to the party leadership at a convention in 1976. His government lasted only until it was defeated in a vote of confidence in the House in December 1979. The Tories were more right-wing than the Liberals, announcing plans, for example, to sell Petro-Canada to the private sector and to introduce mortgage deductibility for taxpayers as the United States had done, providing a benefit of interest only to those with the income required to buy homes. Their monetary and expenditure policies however seemed largely a continuation of the policies followed in the seventies and particularly after 1975. The budget item that got the minority government in trouble was a tax of four cents per litre on gasoline, meant to raise billions to reduce the deficit. The Trudeau government had used state intervention to keep Canadian oil prices below international levels. This meant that Canadian producers, mainly in Alberta, earned less profit than a strictly market regime would have provided them, while federal subsidies were required for the portion of eastern energy needs that were supplied from abroad. The Tories wanted both to reduce the size of the subsidy and to collect the subsidy from gasoline users rather than from general revenues. It was part of a strategy to let Canadian prices rise closer to international prices. As we shall see in Chapter Eight, Trudeau's policies were viewed in western Canada as exploitation of the region in favour of central Canadian industries. The Clark government hoped both to pacify western complaints and to reduce costs to the federal treasury of making up the difference between the imposed price on western oil and the cost of imported oil.

Lacking a majority in Parliament, however, the Conservatives were unable to withstand the combined assault of the Opposition parties. The small Créditiste bloc from Quebec had wanted to sustain the government after its election, fearing the consequences to a declining regional party of an early election, but they could not support higher oil prices for Quebec. The government fell on a loss of confidence vote following the tabling of its budget in December 1979. Pierre Trudeau, who had recently quit as Liberal leader, agreed to return to the leadership and won a majority victory in 1980. "Welcome to the eighties," he told Canadians in his victory speech. He had campaigned on the left, attacking the Tories for caving in to American-dominated petroleum companies and pledging Canadianization of the energy industry. Gasoline prices had risen steadily in Canada since the OPEC price increases of 1973, though at a pace far more modest than western Europe experienced. Canadians were unwilling to pay more and did not buy Conservative Finance Minister John Crosbie's claim that the price increases were "short-term pain for long-term gain." On the whole, Trudeau's campaign was negative, a long series of jibes at Prime Minister Clark, an uncharismatic man who had been labelled "Joe Who?" by the media.

The Trudeau government's single-minded focus on inflation after 1975, while it did not lead to a full-scale Liberal embrace of neo-conservatism, led away from any desire to support further programs for redistribution of wealth. In the early seventies, the government had pursued talks with the provinces on the implementation of a guaranteed annual income (GAI) as a way of dealing with poverty

in the country. The three NDP governments of the early seventies —
in Manitoba, Saskatchewan, and British Columbia — and the governments of the Atlantic provinces supported such a program. In
April 1975, the welfare ministers of all provinces agreed to a two-tier
system for a GAI, with unemployables and those unable to find work
in one tier and the working poor dealt with separately. The federal
government suggested a scaled-down version of the program limited
to families with children and people aged fifty-five to sixty-five. This
would cost $240 million as against the $2 billion required for the
program approved by the provinces the year earlier. Ontario balked
at the federal proposal and the Liberals simply shelved the GAI
concept they had extolled a few short years earlier.[30] In 1979, the
government introduced a refundable child tax credit for low-income
parents, a program which did have connotations of a guaranteed
annual income or "negative income tax" philosophy.[31] This represented one of the few victories of poverty action groups in the
seventies.

The government also tried to reduce its obligations to the provinces under shared-cost programs. In 1977, the matching grants for
health and postsecondary grants were replaced by Established Programs Financing, which gave the provinces half of their federal funds
in these areas through a transfer of tax points and half through cash
which was not designated for any specific program.[32] This provided
the federal government with the leeway to cut cash grants as it saw
fit, though initially total federal spending on transfers to the provinces did not fall. All in all, while the Trudeau government of the
late seventies seemed to want to reduce the scale of federal government responsibility for Canadians' well-being, it appeared to accept
the general philosophy that had developed since the war that made
the state, particularly the federal state, responsible for providing a
minimum level of services and income to citizens. But neo-conservative perspectives were gaining more political credibility by the late
seventies and the Trudeau Liberals did accept the neo-conservative
concept of the NAIRU.

Canada in the World

The "welfare state" measures of the sixties, particularly medicare,
became for many Canadians part of the emerging — and always
contested — identity of Canada. From this perspective, Canada was
— if only compared to the United States, which, after a short War

on Poverty, allowed racism and paranoid anti-communism to abort the efforts of its social reformers[33] — a caring, sharing country, not socialist, but not purely grubby capitalist either. Canada wished to project such an image on the international stage as well, that is, the image of a moderate country moved by compassion rather than by ideology. It only partly succeeded.

Canada's commitment to the American/South Vietnamese side in the Vietnam War, despite its supposed continued neutrality as a member of the ICC, raised questions about that image. Beginning with the Kennedy administration, the Americans joined the South Vietnamese government in using defoliants to deprive the National Liberation Front (NLF), the guerrilla movment of South Vietnamese supporters of unification, of forest cover. They also used herbicides to poison NLF food supplies. This chemical warfare had "devastating ecological consequences," writes Vietnam War historian George Herring.[34] Canada ignored the chemical warfare, continuing to focus exclusively on North Vietnamese violations of the Geneva Accords.

The American government's efforts to shore up the South Vietnamese government without large-scale, direct military intervention unravelled by late 1964. In November 1964, after an American army barracks and helicopter base in the south were attacked by the NLF, Johnson, arguing that the NLF was a North Vietnamese creation, began bombing North Vietnam. Johnson hoped to stop the flow of supplies from the north to the NLF but the bombing, though it killed many people, had little impact on the political dynamics of the region. Lester Pearson, speaking at Temple University in Philadelphia in April 1965, called guardedly for a halt to the bombings to see if the north would agree to peace talks. He was manhandled by the president for his efforts and the two governments soon came to an agreement that neither would criticize the other's foreign policies publicly.[35]

Despite Pearson's speech, Canada continued to support the American effort in Southeast Asia. In May 1965, Blair Seaborn, Canada's representative on the ICC, visited the north and delivered an American threat that bombing, recently halted, would recommence if the north did not stop supporting the NLF. For good measure, Seaborn took advantage of his time in the north to report to the Americans on the morale of the North Vietnamese people (which was high) and the preparedness of Hanoi for more bombing (which seemed minimal). Such spying was inconsistent with Canada's role as a mediator on the ICC but quite consistent with Canada's overall role in the war.

Canada supplied arms to the Americans throughout the war and aid to the South Vietnamese, even testing weapons for South Vietnam.[36]

There was little visible change in Canada's stance on the war when Pierre Trudeau succeeded Pearson. After a limited peace agreement between the Americans/South Vietnamese and North Vietnam with its NLF allies in the south was announced in October 1972, the ICC was replaced by a new commission and Trudeau was reluctant to have Canada serve again. In the end he agreed only to a short-term involvement for Canada. But, according to American writer Gareth Porter, as well as Canadian historian Victor Levant, Canada played a similar role in the new commission to its role in the ICC. Porter suggests that Michel Gauvin, chief of the Canadian delegation to the new ICCS, was "well known as an anti-Communist zealot" and blamed the pro-unification forces in South Vietnam for every violation of the peace agreement, even when there was no evidence to back up his accusations. "Canada made no secret of its belief that the division of Vietnam was necessary to maintain peace, and that any negotiated settlement should be based on a progressive reapplication of the Geneva Agreement's cease-fire terms — but not its political terms," concludes Porter.[37]

For most Canadians, the key phenomenon that suggested the Canadian government was not entirely supportive of the American government was the country's embrace of American draft dodgers and deserters. An estimated 70,000 to 125,000 Americans entered Canada during the war so as not to have to fight in Vietnam. More tried to enter, but the RCMP, ignoring the law, often evicted deserters and draft dodgers who had entered the country legally and returned them to American authorities. In January 1970, an army deserter turned over to American military authorities by the RCMP managed to escape and returned to Canada, confirming on national television the story that NDP member David Lewis had told the House of Commons and the RCMP and Solicitor-General had denied.[38] Afterwards, well-organized groups of Canadian sympathizers with draft dodgers were better able to use the media to limit illegal efforts by the RCMP to deport American immigrants whose politics the police force appeared not to like.

Trudeau did try to assert Canada's independence on a number of foreign policy questions. Though Trudeau maintained the NORAD agreement which put the military protection of the North in joint American–Canadian hands, he asserted Canada's right to protect the northern environment. The Arctic Waters Pollution Prevention Act of 1970 indicated Canada's intent to implement its laws regarding environmental pollution throughout a 100-mile zone north of the sixtieth parallel, an assertion made necessary because American oil tankers often passed through the waters of the area. Despite American objections, Canada exempted this law from the jurisdiction of the International Court of Justice, arguing that protection of Arctic Native communities overrode concerns for normal procedures of dealing with international claims. On this issue, argue two political scientists, "the Canadian government broke decisively with the liberal-internationalist traditions that had dominated Canadian foreign policy since the Second World War."[39]

In 1970, the Canadian government recognized the government of mainland China, two years before the Americans were prepared to follow. One year earlier Canada also cut its NATO troop commitment in half, to the chagrin of the Americans, though Trudeau was careful not to criticize NATO, and therefore American, policies. Trudeau scrapped the obsolescent Bomarcs and after 1970, Canada was again nuclear-free.

But while Canada had no desire to become a nuclear power, Trudeau continued to support the concept of nuclear deterrence.[40] His government also continued the policy of selling nuclear reactors in the international marketplace. Atomic Energy of Canada spent more money producing CANDU reactors than it received in sales, but it promoted sales vigorously. The sales were accompanied by safeguards meant to ensure the peaceful use of the atom but when India exploded a nuclear device in 1974, the hollowness of such safeguards became obvious. An embarrassed Canada tightened its safeguards further, announcing in December 1976 an end to nuclear sales to countries that had exploded nuclear devices or failed to ratify the United Nations non-proliferation treaty on nuclear weapons. Within a year, however, it cancelled this decision, unwilling to offend West Germany and Japan who had been among the countries embargoed by the 1976 legislation.[41]

Trudeau removed government subsidies from firms dealing with the apartheid regime in South Africa, but he refused to heed the anti-apartheid movement's call for a trade boycott. Trade between the two countries was largely unaffected by the government's token action.

Though Trudeau indicated some appreciation of the extreme social disparities that triggered revolutionary movements in the Third World, his government largely supported regimes that reinforced the

status quo and rejected anti-capitalist governments. Like his predecessors, he seemed to make no exception for democratically-elected
left-wing governments, such as the government of Salvador Allende,
a Socialist, elected president of Chile in 1970. The destabilization by
the CIA and eventual overthrow of Allende by Chilean generals with
American support, demonstrated Canada's criteria for support. Notes
historian Stephen Randall:

> Unfortunately, the Canadian response to the Allende admini-
> stration in Chile from 1970 until the coup in 1973 suggests
> that when confronted with a fundamental alternative, Cana-
> dian policy-makers will opt for a collaborative position vis-à-
> vis the United States. Canadian reception of Allende was cool.
> It included a refusal to support the extension of new credits,
> either bilaterally or multilaterally, although old programmes
> were not discontinued. There was an uneasy feeling among
> some officials in External Affairs that relations with Allende
> were somehow incompatible with Canada's role in NATO.
> One official identified Canada's main "interest" in Chile as
> specifically Bata Shoes and generally the protection of free
> enterprise capitalism.[42]

As the next chapter indicates, Canadians in the 1960s and 1970s
were engaged in a great deal of soul-searching about whether Canada
was simply a northern outpost of the United States or whether it
embodied different values than those held by the Americans, whether
indeed "the protection of free enterprise capitalism" was what Canadians valued most. In Canada's case "free enterprise capitalism"
often meant American economic domination and accompanying political domination. But the question Canadians faced was: does it
matter?

Six

English-Canadian Nationalism

Perhaps it was the intense preparations for Canada's Centennial in 1967. Perhaps it was the negative images of the Vietnam War and race riots in America's major cities. Or it may have been the confidence that unprecedented prosperity gave many Canadians, particularly the middle-class strata of baby boomers who had known nothing else. No doubt it was some combination of all of these factors that made Canadians, so complacent about American control in the 1950s, more anxious to assert their independence of the Americans in the 1960s and 1970s politically, economically, and culturally. The degree of foreign control was staggering, and this occasioned a great deal of debate about the ability of Canadians to control their own destiny. While forty-six percent of Canadians told the Gallup organi-

Bobby Gimby leading centennial parade, NAC C-26756.

Expo '67. Over 50 million people visted the Montreal fair, viewed today as a catalyst for Canada's burgeoning nationalism. NAC C-18536.

zation in 1964 that Canada had enough foreign investment, there were many Canadians who did not embrace the new nationalism. The business community, whose leading ranks included the heads of American corporations in Canada, was, on the whole, staunchly continentalist and warned that nationalism would impoverish Canadians. This chapter attempts to recreate the flavour of the debate about nationalism from 1963 to 1980.

It should be stated from the outset, however, that the nationalism that defined Canada's identity, in terms of protection of Canadian businesses and cultural institutions from American control, was mainly potent in English-speaking Canada. For francophones, particularly in Quebec, cultural protection meant preservation and *"l'épanouissement"* of the French language. Though many Québécois supported controls over American investment and trade, the "national issue" in the province largely referred to relations between Quebec and the rest of Canada, as we see in Chapter Seven. Even within anglophone Canada, the nationalist movement had unequal strengths. In both the Atlantic provinces and western Canada, concerns about Ottawa's supposedly overweening powers over the provinces had more political appeal than concerns about foreign control of the economy. Nationalists' claims in the 1970s that foreign control was resulting in the "deindustrialization" of Canada won little support in provinces such as Nova Scotia and Saskatchewan, which had little industry for anyone to take away. In any case, while the resource sector was dominated by foreign capital across the country, the industrial sector outside central Canada was considerably less dominated by non-nationals. This was simply because American manufacturers had chosen to invest in industry in Canada's industrial heartland and had largely ignored the outlying regions. So had everyone else and many Canadians in both the east and west saw no reason to favour central Canadian capitalists over their American counterparts.

Shaping Canada's Economy

The *laissez-faire* approach to Canadian economic development was nicely summed up by Mackenzie King in a diary entry, after a meeting in November 1935 with American Secretary of State Cordell Hull.

> I was able to tell Mr. Hull that the arguments he was putting forth paralleled very completely the line I had taken in the recent campaign in Canada. I let him see wherein I was wholeheartedly at one with him in the point of view he had presented. I spoke of the home market argument, pointing out that the home market of Canada was the purchasing power in the hands of our agriculturalists for manufacturers while the home market in the United States was the purchasing power in the hands of the manufacturers and those employed in industries for the purpose of agricultural products. This, the result of Canada being an exporter chiefly in natural products; the United States an exporter chiefly of manufactured products. I said I thought this fact should make possible the satisfying of all parties in both countries on the wisdom of any policy which permitted more in the way of trade between the two countries, especially those commodities of which they respectively produced surpluses.[1]

In the post-war period, the United States continued to be Canada's major trading partner, and trade continued to be crucial for Canada. In 1968, Canadian exports amounted to twenty-four percent of Canada's GNP, a figure six times larger than the comparable figure for

Table One Foreign Assets in Canada % of total assets by industrial sector		
	1970	1980
Agriculture	13	4
Mines	69	45
Manufacturing	58	48
Construction	16	10
Public utilities	8	5
Wholesale trade	27	24
Retail trade	22	13
Services	22	15
Non-financial industries	36	27
Source: Jorge Niosi,"The Canadian Bourgeoisie: Towards a Synthetical Approach," *Canadian Journal of Political and Social Theory*, 7,3 (Fall 1983), 143.		

the United States. Over sixty percent of those exports went to the United States[2] and, despite government attempts to find new, particularly European, markets for Canadian products, Canada was exporting seventy percent of its exports to its southern neighbour as the 1980s began. In 1980, Canada also received seventy percent of its imports from the United States. The bulk of Canada's exports remained unprocessed and semi-processed products, as they were in King's time. Manufactured goods loomed large in the nation's imports. While the United States imported only ten percent of its manufactured goods, Canada imported thirty-six percent.[3]

But American manufacturers were interested in establishing branch plants within Canada even though the policy of imperial preference, which had drawn them to the country in the pre-war period, had been largely dismantled. *The Star Weekly*, reflecting the post-war concern about jobs regardless of how they were created, reported excitedly in January 1947, "Uncle Sam Moves to Canada." American industrialists told journalist Ross Harkness that "Canada is steering a steadier course than her neighbor through the storm of labor troubles." Many industrialists viewed Canada's unions as less militant than their American counterparts and Canada's government as less interventionist than the American government had become since the Roosevelt New Deal began in 1933. G.D. Mallory, chief of the industrial development division in the Department of Trade and Commerce, noted: "They are looking for an anchor to leeward; they are insuring themselves against trouble in the States by having a source of raw materials and a Canadian plant to fall back on."[4]

By 1970, American corporations and individuals controlled fifty-eight percent of all manufacturing assets in Canada, and thirty-six percent of all non-financial industries, despite a healthy public sector in Canadian utilities and limited American ownership in Canadian agriculture.[5] Foreign ownership, however, declined dramatically in the 1970s as Americans began to look warily at a Canadian policy environment that they viewed as anti-American and more interventionist than in the United States (see Table One). Before looking at the principal players on both sides of the debate in Canada regarding foreign ownership and continental economic integration, let us look at the main arguments that each side mustered in the effort to enlist the support of Canadians.

The Impact of Continental Integration

Supporters of continental integration of industry, and more particularly of access to ownership of Canadian industry by non-Canadians, argued that Canada could not realistically go it alone given its small, spread-out population. Americans injected capital, expertise, and technology into Canada and could take credit for the economy moving further away from its earlier concentration on agriculture and resource industries.

Opponents of foreign investment countered that American capital was not needed because Canada had a sufficient capital base. Lack of controls on capital movements resulted in almost as much Canadian capital being invested abroad as American capital was invested in Canada. Furthermore, by the 1960s, far more money was leaving Canada in the form of dividends for American owners than was being invested in Canada by Americans. Indeed, over time, most of the "American capital" invested in Canada did not emanate from the United States at all. Rather, it was simply retained earnings of US companies already in Canada. From 1957 to 1963, notes economist Kari Levitt, retained Canadian earnings provided seventy-three percent of capital investment in American companies in Canada; financial institutions and other Canadian sources provided an additional twelve percent while new investment from the United States represented fifteen percent.[6]

Calgary in 1964. GAIA NA-2864-1539.

Nationalists countered the argument about technology and expertise by suggesting that foreign ownership had resulted in Canada
having the lowest per capita expenditures on research of all OECD
countries. American firms tended to do their research at home. While
they sometimes hired Canadians to scientific and technical positions,
it usually meant emigration to the United States for the employees.
The result was that Canada itself was deprived both of the high-paying jobs and the possibility of industrial innovation that having an
important research establishment provides many nations.

Foreign ownership advocates suggested that many of the arguments of their opponents were moot because Canadian businessmen
had demonstrated, during the long years of tariff protection that
preceded World War II, that they were a conservative lot who would
only invest in manufacturing when it involved import substitution
and who rarely demonstrated a keenness to innovate. Even in the case
of resources, it was Americans who were willing to take the risks to
develop new industries as the development of Alberta's oil industry
after the war amply demonstrated. While the history of Canadian
business seemed to confirm the view of the anti-nationalists, nationalists sometimes pointed to a different kind of entrepreneurialism that
they claimed had been successful in Canada: state capitalism. During
World War II, for example, the federal government had established
twenty-eight Crown corporations to produce items required for the
war effort. Nationalists viewed the sale of most of these Crown

operations after the war as the product of ideological opposition to state ownership rather than as a comment on the success of these corporations.

Continentalists were usually free traders and free enterprisers for whom state ownership, or even extensive state regulation of industry, was anathema. They claimed that controls over foreign investment would result in a slower rate of growth, and a less competitive, less efficient economy. Their opponents suggested that the prosperity of Western countries after the war, during a period when the state intervened in the operations of industry more than at any other time in peacetime history, demonstrated that unfettered free enterprise was not a prerequisite for economic growth. American ownership had not, in any case, resulted in greater efficiency or useful competition. Instead, it had produced what was called a "miniature replica" effect. Each American corporation in an industry, such as tire manufacturing, established a Canadian branch plant. The result was more firms than the Canadian market required, each operating under capacity, and none developing products for export. Nationalists and continentalists disagreed however about why American manufacturers in Canada did so little exporting. While nationalists pointed out that corporate strategy determined in the United States resticted many branch plants to producing for the national market, continentalists suggested that Canadian-owned firms in the manufacturing sector also concentrated on the home market. From their point of view, it was only natural that Canada, rich in resources, focussed its exports on natural resources for which a ready international market awaited, while limiting its involvement in exports of manufactured products where world markets were often already glutted.

Many of the specifics of the debate between continentalists and nationalists proved of little interest to Canadians generally. Those who sided with the nationalists often had a gut feeling that Canada was becoming too subservient to the United States and that this was harming both Canada's economy and Canadian independence. Continentalist supporters, equally unconcerned with specific economic arguments, felt that breaking the ties with the Americans would cause economic disruptions and saw no real link between economic and political independence. Advocates of foreign ownership argued that American corporations in Canada were subject to Canadian law and paid taxes to Canadian governments. But nationalists rejected these arguments. They pointed out that Americans laws, in many cases, did apply to branch plants in Canada, and suggested that this "extra-territorial" reach of the American government impugned Canadian sovereignty. In particular, the Trading with the Enemy Act, an American law that forbade all trade with most Communist countries, forced American companies operating in Canada to refuse orders of trucks for Cuba, potash for China, and medical supplies for North Vietnam in the 1960s, though Canadian law placed no restrictions on such sales.

Finally, while continentalists maintained that Canada followed an independent foreign policy and attributed similarities in the two nations' external policies to the exigencies of a bipolar world, nationalists seized on evidence that Canada had compromised its foreign policies to accommodate "Big Brother," whose power of economic retaliation was immense. We look now at some of that evidence.

Economic Policy and Foreign Policy

Commenting in his memoirs on charges that the Pearson government bent over backwards to appear compliant with American foreign policy wishes in order to receive economic favours, Paul Martin, who served as Minister of External Affairs throughout the Pearson years, responded combatively. He was proud that Canada won an exemption from an American tax on issues of foreign securities in American capital markets.

> Many observers and analysts have argued that the president's imposition and subsequent modification of the interest equalization tax perfectly illustrated Canada's dependence on American goodwill. Of course it did, but what of it? One of the functions of Canadian diplomacy has been to ensure that the United States will always harbour a special regard for Canada. My own generation of Canadians, conscious of the "North Atlantic Triangle" — so called because of our participation with our great allies in two world wars — has always had a more profound understanding of the special relationship between Canada and the United States than those who grew up in the 1960s. Neither Canada nor the United States can go it alone.[7]

"What of it?" is indeed the issue. Martin, of course, denies that Canada made itself subservient to the Americans in its efforts to ensure the Americans' "special regard." But his evidence often suggests that it did. While he gives the standard Liberal argument about why the Pearson government accepted nuclear warheads for its NATO and NORAD missiles — Diefenbaker had made a promise, and a promise is a promise — he admits that the Liberals' turnabout helped maintain the "special regard." Writes Martin: "The Canadian government's readiness to ensure that we would honour our commitments to NATO and NORAD, despite the fact that our personal reluctance was well-known, did more than anything else to foster good relations between Ottawa and Washington."[8]

Lester Pearson was, on occasion, candid about the impact of close economic relations between Canada and the United States on Canada's policies regarding the Vietnam conflict. He told *Maclean's* magazine in 1967: "We can't ignore the fact that the first result of any open breach with the United States over Vietnam, which their government considers to be unfair and unfriendly on our part, would be a more critical examination by Washington of certain special aspects of our relationship from which we, as well as they, get great benefit."[9] That same year, Pearson defended his government's arms sales to the Americans in a letter to a group of University of Toronto professors who called upon the government to stop selling arms to the Americans until the Americans pulled out of Vietnam. Such arms sales, argued Pearson, must be seen "in a somewhat broader perspective than the problem of the Vietnam war alone." The prime minister elaborated:

> The U.S.–Canadian production-sharing arrangements enable the Canadian Government to acquire from the U.S.A. a great deal of the nation's essential defence requirement at the lowest possible cost, while at the same time permitting us to offset the resulting drain on the economy by reciprocal sales to the U.S.A. Under these agreements, by reason of longer production runs, Canadian industry is able to participate competitively in U.S. research, development and production programmes, and is exempted from the "Buy American" Act for these purposes. From a long-term point of view, another major benefit to Canada is the large contribution which these agreements have made and are continuing to make to Canadian industrial research and development capabilities which, in turn, are fundamental to the maintenance of an advanced technology in Canada.[10]

Although *realpolitik* seemed to guide Pearson and Martin, their government was far from unanimous in its willingness to simply rationalize away Canada's increased economic and political dependence on the Americans. While the nationalist forces in the Liberal party were probably weaker overall than the continentalist voices, popular pressures resulted in some victories over time for supporters of greater Canadian economic independence. Such victories would be largely swept away in the period after the Mulroney election of 1984, as we see in Part Three, but certainly in the 1970s it did not seem entirely implausible that Canada would begin to chart an economic future more and more autonomous from that of the United States.

The Political Battles

Lester Pearson rewarded Walter Gordon's critical role in rebuilding the Liberal Party by naming him Minister of Finance when the Liberals took power. While Paul Martin was working on catering Canadian external and defence policies to American tastes, Walter Gordon was writing a budget that proved to be at odds with his government's desire to make the Americans happy once again with a Canada that had somewhat alienated them in the latter Diefenbaker years. The budget, tabled in the House of Commons on 13 June 1963, introduced a thirty percent takeover tax on foreigners who acquired Canadian corporate assets, and a large tax penalty on dividends leaving the country from firms that had less than twenty-five percent Canadian ownership. The former was meant to discourage American buyers when foreign-controlled assets in Canada were available for buyout, while the latter was meant to encourage a respectable degree of Canadian participation in foreign-controlled firms operating in the country.[11]

Not only the US Treasury but also a chorus of Canadian businessmen and the Canadian Labour Congress objected to these measures. The businessmen made the continentalist arguments noted previously, while labour indicated concerns about the impact on job creation of discouraging foreign investment. The anti-nationalist bias of the chief economic protagonists, so at odds with the growing nationalism in popular opinion, no doubt also reflected the extent of American penetration of Canada's elites. When American capital dominated the resource and manufacturing sectors, it was hardly surprising that the organizations representing these sectors opposed discrimination against investors on the basis of residence. As for the

CLC, in 1963, it was overwhelmingly dominated by Canadian branches of American unions. These were called "international unions," though, outside of Canada, no other nation had members in these American-controlled unions. Some of the unions, such as the United Autoworkers, gave considerable autonomy to their Canadian branches while others, such as the construction and railway unions, treated their Canadian branches as cash cows for headquarters and provided little real autonomy to Canadian members.

Opposition, however, went well beyond the agents of American operation in the country. American investment had become so important within the economy as a whole that it was almost inevitable that Canadian businessmen would, for the most part, oppose measures that smacked of economic nationalism. Ironically, one of the most effective opponents of Gordon was Eric Kierans, then president of the Montreal Stock Exchange, and a few years later one of Canada's leading economic nationalists.[12] Within two months, the turnover tax proposal was withdrawn and the discriminatory tax on dividends reduced to a token.

Ten days after the change was made, the Americans announced an interest equalization tax, meant to deal with the United States' persistent balance of payments problem. Since Canadian governments and corporations borrowed extensively in the United States, the Pearson government went cap in hand to Washington to win an exemption from the legislation. President Kennedy granted a partial exemption. As the quotation from Paul Martin suggests, the need for such an exemption illustrated the importance of Canada following policies that did not disturb the Americans. Whether it was a turnover tax, an independent nuclear stance, or a critical perspective on American involvement in Vietnam, Canada had to stifle itself if it wished to retain its "special relationship" with the Americans.

Gordon remained as Finance Minister until the 1965 elections, focussing mainly on prodding the government to implement the social programs promised in the 1963 election, but also attempting to deal more gingerly with the American economic impact upon Canada. Seemingly taking the approach that "if you can't beat them, join them," Gordon introduced subsidy programs for industry that attracted a variety of American firms, particularly in the automobile and automotive parts industries. When small American businesses in the automotive parts industry complained to Washington of unfair competition from Canada, Gordon set in motion negotiations for an agreement on trade in automobiles and automobile parts with the

United States. The agreement, which some see as "free trade" and others see as "managed trade," guaranteed Canada a minimum share of production of automobiles and automobile parts, otherwise leaving the market to decide where various components of the auto trade were carried out.[13]

After the 1965 election, Gordon, who took responsibility for mistakenly advising Pearson that he could win a majority government by calling an early election, left the Cabinet. His successor, Mitchell Sharp, was a conservative more concerned about inflation than social reform. Indeed the tone of the second Pearson government was more conservative than the first. Pearson, responding to party pressures to give more influence to its reformist wing, urged Gordon to return to Cabinet. Gordon did return in January 1967, but only after extracting a promise from Pearson to have a task force examine foreign ownership and its impact on Canadian economic and political life.

Pearson agreed, and the result was the appointment of the task force on the structure of Canadian industry headed by Professor Mel Watkins of the University of Toronto. The task force largely accepted the viewpoint of the economic nationalists that the disadvantages of foreign control of industry outweighed its advantages, and its report in January 1968 would be extensively quoted afterwards by nationalists. Watkins and his colleagues recommended that the federal government establish agencies to promote the development of Canadian-controlled corporations and to supervise the operations of multinationals in Canada, particularly with a view to ending the application of American laws to branch plants operating in Canada.[14]

Pearson took no action on the recommendations of the task force, but nationalist forces in the Liberal caucus produced two reports in the early Trudeau years that confirmed Watkins' analysis and also urged state action to limit foreign control. Ian Wahn's report for the Standing Committee on External Affairs in 1970, and National Revenue Minister Herb Gray's commissioned report in 1972, both called for government action. Public opinion polls suggested Canadians wanted action; in 1970, eighty percent of Canadians favoured the establishment of a Canada Development Corporation to increase Canadian control over the economy.[15]

Trudeau established the Canada Development Corporation in 1971 with a modest budget to finance new Canadian firms and buy designated American-controlled firms. In 1974, the Foreign Investment Review Agency (FIRA) was established to review all takeovers of firms in Canada by non-Canadians, regardless of whether these firms were already controlled by foreigners, to determine whether the takeover was likely to be of benefit to Canadians. One year later FIRA was also given the power to investigate new foreign-controlled firms in Canada.[16]

FIRA proved quite magnanimous in its judgments, only rarely deciding that a takeover was against the Canadian interest. But bureaucratic interference in their affairs, with the concomitant necessity to plan takeovers or new companies in ways that added to the Canadian stock of jobs or otherwise demonstrated a positive impact on the Canadian economy, infuriated many American businessmen. They also feared that, with the nationalist movement well organized, FIRA was only the tip of the iceberg. Indeed, especially in Ontario, nationalist movements were well entrenched. The Committee for an Independent Canada (CIC), a non-partisan organization whose membership included a star-studded set of Canadian personalities, led by Walter Gordon, called for repatriation of the Canadian economy. Canada's largest-circulation newspaper, the *Toronto Star*, often seemed to be a mouthpiece for the CIC. On the left, the Waffle group within the New Democratic Party carried one-third of the delegates to the 1969 national party convention with a resolution that would have used nationalization as a means to guarantee Canadians meaningful control over their economy. The party leadership fended off this resolution partly by conceding a more stridently economic nationalist position, though stressing government control rather than ownership of industry. Three NDP governments — in British Columbia, Manitoba, and Saskatchewan — were in power in the early 1970s. These governments, as well as the Parti Québécois government elected in 1976 in Quebec, seemed too statist to many American investors. Americans began looking for other places to invest, while Canadians, for whom tax laws and the CDC made investment within Canada more attractive, acquired more of the nation's economic assets. American control of Canadian assets declined by twenty-five percent from 1970 to 1980. Government statistics meant to demonstrate to the Canadian public that a problem was being resolved ought, however, to be taken cautiously. As historian Robert Bothwell, who largely disagrees with the nationalists' arguments, nevertheless points out:

> Sometimes administrative decisions helped. In 1971 the International Nickel Company was reclassified as Canadian rather than foreign by the government; as a result, "foreign control"

of the Canadian mining industry dropped from 71 percent to
58 percent. Statistics are, after all, "State Arithmetic."[17]

Prime Minister Trudeau also made efforts to diversify markets for
Canadian goods, particularly after President Nixon introduced a ten
percent surcharge on existing tariffs in August 1971, in yet another
American effort to deal with balance-of-payments difficulties.
Though Canada once again lobbied the American government for a
Canadian exemption, the "special relationship" had sufficiently
soured that Nixon said no. A year earlier, in a White Paper on
Canadian foreign policy, the Trudeau government had announced
that it wanted to consider an option other than either the status quo
or even closer integration of the Canadian and American economies.
It favoured a Third Option, which was to "pursue a comprehensive,
long-term strategy to develop and strengthen the Canadian economy
and other aspects of our national life ... to reduce the present Canadian vulnerability."[18] Increasingly, after the new American protectionism was announced in 1971, Trudeau attempted to create a
special link between Canada and either the European Common Market or Japan. But both the Common Market countries and Japan were
largely uninterested. They were unprepared to risk the antagonism
of the United States that would surely result from granting Canada
trade privileges that were denied to the Americans. Throughout the
1970s, the proportion of Canada's trade with the United States increased; efforts to establish a Third Option yielded little that was
concrete.[19]

The movement for greater economic independence from the
United States sparked unprecedented nationalism among Canadian
workers as well. Breakaways from American unions occurred where
union members felt the American headquarters gave the Canadian
arm of the union too little autonomy or proved too tight-fisted when
the Canadians were on strike. Pulp and paper workers, retail workers,
hard-rock miners, chemical and oil workers, in varying numbers,
chose to form independent Canadian unions. While some of the
breakaways reflected nationalism less than deep-seated criticisms of
a growing trade union bureaucracy that seemed less interested in
consulting union members than in developing good relations with
management, the "foreignness" of the unions sometimes seemed to
highlight the estrangement between leaders and rank-and-file unionists. The breakaway movement and the growth in the sixties and
seventies of public service unions, which were invariably Canadian

unions, gradually transformed the trade union movement in many ways, one of which was that the majority of Canada's workers now belonged to Canadian unions.[20] Workers' loyalties, however, like those of other Canadians, were often divided between regional and national sentiments, depending on the issue. As we see in Chapter Eight, regional antagonisms in Canada were heightened by the growing north-south character of economic development in the post-war period.

Cultural Nationalism

Canadian nationalists believed that the United States represented not only an economic threat to Canada's national existence, but also a cultural threat. Such concerns had led the federal government in 1949 to establish the Royal Commission on National Development in the Arts, headed by Vincent Massey. Massey's report in 1951 called for the creation of the Canada Council to subsidize development of the arts in Canada, for federal financial support of universities, and for more money for the CBC. The federal government implemented all of these recommendations.[21] CBC Television, which began operation in 1952, technically had a monopoly over television broadcasting for a number of years, though, in practice, Canadians who lived close enough to the American border could tune in American stations. By the 1960s, faced with competition from both Canadian private broadcasters and American stations, the CBC developed a seemingly permanent identity crisis. Though its mandate was to help Canadians know themselves better, the public broadcaster was under pressure to do so without costing a great deal of money. It could generally attract its largest audiences and therefore its biggest advertising revenues by buying broadcasting rights for American-produced "sitcoms."

Apart from Hockey Night in Canada and the National News, the CBC only rarely had a "hit" show that it had produced itself. A significant exception was the Sunday night news feature, "This Hour Has Seven Days," which had audiences of about three million per show from 1965 to 1967. Political interference by the Liberal government killed the hard-hitting news show, and while supporters of the CBC called for the public broadcaster to be put even further at arm's length from government control, the view of the CBC as, in part, a government agency, was strengthened by the cancellation of the CBC's most popular news show ever. Shows that had large audiences over long periods included "Front Page Challenge," which endured from 1956 to 1995, and "Don Messer's Jubilee," whose cancellation in 1974 after eighteen years on air lit up CBC phone lines with protests. Both shows indicated a market in Canada for homey entertainment with no trace of American glitz. On "Front Page Challenge," brainy panelists guessed the stories, new and old, that mystery guests represented. Don Messer's show featured down-home Maritime fiddling, singing and dancing. The removal of the show, which was not only a sensation in the Maritimes but the CBC's biggest draw in blue-collar cities like Hamilton, Ontario, was the result of CBC management's view that it was too old-fashioned rather than a consequence of low ratings.

The Pearson and Trudeau governments were concerned about accusations that Canadian television, including the CBC, was focussing too much on rebroadcasts of American shows. In 1968, the government established the Canadian Radio-Television Commission (CRTC). The CRTC required that sixty percent of shows broadcast on Canadian television stations from six p.m. to midnight be Canadian-produced or joint Canadian productions with a broadcaster from another country. Neither CBC nor its main competitor, CTV, proved willing to spend large amounts of money producing Canadian programming and, apart from news and sports shows, where both broadcasters generally did a good job, much of what Canadian stations offered was low-budget copies of American sitcoms. Canadian actors complained that the country's TV stations created few jobs for them and many continued to emigrate to the United States in search of work.

While CBC Television never really resolved its purpose, by the 1970s, CBC Radio had become an advertising-free medium focussing on news and the arts. Peter Gzowski emerged as a quintessential Canadian radio host, his popular three-hour morning program on CBC Radio establishing that many Canadians were quite happy to listen to discussions centring mainly, though not exclusively, on Canadian news, artistic developments, and personalities. "As It Happens," an evening radio program with Barbara Frum as its first host, focussing on interviews with a combination of newsmakers and eccentrics, was also quite popular.

While CBC radio appealed to a sub-section of educated Canadians, most Canadian radio listeners tuned in private stations that played music, little of it performed or written by Canadians. The economic impact of this was clear. The huge record-buying industry

John Grierson, creator of the National Film Board of Canada, 1939–45. NAC PA 169782.

simply drained money out of Canada to the United States and Great Britain. Influenced by Canadian performers and by the growing nationalism in the country generally, in 1971 the Trudeau government, via the CRTC, created a "thirty percent rule" for Canadian content on radio stations. While stations were given some time to reach the new quota, and there were debates on what constituted a Canadian recording, by the end of the 1970s, Canadian artists were prominent on Canadian radio stations. The result was not only the making of a variety of stars in Canada such as Anne Murray, Joni Mitchell, and Bachman-Turner Overdrive, but success for many of the Canadian stars in the United States as American radio took an interest in records that were clearly selling well in Canada.

Attempts to create an independent Canadian film industry proved less successful than efforts to produce a Canadian recording industry. The federal government offered tax writeoffs to business people who sponsored movie production, but few of these movies got mass distribution. This was unsurprising since American film distributors pretty much monopolized decisions about what films were screened. A few movies such as *Wedding in White, Mon Oncle Antoine*, and *Les Ordres* were highly acclaimed both inside and outside Canada, but there were few box office successes. The "Canadian" movies that did best at the box office were those that imported American stars for lead roles, such as *The Apprenticeship of Duddy Kravitz* and

Atlantic City, with Canadian actors in secondary roles. The Canadian movie industry created the Genies, Canada's answer to the Oscars, in an attempt to create some publicity and excitement about the best work being done in Canada. But Canadians generally appeared happy with imported movies, with most moviegoers favouring American films, and an arty sub-set of movie patrons favouring European and other foreign fare. Outside of the Quebec francophone film industry, which did tend to focus with some success on local stories, Canadian film-making was perhaps defeated by its efforts to produce movies which would have appeal outside Canada as well as inside the country. Unlike Australian movies, also produced with large state subsidies, but appealing to a mass market within and eventually outside the country, Canadian films rarely dealt with themes that were drawn from Canadian history and Canadian places. The attempt to produce American-seeming films in Canada with budgets that were a fraction the size of Hollywood budgets was largely doomed.

If Canadians were unwilling to see Canadian films, and distributors were unwilling in most cases to give them many opportunities, they were willing to read Canadian books. A great deal of "CanLit," unlike Canadian movies, dealt with themes, places, and people with whom Canadians could identify. Canada Council grants, university writer-in-residence programs, and government assistance to publishers all helped. But, in the end, it was talent and the willingness of Canadians to buy books written in the country that produced the commercial success of such authors as Margaret Laurence, Margaret Atwood, Hugh MacLennan, Michael Ondaatje, Robertson Davies, Timothy Findley, Alice Munro, and a host of other authors. Minority authors such as Austen Clarke and F.G. Paci, enjoyed popularity well beyond their own communities. The nationalist movement forced Canada's university English departments, which once regarded Canadian literature as too parochial to be worth serious study, to set up courses in Canadian literature at all levels. Eventually whole programs of Canadian studies were offered at many universities. The focus on Canadian literature in universities, and later, schools, revived many works, such as Sinclair Ross' *As for Me and My House*, which had had little success upon first release. New editions of authors' work in series like the Carleton University Library series brought the works of great Canadian writers, past and present, to a wide audience.

Canadian playwrights also thrived to a certain degree. Regional troupes, including Newfoundland's Mummers, Saskatchewan's 25th

Actress and teacher Dora Mavor Moore (1888–1979), the namesake of Toronto's annual theatre awards. NAC PA-137084.

Street Theatre, and Toronto's Theatre Passe Muraille, performed works across the country that were coloured by the history and cultures of their regions. Plays increasingly dealt critically with social problems such as racism experienced by Native people, the subject of *Ecstasy of Rita Joe* by Vancouver's George Ryga, and the oppression of working people, the focus of *On the Job* by Montreal's David Fennario.

Of course, many Canadians watched no plays or only went to flashy musicals that had been successful on Broadway, watched only American movies and American television, and read only American pot-boilers. By the end of the seventies, however, a large section of Canadians patronized, at least to some extent, Canadian cultural productions. There were some debates about how different these cultural products were from their American counterparts. Margaret Atwood, for example, claimed to see a theme of survival in Canadian writing throughout the country's history, at odds with the more combative themes present in American writing. But others, such as Northrop Frye, asked whether Canadian and American writing were not the products of a common North American culture. One Canadian province that seemed particularly adamant that it would not simply blend in with the larger North American culture, even as it strove to catch up with the material success of much of the rest of the continent, was Quebec.

Seven

From the Quiet Revolution to the First Sovereignty Referendum

While the extent of social change in English Canada in the 1960s and 1970s was far-reaching, the extent of social change in francophone Quebec was even more dramatic. Though the economic forces undermining Quebec's existence as a rural, Church-dominated society were evident before the turn of the century and the social forces that favoured a greater degree of emulation of North American norms strengthened in the post-war period, it was not until the 1960s that old social values and ways of doing things were swept away. The "Quiet Revolution" from 1960 to 1966 — the period of the political regime of Jean Lesage's Liberals, with its goal of *"rattrapage,"* that is, catching up to the rest of North America — is often credited as the catalyst for the social changes. But the Quiet Revolution was itself part of a larger *"projet de société,"* or society-wide movement that embraced the trade unions, the women's movement, and even the Church. The winds of change blew across Quebec after the war and it seemed to take only the fall of Duplessis to put in power a government that had these winds in its sails.

Quebec's *projet de société*

The character of French Quebec's *projet de société* after 1960 is open to debate. Many anglophone commentators at the time, both Canadian and American, focussed on Lesage's use of *rattrapage* in the 1960 election and suggested that Quebec wanted to become like the rest of North America while remaining French-speaking. Families in Quebec, once the largest in the country, became smaller, and by the mid-seventies, the province had the lowest birth rate in the country. Consumerism became as rampant as anywhere else on the continent.

Francophone Québécois watched as much television as their English-speaking confreres, bought as many popular records, and attended as many movies. With censorship relaxed, the cultural offerings available to francophones became as secular as those available to anglophones and French-language films and television shows, whether produced in France or Quebec, were generally as salty and as irreligious as their English-language counterparts.

It is misleading, however, to see the changes in Quebec society solely in terms of *rattrapage* with its implications of becoming like everyone else. Among the middle classes of Quebec society, nationalism had taken root early in the nineteenth century and while its form was sometimes secular and sometimes religious, the sense that the Québécois had a mission to remain a distinct entity was firmly rooted among the intellectuals, if not always among the masses.[1] During the Quiet Revolution too, the intellectuals were concerned that Quebec's embrace of North American social values not result in the abandonment of the dream of nationhood, which many increasingly saw in terms of having separate statehood. The nationalist cause had firm support within Quebec society as a whole, because of a belief that the French language was treated as an inferior language even within the province where it was the language of the majority. Most francophones wanted the opportunity to work in their own language without having to pay the price of being excluded from consideration for most management and professional jobs. As more and more francophones worked in large, foreign-owned companies, the question of the language of work became an issue for the majority. Increasing levels of education also created a growing middle class whose expectations with regards to salary and status far exceeded those of their parents. Many felt that their language limited their success and that their dreams would only be possible if there were strong Quebec laws requiring that the language of work at all levels of corporations, right up to the board of directors, be French. The educated middle classes, resentful of discrimination in favour of anglophones, and certain that an independent Quebec would offer them important opportunities, became the most solid support of the sovereignist movement.

Both *rattrapage* and *nationalisme* were part of a single phenomenon in French Quebec: the attempt of a people and of individuals to find a new identity as they shed the certainties of the past. The search for identity, however, is always complex, and at no time were francophones in Quebec, any more than English-Canadians in Quebec or in Canada, united around a single understanding of who they were as a people and what their future should be. Among those who advocated separation from Canada and the creation of a Quebec nation-state were those who wanted to return to a (partially imaginary) past where Quebec defined itself not only by language, but by religion. Socialists wanted to alter Quebec far more than the architects of the Quiet Revolution found acceptable. Every shade of social opinion in between was also represented within the budding sovereignist movement. Francophone federalists spanned the political spectrum, ranging from old-style nationalists who feared the revolutionary appeals made by some separatist groups, to free marketeers who thought nationalism stood in the way of capitalism, to Marxist-Leninists who regarded nationalism as a diversionary tactic of the bourgeoisie to convince people to divide on ethnic rather than class lines. So one must be careful in assessing at any given moment what federalists or sovereignists stood for in Quebec.

Among both federalists and sovereignists, there were splits as well on the question of how much federalism and how much sovereignty their adherents wanted. Some federalists, particularly the entourage of Pierre Elliott Trudeau, were Pearsonian liberals who wanted a strong federal government and defended the social interventionism of the Pearson period. Others, while opposing the break-up of the federation, wanted a return to what they regarded as the spirit of the Confederation agreement of 1867: autonomy of the federal government within a few jurisdictions, and autonomy for the provinces within most jurisdictions, including all social services. The decentralizers objected to the tendency since World War II for the federal government to exercise control over provinces through shared-cost arrangements for social programs, with penalties for provinces whose programs violated principles set out by the federal government. One wing of the separatists was not far from the decentralizers in the arrangements it hoped to see with the federal government. "Sovereignty-association" supporters led by René Lévesque argued that the remaining nine provinces were pulling in a direction that was producing greater centralization, and Quebec could only assert its autonomy in a variety of fields by becoming a nation-state, and then contracting with the rest of Canada to associate in certain areas of mutual interest. Radical sovereignists rejected this vision of a sovereign Quebec as too confining and called for an independent Quebec which would redefine its place in the world without focussing on the new nation-state's relations with the country from which it was liberating itself.

Before outlining the evolution of the sovereignist and federalist options and the impact of constitutional wrangling on the texture of Quebec politics, it is important to look more closely at the changing character of the Quebec society that produced these debates. Religion is a useful starting point. In 1960, slightly over sixty percent of Montrealers who identified themselves as Catholics were regular church attenders. Within a decade, that number had dropped by half and it continued to drop in the 1970s.[2] Observers noted that most of the regular church attenders in 1980 had grey hair despite a variety of efforts by the churches to make attendance attractive to younger people. Church attendance did not drop as precipitously in rural areas, but throughout the province, it was obvious that the once seemingly omnipotent Roman Catholic Church was in crisis. The number of priests declined by half — from 8400 to 4285 — from 1960 to 1981, while the number of cloistered priests and nuns fell from over 45,000 in 1961 to just over 29,000 in 1978. Worse, re-cruitments to the priesthood and the religious orders had virtually dried up. In 1946, there were 2000 new priests in Quebec; in 1970, just 100.[3] Some churches were forced to close their doors, while others stayed alive by running bingoes during the week, ignoring past condemnations from the pulpit of the sin of gambling.

What was left of the Church however, had also changed. The death of the conservative pope Pius XII in 1958, and his replacement by the liberally minded Pope John XXIII, led to a shift, however tem-porary, in the balance of contending ideological forces within inter-national Catholicism. The Papal encyclical of 1961, *Mater et Magistra*, supported state intervention to create social justice,[4] and the Second Vatican Council, which met between 1962 and 1965, produced a redefinition within the Roman Catholic Church of the religious calling. Within Quebec, the post-war church had been somewhat divided between traditionalists and reformers.[5] The appeal of the reformers became clear in 1960 when a cleric, Jean-Paul Desbiens, produced a runaway bestseller called *The Impertinences of Brother Anonymous*, which provided a scathing indictment of the operations of the Church in Quebec and accused the Church of preventing the development of an education system for Quebec Catholics that would prepare them for the modern world. Tradition-alists wanted the impertinent priest defrocked, but Cardinal Paul-Émile Léger, archbishop of Montreal, who had gradually become

Paul-Émile Léger, 1953, cardinal of the Roman Catholic Church. Archbishop of Montreal from 1950–1967, Cardinal Léger was recognized in Quebec and beyond for his attention to a city struggling with the stress of social change. ACAM.

more reform-minded since his appointment in 1950, intervened to prevent such a reaction.[6]

Canada's Catholic bishops, including the Quebec bishops, began increasingly to take progressive positions on social policy questions. The bishops joined a coalition of churches, unions, and social welfare organizations to lobby for medicare in 1965. By the seventies, Roman Catholic churches and religious orders were involved in most of the social justice movements in Canada.[7] Traditionalists remained influential within the Church,[8] but they no longer held the levers of authority within Quebec's Roman Catholic hierarchy. With the liberal wing of the Church supportive of the wave of social reforms in the 1960s, the conservatives were in no position to mount a campaign against the Lesage government's plans to transfer effective control over schools, hospitals, and social services from the Church to the state.

Church conservatives were also largely unable to impose upon women the Church's longstanding view of the proper roles for each of the sexes. As we have seen earlier, the Roman Catholic Church, hardly alone within Canadian society, but more rigid than most other organizations, believed that the duty of a woman who did not become a nun was to marry and to devote her life to serving the needs of her husband and children. Francophone women's organizations in Quebec usually operated within the Church and were expected to conform to the Church's expectations regarding areas of proper concern for women.[9]

By the mid-sixties, the Church's ability to dictate to women was limited and, in any case, reform elements were less certain that the Church's former doctrine regarding gender roles had much to do with religion as opposed to misogyny. The Quebec hierarchy, like the Canadian hierarchy generally, while never openly defying Rome, was often less than keen to propagandize the Pope's edicts. In 1968, Pope Paul VI's encyclical, *Humanae vitae*, reminded the faithful that the Church continued to regard the use of artificial contraception as an unpardonable sin. The Canadian and Quebec bishops, aware that Catholic women were increasingly making use of effective means of birth control, neither regretted Rome's decision nor instructed women in their duty. Quebec women indicated their indifference to the Pope's views on their intimate lives by reducing their birth rate by half from 1957 to 1971,[10] bearing on average fewer than two children per adult woman during a lifetime. The province had the highest birth rate in Canada before World War II but the lowest by

1980. With fewer children at home, and higher material expectations than their mothers, Quebec women increasingly ignored the propaganda they had imbibed in their youth against working outside the home. By 1980, Quebec francophone women were as likely as their anglophone counterparts to hold a job. But most were poorly paid. In part, this was a result of systemic gender bias in the labour force from which all women suffered. But, for women who had been educated in the period before 1960, it was also the result of the inferior education they received. The Church had used its power over Catholic education to stream most girls into dead-end educations. Until 1961, for example, the "Instituts familiaux," which trained girls to be *maîtresses de maison,* but gave them no chance to enter universities, had been popular with Catholic leaders and many parents. The classical colleges, which were the educational stream leading to university, were divided along gender lines, with only the boys' schools receiving Church subsidies; only well-off parents could realistically consider paying the costs of sending their girls to such schools.[11]

The Fédération des femmes du Québec, formed in 1966 as an umbrella group of women's organizations in the province, had no ties to the Roman Catholic Church or any other Church body. It quickly established itself as a voice for women in the province and within a few years a variety of more radical women's groups, usually tied to campus movements, proclaimed the arrival of the women's liberation movement in Quebec. The Fédération des femmes did have important links with past manifestations of feminism in the province. Thérèse Casgrain, who had been a thorn in the side of governments and the Church with her persistent and eventually successful campaign for women's suffrage in the province, played a key role in its founding. The Fédération declared that its aim was to co-ordinate the activities of all women working in the field of social action, to sponsor forums, conferences, and other means of exchanging information, and to publish materials to inform the public about why reforms were needed.[12]

The Fédération outlined some of the reforms it wanted to see at both the provincial and federal levels when it appeared before the Royal Commission on the Status of Women in 1968. Clearly rejecting traditional Quebec Catholic views of the desirability of separate spheres for men and women, the Fédération brief called for equal opportunities for the sexes in education and employment. It wanted the education system to train girls to see themselves as future citizens who would have careers and the same opportunities and responsibilities as boys could expect. Recognizing that working women faced the "double work day" of home and paid work, the brief called for socialization, preferably at the local level, of a variety of services such as childcare, restaurants, and domestic services. It wanted daycares to be attached to places of study and work and paid maternity leave to be legislated.[13]

Not all Quebec women wanted to go so far as the Fédération des femmes in having the community assume responsibility for duties otherwise relegated to households, with women generally carrying most of the load. But even groups that defended the traditional role of women in the household tended to recognize that women increasingly wanted to combine mothering with paid work and that society had to take some responsibility to make this possible. The Association féminine d'éducation et d'action sociale, a French-Canadian Catholic organization which had close to 30,000 members, mainly in rural Quebec, told the Commission that its members believed that the mother's duty and main contribution to society was staying home to look after her young children. The organization wanted mothers who stayed at home to receive a special allowance. But it also wanted working women to have access to quality daycare at a reasonable cost, with provincial governments and private bodies co-operating to provide such a service. It also supported maternity leave with seniority protected and the provision of social benefits for part-time employees, who tended to be women.[14] The Fédération, it might be noted, also supported the right of mothers to remain at home with their children and to enjoy *une certaine indépendance financière*. As they indicated to Premier Robert Bourassa in a brief in 1970 calling for the creation of a provincial women's bureau, they wanted the bureau to organize activities that would reduce the social isolation of married women, including television courses geared to career training, drop-in centres, and subsidized family vacation camps.[15]

Some women's groups, particularly in rural areas, or in conservative Catholic organizations, were uninterested in policies that encouraged women to work outside the home and wanted the focus of state policy to be on preserving the traditional home, in part by raising family allowances. The Quebec Farm Wives' Circle, with 45,000 members, most over the age of forty, believed that it was wrong for society to be pushing women with small kids into the work force, rather than financially aiding families so that these women could stay home.[16] The Ordre des dames Hélène de Champlain, affiliated with the family-centred Union mondiale des organisations féminines catholiques, appeared before the Commission not only to defend women's traditional role, but also to oppose abortion and the legalization of homosexuality, which the organization regarded as "a mental disorder."[17]

The trade union movement, if only half-heartedly at first, gradually came to support feminist demands. Women activists within the unions fought well-entrenched sexism, which had caused the Catholic trade union movement, in particular, before the fifties, to oppose married women's right to work.[18] The unions in the 1950s, whether international or Catholic and Québécois, were opponents of the Duplessis regime, demanding fewer restrictions on union certification rights and on the right to strike. They also supported demands for an expanded welfare state that were anathema to Duplessis and traditionalist elements within the Church. The unions, along with the liberal intelligentsia and liberal clergymen, provided the catalyst that pushed post-Duplessis Quebec in the direction of greater state interventionism to achieve economic growth and a degree of redistribution of wealth.

The Lesage Years

The Lesage government became the instrument for the francophone middle class's collective self-realization. Using the slogan *maîtres chez nous*, the province created new economic institutions that were directed by francophones and employed mainly francophones at all levels. This gave rise among the middle classes, and much of the working class as well, to the notion that the Quebec state could best defend francophone rights not simply by attacking federal programs in the *duplessiste* manner, but by establishing programs and institutions of its own. Many francophone managers and professionals complained that both the private sector and the federal government scorned their skills, preferring to hire anglophones, especially at higher levels. The provincial government, by contrast, beginning in the Lesage years, was an ever-growing source of jobs, many highly-paid and prestigious, reserved virtually exclusively for francophones.

Among the Lesage government's economic achievements, two stand out. One was the creation of Hydro-Québec, a public monopoly over hydroelectric power in Quebec, similar to the model of Ontario Hydro. The Lesage government, on the urging of the popular Cabinet minister, René Lévesque, made nationalization of private utilities its key election issue in the 1962 provincial election. The newly-nation-alized utilities were merged with existing public utilities to create the utility giant called Hydro-Québec. Staffed from top to bottom with francophones, Hydro-Québec became a symbol of the ability of francophone Québécois to manage a huge corporation without an-glophone involvement.[19] For many it became a model suggesting that Quebec need not remain within Canada; the Québécois could run their own economy. The building of huge dams at Manicouagan, hardly a romantic occurrence, became part of nationalist lore, with "La Manic" becoming the subject of a popular tune written by Gilles Vigneault and recorded by nationalist chanteuse Pauline Julien.

Even more far-reaching in its economic impact was the Lesage government's decision to create its own provincial pension plan rather than participate in the Canada Pension Plan. Though the two programs were harmonized to provide equivalent benefits, Quebec's decision to run its own program meant that the province, through employee deductions, collected vast amounts of money. These were used to create a provincial investment fund that was used by the province to promote private, Quebec-owned and usually francophone manufacturing companies, to build infrastructure for resource indus-tries, and to otherwise encourage the development of the Quebec economy. Other economic instruments established by the Lesage government included the Société générale de finance, which pro-vided low-interest loans to companies seeking to establish in Quebec, and the Société québécoise des minéraux, which became the largest mining exploration outfit in Quebec.

Some scholars have noted that the major beneficiaries of the Quiet Revolution's economic reforms were large and medium francophone businesses. While every worker paid into the pension plan, and those who lived long enough would draw benefits from the plan, it was large businesses that received an infusion of capital in the short-term from the Caisse de dépôts et de placements, the investment arm of the provincial pension plan. Businesses also received cheap power from Hydro-Québec, since business rates for hydroelectricity contin-ued to be far lower than residential rates. Yet it is simplistic to dismiss the Lesage Liberals as tools of the francophone bourgeoisie. The government liberalized labour law in the province, and union organizing in the province became far easier than it had been in the Duplessis years. Public servants received the right to unionize and to strike.

Outside of the economic sphere, the government's reforms were equally sweeping. A provincial Department of Education was created to replace the Catholic and Protestant commissions that had previously determined curriculum and standards. Though the churches remained nominally in control of the schools, the state made the important decisions about what the schools taught and how, the qualifications required by teachers, and the distribution of funds among schools. Social services also came under state control. Though church-run charitable organizations were not shut out of the new system of delivery of services to the poor, disabled, and aged, professional civil servants and social workers quickly came to dominate the social service area in the province. Hospitals, even where they remained nominally under church direction, became increasingly controlled by state policies and run by state funds, though state funding in this area was already considerable under Duplessis.

The Lesage government proved particularly willing to effect *rattrapage* in the area of education. The new provincial curriculum focussed far more on science and technology and the social sciences than the curriculum that had been followed by the Catholic schools. Segregation of education and educational programs by sex gave way to co-educational programs. Millions were spent building high schools so that a large portion of the population could achieve high school matriculation. A new community college system, the "CEGEPs," was established to provide greater post-secondary opportunities in a province where Catholics had been only one-fifth as likely as Protestants to receive post-secondary education. The CEGEPs offered diploma programs in various professions and the first two years of university in arts, science and commerce. This relieved some of the pressure on the university system to provide facilities for a quickly expanding student body, though the universities, as well, received a massive infusion of cash from the province, along with their federal grants, to build satellite campuses and add buildings to existing campuses. All of this activity resulted in staggering increases in the number of full-time students in Quebec in the sixties: secondary school enrolments in 1969 were up 101 percent over 1960, college enrolments had risen 82 percent while university enrolments climbed 169 percent.[20]

The large number of new postsecondary teachers made clerics, who had once dominated university life in the province, a modest minority within the postsecondary system, just as they had become in the schools.[21] In the latter, the nuns, who once had dominated

Beginning in 1963, the Front de Libération du Québec bombed federal and anglophone targets, like this mailbox, in Quebec. NAC PA-157323.

teaching in the lower grades, gave way to university graduates. Liberal Catholic intellectuals, who had sparked many of the post-war debates about the direction of Quebec society, remained within the university setting. But increasingly, debate in intellectual circles was not framed in terms of Catholic teaching. Liberalism, Marxism, Keynesianism, and indeed all the intellectual trends that were important in Europe and the rest of North America, began to dominate Quebec debates far more than Catholicism. Those who espoused sovereignty for Quebec were more likely to draw upon the liberation rhetoric of Third World countries that were breaking away from European colonial domination, than to repeat the tired arguments of the fascistic Abbé Lionel Groulx, who, for many years, had argued for creation of a sovereign Quebec as a way of preserving a traditionalist Catholic francophone society.

The Quebec government's desire to have greater provincial control over the direction of the Quebec economy led to inevitable friction with Ottawa, particularly over the relative share of taxes taken by the federal and provincial governments. First Diefenbaker and then Pearson made substantial concessions to the provinces, mainly to appease Quebec. The provinces received sixteen percent of the income, corporation, and succession taxes collected by Ottawa in the late fifties, a large increase from the five percent transferred during the war; in 1964, the figure had reached twenty-four percent. The Pearson government also yielded to the constant demand of Lesage and Lévesque for the right of provinces to opt out of shared-cost programs in which the federal government paid a percentage of the costs incurred by a province that agreed to establish a particular program in line with principles laid out by the federal government. Most such programs were in the social services area — the Canada Pension Plan and medicare were to become the largest — and the Quebec government argued that federal intervention in areas of provincial jurisdiction violated the spirit of the British North America Act, even if it did not break the letter of the constitution.

The Sovereignty Movement Appears

Though Quebec won considerable autonomy as a result of its negotiations with the federal government, nationalists believed it was degrading for Quebec to go cap in hand to Ottawa, constantly asking for favours. While federalists applauded "opting out" and federal tax concessions, suggesting that they demonstrated the flexible character of the Canadian Confederation, a sovereignist movement arose that argued that Quebec did not need the federal government at all and that the nationalist dream of reversing the defeat of 1760 was no longer wishful thinking. If federalists regarded Hydro-Québec and the Quebec Pension Plan as emblematic of programs that Quebec could initiate while a province within Confederation, sovereignists regarded them as symbols of what Quebec could do on its own.

The first separatists who received media attention were atypical of separatists as a whole. They were members of underground groups, composed mainly of university students, who used violent acts to compel publicity for their cause. The Front de Libération du Québec, in particular, became notorious for a campaign of sporadic planting of bombs in federal buildings from 1963 onwards. The campaign resulted in the deaths of several innocent by-standers, ironically all francophone workers. While the FLQ became a romantic symbol of Quebec's attempts to emerge as a nation, drawn upon by important authors such as Hubert Aquin and Roch Carrier, and praised by radical university student newspapers, the organization appears never to have had more than a handful of members at a given time. Because the "cells" of the FLQ were sometimes penetrated by the RCMP, contacts between the small groups that composed this illegal organization were limited. FLQ propaganda suggested that they were influenced by Third World liberation struggles and saw a parallel between Quebec's struggle for independence and the successful independence struggle of the Algerian people against France. The attempt to apply the same techniques of revolutionary terror in Quebec yielded less fruit, because whatever the FLQ believed, conditions in Quebec were not as terrible as in Algeria and the province had a flourishing democratic tradition.[22]

That tradition, however, was becoming increasingly nationalist by the mid-sixties, and the FLQ took some credit for forcing the political debate in the province to increasingly include the possibility of Quebec leaving Confederation. Though the political parties all denounced the FLQ's campaign of terror, the 1966 provincial election demonstrated the strength of nationalist ideology during this period of rapid social change and the increasing credibility of the sovereignist option. Both the Liberals and the Union Nationale ran on strongly nationalist platforms, trying to outdo one another in asserting Quebec's intention to run its own economy and social programs, and to keep Ottawa at bay. Lesage called for Ottawa to surrender to Quebec provincial control over job training, family allowances, and old-age pension supplements, and to give Quebec monies unconditionally when the province dropped out of shared-cost programs rather than requiring that the province establish a parallel program. The Union Nationale wanted the federal government to surrender or share with provincial governments some of its exclusive powers such as the control of currency and credit, tariffs, broadcasting, and the appointment of members of higher courts.[23] The Union Nationale leader Daniel Johnson let the voters know that, while he did not support separation of Quebec from Canada in the short term, he did not reject the sovereignty option. He warned that a Union Nationale government would expect concessions from Ottawa and would use the threat of Quebec separation to get them; if the federal government proved intransigent, his party would campaign for separatism.

Two parties in the 1966 election did campaign for sovereignty. The Rassemblement pour l'Indépendance Nationale campaigned on the left, calling for a vast extension of the economic and social policies of the Quiet Revolution, which they argued could only be implemented by a nation-state in control of its own economic destiny. By contrast, the smaller Ralliement National represented traditional nationalist views. Together these *indépendantiste* parties polled nine percent of the vote despite having limited means at their disposal to air their message, unknown leaders, and no candidates in many ridings. The vote leader remained the Liberals, with forty-six percent of the vote. But the Union Nationale, with forty percent of the vote, carried a majority of seats, a reflection of an electoral map that favoured rural areas and small cities over Montreal and Quebec City. Support for the Union Nationale suggested that traditional nationalism of the non-separatist variety was not yet dead in Quebec. It also indicated that many Québécois did not like the social reforms that the Lesage government had undertaken, or that they saw no benefit to themselves from programs that appeared targeted to large businesses. Even the government's favourable attitude to unions, while it won unionized worker support for the Liberals, gave the government few votes among farmers or among workers in small, difficult-to-organize shops. Many voters blamed high unemployment in Quebec relative to the rest of the country on the government and its technocratic preoccupations.[24] The temporary surge of Réal Caouette's Créditistes, Quebec's Social Credit party, which won twenty-six of the province's seventy-four federal seats in 1963, was another sign of the alienation of rural and working-class Québécois from the politics of parties that promoted modernization but gave little thought to redistribution of wealth.[25]

Daniel Johnson proved a thorn in the side of both Lester Pearson and Pierre Trudeau because, unlike Lesage, he appeared unbending in his demands for greater provincial control over most important jurisdictions, whether they were constitutionally in the provincial sphere or in the federal sphere. He also insisted on sending Quebec delegates to international francophone conferences despite federal warnings that only a nation-state had such a right. Quebec rejected suggestions that it work with the federal government to determine representatives and issues for such conferences. Johnson's death in late 1968 appeared to bring to a close a quasi-separatist phase in Quebec's evolution when the provincial government seemed, at every opportunity, to be questioning the legitimacy of the federal goverment's presence in Quebec. His successor, Jean-Jacques Bertrand, was less ideologically zealous and more disposed to seek accommodation with the federal government.

Beneath the surface, however, the separatist forces in the province were growing. In the fall of 1967, the Quebec Liberal Party, pondering its future from the Opposition benches, was rocked by an attempt

France's president Charles de Gaulle, in Quebec City, 1967. NAC PA-185519.

by René Lévesque to win the party over to his vision of "sovereignty-association" for Quebec. Lévesque's constitutional option, which would create an independent Quebec state but with a close association with Canada, received little support from the Liberal Party's convention. But the popular former Cabinet minister left the party and formed the Mouvement Souveraineté-Association to promote his goal, which involved Quebec and what would be left of a Quebec-free Canada sitting together as two equals to determine policies in areas where the federal government ruled. At first Lévesque's ideas were ridiculed both by sovereignists and by federalists inside and outside Quebec. It was a pipe dream, argued sociologist and separatist Hubert Guindon, to think that the rest of Canada would ever accept Quebec, which had only one quarter of the total population of the country as a whole, as equal to the rest. Quebec, if it wished to be a nation-state, had to work out its own destiny rather than try to pull a constitutional sleight of hand that would make it a *de facto* part of Canada, but with greater powers than the other provincial governments. Lévesque, however, could take some comfort from the New Democratic Party's commitment in the late sixties to "special status" for Quebec, which seemed to imply that Quebec could have greater provincial powers than other provinces, though it did not go as far as Lévesque and endorse equal powers for the Quebec and federal governments. The discussions in the Conservative Party in 1967 over declaring that Canada was composed of "two nations" proved fairly vague and did not result in a "two nations" policy for the party. Still, Lévesque could point to murmurings in the national parties to suggest that eventually Canada would come around to an acceptance of a sovereign Quebec in association with the rest of Canada.

Lévesque's constitutional option was more popular with francophone Québécois than the notion of outright separation of Quebec from Canada. Popular fears of a post-separation depression as anxious non-Quebec francophone investors pulled out their investments limited support for independence to between ten and fifteen percent of the Quebec population by the end of the sixties. Sovereignists had little choice but to follow the leadership of the one individual and the one policy that seemed to attract "soft nationalists," that is, those who were willing to support Quebec independence only if they could be reasonably assured that it would not produce economic hardship in the short term. By October 1968, Lévesque could count on sufficient public support to create a new political party, the Parti Québécois, which was dedicated to his vision of sovereignty-association. Supporters of all shades of sovereignty options flocked to the new party, which offered the realistic hope of a sovereign Quebec within the foreseeable future.

The PQ received a boost from generalized fears among francophones that their culture was threatened by immigrants' preference for educating their children in English, the language of the North American majority and of economic power within Quebec, rather than French. Clashes occurred in Montreal suburbs, most notably in Saint Léonard from 1967 to 1969, between immigrants and francophones "*de vieille souche*," that is, old-stock francophone Québécois who traced their roots to the pre-1760 population, over the question of language of instruction in local schools. The local Catholic school commission's decision to require all immigrant children to be educated in French angered many immigrants and led to huge demonstrations, counter-demonstrations, and scuffles at school board meetings for several years. The tendency of most immigrants to choose English over French as their language of choice in their new home was hardly new. But it had made little difference to the dominance of French in the era of large French-Canadian families. Now

The Canadian army in the streets of Montreal during the 1970 October crisis. NAC PA-129838.

that the francophones were the group in Quebec with the smallest families, there were legitimate fears over how long Quebec, or, at least Montreal, which received the bulk of the new arrivals, would remain francophone if the state did not intervene. While Bertrand was willing to guarantee a continued right to allow individuals the right to choose their language of education, though he wished to strengthen the position of French as a language of work, his Liberal successor as premier, Robert Bourassa, recognized that language concerns were key to the growth of sovereignist opinion. Wanting to stem the tide, he introduced a language bill (Bill 22) in 1973 that made French the language of both government and most workplaces in Quebec, and restricted the right of education in English to those who had English as a first language, or who could pass a proficiency test in English. This pleased no one since the immigrants objected to having to get their children trained in English before sending them to English schools, and nationalists insisted that all new arrivals in the province should have their children educated in French with no exceptions made.

Bourassa was hardly a nationalist. Elected Liberal leader in 1969 after the resignation of Lesage, and winning the provincial elections of 1970 and 1973, he was largely interested in attracting private capital to the province. He was unenthusiastic about expanding the state-building efforts of the Quiet Revolution, except in the area of hydroelectricity, and appeared to have no strong personal convictions on the language issue. But the PQ had won twenty-four percent of the vote, though only seven seats, in their first electoral contest in 1970, and Bourassa wanted to prevent the language issue from gaining them even more adherents. Bertrand had faced 50,000 demonstrators when his language legislation in 1969 providing choice in education was passed, and Bourassa hoped to do better than his predecessor by taking a tougher stance on French as the primary language of instruction in the province. He succeeded only in alienating both sides of the argument.

From the October Crisis to the Election of the PQ

Bourassa's problems with nationalists were especially evident during the "October crisis" in 1970. The crisis began when a cell of the FLQ kidnapped James Cross, a British diplomat, in Montreal. Several days later, a second cell of the terrorist organization, apparently acting without contact with the first cell, decided to kidnap provincial Labour minister Pierre Laporte. Bourassa, his plans to attract capital to Quebec suddenly shattered by such a display of Quebec's apparent political instability, did not know how to react to this wave of violence. He was persuaded however, by Pierre Trudeau, to make a request to the federal government to declare the War Measures Act.

On 15 October 1970, the Act was declared, the first time it had been invoked in Canada in peacetime. The Act gave the federal government and its agencies, including the RCMP and the military, the power to arrest and detain individuals without stating a cause. A few days after it was declared, the kidnappers of Laporte murdered their victim. Meanwhile the Quebec government had ordered the arrest of more than 500 people, many of whom were held for several months with no charges ever being laid.

Trudeau claimed that an "apprehended insurrection" had forced the government to react boldly. Caches of arms for an intended revolution had been found, he claimed, along with evidence of a conspiracy to overthrow the government of Quebec. Canadians, and especially Québécois, he argued, were tired of the FLQ's deadly antics and wanted to see it suppressed. But, as Quebec newspapers pointed out, most of those arrested were unlikely to be part of an underground conspiracy. Celebrity separatists such as Pauline Julien and journalist Gérald Godin were among those arrested but never charged. Michel Chartrand, a firebrand Montreal labour leader, quipped that the Quebec media made it difficult for him to share intimate moments with his wife, much less to find time to conspire with revolutionaries. In the years that have followed, no proof of the "apprehended insurrection" has ever been published.[26]

At the time of the declaration of the War Measures Act, most Québécois, like most Canadians, told pollsters that they believed the government had done the right thing. But opposition to the Act, at fifteen percent in Quebec, was three times as high as in the rest of the country, and within weeks, had doubled. It would become part of sovereignist mythology that the Quebec government had humiliated the people of Quebec by allowing the federal government to place them under military authority.

With the release of Cross by his kidnappers and the gradual freeing of those arrested under the War Measures Act, the crisis petered out. Trudeau and his Cabinet ministers tried to tarnish the reputation of the sovereignty movement generally by suggesting that their cause inevitably led to terrorism. They largely failed to persuade francophones of any connection between the FLQ and the PQ. The latter grew apace.

During the crisis, the FLQ had released a manifesto which they demanded that all media report as their price for keeping Cross alive. It was an angry document that condemned the high unemployment, poverty, and hopelessness that remained the lot of many Québécois, and blamed both colonial domination of Canada over Quebec and the operations of the capitalist system for social injustice. It struck a responsive chord, with many ordinary people calling hot-line radio show hosts to indicate that while they opposed the FLQ's violent tactics, they endorsed much in the radicals' description of the exploitation of ordinary Québécois by business and government. Economic growth since the end of the war and the reforms of the Quiet Revolution had improved the lives of much of the population, but the lives of those left behind were often quite miserable. In the mid-sixties, a University of Montreal report claimed that thirty-eight percent of city residents lived in poverty or privation. Regions such as Lac Saint-Jean, Abitibi, the Lower St. Lawrence, and the Gaspé experienced little economic development and their residents suffered staggering rates of unemployment.[27]

Poverty was by no means restricted to francophones. There had always been an anglophone working class in Montreal, much of which was unskilled and poorly paid. Immigrants who spoke neither English nor French ("allophones") were among the most exploited workers in the post-war period. In the sixties and seventies, thou-

A Common Front demonstration in 1972, led by the presidents of the three union federations representing Quebec public employees. NAC PA-116453.

sands of immigrants from the Caribbean, Latin America, India, Pakistan, Greece, Portugal, and Italy were earning the minimum wage, which was virtually a starvation wage, or even less. Unable to speak French or English, and sometimes illegally in Canada, these workers were often unaware that there was a legislated minimum wage or were afraid of being fired or deported if they demanded the minimum provided by law. In 1974, journalist Sheila Arnopolous prepared a series for the *Montreal Star* that revealed the working conditions and lives of these exploited immigrant workers.[28]

Luigi M., a dish washer, worked sixty hours a week in an Italian restaurant and was paid fifty dollars, whereas the minimum wage legislation required that he be paid $1.85 per hour for forty hours, and time and a half for overtime, for a total of $129.90. Maria V., a sewing machine operator, working piece rates, did even worse, clearing only thirty-seven dollars in three weeks, working 135 hours. Dust in hosiery factories, smoke from polyurethane and vinyl machines in unvented vinyl factories, sexual assault, limited safety expenditures, and lax public enforcement of fire hazards (Montreal had forty fire inspectors to deal with 88,000 commercial establishments) were all part of the work scene for immigrant workers.

Arnopolous, wanting an intimate view of the work lives of the unskilled, briefly worked in a hosiery operation that was situated in "a black windowless basement smelling of oil and dust where about sixty noisy machines were making snow-white stockings." The women working there worked by the piece and ate their lunches in the furnace room. The women counted and then bundled stockings. Joan, an immigrant from Guyana, commented to Arnopolous: "What do they think that we are, horses or something — no breaks, no chairs — and it's filthy." Arnopolous, working her fastest, managed to earn five dollars and eighty cents for a nine-hour day. A few women earned up to fifteen dollars a day by working non-stop, never stopping to talk or go to the washroom, which was, in any case, foul-smelling.

In the climate of social change in the sixties, community groups, focussing on the problems of the poor generally, of single mothers, or of renters, sprang up throughout the province. Supported by the trade unions, the women's movement, and by liberal Catholic groups, these new social organizations fought for better medical and dental care for the poor, for more generous social assistance programs, for childcare and the like. The FLQ Manifesto echoed the frustrations that many of these groups felt as successive governments focussed more on creating a political climate conducive to the attraction of capital than on helping ordinary people get by. The manifesto's mention of the "*gars de Lapalme*," truckers in a firm with a contract to the post office who lost their jobs when the company lost the contract, as examples of victims of a heartless capitalist, federal system, reminded many Québécois of the unfairnesses they faced in their everyday lives. The Lapalme "guys" had gone to Ottawa to protest the removal of their jobs. On Parliament Hill, Pierre Trudeau greeted their taunting by telling them: "*Mange de la merde*," that is, "eat shit." The FLQ angrily denounced those who thought the workers would be content to eat shit forever.

In fact, the Bourassa years witnessed a great deal of worker radicalism, most notably in the public sector. In 1972, the three major union federations united their public service components to create a Common Front in bargaining with the provincial government. Teachers, hospital workers, clerical workers, highway employees, professionals, and many others, 200,000 in all, made a common set of demands. Most progressive was their call for a minimum wage for government employees of $100 a week; many government workers at the time were making as little as $56 a week. When negotiations with the provincial government reached an impasse, Quebec's civil servants virtually shut down the province, though essential services, particularly in the health area, were maintained. Rather than bargain, the government ordered the workers back on the job. When the leaders of the three union federations preached defiance of the back-to-work order, the Bourassa government had them arrested. The arrests caused a storm of worker protest, with labour actions both in the public and private sector. Where had the right to free speech gone in Quebec? unionists asked angrily. Was Quebec returning to the age of Duplessis? The state intervened on management's side not only against public-sector workers but also, at times, against private-sector workers engaged in bitter strikes. Production workers at Pratt and Whitney Aircraft, for example, endured a long and bitter strike in 1974 and 1975, and at one point police ran amok among strikers who were keeping out replacement workers, cracking the skulls of fleeing strikers.[29]

Neither union militancy nor community activism need necessarily have translated politically into support for the sovereignist PQ. But the PQ, before it reached office, though composed mainly of solid middle-class elements, embraced a social democratic perspective, and its representatives in the National Assembly identified the party with popular causes. With the Liberals firmly in the pockets of big business, the Union Nationale in disarray, and the federal parties other than the Liberals of no significance in Quebec provincial politics, the PQ was able to win the votes not only of committed sovereignists, but also of working people who were more interested in its social policies than its constitutional promises.

By 1976, the Liberal party of Robert Bourassa was in deep political trouble. His language law had won him no friends and many enemies among both francophones and anglophones, and especially among allophones, many of whom turned to the Union Nationale. His social policies alienated trade unionists and the poor. Scandals involving the construction industry and the construction unions made the government appear cynical, corrupt, and incompetent.

The PQ, by this time, had gathered a membership of 300,000, making it easily the largest political party in the province to that time. It had also accepted a strategy devised mainly by Claude Morin, a former constitutional advisor to the Lesage government who had become Lévesque's advisor. It would not ask the electorate for a mandate to separate Quebec from Canada during an election. Rather it would simply ask for a mandate to govern the province progressively and efficiently and indicate that it would call a referendum not on sovereignty but on sovereignty-association at some point during the tenure of its administration. This would allow the party to attract the votes of those who were unsure where they stood on the sovereignty question, and even those who were dead set against the break-up of Canada but unwilling to see the Liberals remain in power. It would give the party a chance to prove that it could provide credible government for the province, and to use that credibility to press more forcefully on the population its view that sovereignty had to be the next step in the Québécois nation's evolution. The strategy proved successful. On election night in November 1976, Quebec elected its first government composed of sovereignists. The Péquistes won only about forty-one percent of the vote, but with the Liberals garnering a mere thirty-four percent (the Union Nationale took eighteen percent and smaller parties won most of the rest of the vote), the PQ won a crushing majority of legislative seats.

The PQ's victory was the result of a cross-class alliance of francophones excluding only industrial managers and entrepreneurs, who remained faithful to the Liberals. It should not be supposed, however, that the period beginning with the Quiet Revolution had done little to improve the position of francophones in the Quebec economy, or, despite the poverty of many Québécois, that no social advances had occurred. The earnings gap between francophones and anglophones had narrowed considerably. In 1961, male workers in Montreal on average earned fifty-one percent more if they were anglophones than if they were francophones. That figure had declined to thirty-two percent in 1970 and fifteen percent in 1977.[30] Increased opportunities in the public and para-public (hospitals, schools, universities) sectors accounted for much of the new-found francophone prosperity.[31] Employees in these sectors gave the PQ its staunchest support, because they regarded it as the best guarantor of their jobs. Indeed, many believed that sovereignty-association would enhance the importance of their own jobs, or at least provide job stability, since an emerging nation-state was likely to wish to demonstrate its close link with the people through a variety of new social programs.

The PQ and the 1980 Sovereignty Referendum

During its first term in office, the PQ appeared to be, as René Lévesque suggested, a social democratic party. The party indeed applied for membership in the Socialist International, the organization of social democratic parties in various nations, but its application was blocked by the NDP which claimed a franchise on Canada even though its Quebec support was negligible. NDP leader Ed Broadbent convinced the international body that, at bottom, it was sovereignty and not social democracy that provided the *raison d'être* of the Parti Québécois.

Nonetheless, in the years leading up to the referendum, there seemed much in the PQ legislative agenda to suggest that the party had a social democratic orientation. It raised the minimum wage in the province to the highest level of any North American jurisdiction; it reformed the labour laws in a manner largely pleasing to the labour federations, abolishing, for example, the right of employers to hire scabs to replace workers engaged in a legal strike; it increased consumer protection and partly nationalized the automobile insurance industry. Furthermore, the government instituted maternity leave and expanded the provision of daycare in Quebec.[32]

The party's nationalist legislation seemed, on the whole, to complement its social democratic initiatives. Aid to small francophone businesses and co-operatives, preservation of agricultural land, and grants to cultural groups all focussed on the strengthening of the French fact in Quebec, and emphasized the PQ's belief that intervention in the marketplace, whether economic or linguistic, yielded good results for the majority of the population.

Unquestionably, the most controversial piece of Parti Québécois legislation was Bill 101, the Charter of the French Language in 1977. Though some sections of the legislation were only an extension of what Bourassa had tried to accomplish in 1973, the PQ charter was uncompromising in its desire to make French not only the dominant language of work and education in Quebec, but the only visible language. Store signs, billboards, and other public signs were to be exclusively in French. René Lévesque wrote in his memoirs that he had wanted only to apply a sign law to downtown Montreal since he recognized a right of anglophones and allophones to have signs in their own language in the areas where they lived. His intention was to let both Québécois and the world know that Montreal was a French city even though its downtown at that time looked like the downtown

René Lévesque's bid to win a mandate to negotiate sovereignty-association was defeated in the 1980 referendum. NAC PA-115039.

of other major Canadian cities with most outdoor signs posted only in English. But the government's legal department advised that it would not be possible to draft legislation that targeted only one area of one city; so Lévesque consented to the draconian solution of keeping languages other than French off signs everywhere in the province.

The language charter also limited the right to education in English for children of parents born in Quebec having English as their first language. The courts would later extend that right to children of parents born anywhere in Canada. The PQ abolished the language tests that had allowed some allophones to make it into the English schools.

Most anglophones and allophones were hostile to the PQ government's language policy and to its campaign for sovereignty. Indeed, while the PQ and its supporters spoke of sovereignty as the PQ goal, anglophone and allophone opponents almost always used the word "separatism," which emphasized that Quebec independence meant leaving Canada, the country to which most of them remained strongly attached. An estimated 200,000 of them left the province during the first four years of the PQ in office, that is, almost ten percent of the non-francophone population. Their numbers were replenished by new immigrants, many of whom also proved hostile to the PQ philosophy. There was a particularly large exodus of young

Jewish people, many of whom were uncomfortable with hints in PQ rhetoric that only white francophone Christians tracing their heritage back to the period before the Conquest had real roots in Quebec. The Péquiste leaders, particularly Lévesque and his Minister for Cultural Communities (that is, non-francophones), Gérald Godin (one of those arrested by Bourassa's government during the October crisis, he had his revenge when he defeated Bourassa in his own seat in 1976), worked to convince the anglophones that their schools and hospitals would remain English-speaking and under their own control after sovereignty was achieved. Their assurances meant little to groups that mistrusted Lévesque and all that he stood for.

In December 1979 came an announcement that had been anticipated ever since the election of the PQ. There would be a referendum on sovereignty-association and it would be held in May 1980. The question posed to the voters was not particularly straightforward. They were asked whether they gave permission to the provincial government to negotiate sovereignty-association with Ottawa. The soft wording of the question indicated the government's understanding that it was not possible to convince a majority of the population to simply secede from Canada without an agreement between the seceding province and the rest of the country about future arrangements.[33]

The referendum legislation called for supporters of a "oui" in the referendum to unite under one banner to promote their option, while supporters of a "non" would similarly be grouped under one umbrella. René Lévesque became the leader of the "oui" forces, while Liberal leader Claude Ryan was leader of the "non" alliance. Apart from the Péquistes, the "oui" side enjoyed the support of Rodrigue Biron, leader of the Union Nationale, who had opposed sovereignty at the time of the 1976 election. The "non" side included all four federal parties, as well as the provincial Liberals.

Many francophone nationalists who wanted a more decentralized Canada in which Quebec would control more jurisdictions but still enjoy the advantages of being part of the Canadian economic union — including Canadian tariffs, quotas for agricultural producers, and relatively easy access to markets in the rest of Canada — were unsure how to vote. Many felt that it would be humiliating for the Québécois to vote negatively in a referendum that asked them to declare proudly their right to existence as a nation, rather than simply as a province in the Canadian federation. But many others believed that, confronted with a choice, they had to consider the possible economic chaos that might follow a "oui" vote. Polls suggested that a majority of francophone Québécois still felt some emotional attachment to Canada that went beyond dollars and cents. Francophone business people, while supporting the government's efforts to make French the language of the Quebec economy, were too dependent on both English-Canadian and foreign markets to be willing to risk the instability that might follow Quebec's break with the rest of Canada.[34] So, the sovereignists had their work cut out for them, trying to persuade over sixty percent of francophones that there was a compelling reason to support sovereignty-association. Since it could be assumed that most of the anglophones and allophones, who together made up almost twenty percent of the electorate, would vote to remain Canadian, it was incumbent upon the "oui" side to galvanize a large majority of the francophones of the province. In the end, they could not, though poll results suggested just under half of francophone voters supported the "oui." The split in terms of all voters was sixty percent in favour of the "non" side. The soft question appeared to make little difference. Most voters assumed that they were being asked to endorse sovereignty rather than simply negotiations about sovereignty, though public opinion surveys were clear that if no association with Canada proved possible for an independent Quebec, support for sovereignty was limited to about twenty percent of the total Quebec population.

The defeat of the sovereignists in Quebec's first referendum on sovereignty did not put an end to the issue. But it demonstrated that momentum in the battle of federalists and separatists could shift. Federal actions had an impact both on the growth of the sovereignty movement and on braking its growth.

Trudeau and Separatism

Pierre Trudeau was Quebec's best-known federalist, and his opposition to the sovereignists and even the milder nationalists who wanted special status for Quebec was bitter. Trudeau still equated Quebec nationalism with the spirit of Duplessis and conservative Catholicism, and believed that Quebec's best route for development was one that embraced Canada and was open to international influences as well. His efforts to patriate the constitution in 1971 ran up against Premier Bourassa's unwillingness to give the nationalists a cause. After agreeing to a formula in Victoria for patriation, Bourassa bowed to nationalist pressures and made demands for extra jurisdictions for Quebec that ensured the collapse of the negotiations between the provinces and the federal government. Trudeau denounced Bourassa as gutless, and relations between the two men were strained from that time on, with Bourassa accusing Trudeau of supporting the kind of centralization that had produced the separatist reaction in the first place, and Trudeau accusing Bourassa of kowtowing to narrow-minded chauvinists.

Apart from defending the economic rationality of Quebec remaining within Confederation and the responsibility of the federal government for ensuring the soundness of the Canadian economic union, Trudeau claimed that Quebec nationalists had a fortress view of *la francophonie canadienne*. If Quebec were to leave Confederation or become a *de facto* nation within the nation-state of Canada, the rights of anglophones within Quebec and francophones outside Quebec would suffer. There were one million French-speaking Canadians who lived outside Quebec, and they had a right to protection of their language, in his view, every bit as much as francophones within Quebec.

One of Trudeau's main goals then became making francophones feel at home everywhere in Canada. For starters, if they were to feel at home in the nation's capital or in their contacts with the federal government wherever they might live, it was necessary for the civil service to be fully bilingual. The Official Languages Act of 1969 created the position of Official Languages Commissioner and committed the federal government to achieving bilingualism within the civil service. Government hiring policies began to emphasize the hiring of more francophones and unilingual anglophone civil servants received language courses at public expense so that they could deliver services in French as well as English. Trudeau's legislation followed hard on the heels of the report of the Royal Commission on Bilingualism and Biculturalism, a commission established by Pearson in 1963 to recommend ways to heal the divide between anglophones and francophones in Canada. Trudeau rejected sections of the report that supported greater powers for Quebec so that French could be preserved in its Canadian heartland, focussing only on sections of the report that promoted greater bilingualism in the country. Trudeau also initiated federal grants to francophone schools in areas where there was a significant concentration of French speakers, but not a majority of the population, and grants to French immersion schools for non-francophones.

The success of federal efforts to make francophones feel *chez nous* across the country is much debated. Certainly, by 1980, there had been results, but many thought they were unimpressive. Though twenty-six percent of federal employees in 1978 were francophones, about the proportion of francophones within the Canadian population, francophones were greatly under-represented at middle and upper levels of the civil service.[35] For ambitious members of the educated middle classes, the federal government often looked like an anglophone closed shop while the Quebec government was becoming, in fact, a francophone closed shop.

Trudeau's efforts to make francophone Québécois feel at home within Confederation went beyond language legislation. Proudly speaking of "French power" in Ottawa, Trudeau and his ministers argued that French Canadians had become important decision makers in Canada and had been able to direct billions of dollars in government projects towards Quebec. During the 1980 referendum, the federal government blatantly advertised the benefits which Quebec had received from Confederation. Unfortunately, other sections of the country tended to exaggerate the same benefits that many Québécois dismissed as token. Atlantic Canadians and Westerners both felt that the economic problems of their regions were being ignored by a federal government apparently obsessed with placating Québécois demands. Our next chapter looks at the reasons why Canadians outside central Canada increasingly felt alienated from the federal government during the sixties and seventies.

Eight

The West and the East in the Period of Centralization

Quebec nationalists resented not only anglophone domination over economic life in their province — which, thanks to the Quiet Revolution and PQ economic and linguistic policies, had weakened by 1980 — but the inferior economic performance of Quebec relative to Ontario. Québécois observed the comfortably higher average incomes of their immediate western neighbour and Ontario's far smaller rate of unemployment. But, to Canadians in the provinces west and east of central Canada, both Ontario and Quebec seemed to have done rather well. In 1971, fifty percent of all manufacturing dollars in Canada were earned in Ontario and thirty percent in Quebec. The "hinterland" provinces wanted to diversify their economies as well and put behind them the memories of the Great Depression when the collapse of export markets meant the collapse of provincial economies geared to the sale of resources. This chapter looks at the attempts of various provinces to maximize their returns from resources and create economic diversification. It is a tale of unequal successes, ranging from Alberta's brief moment in the sun after OPEC unleashed a spiral of energy price increases at the end of 1973, to the dismal tales of failed mega-projects in several provinces that enriched private investors but left taxpayers and workers to suffer the consequences of desperate attempts to diversify at all costs.

The Atlantic Provinces

For the Atlantic provinces, the 1960s was a decade of some hope, while the 1970s seemed more a decade of cynicism as the big plans of the previous decade failed to yield the promised jobs. In the 1960s, the federal government committed itself to going beyond the equalization payments of the fifties that allowed poorer provinces to provide reasonable education, health, and social services. In addition to a number of new national programs that would provide better pensions and health care that poor provinces could ill afford to finance on their own, the federal government established a variety of economic development programs targeted at areas of low income and high unemployment. Though the philosophy of the economic development programs varied somewhat over time, they seemed to be united by two threads. The first was that the basic infrastructure, physical and human, of a poor region such as the Atlantic provinces had to be improved to attract industries. This meant large expenditures on industrial parks, highways, harbours, airports, schools, technical training institutes, and universities. The second assumed that the provision of a more skilled labour force and better transportation facilities alone would be insufficient to convince large investors to look beyond traditional areas of investment. Direct state aid, in the form of subsidies, loans, tax writeoffs, lax pollution rules, free building space, and the like would be needed to bring in enough industrialists to establish the Atlantic region as an attractive place to invest. By 1980, however, it was clear that while many industrialists were happy to collect such generous giveaways, they were not necessarily committed to maintaining their operations in the region over the long haul.[1]

In the process of trying to offer their citizens similar levels of service to those enjoyed by other Canadians, the Atlantic governments became quite dependent upon Ottawa. "By the 1970s the Atlantic governments were obtaining more than a third of their revenues from federal equalization payments, while comparable amounts were transferred into the regional economy through federal social and development programs."[2] The infusion of money from the federal government was generally welcomed, but there were many reminders that the piper called the tune. The federal government had an inordinate say in the strategies of economic development that the Atlantic provinces were to pursue. Nor did the federal government give much consideration to the hinterland regions when freight rate policies, the bank rate, or other macro-economic policies were made.[3] It would be easy, however, in retrospect, to overstate federal blame for poor decisions that were made or for the overall philosophy which emphasized economic growth over all other values, including preservation of communities and the natural environment. Provincial governments largely shared the same values as the federal government and popular opinion, while hardly unanimous, tended to focus as well on the benefits associated with economic growth. Atlantic

Canadians had known poverty and while there was a great deal of cultural pride in the communities that survived on fishing and farming, most people wanted the same kinds of opportunities and advantages that they imagined people in the more prosperous provinces enjoyed.

Provincial efforts to attract industry were evident from the late fifties and early sixties as each provincial government established an agency whose central purpose was to woo investors. In Nova Scotia it was Industrial Estates Limited, in Newfoundland the Newfoundland and Labrador Corporation, with New Brunswick's Development Corporation and Prince Edward Island's Industrial Enterprises Incorporated completing the picture.

Federal government assistance targeted at poorer regions began in a big way in 1961 with the legislation of the Agricultural and Rural Development Act (ARDA). ARDA's mandate was limited to improving the economic performance of rural areas and, at the urging of the Atlantic premiers, the Atlantic Development Board was established in 1962 to promote industrial growth. In the next year, Lester Pearson gave the fund $100 million to distribute for Atlantic projects whose objectives were economic growth. By 1968, a total of $188 million had been disbursed. Programs for improving infrastructure were favoured, including the completion of the Trans-Canada Highway in Newfoundland, the expansion of airports, expansion of the harbours of Saint John and Canso for bulk cargo, the opening of a container port for general cargo in Halifax, and a variety of hydroelectricity developments.[4]

Such projects created a host of short-term construction jobs and a smaller number of long-term jobs. They did not persuade industrialists to look away from the industrial heartlands when they established new plants. By the time the federal government established the Department of Regional Economic Expansion (DREE) in 1969, to replace the alphabet-soup of agencies promoting economic growth, the Atlantic provinces were beginning to look desperate in their efforts to attract investors. With the aid of DREE or its predecessors, the provinces promised millions in giveaways to a series of mega-projects and apparently innovative investments. By 1980, the list of failures was far longer than the list of successes and the public monies wasted, federal and provincial, ran into the billions. Among the more spectacular losses were the Deuterium of Canada heavy-water plant at Glace Bay, Nova Scotia, which involved public losses of about $90 million, and never created more than a hundred full-

time, post-construction jobs; Clairtone Sound's television manufacturing plant at Stellarton, Nova Scotia; the estimated $100 million
lost in subsidizing the Come by Chance refinery in Newfoundland;
and the $20 million lost by New Brunswick on Malcolm Bricklin's
dubious effort to produce a luxury sports car in Saint John and
Minto.[5]

Newfoundland's linerboard mill fiasco illustrates why so many
failures occurred in Atlantic Canada at a time when North American
capitalism was in its most robust stage ever. The mill's construction
in Stephenville cost $144 million, but the major private investor,
John C. Doyle, an American, only put up $29 million. The federal
and provincial governments gave grants and loan guarantees to the
banks for most of the rest. The province was stuck with $114 million
in loan guarantees before they removed Doyle from the project in
1972, but five years later had to shut the mill down.[6]

Some companies lured by giveaways did stay, but often with a
price that showed they thought they were doing the province in
question a favour rather than the reverse. Michelin built factories at
Granton, Bridgwater, and Waterville, in Nova Scotia, with two-thirds
of the capital for the first two plants provided by governments. These
tire plants employed 3500 people at the end of the seventies. Yet
Michelin threatened to leave the province if trade unions successfully
organized any of its plants. When the United Rubber Workers signed
up a majority of the Granton employees, the government changed its
labour law in 1979 to require that, when a company had more than
one branch in Nova Scotia, a union had to win support of a majority
of the company's Nova Scotia employees to be certified and could
no longer simply sign up one plant. This was a thinly veiled and
successful attempt to nullify the union's efforts at Granton, since it
was generally known that the other two plants were in rural areas
with little experience of or sympathy with unions.[7]

Critics suggested that the DREE approach, marrying public capital
and private initiative, invited quick-buck artists to take the money
and run. But the desperation of Atlantic premiers to have big projects
to present to their electorates, rather than focussing on smaller local
projects that might have more potential for enduring job creation but
less lustre in the mega-project–minded media, made such observations pointless. Only as the national economy slowed down in the
mid-seventies and the federal government became less willing to
provide aid to poorer provinces for industrial development, or much
else, did the giveaways begin to become more modest.

The Parade of Concern, protesting the planned closure of Hawker Siddeley steel mill, Sydney, Nova Scotia, 1967. NAC C-98715.

The need to win votes and to preserve local economies led to other state expenditures that, with the benefit of hindsight, appear pointless. In the mid-sixties DOSCO decided to abandon its coal mines on Cape Breton Island and its steel plant, which was Sydney's main employer. Almost the whole town of Sydney showed up at a rally in 1967 to save the mill, putting tremendous pressure on the provincial government to act. The federal government took over the coal companies and the province bought out the steel company. But, while each government suffered enormous losses running the Crown corporations that replaced DOSCO, neither was willing to spend the larger sums required to modernize these firms and make them potentially profitable in the long run. Many people in industrial Cape Breton found it depressing that they were living on glorified welfare and were unsure whether to thank the governments that had saved their jobs or curse them for having no long-term plan to make either the industries viable, or to provide other long-term job opportunities for islanders.[8]

While industrial development was off to a shaky start in the Atlantic region, fishing and farming provided employment to a declining number of people. Prince Edward Island's farm population fell from one-third of all Islanders in 1960 to fewer than one-tenth in 1980, while only about four percent of the population of the other three provinces farmed in 1970. Farms were bigger and better capitalized and agri-business had entered the region quite forcefully, with McCain's modest french-fry and frozen vegetable facilities in New Brunswick, for example, expanding significantly.

Fisheries policy, like industrial policy, favoured large companies over individual operators. In Newfoundland, the offshore fishery was favoured over inshore fishing and National Sea Products and Birds Eye Fisheries, among others, increased their trawler fleets as well as their processing activities. Meanwhile, federal and provincial funds were used to relocate about 30,000 Newfoundlanders living in 250 communities, almost one Newfoundlander in ten, from small outport communities into designated regional growth centers supposedly geared towards the offshore fishery. Most of those moving had little choice, because the provincial government made clear its intention to subsidize health, education, and other services only in the designated centres. For many, the trade off for losing their community was supposed to be a higher standard of living.[9] Many of the growth centres, however, fared poorly as the offshore fishery faced difficulties of supply in the 1970s as a result of poorly controlled foreign overfishing off the Grand Banks.

Northern cod harvests tell the story. Having risen from 393,000 tons in 1960 to 807,500 tons in 1968, they fell to 432,500 tons in 1971 and a dismal 138,600 tons in 1978.[10] The federal government's lame response to over-fishing caused Newfoundland Premier Brian Peckford to call for provincial control over the offshore fishery. The Maritime premiers concurred.[11] There was resentment among Atlantic Canadians generally that the federal government seemed less interested in defending the fishery than in avoiding alienation of nations with whom other regions of Canada had extensive trade.

Lobster catches, once the mainstay for south shore fishermen in Nova Scotia, were also down. The instability of the fishery led many fishers to seek wage labour outside of the fishing season. It also persuaded many of the need to unionize. The Maritime Fishermen's Union organized 2000 fishers in New Brunswick, Prince Edward Island, and northeastern Nova Scotia in the late seventies as fishers recognized that their co-operatives lacked the bargaining clout with an increasingly oligopolized industry that unions potentially had.[12] In Newfoundland, the Newfoundland Fishermen, Food and Allied Workers Union, formed in 1971 under the leadership of the colourful

Richard Cashin, organized independent fishers, trawler crews, and shore workers.

The dramatic growth of government and the halting steps towards industrialization in the Atlantic region, combined with the decline of fishing and farming, meant important changes in how most people lived and worked. Like most other Canadians, Atlantic Canadians by 1980 were more likely to live in a city than in a rural area, and more likely to have industrial, private-sector service, or government jobs, than jobs in primary industries. Federal government monies, in the form of national social transfers, equalization payments, industrial programs, and military expenditures, all ensured that a large number of people were employed even as traditional employments fell away. Still, unemployment rates in the region were far higher than in Canada as a whole, while labour participation rates were much lower. In Newfoundland, for example, in 1979, 15.1 percent of the labour force was unemployed on average throughout the year, while the comparable rate for all of Canada was 7.4 percent; 52.3 percent of Newfoundlanders were in the labour force, against 63.4 percent of Canadians generally.[13] Over 55,000 Newfoundlanders left the province during the 1960s and 1970s, while New Brunswick lost 35,000 residents from 1966 to 1971 alone. As the popular movie *Goin' Down the Road* suggested, the lack of prospects for work caused many young Maritimers to head for central Canada, often with unrealistic expectations.[14]

Atlantic cultural expression in this period, aided by state grants, produced notable achievements in literature, music, and art. The tendency, whether in the works of Acadian author Antonine Maillet, the music of Cape Breton singer John Allan Cameron and Acadian composer-singer Edith Butler, or the art of Alex Colville, was to deal with historical traditions and with the landscape, rather than with current realities. This was less true of drama groups such as Newfoundland's Mummers and Codco who made current issues the subject of much of their dramatic fare. Preservation of the region's history became an important component of the burgeoning tourist industry, which provided an increasing number of jobs. The eighteenth-century fortress of Louisbourg had been restored as an employment project in the Diefenbaker years, and historic Acadian villages were established in Prince Edward Island and Caraquet, New Brunswick. Battle sites, a miners' museum in Glace Bay, a reconstruction of Champlain's Port Royal settlement at Annapolis Royal, and Peggy's Cove, an idyllic fishing village near Halifax, were all tourist

Lobster traps at Halifax Harbour in the 1960s. PANS, Norwood Collection.

attractions. The region immersed itself in its history in an effort to attract tourists to "quaint" locations. Of course, the region also had a history of class warfare, particularly in the coal fields, of extremes of poverty and wealth, and of gradual industrialization. Much of this was hidden as the tourist industry gained the upper hand in recreating a regional past that was made to seem charming and without controversies.

Glorification of rural communities was set aside when the demands of tourism suggested the need to bulldoze existing communities. The expansion of national parks in the region inevitably resulted in the expropriation of homes and the destruction of communities, often with minimal financial compensation for those forced to move. The most contested development was Kouchibouguac National Park in New Brunswick, opened in 1969. One property owner, demanding about seven times as much compensation as the federal government offered, refused to move and the government finally bulldozed his home and charged him and members of his family with criminal offences for trying to save their home.

Another controversial bulldozing of a community involved the historic African-Nova Scotian neighbourhood, Africville. Once separated from Halifax by bush and rock, Africville was established before 1850 by African-Americans fleeing slavery in the United States. They and their descendants farmed and fished to make a subsistence living. Ignored by Nova Scotia and Halifax when it came to supplying basic services, Africville, populated mainly by descendants of the original settlers, came to Halifax's attention in the early sixties as a potential area for industrial redevelopment. The city provided no paved roads, sewerage, water, or garbage collection to Africville, though it had long since come under municipal administration. In the 1950s, the city located an open dump just outside Africville. Campaigns by residents for services were ignored. So were their pleas to let them stay in their community. The city council agreed in 1964 to raze Africville. In 1969 and 1970, its residents were relocated with little thought given to employment for those relocated, or efforts to keep them together.

By 1969, African-Nova Scotians, taking their cue from the "Black Power" movement in the United States, formed the Black United Front to press for an end to discrimination against Nova Scotia's blacks. On 6 August 1972, about 1200 people gathered on the site of the gutted Africville community for a memorial service sponsored by the Cornwallis Street Baptist Church. It would be a long struggle for equality for African-Nova Scotians but the days of turning the other cheek or simply going to the courts had passed.[15]

Acadians had also become more militant, particularly in New Brunswick, where they composed thirty-eight percent of the population in 1971. Some of their anger was focussed on the poverty that plagued northern New Brunswick where Acadians were a majority. When Nigadoo Mines announced the closure of its mine near Bathurst, eliminating 300 jobs, close to 3000 people attended meetings on a Day of Concern at Bathurst College. Shortly afterwards, about 100 demonstrators occupied the Unemployment Insurance Office in one of a series of demonstrations against the company and government who were sealing their fate. Outside Acadia itself, a concern of the French-Canadians was the preservation of their language. Moncton mayor Leonard Jones and his council had refused to make city services available in both French and English in 1968. After the National Film Board film *L'Acadie, l'Acadie* was telecast in January 1972, about 200 students marched through the streets and the campaign for a bilingual Moncton was on again. But Jones held firm, speaking for unilingual anglophone residents who opposed giving French speakers equal rights in their city. The provincial government of Richard Hatfield, a Conservative who had defeated Liberal and Acadian Louis Robichaud in 1971, surprised many by proving a strong supporter of bilingualism. In 1981, New Brunswick became officially bilingual.[16]

Some leading politicians and business people in the Atlantic region believed that part of the reason for the region's difficulties lay in having so many governments for so few people. Louis Robichaud, in particular, was keen to have the premiers go beyond looking at ways of co-operating on projects and consider formal amalgamation of the four Atlantic provinces into one. This would result, he believed, in the need for smaller numbers of bureaucrats to organize public services and a rationalization of the region's health, social services, and advanced education facilities. But local feelings, and the resistance of politicians and officials who regarded amalgamation as a threat, ensured that discussions on creating one Atlantic province went nowhere.[17]

Manitoba and Saskatchewan

While there were differences of opinion on some questions among the Atlantic provinces, there was a general regional consensus supporting equalization payments, regional development grants, and federal social programs. Within these provinces, political debate was often lively, but with little fundamental difference between the two old-line parties, who alternated, Tweedle Dum and Tweedle Dee, in power. Among the western provinces, there had been differences even in the pre-war period between the agricultural Prairie provinces and British Columbia, for which forests and mines were more important than agriculture and whose agriculture was more diversified. The coastal province retained its own identity in the post-war period, and increasingly, Alberta also became a region unto itself, thanks to the development of its energy industry, though rhetorically it often claimed to speak in the interests of the Prairie region. Alberta stood out as the one province where politics were not polarized. The Social Credit party reigned provincially from 1935 to 1971, without a serious challenge in the post-war period from the left. When the Conservatives emerged as the Official Opposition under Peter Lougheed in 1967 and as the government in 1971, they presented themselves as a youthful, more urban, and educated alternative to the grey-haired, Bible-belt politicians of the Social Credit era. Policy differences between the two "small-c" conservative parties were not obvious during either election. By contrast, politics in Saskatchewan was hotly contested between the socialist NDP and the right-leaning Liberals (and by 1979, the Conservatives). Manitoba politics were three-cornered until 1969 when they developed, for two decades, along the Saskatchewan two-party model. The urban working class, state employees, and smaller farmers tended to favour the NDP while the wealthier among the farmers and urban dwellers usually gave their votes to the major right-wing party that squared off with the New Democrats.

In the 1960s, Manitoba and Saskatchewan behaved towards the federal government and private corporations much as the Atlantic governments did. Winnipeg had enjoyed a relatively healthy manufacturing sector before World War II with its railway metal shops, meat-packing plants, and clothing industry particularly strong. After the war, however, all of these sectors experienced a gradual decline and Winnipeg's two large railway yards, CN and CP, which employed about 10,000 workers in the late fifties, had begun to shed staff by the end of the sixties, as competition from other forms of transportation reduced demand for railway transport. New manufacturing companies, particularly in the aircraft and motor coach industries, replaced declining sectors, but new job creation barely kept pace with the jobs that were being lost in the pre-war sectors of strength. The city's oil refineries and packing plants closed in the seventies in a wave of corporate consolidations. Outside of Winnipeg, the job-creation situation was even less bright, though Manitoba joined other provinces in expanding its hydroelectricity production. In Manitoba's case, it was mainly for export markets to the south. Southern Manitoba, outside of Winnipeg, lost some of its population as the number of farms declined, while the population increased in northern Manitoba, where there was some expansion of metal mining. Failure to balance this decline left the province with a steady population of about one million while the country as a whole continued to grow.[18]

Manitoba's Conservatives, first elected in 1958, had greatly increased public spending relative to their Liberal-Progressive predecessors, whose support came mainly from rural areas. They built schools and roads, poured money into universities and technical schools, and developed hydroelectricity, just as their Atlantic counterparts were doing, and expected that industrial development would be the taxpayers' reward for the taxes required to pay for all of this. But little industry appeared. Premier Duff Roblin became desperate as the time approached to face the electorate in 1966. Roblin had established the Manitoba Development Fund to search out prospective industrialists for Manitoba, but its achievements before 1966 were mediocre. As the election approached, Roblin and the MDF suddenly made a big announcement: a huge integrated forestry complex was to be built at The Pas by Churchill Forest Industries (CFI). The government told the public little about who the investors were or what the terms of the deal were, but they insisted that no public money would be involved and that the deal was a vindication of the government's approach of building expensive infrastructure but leaving the role of industrial development to entrepreneurs rather than the state.[19]

Apart from articles in the *Financial Post*, which government insiders suggested were planted by jealous forestry competitors, the only critical articles on the project appeared in a special joint edition in 1970, of *The Manitoban*, the University of Manitoba Student Union's newspaper, and *Omphalos*, a community newspaper largely devoted to the arts.[20] CFI immediately sued them for libel and won a court order to restrain them from revealing more. But most of their charges were subsequently proven to be true.

The principals of CFI had built a pulp mill in Catania, Sicily, and Premier Roblin used a visit to the Catania mill as a photo opportunity to demonstrate that Manitoba had attracted able entrepreneurs to build the mill at The Pas. In fact, the Catania mill had gone broke by 1970, and was revealed to be a scam. Backed by state funds, the owners had purchased outdated machinery from a firm they owned at inflated prices and sold the pulp produced by the mill to another of their firms at rates below the cost of production. They made a fortune with other people's money and then abandoned the mill. In Manitoba, they did substantially the same thing and $140 million of provincial and federal money had been spent before Ed Schreyer's NDP government finally felt compelled to take over the forestry complex. Criminal charges were laid against the principals of the firm but no one could be extradited from Austria and Switzerland, where CFI owners lived. Not only had the provincial government played fast and loose with public money, but the city council at The Pas showed how desperate some communities were for development by exempting CFI from property tax and by waiving the right to impose pollution controls on the mill.

Questionable forestry developments were not limited to Manitoba. Saskatchewan's Liberal government under Ross Thatcher wanted to demonstrate that the previous CCF-NDP government (1944–64) had been wrong to rely on the public sector to create industry. But, like the Atlantic and Manitoba premiers, he found that infrastructural improvements and even low taxes and low wages were not enough to attract new investors. So, he gave them more. Thatcher agreed to supply much of the capital for a pulp mill project near Prince Albert in return for a partnership arrangement with Parsons and Whittemore, an American forestry giant. While the province was supposed to receive thirty percent of the profits, it played no role in the management of the mill. But the mill reported only losses. Critics charged that the mill was inflating its costs and deflating its revenue, easy enough for a vertically integrated company to do[21], and thereby depriving Saskatchewan of its just return. Yet Thatcher contemplated going into partnership with the company for a second mill. Only the re-election of the NDP in 1971, under Allan Blakeney, ended this possibility.[22]

Though the Manitoba New Democrats proved cautious about extending public enterprise, doing little beyond creating a public auto insurance program in 1970, the Blakeney government was a bit bolder. It nationalized about forty percent of the potash industry in Saskatchewan and, when oil prices were high and Saskatchewan's energy royalties briefly soared, the government set aside some of this revenue to launch a steel fabricating plant in Regina.[23] For part of the late seventies, Saskatchewaners believed the days when the price of wheat alone determined the fate of their province[24] was behind them.

The NDP governments in the two provinces (Manitoba, 1969–77, and Saskatchewan, 1971–82) could boast some progressive achievements on the social policy front. Saskatchewan introduced free prescription drugs as part of the provincial medicare scheme; Manitoba established an extensive public-housing program. Yet the differences between the social programs introduced by the NDP and those implemented in other provinces can easily be exaggerated. Though the Manitoba NDP increased social assistance rates by twenty percent shortly after its election, it failed to raise them over the next four years, despite rapid inflation. The Saskatchewan NDP broke its promises to expand daycare spaces and had a worse record in the daycare area than many other non-socialist provinces.[25] It proved largely indifferent to efforts to have employees of Crown corporations involved in management, preferring to run public corporations in much the same bureaucratic manner as private corporations were run.[26] Neither government followed Quebec in banning the use of scabs during strikes. In the case of Manitoba, there was considerable disillusionment on the part of working people when the Schreyer government refused to intervene as police confronted picketers at Griffin Steel, where poorly paid workers were striking to end the company's practice of requiring compulsory overtime.[27]

The obsession with economic growth that had produced the CFI and Parsons and Whittemore deals also caused a controversy in Saskatchewan over uranium mining. Many New Democratic Party members joined environmentalists and peace activists in opposing the mining of a substance that was hazardous to the health of the workers and the surrounding community to extract a product that was used to make nuclear bombs and whose utility for "peaceful uses" was increasingly open to question. The government ignored such complaints and spent about a billion dollars to open up several uranium mines in the North. With agricultural communities in decline, governments in Saskatchewan and Manitoba were afraid that, if they did not diversify their economies quickly, their provinces would become ghost provinces. Predictions in the late sixties by the Economic Council of Canada that Saskatchewan's population could decline by half by the end of the century while the national population doubled only reinforced the often myopic focus on growth for growth's sake.[28]

Manitoba gave the country a first taste of neo-conservatism when the Conservatives under Sterling Lyon won provincial office for one term in 1977. Though Lyon had been a member of the Roblin Cabinet, he now turned his back on the notion that the state had an important role to play in either fostering economic growth or helping the casualties of the marketplace. He fired a large section of the civil service, tightened eligibility requirements for social assistance recipients, and reduced funding for health, social services, and education. The Roblin giveaway approach discredited, Lyon argued that industry would be tempted to come to Manitoba if it knew that its government was uninterested in interfering in the operations of the private sector by charging high taxes and regulating the environment closely. In fact, industry remained as uninterested in Manitoba as ever.[29]

Whether the right or the left ruled in Manitoba and Saskatchewan, governments in these provinces, like Atlantic governments, defended federal equalization and federal social programs because these provided net benefits for the citizens of these disadvantaged provinces. Alberta, by contrast, resented such programs as a redistribution of funds from Albertans, especially rich Albertans, to other Canadians.

Alberta — Blue-Eyed Sheiks of the North

Alberta accounted for only a third of the Prairie population in 1941. By the 1981 census, its population had almost tripled. With 2.2 million people, it was larger than the other two Prairie provinces combined. The energy industry largely accounted for the difference. Though Alberta made efforts to diversify its economy, manufacturing accounted for only eleven percent of the provincial workforce in 1976, two percent less than in 1961.[30] By contrast, the oil and gas sector accounted for over fifty percent of all income generated in the province in 1981, up from forty percent in 1971.

Efforts to industrialize Alberta had been fairly desultory under the Social Credit regime. Ernest Manning was skeptical about Alberta's prospects for industrialization, even in the petrochemical sector, because it was so far from the major markets. Unlike the premiers of the other Prairie provinces and the Atlantic provinces, Manning's province was experiencing more in-migration than out-migration, and he saw no reason to subsidize industries.[31]

The Social Credit regime largely took a back seat to industry in the development of the energy resources of the province. Uninterested in the exploration, production, or marketing of oil, Social Credit was content to collect royalties. Yet, while these royalties collected on oil companies' production provided over half the Alberta budget by the late sixties, they were low in comparison to those assessed in all other jurisdictions in North America.

Peter Lougheed's Conservatives more than doubled the royalty rate, putting some of the profits into luring petrochemical industries into Alberta, and joining with the federal government and private industry to develop the tar sands of northern Alberta. The Alberta government proved willing to pour hundreds of millions of dollars into the development of Syncrude in Fort McMurray, in return for only a fifteen percent share of ownership of the tar sands develop-

Construction of the Students Union Building, December 1965, University of Alberta. UAA 79-149 3A.

ment. Provincial subsidies included equity and debit financing, work force training, the provison of infrastructure, and the underwriting of environmental studies and costs. A report to the government by top civil servants suggested that the government's policy on Syncrude, along with energy policies more generally, constituted "policies ... creating tremendous and unregulated growth and developments resulting in short-term benefits accruing to the province as well as the long-term costs arising from exported energy, technology, job opportunities and environmental damages in addition to the depletion of non-renewable resources."[32]

The large increase in provincial revenues that accompanied the OPEC increases in oil prices after 1973 gave the Alberta government the luxury of being able to subsidize both energy-related and non-energy-related developments, though the former were favoured, with Lougheed's emphasis on industrialization focussed on the petro-chemical industry. Lougheed wanted Alberta to diversify in the near future, fearing that if it waited twenty years, its energy supplies would have dwindled and its opportunity to plan the post-oil Alberta economy would be lost. Inevitably, he clashed with the federal Liberal government, which saw the OPEC-induced oil price increases as a windfall in which all Canadians should share. The Alberta government rejected such an inference, observing that mineral and forestry profits in other provinces were not treated as windfalls. For Lougheed, it seemed indecent that the federal government, whose policies, historically, had allegedly restricted the economic development of Alberta, should try to strip Alberta of the financial resources it needed to create a diversified economy like that of Ontario.

It was perhaps inevitable then that the governments of Alberta and Canada clashed when Prime Minister Trudeau introduced his National Energy Policy in the fall of 1980. The NEP envisaged the Canadianization of the largely foreign-owned energy industry, and a greater share of petroleum revenue for Ottawa from Alberta oil sold to Canadians 25 percent below the world market price. Lougheed attacked the NEP stridently, claiming "the Ottawa government — without negotiation and without agreement — simply walked into our homes and occupied the living room."[33] He reduced the flow of oil from Alberta to the rest of Canada for almost a year while the federal and provincial governments worked out a compromise. In the immediate aftermath of the announcement of the NEP, Alberta separatism, a notion once restricted to the province's lunatic fringe, briefly gained a great deal of support. Polls at the end of 1980 suggested that almost one Albertan in four believed that the province should separate from Canada if the NEP was not abandoned.

Many of the Albertans who bitterly opposed the NEP were not Albertan by birth. They had migrated to Alberta to be part of the oil boom and experience the province's amazing prosperity.[34] In Alberta in the seventies, it was not uncommon for oil rig workers to earn as much money as physicians in other provinces, or for construction workers in their twenties to purchase mansions. There was little unemployment, and though poverty persisted in the northern and rural areas, and in Native communities, which the energy industry by-passed, only the voices of the well-off and the middle classes counted in political discourse. Trudeau's plans to provide cheap energy to Canadians outside Alberta and to enrich the federal treasury threatened to kill the goose that laid the golden egg. Individual fears were easily married to mythologies of Ottawa's persistent screwing of the West to create righteous indignation. Indeed, the reaction to the NEP revealed a great deal about the peculiar political culture of Alberta. Though Alberta had become an urban, industrial, and increasingly multicultural society, many of its citizens, even if

Peter Pocklington, Alberta businessman and Conservative politician. PAA J-5268-1.

they were recent arrivals, identified with a nostalgic view of the province as a frontier, cowboy society, where individualism reigned supreme and the interventions of an outside government were unwelcome. In practice, most Albertans worked either for large multi-national corporations, for small companies dependent upon the multi-nationals for their contracts, or for government. Only pockets of the province could claim to have cowboys other than "midnight cowboys." But the notion that they were living in a modern version of the Wild West attracted many Albertans, and made their quarrel with the federal government, which was motivated by selfishness, justified or not, appear to be one of high principle. The right-wing vision of Alberta's interests was particularly fostered by "the growing number of white-collar professionals in the oil industry and of financier-developers" whose Epolitical ideology was built on a social-Darwinian faith in the efficiency and morality of an economy based on individualism and rooted in a vision of western Canada, particularly Alberta, as one of the last frontiers of economic opportunity."[35]

British Columbia: Economic Growth and Political Polarization

While Alberta often seemed like a one-party province where left-wingers and the poor were shut away from public view, British Columbia continued to be as class-divided socially and politically as it had ever been. British Columbia's post-war prosperity had, perhaps, blunted the edge of class warfare, but the political culture that made both workers and capitalists class conscious and prepared to defend their perceived interests against one another continued.

Most of the time, the right-wing was dominant. The Social Credit party governed the province from 1952 to 1972 and then again from 1975 to 1991. It owed its success to the staunch support of the corporate sector and the large number of well-paid jobs that expansion of the province's resource sectors produced. This did not happen without a price for the province's long-term interests. W.A.C. Bennett, premier from 1952 until Social Credit met defeat at the hands of Dave Barrett and the NDP two decades later, wanted growth at all costs. He levied modest royalties on the forestry companies, and did little as these companies followed lax reforestation practices, replanting on average only one tree for every seven that they cut down in 1970.[36] He did nothing to preserve agricultural land from being taken over by industrialists and land developers building suburbs. Political scientist Martin Robin summarizes the environmental record of the Bennett years:

> ... the companies emptied their bowels and bladders with impunity across the province: at Buttle Lake where Western Mines fouled the water with its tailings; at Port Hardy where Utah Construction created a few jobs and besmirched the land; in Burnaby where Shell and Imperial refineries sickened the air for suburbanites; in the instant pulp towns of the north and central interior covered over by palls of effluent emitted by integrated mill complexes like Northwood Pulp and Weldwood; at the Harmer's Ridge site of Kaiser's violation in the East Kootenays where millions of yards of overburden and waste coal, pushed aside by the strip-mining operation, slid down into the creek system feeding the Elk River Valley.[37]

A slump in the market for British Columbia's resources in the early seventies resulted in a recession even more severe than the one the country was experiencing as a whole. In January 1971, provincial unemployment reached 9.4 percent, almost four percent more than the national rate.[38] In the 1972 provincial election, the aging Bennett faced not only his traditional NDP rival but vigorous Liberal and Conservative opponents. Though the NDP won only thirty-nine percent of the vote, about six percent more than it had won in the previous election, that figure proved good enough to win a large majority of seats, as the right-wing vote in most ridings was split among two or three parties.

The NDP government in British Columbia greatly expanded day-care for the neediest of mothers and increased seniors' benefits and the minimum wage. It also implemented a public automobile insurance program. Barrett substantially increased mine and forestry royalties, and introduced and enforced new conservation measures, also protecting agricultural land by allowing its sale only for agricultural purposes. The government, however, trying to win greater support from the middle class, distanced itself from its union supporters and even legislated several groups of strikers back to work. This did not win the NDP any new friends. When Barrett called an election in late 1975, two years before he was required to do so, the NDP vote remained stuck at thirty-nine percent. But the right-wing vote had largely coalesced around Social Credit again, and that party won forty-nine percent of the vote, this time with Bill Bennett Junior at its head. Bennett had blamed the NDP's interventionism for the continuing malaise in the British Columbia economy, but over the next four years it became clear that international markets, rather than British Columbia politics, explained the relative health of the British Columbia economy at a given moment. In the 1979 provincial election, although the NDP vote reached forty-seven percent, Social Credit retained power. The province was more politically polarized than ever.

Nine

The Women's Movement: A "Second Wave"

Surveying the position of women in Canada in the early seventies, long-time feminist Thérèse Casgrain, a link between the feminists of the pre-war period and those of the sixties and seventies, commented:

> Even the few forward steps made by women along the road to their emancipation do not prevent them from remaining prisoner of a bunch of prejudices. We confront a society that has to rid itself of its old racist, violent, and snobbish concepts. We are too afraid to abandon the past perspectives that equated patriotism with obedience, ripe old age with wisdom, and women with abdication. True women's liberation cannot occur without men's. At bottom, the women's liberation movement is not uniquely feminist in its inspiration; it is also humanist. Let men and women look at each other honestly and let them try together to rethink society's values.[1]

The position of women in Canadian society changed substantially in the 1960s and 1970s. By 1980, many women and men no longer accepted the notion of a strict division of gender roles and abilities. The view that a woman's destiny was to marry and become a stay-at-home housewife, raising children and tending to the needs of her husband, was increasingly questioned. Many women chose neither to marry nor to have children; many chose to do one but not the other. Among those who married and had children, it became common to work outside the home for all or a substantial number of years of child-raising. But, while more and more women worked for pay, "pink ghettoes" of low-paying women's jobs and different rates of pay for women and men who performed the same work defined much of their work force experience.[2] For many, having a paid job simply meant a double work day since they were expected to come home

Thérèse Casgrain (1896–1981) fought for women's suffrage and led the CCF in Quebec from 1951–1957. She was named to the Senate in 1970. NAC PA-126768.

and do all or most of the housework and tend to the children when their paid work was done.

State policies continued, for the most part, to pretend that the television "sitcom" model of the family was still prevalent in Canada, and little was done to help working families with childcare, or to aid single-parent and low-income families. With divorce more common, the number of single-parent families rose annually, and female-headed single-parent families were generally poor. The National Council of Welfare reported in 1975 that 69.1 percent of such families lived in poverty, compared to 21.2 percent of two-parent families, and 33.7 percent of male-headed single-parent families.[3] It did, however, become easier for women to enter professions such as law and medicine, and unionization resulted in better paycheques in traditionally female professions like teaching, nursing, and social work. Many of the gains women made were the result of a revitalized women's movement which, although divided regarding both ends and means, was united in a belief that women required full equality with men.

Women's labour force participation, as we have seen earlier, increased in the post-war period, despite the state and media strictures on married women working outside the home. By 1951, one in nine married women was in the work force, a three-fold increase over 1931, and married women were 6.6 percent of the female labour force. By 1961, one married woman in five held a paying job and in 1979, 47.4 percent of married women were employed, accounting for one in four employed women. Another forty percent of the women working for wages were separated, divorced, or widowed.[4] The availability of better contraception, especially after the birth-control pill became available in 1960, contributed to the erosion of the view that lifelong bearing and raising of children was a woman's destiny. While the average mother of the late fifties bore four children, her counterpart just a generation later had only two. Greater use of contraception, the large increase in divorces after the laws were changed in 1969 to make divorce easier, and the greater availability of educational opportunities for women all contributed to a rethinking of the notion that women were destined to marry, and live happily ever after raising children and then doting on grandchildren, all the while attending to the whims of their husbands and keeping the house spotless.

Female labour participation in the work force had increased from 23.4 percent in 1953 to 48.9 percent in 1979, while male participation had declined from 82.9 to 78.4 percent during the same period. While many women now worked because they had made a conscious choice to have a career, many worked mainly out of economic necessity. The National Council of Welfare estimated in 1979 that there would be a fifty percent increase in the poverty rate for two-spouse families if none of the women in the two-spouse family category had jobs.[5]

Given the continued gender-typing of jobs, it is unsurprising that the average full-time woman worker earned only fifty-eight percent of a man's earnings in 1972. Women were also far less likely than men to have full-time jobs. That year, twenty-five percent of employed women worked part-time, while only six percent of employed men did not have full-time work.[6] For many women, the option of full-time work was unrealistic because of the high costs and poor availability of decent childcare. It was against such a background of changing gender roles, but with continuing discrimination against women, that a "second wave" women's movement arose in Canada.

The Women's Movement

Canada's "first wave" of feminists had been the supporters of suffrage at the turn of the century. The suffragettes argued that women should have the same rights of participation as citizens that men did. This included the right to vote and to run for public office. Many of the first-wave feminists were "maternal feminists" who believed that, as mothers, women had special insights and abilities for nurturing society and ensuring that its weakest elements, particularly children, received the attention of legislators. Most also believed that professions should be open to women, but they usually had unmarried or, at least, childless women in mind. They generally accepted that the raising of children was a full-time job, and that it should be done within the family home by mothers, who they believed were best-equipped emotionally to deal with children. After votes for women were conceded by the federal and most provincial governments during and immediately after World War I, no other single cause united the efforts of either feminists or women's organizations more generally. Women were, however, politically active. In Quebec, feminists had to fight for another generation to win the vote. On the Prairies, women were active in the movement to build co-operatives to market farmers' products, in campaigns for greater equality with men, and for more control over their reproductive lives. The United Farm Women of Alberta, for example, campaigned in the inter-war years for a farm wife to have equal ownership of all farm property with her husband, for birth control clinics, and for legalization of mid-wifery.[7]

The National Council of Women of Canada (NCWC), and its provincial and local component groups, pressured government and employers to remove all legal and informal barriers to the employ-ment of women. But most of the NCWC leaders took this to mean either single women or rich women who could hire servants to raise their children. In the late forties, some NCWC leaders seemed to believe that stay-at-home mothers were part of the necessary arsenal to fend off Communist ideology. Even more vigilant in pressing the rights of women to work and receive the same opportunities for career advancement as men was the Canadian Federation of Business and Professional Women's Clubs. Until the 1960s, however, the Federation restricted its discourse to equal rights feminism, calling for equal pay for equal work, while ignoring the special problems that married women without servants had in the labour force. They were afraid that by highlighting the different needs of a certain group of women they would undermine their underlying argument that the state and employers should treat men and women the same.[8]

In the 1960s, with more and more women working, a new genera-tion of feminists began to question directly the patriarchal assump-tions that infused state and employer policies. The "second wave" of feminists, unlike the "first wave," rejected the notion that women must choose between children and careers. While only a few suffra-gettes questioned women's obligation to perform all the chores of the household, the new feminists argued that sex, a biological fact, did not naturally produce a division of labour. Rather, the socially produced norms of behaviour for the sexes determined the degree of similarity and difference in gender roles within societies. The great variation in gender differentiation among societies historically gave the 1960s feminists hope that male oppression of women could be ended. Liberal feminists looked to state legislation that would create a level playing field for women, including affirmative action, equal pay for work of equal value, and state-subsidized childcare facilities. Radical feminists believed that the nuclear family was the source of women's oppression and called for new family forms in which col-lective sharing of duties replaced the ideal of a married couple with their children, with the father earning the income and the mother raising the kids and looking after the father's needs. Socialist femi-nists suggested that the capitalist economic system, with its competi-tive ideology, worked against the achievement of equality within or between the sexes and called for an end to both capitalism and patriarchy. Unsurprisingly, the liberal feminists had the most influence, though mainstream feminist organizations reflected the input of all three streams of feminism.

Mainstream feminist thinking just before the second wave took wing is exemplified in a letter from Grace MacInnis, New Democrat MP for Vancouver-Kingsway and the only woman in the House of Commons after the 1965 election, to Quebec's best-known feminist before the 1970s, Thérèse Casgrain. While MacInnis championed women's right to work, her assumptions that they would stay home during their child-bearing years and do gender-specific paid labour the rest of their lives is clear in the letter. MacInnis asked Casgrain to support a proposal she was making in the House for Canada Manpower to extend a program that trained women as nursery school aides. She wrote:

> It would seem to me highly advisable that other large cities across Canada should take steps to see that such training is available for older women and young girls who wish to avail themselves of it. This should provide a career for many women whose children have grown beyond needing their constant care. It should also be excellent training for young women who will be having families of their own.[9]

The notion of feminist waves, while it helps to trace changes in the position taken by advocates of women's rights in Canada over time, may overstate the speed of change in feminist positions. It also, perhaps, disguises the fact that there was a continuity of militants from the first to the second wave. Long-time feminists such as Thérèse Casgrain and Laura Sabia were the leaders of the campaign that produced the Royal Commission on the Status of Women, established by Lester Pearson in 1967 and chaired by broadcaster Florence Bird. Aviation engineer Elsie Gregory MacGill, generally viewed as the most influential of the Commission members in producing the final report, was a former president of the Canadian Federation of Business and Professional Women's Clubs, and the daughter of turn-of-the-century British Columbia feminist Helen Gregory MacGill. Like her mother, Elsie MacGill wanted to remove all the barriers that restricted women's equality with men, and the Commission report reflected her growing belief that state action was required to achieve this objective. The hearings and findings of the

Commission together tell us a great deal about the changing views of women about their lives in the late sixties.

The Royal Commission on the Status of Women

Sherrill Jackson, a working mother of two children in Montreal, was separated from her husband, who made no financial contribution to his former family. When she appeared before the Royal Commission in June 1968, she made it clear that she did not accept the once-common view that a woman who lost her husband faced a purely private tragedy. She believed that society, and, therefore, government, had an obligation to assist her children and herself. She told the Commission, in part:

> In my opinion there should be free nursery and after school care for children in situations such as mine, to ensure that they are well cared for, and protected from the many haphazard arrangements that can result when a mother is desperate and cannot locate the kind of babysitting best for her child, or is hard pressed to pay for it ...
> There is also the difficulty of women ... to find and pay babysitters in the evenings to enable us to get out and make social or educational contacts and enrich our lives or invest our time towards a better life ...
> It is to the advantage of the children that she be fulfilled, to divert the resentment she might otherwise build up at having to devote her life and, as in my case, youth to her children. Our work is a very important one ... the shaping of future citizens and hopefully the prevention of delinquents in the future. An investment in the easement of our problems is an investment in the future welfare of our country.[10]

Nancy Bryan of Fredericton, another single mom, wanted to "increase the individual worker's mobility, and to increase the degree of public participation in child-raising." She advocated a fully-integrated pension system, making pensions completely portable, expanded training and retraining programs, and a government-initiated expansion of affordable daycare.[11] Such demands, along with many others, were made by a group called The Minus Ones, a group of sole-support mothers in Manitoba who had been brought together under the auspices of the Knox United Church and the Neighbourhood Services Centres in Winnipeg, to improve the lot of women raising children alone. They called for a guaranteed basic income for sole-support women, upgrading and retraining opportunities, enforcement of equal pay legislation, "mothers to have a pension in their own right," and a pregnant woman's right to choose whether to have an abortion.[12] The Manitoba Volunteer Committee on the Status of Women, an umbrella group of Manitoba women's organizations that came together to prepare recommendations for the Commission, called on government to build apartment blocks for deserted and widowed women with educational, recreational, medical, and childcare services incorporated within the building.[13]

The Anglican Church of Canada went further, calling for equal treatment of the sexes. The Commission on Women's Work, an interim body appointed by the General Synod and including the leaders of the principal women's organizations in the Church, supported equal rights to work, and joint responsibility in the home for women and men in raising children and doing housework. Regarding childcare, the Church concluded:

> While women in growing numbers go out of the home to work, little has been done to make available adequate day care services for children or in other ways to lighten the load of their family responsibilities. The result is that too often the essential quality of women's presence is lost both at home and at work.[14]

The Anglicans' apparent willingness to embrace liberal feminist perspectives did not reflect the views of churches in general. As we saw in Chapter Seven, while many Quebec women's groups of the mid-sixties had adopted a feminist viewpoint, mainstream Catholic organizations remained committed to the view that women should remain home during their child-raising years. While the Canadian Federation of Business and Professional Women's Clubs wanted full equality for women and men, the Ontario Jaycettes surveyed their members and "100% agreed that women with small children should not work, unless it is essential." They were willing to support daycare centres only for those women for whom it was "necessary" to work. The Primrose Club, a women's club promoting the welfare of the Conservative Party throughout the country by acting as hostesses to visiting Tories, had nothing to say about daycare or working women, though they lamented a shortage of domestics for hire.[15]

But equality-seekers vastly outnumbered traditionalists in the briefs heard by the Commission. The Indian and Metis Ladies committee of the Manitoba Volunteer Committee on the Status of Women were blunt about what Native women wanted, both as women and as Natives.

1. We want equal opportunity with other Canadians.
2. We want full educational opportunity for all our children.
3. We want job opportunity for our people.
4. We want job training for housewives.
5. We want nursery schools for all.
6. We want day nurseries for children of working mothers.
7. We want housekeeping consultants to assist women in learning to spend wisely the food and clothing dollar.
8. We want to get into decent homes away from the "Social Disorganization" of the slum.
9. We were shocked to hear some time ago that Canadians spend twice as much on dog-food as is spent on public housing.
10. The Indian Act of Canada shows real discrimination toward women — Section 12, sub-section B, Section 14[16] (Point 10 of the brief refers to a section of the Indian Act, only removed in 1985, that deprived Native women and their children of Indian status if they married a non-status man, though no such penalty was imposed upon Native men who married non-status women.)

On the whole, the commissioners, reporting in 1970, sided with the majority of the witnesses who had appeared before them, that is, the equality seekers. Under "criteria and principles," they indicated their acceptance of the second wave's rejection of strict gender roles for married couples with children. "The care of children is a responsibility to be shared by the mother, the father and society," they announced. "Unless this shared responsibility is acknowledged and assumed, women cannot be accorded true equality."[17] The commissioners' recommendations were aimed at providing equal opportunities for women, and in boosting the incomes available to women, particularly disadvantaged women. The centrepiece of the recommendations was a call for a national network of daycare centres with sliding fee scales that would ensure that low-income women did not have to spend a disproportionate share of their wages on childcare.

A women's centre in 1975, Kitchener–Waterloo. CWMA.

Other recommendations included the splitting of pension benefits with a spouse, an end to discrimination against women in the unemployment insurance system, maternity benefits, greater public investment in public housing, enforcement of strictly interpreted laws on equal pay for equal work, and a larger family allowance.

NAC: The National Action Committee on the Status of Women

The Trudeau government implemented a few of the Commission's recommendations, in particular moving in 1971 on maternity benefits, and ending many discriminatory practices in the awarding of unemployment insurance. But, as the economy stagnated and the government's liberalism was found to be wanting, many feminists became disillusioned. They were not willing to accept government excuses that there was no money for better daycare or for family allowances that would at once recognize the important work of women in the home and reduce the poverty rate.

A conference in 1972 launched the National Action Committee on the Status of Women (NAC), an umbrella group whose purpose would be to fight for implementation of the Commission's recommendations and for other measures supported by feminists generally. Feminists were unhappy, for example, with the limited reform of the abortion laws in 1969. While the reform expanded the availability of the procedure, it left committees of hospital doctors, rather than a pregnant woman, with the decision about whether a woman would carry a baby to term. They demanded the removal of abortion from the Criminal Code, and the recognition of a woman's right to choose whether or not to have a baby. Laura Sabia, the prime mover of the 1972 conference, was elected the first president of NAC.

NAC proved to be capable of uniting the various factions of the feminist movement in Canada, which distinguished the Canadian women's movement from its American counterpart, noted for its factiousness. The American movement often seemed hostile to state action. Its right wing was influenced by American individualist traditions, and its left wing was steeped in the ideology of the New Left, which found little reason to believe in the possibility of reform of the imperialist state which was raining destruction on Indochina. By contrast, the Canadian women's movement was influenced by the social democratic traditions of its first-wave foremothers.[18]

NAC included the women's committees of political parties ranging from the Conservatives to the Communists, labour and business women's organizations, service groups, and radical feminist networks. Its leaders in the 1970s included Sabia, a Tory, and Grace Hartman, a labour leader and left-wing New Democrat. Both NAC and its provincial branches, the Action Committees on the Status of Women, lobbied politicians, organized demonstrations, and conducted public education campaigns to put women's issues on the political agenda of the nation. Though they met with a great deal of resistance from patriarchal-minded politicians and from fiscal conservatives who rejected the statist approach of Canadian feminists, they could boast, in 1980, of an expanded — though vastly insufficient — network of publicly subsidized daycare "spots" for low-income mothers, better enforcement of equal pay laws, and the introduction, in 1979, of the refundable Child Tax Credit, which effectively served as a supplement to family allowances for women whose family income was limited. The latter, available to both the

Celebrating International Women's Day, as depicted on the cover of The Other Woman newspaper, 1973, Vol. 1, No. 6. CWMA.

working poor and social assistance recipients, differed from its American counterpart, the Earned Income Tax Credit, which specifically excluded families without a member in the paid labour force.[19] Still, for many women, the progress that was occurring seemed negligible. In 1980, for example, fifty-eight percent of female single parents headed families living in poverty.[20] Women struggled not only to make government and employers take heed of their needs, but the trade union movement, which was supposed to represent all workers, as well.

Women and Unions

By 1978, women made up forty percent of the workforce, but accounted for only 28.5 percent of unionists. Still, this represented a considerable improvement. From 1966 to 1976, the rate of women's unionization had increased by four times as much as the rate of men's unionization. Indeed much of the growth of unionism in the 1970s was the result of organization of women workers. The benefits of unionism were palpable. In 1982, it was estimated that unionized women earned on average fourteen percent more than their unorganized sisters doing comparable work. The wage differential between men and women in the same occupations was seventen percent for non-unionists, but only ten percent for unionists.[21]

The representation of women on union executive boards also increased. But some unions proved more resistant to placing women in responsible positions than others. In 1980, there were no women in the executive officer positions of the Public Service Alliance despite the fact that forty-three percent of the union membership were women. The executive in the Canadian Union of Public Employees, where forty-four percent of the membership were women, reflected the gender composition of the membership. Yet, although the union president was Grace Hartman, a committed feminist and socialist, only eleven percent of staff representatives were women.[22]

Most unionized women either worked for the state or in large manufacturing concerns. But the large number of women concentrated in retail, secretarial, hospitality industry, and other private-sector service occupations, had little success with union drives. Their employers were only too willing to replace them with more compliant workers. Less than one percent of Canada's 145,000 bank employees, for example, were organized. A Canadian Labour Board ruling in 1954 discouraged union efforts to organize bank workers. The Board ruled that a single branch of a bank could not constitute a legitimate bargaining unit. A union would have to organize all the workers of that bank in a particular province, and could not organize unit by unit to get a toehold in the industry that would cause other bank workers to apply for union membership. The prohibitive costs and unlikely success of such an endeavour dissuaded unions, steeped in any case in "male breadwinner" ideology, from trying to organize bank workers. The CLC did make some half-hearted attempts in the 1970s to organize office workers. But the union chose to use sexist advertising to draw attention to its organizing efforts in Toronto, calling on women workers to "get in the ACTE." ACTE was an acronym for Association of Commercial and Technical Employees, but the double entendre of the ads turned off more women than it persuaded to organize.[23]

Women and "The Chip"

Unionized or not, many female workers faced "de-skilling" of their jobs by the 1970s, that is, the turning of jobs requiring skill and discretion into routinized, repetitive-motion work. With the development of the microprocessor in 1971, many office jobs were automated. The position of secretary, which valued the knowledge of a variety of office procedures and flexibility in the performance of job tasks, gave way to a factory-like regime where work was broken down into component parts. Workers at "work stations" complained of boredom, as well as eyestrain from sitting for hours before computer screens. Automated cheque processing reduced three jobs — bank teller, supervisor, and keypunch operator — to one. Insurance claims were analyzed by machines. Local filing systems were centralized in one Canadian location. As for cashiers, they were:

> ... deskilled by the transfer of price information and change calculation into the memory and processing components of the cash register. Like the weaver in the industrial factory, the cashier valued for good price memory and arithmetic efficiency is no longer needed; the cashier becomes a highly replaceable unskilled worker.[24]

In manufacturing, microprocessors also eliminated jobs both for women and men. By 1980, microprocessors controlled systems that automatically cut boards, stitched seams, and assembled parts for a variety of products. It is no wonder, then, that the women's movement put great emphasis on providing women with the same educational opportunities as men at all levels, and in all institutes of learning. Not only were pink ghettoes a violation of women's rights to equality in the labour force, but there was a great likelihood that these ghettoes would soon employ a smaller and smaller number of women workers. Women had to be flexible and willing to break into formerly all-male domains if they were to have equality with men in the labour force.

Changing Sexual Norms

"Good girls don't" was still the common admonition to unmarried women in the early 1960s. Young women who had babies out of wedlock were expected to give them up for adoption, the stigma of "illegitimacy" and the state's unwillingness to make a financial contribution limiting their options as they tried to decide whether to keep their children. By the end of the sixties, however, there had been considerable relaxation of sexual attitudes. Over half of unmarried university students reported to pollsters that they were sexually active, and with better birth control information and the greater availability of condoms, diaphragms, and especially the pill, pregnancy was easier to avoid. However, surveys suggested that most young people did not practise birth control on a regular basis, and the rate of unplanned pregnacies actually increased. Though the abortion laws were liberalized in 1969 and many young women chose to terminate pregnancies safely, the percentage of births for unmarried women was higher in 1980 than 1960. Single women without husbands had become eligible for social assistance, and the stigma attached to raising a baby born out of wedlock had diminished significantly. As we have noted, however, most single mothers lived in poverty.

Women could choose to have one or many sexual partners outside of marriage without fear of pregnancy. But the "sexual liberation" of the sixties and seventies had its negative side. Men and teenage boys came to expect that their dates would "put out." The spread of sexually transmitted diseases increased. Date rape became common, and young women often found that police and courts were skeptical about their claims of having had sex forced upon them. A woman who used birth control and was sexually active was, it appeared, viewed by males and the state as "asking for it" whenever she dated any man. Women's groups, while pleased that better contraception meant greater control for women over their reproduction, argued that, to some degree, women still had not won control over their bodies. They demanded that law enforcers take accusations of date rape seriously, and began educational campaigns to persuade both young men and women that "no means no." The most effective birth control devices also proved to have side effects on women's health. The intra-uterine device (IUD) was eventually removed from the market as a danger to women's physical and mental health, because it produced so many side effects, including the danger of sterility. Users

Canadian finals rodeo queens in Alberta, 1976. PAA, Edmonton Journal Collection, J-2851-1.

banded together to demand compensation from the former manufacturers on the grounds that the manufacturers had either tested the IUD too poorly, or hidden information they had gathered from the testing they had done. There were also reasons to pinpoint the pill as the cause of various medical problems that women faced, though it wasn't until after 1980 that links between the pill and various cancers were discovered.[25]

Lesbians were more likely to come out of the closet after homosexuality was removed from the Criminal Code in 1969, and when notions popular in the early post-war period that postulated that homosexuality was a mental disorder were discredited. In the 1950s, lesbians did have their own underground "scene" in Canada's largest cities. But they covered their tracks by adopting butch and femme roles in which the butch dressed like and behaved like a man. By the 1970s, many lesbians had rejected this re-creation within their relationships of traditional, hierarchical relations between men and women. Lesbian couples were more likely to treat each other as equals and to reject butch/femme role-playing. Gay and lesbian clubs became more open in the major cities, though police harassment of gays, particularly men's gay bathhouses, became common.

Unfinished Revolution

The 1960s and 1970s were decades of major change for Canadian women. The notion of a life devoted solely to motherhood, a life of financial dependence, became weaker, though it did not disappear. By 1980, women were more likely than ever to be in the paid workforce, or in higher education, and to be planning to combine careers with motherhood. Young women bore only half as many children as their mothers had, and the greater availability of divorce reminded them that lifelong financial dependence on a man was risky. While job opportunities expanded and the women's movement made government and employers aware of the need for affirmative action programs, the fact remained that low pay and job ghettoes were the fate of most women. Still considered responsible for child-care and housework, many women faced the double work-day of paid labour and house labour with little help from either the men in their lives or from the state. Though the need for better daycare facilities was widely recognized, government programs in this area were ane- mic, reflecting the view that work outside the home was a woman's private decision to make, and the care of her children was an equally private decision. The result was that horror stories of children being raised in terrible conditions were commonplace. The women's move- ment struggled for complete equality for women and men, and a collective, societal responsibility for childcare. But though the women's movement won many victories, in 1980, it still had far to go to change patriarchal assumptions that were deeply embedded in Canadian culture.

Ten

Canada's First People Rebel

In 1960, Canada's Native people were still treated as wards of the state, the Queen's "red children," as the treaties in the nineteenth and early twentieth centuries called them. They lived only half as long as most other Canadians, and their lives were made miserable not only by dire poverty, but by systemic discrimination that denied them jobs, and in many regions, took their children away from them for ten months of the year. But, by the late 1960s, the various local Native organizations had coalesced into a national body. Natives became vocal in asserting their rights to practise their traditional ways, and to have control over their resources, schools, and health. By 1980, Natives were, on the whole, much poorer than non-Natives, but a large Native leadership had emerged throughout the nation to inspire their people to work collectively for their rights, and to make their demands upon government as clear as possible.

It was hardly happenstance that the Native movement appeared when it did. Like the women's movement and the Quebec nationalist movement, the timing of the Native movement coincided with the upsurge throughout the Third World against colonialism, the African-American movement for civil rights, and the student movement for an end to the war in Vietnam. The challenges to constituted authority that marked the 1960s found a strong echo among Canadian Natives, who were some of the most oppressed people on the North American continent.

Terrible Memories

Mary Anne Nakogee-Davis was a student at St. Anne's Residential School on the west coast of James Bay from 1961 to 1969. There, like many of her fellow students, she suffered sexual abuse by priests, and humiliation and physical assaults by nuns. One of the priests had the girls sit on his lap and "touched where he was not supposed to touch," giving Mary Anne, who was only six when she was first

Preparing to hunt seal, Moose Factory Island, Ontario, 1946. NAC PA-145171.

subjected to this abuse, candy as a reward. Nakogee-Davis was also
a victim of one of the instruments of torture used by some of the
priests and nuns: a homemade electric chair. "It was done to me on
more than one occasion. They would strap your arms to the metal
arm rests, and it would jolt you and go through your system. I don't
know what I did that was bad enough to have that done to me."[1]

Mary Anne witnessed other students being punished by the priests
and nuns by being punched, kicked, strapped, scalded, forced to sleep
alone in a dark basement, having their hair pulled or their heads
pushed into the wall. Her story, and that of her fellow classmates,
would not be revealed until the 1990s. By then, it became clear that
such experiences were common in the residential schools operating
from the late nineteenth century until the early 1970s. Native children
in western Canada and northern Ontario were generally forced by
Indian Affairs to attend these schools. In British Columbia, newspa-

per reports in 1996 suggested that sexual and physical abuse were common in all of the residential schools operating in the province. Not every priest or nun participated in the abuse, but all knew about it and few, if any, reported any concerns to the Church hierarchy. The racism directed towards Native culture and Native people was just too strong for many individuals to recognize any special evil on the part of the perpetrators of abuse.

Students left the residential schools, where they lived for ten months of the year away from their parents and communities, confused and embittered. The religious people who had controlled them during their school years had done their best to make them ashamed of Native traditions and languages. As if this was not sufficient psychological damage, the memories of abuse contributed to feelings of self-contempt. The return to the reserve with its limited employment opportunities further contributed to a negative self-concept for many Native people. Drunkenness was common on reserves, and many children were abandoned by parents too emotionally scarred to parent successfully. Suicides and early deaths from liver and heart disease were the fate of many Natives. In remote communities, where the children sniffed glue and many of the adults were alcoholics, the situation seemed particularly despairing. Many Natives moved to the cities, but they lacked the skills required for the better jobs available and faced severe discrimination in their efforts to get semi-skilled or unskilled jobs. Discrimination also dogged them as they looked for housing, or attempted to get help with children who were "acting up" or doing poorly in school. Racism was rampant in Canada, and most Canadians seemed content to believe that the drunkenness and poverty common to Native people demonstrated that Natives were, in essence, inferior beings. They paid little attention to the role that state bodies, religious organizations, and individual Canadians had played in creating the devastation that marked most Natives' lives. Largely oblivious to the efforts of many Natives either to make it in the larger society despite the odds against them or to recover their lost culture, they were unaware, and perhaps unconcerned, that many Natives who did not fit the convenient public stereotype were being assaulted by state policies.

Throughout the country, in the 1960s, new hydroelectric developments, pulp mills, and mines were hailed as evidence of Canada's continuing post-war prosperity. "You can't stop progress" was the cliché with which most people answered the fledgling environmental movements that questioned the environmental sustainability of the

Métis leader Jean Cuthand, Malcolm Norris, and Jim Brady at an anti-nuclear demonstration in Regina, April 1961. GAIA PA-2218-943.

new developments. Native people who still had self-sufficient life-styles, and who, despite the impact of the residential schools and other state interference, were not alcoholics, were often victimized by such developments. Where Native hunting and fishing conflicted with "progress," the latter always had state support. Sometimes the Natives were simply ignored and left to fend for themselves in territories suddenly stripped of game and fish; sometimes the Natives were moved to new reserves, usually in areas where there were no longer game or fish for industry to chase away. Some Native leaders were willing to welcome industries into their area, despite the impact on traditional subsistence patterns, if jobs were offered to the First Nations people of the area. Native people were anxious to have job training if they were no longer allowed to live the lives that their ancestors had lived from time immemorial. But most employers, whether for racist or pragmatic reasons, preferred to bring in skilled workers from outside the area, leaving Native people on the outside looking in.

For example, while the building of the St. Lawrence Seaway in the 1950s was a media event for many years, with the focus on the many benefits to both Canadians and Americans in terms of both shipping and hydroelectricity, the Mohawk who were displaced from their homes rarely received a mention. Nor did many people hear the story of the Ojibwa of Grassy Narrows in northwestern Ontario. Once relatively prosperous from commercial fishing and from catering to tourists attracted to their home to fish and hunt, they were removed to a new reserve in 1964 which provided fewer economic prospects. Even these were dashed in 1970, when it was discovered that effluent from the Reed Paper Mill in Dryden had contaminated the English-Wabigoon River system, the source of their water and fish, with mercury. "The closure of the waterway for fishing destroyed the band's fragile economic base, and social problems soon followed economic troubles in a depressing cascade of misery."[2] Though the Ojibwa established, with the aid of Japanese specialists, that mercury poisoning was the cause of Minamata disease, a deadly nervous system and motor disorder, Reed Paper Mill was able to persuade the Ontario government to allow yet another mill to be established in the area in 1976.[3]

The changes in the lives of the Grassy Narrows Ojibwa over a short period of time were dramatic, whether the media noticed or not. A seventy-year-old man could hardly believe the changes he had witnessed over a lifetime:

> On the old reserve, the Indian Agent used to supply us with all the things that we needed to make a living for ourselves — I mean garden tools and seeds, gill nets for fishing, shotgun shells, and things like that. This was good. Why did this stop? Everybody had enough, they could provide for their own potatoes and other vegetables. A lot of families had very good crops, enough to last the winter. They used to build a root house, put straw in it, and keep the vegetables there. People had enough to eat. They didn't need welfare.
> Now we can't make a living for ourselves anymore. The new reserve is on dirt and rock. We can't have gardens ... the fish is poisoned, there are not as many moose and deer ... and our people have to depend on government. This is not good. We used to be a proud and independent people. But everything has changed in my lifetime.[4]

Somewhat more media attention was given in Manitoba to the Natives of South Indian Lake, a relatively wealthy northern community, thanks to the publicity generated by a group of University of Manitoba science professors. They recommended, in 1967, that the provincial government not proceed with a planned hydroelectric dam that would flood the community. The community had no welfare recipients and few alcoholics, and the average family money income from fishing was higher than the average for families in Manitoba, even without considering the considerable non-money income that the community generated from its use of animal resources for subsistence purposes. In the end, however, the lake was flooded and residents of the community were moved south to a new community without an economic base. Inevitably, within a decade, their community was plagued with many of the social problems that beset Native communities in the south and contributed to the facile stereotype of the "drunken Indian."[5]

The despair that many Native people felt was reflected in an outpouring of poems, novels, and autobiographies that began to appear in the late 1960s. Emma LaRocque, a Métis scholar, essayist, and poet, reflected that despair and anger in a 1977 poem entitled "Eulogy for Priscilla," which reads in part:

> You are a thousand of us
> us
> us brown people
> who die by fire
> who die by water
> who die by waterfire
> firewater
> or however —
> we die.
> We excel in death.[6]

But just as Native people like LaRocque were giving voice to their collective sense of injustice, they were also beginning to organize to fight injustice.

The White Paper of 1969

The event that seemed to galvanize Native people was the publication by the Government of Canada of a "White Paper" — the irony was often mentioned by Native spokespersons — on Indian Policy in 1969. The White Paper, prepared for the Indian and Northern Affairs minister, Jean Chrétien, reflected Pierre Trudeau's insensitivity, and indeed hostility, to ethnic nationalism. Just as Trudeau believed that French-Canadian nationalism in Quebec was "tribal" and retrogres-

Jean Chrétien, minister of Indian Affairs, and prime minister Pierre Trudeau, June 1970. NAC PA-170161.

sive in a period when the world was becoming a "global village," he believed that Native people were held back by their segregation from the rest of society. The White Paper correctly identified racial discrimination as a phenomenon that robbed Native people of participation in the larger society. Controversially, however, it suggested that segregation on reserves contributed to the separation of white and Indian that produced stereotypes and made Indians at once wards of the state and pariahs in the larger society. The solution suggested by the White Paper was the gradual elimination of reserves with Native people coming under the jurisdiction of the provinces. The treaties and the Indian Act, products of federal control over Native affairs, were to disappear.[7]

Native people responded furiously to a document which, whatever its good intentions, ignored the desire of Native peoples to retain their identities and to maintain living links between their pasts and their present. At a conference in Winnipeg in June 1969, representatives of the various provincial treaty Native organizations conferred upon the fledgling National Indian Brotherhood the status of a voice for national Native aspirations. Led by the NIB, the Native organizations of Canada let the government and people of Canada know that they considered the "solution" suggested by the White Paper to be a "final solution": while Native people would not be physically destroyed like the Jews of Europe, they would cease to have a true corporate existence. Native people, they argued, wanted change too. But what they wanted were resources and education for their communities, so that they could rise out of poverty. They wanted an end to violations of the treaties, such as the location of industries in areas where they had impact on Native abilities to trap, hunt, and fish. The Native leaders pointed to an extensive study of Native living conditions done for the federal government from 1963 to 1966, headed by University of British Columbia anthropologist Henry Hawthorn, to buttress their case. The Hawthorn Report called for hundreds of millions to be spent to ensure that Natives, whether on reserves or off, enjoyed the same standards of housing, health, and education that other Canadians enjoyed. When the NIB drafted a Red Paper to counter the White Paper, they drew on Hawthorn's notion that Natives in Canada had become "citizens minus," who needed to be treated as "citizens plus" for some time in order that they catch up with average Canadian living standards.[8]

The federal government backed away from the White Paper once it became clear that the firestorm it had provoked would not abate. But it did not embrace the philosophy of the Hawthorn Report, in part because of the costs required to implement Hawthorn's recommendations and, in part, because of a continued desire not to encourage Native nations to be self-assertive. Native successes in the courts may, in the end, have done more to cause a shift in the federal government's position regarding Native issues, than the militancy — mostly verbal in any case — of the official Native leadership.

The Calder decision of the Supreme Court of Canada was particularly important in this regard. Frank Calder, a Nishga chief from British Columbia and long-time CCF-NDP MLA in that province, was one of several Nishga chiefs who asked the Supreme Court of Canada to rule on Native land rights in Canada. The Nishga court effort had begun in the early 1960s, when two Nishga men had been arrested for violating British Columbia's game laws by hunting deer out of season and without a licence. The men argued that they were exercising their rights under a treaty signed with the British in 1854 which gave them unrestricted rights to hunt and fish on unoccupied land. To the delight of the Nishga, all the courts that heard the case, right up to the Supreme Court of Canada, accepted the Natives' argument. The Calder case was a bold follow-up, asking the courts to recognize the Nishga title to a large area of British Columbia. Since they had never renounced their land rights, argued the Nishga, Europeans had no right to occupy these lands without negotiating

Judd Buchanan, Minister of Indian Affairs, joins Charlie Watt, president of the Northern Quebec Inuit Association, to celebrate the signing of the James Bay Agreement, 1975. NAC PA-164787.

terms with the Natives. They used the Royal Proclamation of 1763, which included a section on the rights of Native people after the British Conquest, to defend the view that negotiation was required before a European government operating in former Native territory could lay claim to the land. The British Columbia government argued in the courts that the Royal Proclamation, which mentioned territories that drained into Hudson Bay, did not apply to the coastal province and that provincial legislation had extinguished Native land titles. This time, the province's courts were firmly against the Native position. But when the case made the Supreme Court, six of seven judges agreed that Natives in British Columbia at the time of contact with the Europeans could claim aboriginal land rights. Nevertheless, with one judge abstaining, the remaining judges divided three-three on the pivotal issue of whether provincial legislation could have extinguished such rights.[9]

Pierre Trudeau began to recognize, finally, that Native land claims had legitimacy and could not be treated dismissively. After meeting with Native representatives, he set up mechanisms that would allow Native people to have their day in court to argue their land rights, with some government funds being made available to help them make their case. Native people greeted the establishment of the Office of Native Claims enthusiastically. Within a decade they had staked comprehensive claims to northern Canada and most of British Columbia. But the wheels of justice moved slowly, with only a few celebrated settlements occurring.

One of these was the James Bay and Northern Quebec Agreement in 1974, between the Grand Council of the Crees of Quebec and the Inuit, on the one hand, and the Quebec and federal governments on the other. Premier Robert Bourassa's government had announced a multi-billion dollar hydroelectric project in the James Bay area in 1971, a project that threatened the ruin of the best fishing and trapping areas of the Cree and Inuit of northern Quebec. Only after initial court decisions suggested that the Natives might be able to halt construction of the dams which Hydro-Québec planned to build did the provincial government agree to sit down and negotiate with the Natives. The agreement gave the Natives $225 million in compensation over a twenty-five-year period and exclusive rights to hunt and trap in a large area of northern Quebec. The agreement was and is controversial among Native rights advocates. On the one hand, the compensation monies allowed the Cree and Inuit to build education, health and recreational facilities of benefit to their people. But, on the other, the diminished resources of land and water available once flooding began limited their ability to pursue a traditional lifestyle. With few other sources of employment available in their remote region, many once-independent Natives became dependent on social assistance for survival.[10]

Native Self-Assertion

In the 1970s, Native peoples struggled for their collective and individual rights in various ways. Their political organizations lobbied politicians and filed land claims; some younger Natives seized disputed properties to demonstrate their frustration with the conventional political route which seemed to yield few positive results; community activists forced Indian Affairs and the churches to give Natives control over their own schools; and various individuals wrote books and poems that gave personal accounts of the rage that many Native people felt about their mistreatment by the country in which their ancestors were the first residents. Native women on reserves organized campaigns to encourage individuals or the entire reserve to abstain from alcohol, and pressed both civil servants and band leaders to provide daycare for working mothers and students, while off-reserve Native women worked to win the repeal of the 1869 amendment to the Indian Act that stripped treaty status from Native women (but not men) who married men who were not treaty Indians.

The most publicized land claim pitted the Athapascan-speaking First Nations of the Northwest Territories (often called Dene), and the Métis of the region, against oil companies planning to move northern oil by pipeline to the United States. Aided by local church groups that had adopted the Native cause, the Dene declared themselves a nation within the Canadian nation-state and insisted that the proposed Mackenzie Valley Pipeline could not go ahead in the form proposed by the major oil companies that sponsored the plan. Steps had to be taken to ensure that the Natives' food supply, which the northern habitat still supplied, was not interrupted by the pipeline. Trudeau, leading a minority government dependent on NDP support from late 1972 to the summer of 1974, acceded to an NDP demand for a royal commission to investigate the impact of proposed pipeline projects on the Mackenzie Valley. He placed Justice Thomas Berger of British Columbia, a former leader of the province's NDP and the lawyer for the Natives in the Calder case, in charge of the Commission. Berger travelled through the Territories, talking to hunters, trappers, and fishers in remote communities who explained in detail the ways in which they still maintained a traditional Native way of life, living off "country food" rather than expensive foodstuffs imported from the south. His 1977 report was a sympathetic account of northern Natives' efforts to retain a traditional lifestyle and still maintain links with Canadian society as a whole. He recommended a ten-year moratorium on pipeline development in the Mackenzie Valley to give the Dene and Métis time to work out mutually acceptable arrangements between themselves, and the companies and governments involved in building pipelines.[11] A parallel study of the impact on Natives of the southern Yukon of a proposed Alaskan pipeline by Ken Lysyk proposed a four-year moratorium for the same purpose.

Of course, moratoria simply meant delays and implied that ultimately projects that altered the northern ecology and forced major changes in Native lifestyles would go ahead. But the notion that Natives had some say in the timing and character of development projects was itself a victory, since even a decade earlier profits for southern businesses and jobs for southern workers drove the agenda in northern Canada, with Natives being treated as the white man's garbage to be tossed out whenever it was convenient to the whites.

Both the Dene and the Inuit increasingly began to demand Canadian government recognition for themselves as national entities, albeit national entities pleased to remain within the Canadian Confederation and anxious to participate within Canadian government decision-making. The Dene Declaration of 1975 proclaims:

> We the Dene of the N.W.T. insist on the right to be regarded by ourselves and the world as a nation.
>   What we seek then is independence and self-determination within the country of Canada. This is what we mean when we call for a just land settlement for the Dene Nation.[12]

The Inuit Tapirisat, the product in 1970 of the same ferment among Natives that had produced the NIB just two years earlier, proposed a settlement of Inuit land claims in the Northwest Territories and the Yukon in 1976 that would give Canada's Inuit a homeland that they called Nunavut.

> In brief, the basic idea is to create a Territory, the vast majority of people within which, will be Inuit. As such, this Territory and its institutions will better reflect Inuit values and perspectives than with the present Northwest Territories. The Inuit should have actual control through their voting power, at least for the foreseeable future.[13]

Slowly but surely, the National Indian Brotherhood and other organizations were able to pressure the federal government to set aside the racist (or "paternalist," as some commentators, more comfortable with a milder term, prefer) assumptions that had produced what author Robert Davis angrily labelled *The Genocide Machine in Canada*.[14] Apart from recognizing that Natives had a legitimate right to pursue land claims in the courts, the government began to shift some of Indian Affairs' responsibilities to the bands themselves. In 1973, after lobbying by the NIB, the federal government gave Native bands control over education on reserves. The nightmare of the residential schools came to an end. Social services and services normally provided by municipalities, such as garbage removal and sewage, were also gradually devolved to the bands. Though the legacy of poverty and maltreatment remained, Native people were able more and more to take control of their lives, rather than having interfering Indian Affairs officials tell them what they could and

Sarcee chief Gordon Crowchild opening a snowmobile area at Bragg Creek, Alberta, near Calgary. GAIA, NA-2864-20418a.

could not do. While overall educational attainments of Native people would take time to improve, reserves, with Indian Affairs funds, were able to sponsor literacy and retraining programs for adults and teenagers, and to open university programs. On the Saddle Lake Reserve near Saint Paul, Alberta, for example, band members seized control of the Catholic-run school on the reserve in 1970, rather than let the Church simply close it down when the local children were bused to school in town. By the end of the decade, Blue Quills School on the reserve offered postsecondary programs for First Nations people across the Prairies in arts, education, and administration, in conjunction with the universities in the province. Administrators, teachers, and other professionals who worked on reserves increasingly were graduates of programs such as Blue Quills rather than outsiders sent in by Indian Affairs.

For many Native women, however, these developments, while important, did not strike blows against the subordinate position to which Native women, powerhouses in traditional society, had been relegated during the years when Europeans had imposed their view of the natural hierarchy of the sexes upon Native people. Native men, degraded by the larger society, often dealt with their anger by drinking too much and then assaulting their wives and children. The Indian Act gave the men control over the family home and its possessions while women who fled abusive husbands or were thrown out by them were left with nothing in their efforts to keep themselves and their children alive. Their grim choices were to return to abusive husbands, live with relatives in their overcrowded homes on the reserves, find a condemned house to live in, or to resettle in cities and towns where they might get social assistance but lost their contact with their reserves.

In 1977, the Maliseet women of Tobique Reserve in New Brunswick had had enough of women being evicted from their homes by their husbands with no reaction from Indian Affairs officials. Eva Saulis and Glenna Perley began to organize women to demand changes from the chief and band council. The men were unwilling to listen or act upon the women's complaints and so, on August 4, the women seized control of the band office and continued their occupation for four months. The occupation was marked by occasional violence and divided the community between supporters of the band leadership and supporters of the women. Among the women's staunchest supporters were women who had left the reserve and married non-status males, only to find that the Indian Act thereby stripped them of their Indian status and prevented their return to the reserves. Jeanette Lavell and Yvonne Bedard, two Native women who had married whites and subsequently attempted unsuccessfully

Inuit woman sewing with child, Padlei, Northwest Territories, late 1940s. NAC PA-166823.

to return to their home reserves, tried to get the courts to end such discrimination. Their lawyers argued that the Canadian Bill of Rights passed in 1960, applying to all federal government operations, prohibited discrimination on the basis of gender. But the Supreme Court ruled by five to four in 1973 that the Indian Act superseded the Canadian Bill of Rights.

The Tobique women took the case of Sandra Lovelace, which paralleled that of Lavell and Bedard, to the United Nations in 1977. Four years later, they won a ruling from the UN Human Rights Committee that the International Covenant on Civil and Political Rights, of which Canada was a signatory, forbids the kind of discrimination Canada was practising against Native women. It would not be until 1985 however, that Parliament, after a cross-party caucus of all the women members of Parliament demanded it, agreed to remove the offending clause from the Indian Act.[15]

The Tobique women finally got promises of houses from the band administration. Their efforts also helped to mobilize both veterans and elderly people who had been having difficulty getting the band administration to give them funds to make repairs to dilapidated dwellings. The Tobique women then organized a Native Women's Walk to Ottawa in July 1979, where they confronted the federal government with the poor living conditions that Native people generally faced, with emphasis on the plight of women and children. The

Clark government gave them $300,000 for housing, though it would not act on their request to reinstate treaty status to Native women who had married off-reserve.

While the leaders of the NIB and the provincial Native federations were increasingly vocal in their criticism of government treatment of Native people, the Tobique women were hardly alone among Native people in suggesting that their leaders were bureaucrats who were not looking out for the interests of Native people. The federal government, anxious to co-opt the Native leadership, funded the NIB and its provincial wings. Many Native leaders seemed to understand the bargain with the "feds" as one in which they were to limit their criticisms to broad generalities. For example, David Courchene, leader of the Manitoba Indian Brotherhood, was always available to provide the media with clichés about the history of European exploitation of Natives. But Natives who wanted to expose the horrible working and living conditions of the Native workers in Manitoba's sugar beet fields found Courchene unwilling to participate in their campaign.[16]

While the plight of the Manitoba sugar beet workers and of many other Native groups still only vaguely touched the consciousness of most Canadians, some Natives were publishing works that exposed the precarious lives of their people. Harold Cardinal's angry tract against the White Paper, *The Unjust Society*, appeared in 1969, and became the first of many works to appear by a people whom publishers had largely shunned.[17] George Manuel, a Shuswap who played a key role in organizing British Columbia Natives and served as president of the NIB for a period during the seventies, published *The Fourth World* in 1974. Canadian Natives, he explained, lived in virtual Third World conditions, within a country whose wealth made it easily a member of the First World of industrialized capitalist nations. This anomaly made them part of a fourth world which existed in many First World countries: an aboriginal group that was despised and marginalized, and allowed neither to live as it had in pre-contact times nor to share in the wealth of the conquering European society.[18]

If George Manuel spoke for male status Indians, Maria Campbell, whose best-seller, *Halfbreed*, appeared in 1973, spoke eloquently for Métis and non-status Indian women. She described a life of poverty, racism, alcoholism, beatings by a drunken white husband, prostitution, her unsuccessful struggle to hold together her birth family after her mother's death, and finally her efforts both to put her own life back together and to work with Métis organizations to fight for social justice for Native people.[19]

While the degree of success that Native struggles achieved in the 1960s and 1970s is debatable, it is clear that Canada's first peoples had learned to work together to pressure the Canadian authorities to end their long campaign to destroy the Natives' separate identity and economic independence. If Canadians, and particularly corporations that were enriching themselves at Native expense, were not necessarily prepared to accede to Native demands for a huge land base, most no longer believed the "cowboy" version of North American history in which Natives were "savages" whom "civilized" Europeans had to defeat and marginalize so that "progress" would not be impeded.

Naskapi painted caribou skin, collected in the 1740s. MC III-B-588; S75-383

Eleven

The Salience of Class

To Canadians living in the second half of the century, gender, race, and ethnicity continued to matter in determining an individual's life chances. Increasingly, in the 1960s and 1970s, they also became an important component of an individual's political identity and defined much of the public policy debate in Canada. At times, the focus on gender and ethnicity on the one hand, and the politicians' propaganda about growing prosperity for all on the other, obscured the class divisions that had always been at the heart of Canadian society. It was not that the class composition of Canada was unchanging, or that membership in a particular social class, such as the working class, had an eternal meaning. But it remained the case that much about people's lives related to their position within the economy. While Canada was a political democracy, its economy was not controlled by the common consent of the governed. For the most part, it was controlled by corporations and individuals operating in the marketplace. They were usually subject to government regulations, but the economically powerful had had a large hand in drawing up most of them. Individuals who did not own or manage companies worked for those who did, unless they had a profession or trade that allowed them to operate independently. The widespread foreign ownership of the economy discussed in Chapter Six was simply one indication of the extent to which average Canadians did not control their economic destiny.

Over two-thirds of Canadian taxpayers worked for an employer rather than for themselves, and many of the remaining third were only nominally self-employed, working as sub-contractors or *de facto* sub-contractors for major employers who nonetheless did not put them on the permanent payroll. Small-boat fishers, for example, did "not operate under formal subordination," but capital had achieved command over them "through control over the products of their labour and over the sources of capital, equipment, and supplies."[1] Nova Scotia fishers fought a long battle in the 1970s to get recognition as workers eligible to form unions, rather than self-employed business people forced to deal with the large processors as individuals. Mac's Milk operators in Ontario won similar recognition from the courts as *de facto* employees rather than independent managers. But most operators of chain stores and sub-contractors in the construction and garment trades, the latter often simply exploited home workers making less than minimum wage, were beyond the reach of unions. Many were afraid of losing their franchises or employment if they organized, while many others regarded themselves as indeed self-employed and did not want to have a union representing them as they struggled to make a living.

While almost two Canadian workers in five belonged to unions in 1980, the three in five who did not were often subject to harsh regimes under stern employers. Even unionized workers faced a hostile political environment during strikes that gave the edge to their employers. Unionization had become more prevalent among public-sector workers than private-sector workers. Even in Alberta, where only sixteen percent of private-sector workers held union cards, seventy-nine percent of public-sector workers were organized. The low rate of private-sector trade unionism in Alberta was partly the result of the fact that most private-sector employers ran small enterprises. Indeed, fifty-one percent of the provincial labour force worked in firms with less than twenty employees.[2] It was difficult to organize in such firms, since union sympathizers feared being singled out by an employer who generally knew them, and then being ostractized and perhaps fired. The Alberta Labour Relations Board had established a reputation for being pro-employer in cases where workers accused management of dismissing employees for union activity.[3]

An individual's race or gender was a limiting factor on where she or he might end up within the economy. But whatever advantages a white male of Anglo-Saxon descent might have statistically over other Canadians in becoming a member of the corporate elite, most white male Anglos, like Canadians as a whole, were not part of that elite. Most were either working class or lower middle class, though within these social groupings they were likely to have a higher status and a higher income than other members. Neither of these social classes was, in any case, homogeneous. There was a decrease in the number of traditional blue-collar jobs that once had defined the "working class" in terms of "male breadwinners" who were neither professionals nor self-employed. White-collar jobs, both in the public sector and the private service sector, took up much of the slack, but not all of it. The average rate of unemployment, which had been below four percent in the late sixties, had reached 8.5 percent in 1977–8. By then, one in every five adult employees worked less than twenty hours per week. Part of the explanation for this was that many workers were mothers of young children. But surveys suggested that many mothers in part-time work, particularly of school-age children, would prefer full-time employment if it was available and if affordable, quality daycare was available.

In the 1960s, the relative availability of jobs emboldened Canadian workers to demand what they considered a fairer share of the economic pie. Strikes in both the private and public sectors, sporadic in the equally prosperous fifties, became more common. Commentators suggested that while workers who had experienced the Depression had been satisfied with the modest wage increases their employers offered in the fifties, the younger workers entering the job market in the sixties measured employers' offers on a different scale. Never having experienced the Depression and unafraid of losing their jobs in a booming economy, they expected to receive a significant share of a company's earnings and asked questions that their parents had not about the relative distribution of such earnings among profits, dividends, salaries, perquisites for managers, and workers' wages.[4] By the late sixties, Canada had the second highest rate of days lost per worker through strikes in the industrialized capitalist countries, led only slightly by Italy where the Communist Party was the dominant force in trade union politics. The media were forever reporting on the inconveniences caused for the public by strikes by postal workers, longshoremen, and railway workers, as well as the economic losses from strikes by steelworkers, forest workers, and autoworkers. Trade union leaders denounced such reports, citing figures that noted that ninety-five percent of trade union contracts in Canada were negotiated without a strike occurring. Yet the federal government, concerned that national and international investors were chafing about the restiveness of Canada's workers, appointed a task force on industrial relations in 1966 with Dean H.D. Woods of McGill University as chair. Woods recommended greater use of federal government arbitration services, and better consultation procedures between management and labour. But the 1970s were as restive on the industrial front as the 1960s, perhaps more so, because public-sector workers were more militantthan they had ever been before. Also, as the low rates of inflation of the fifties and sixties were replaced by double-digit inflation, workers whose incomes had been eroded by inflation entered negotiations with employers for new contracts with the express intention of getting back their losses and staying ahead of inflation in the year to come. Longer-term contracts, desirable during the years of low and predictable inflation, became harder to achieve because neither management nor labour was certain about the economic future. Some employers agreed to "Cost of Living Adjustment" (COLA) clauses in order to get longer-term contracts and enjoy some stability on the labour front; many others settled for one-year contracts and tried on an annual basis to compel workers to accept a wage and benefits increase that did not match the increase in the cost of living.

Workers' militancy did not necessarily imply disillusionment with the prevailing economic system, and the vote for the New Democratic Party, labour's political arm, was never greater than twenty percent in a federal election in the sixties or seventies. Certainly, a sub-set of workers, including many union leaders and the leaders of the "wildcat" strikes of the period — strikes unauthorized by union officialdom — supported some form of socialist organization of the Canadian economy. But much of the rank-and-file simply wanted better wages, shorter hours, and safer workplaces. They believed that strikes, rather than their votes, were the means to win such results, and were hostile or indifferent to attempts to link trade union struggles with ideological battles. Though social solidarity in workplaces and in working-class communities was still important, many workers had bought into the consumerist model of citizenship that media messages embodied: individuals were to see themselves and their families simply as human consumption functions rather than human beings rooted in particular communities and class identities.

The individualist ethic that often lay behind collective actions by workers was cold comfort to private employers who were unwilling to let their rates of profit drop, or to public employers who did not want to face the question of who should be taxed to pay more for public servants' wages. As we have seen in Chapter Five, public policies from the mid-1970s focussed less on job creation than on controlling inflation. For many conservative (including Liberal) politicians, "controlling inflation" and reducing wage increases below the increase in the cost of living, that is redistributing wealth to employers, were synonymous. That meant assaulting the expectation of unionized workers that if wages were not keeping pace with the cost of living, they would strike to win back their losses and even try to make some gains. The combination of monetary policies that produced job losses[5] and enforced maximums for wage increases (during the period 1975–8) was arguably little more than class legislation designed to put workers back in their place. Of course, the Trudeau government claimed that these were measures to improve economic performance as a whole and therefore of benefit to the entire Canadian people. But this ignored the underlying notion of "economic performance," one in which capital received greater returns. It could do so only at labour's expense. By the end of the seventies, strikes had become rare and the trade union movement faced a crisis. We look now at Canada's trade union movement in the sixties and seventies and its strengths and weaknesses.

The Trade Union Movement

On the surface, it might appear that strikes were the method used by most workers to get their wage increases in the 1960s and 1970s. In 1966, for example, 410,000 workers staged 617 strikes that cost employers 5 million worker days.[6] But during the 1960s and 1970s, over half of the person days lost and over two-thirds of the drawn-out labour disputes were accounted for by workers in six industries that together employed less than fifteen percent of Canadian workers. The industries were construction, mining and smelting, transportation equipment manufacturing, primary metals manufacture, and the wood products industry.[7] These were industries that were almost completely unionized. They were also, with the partial exception of the construction industry, "capital-intensive," that is, the amount of capital equipment deployed per worker was high. Workers in such industries had a stronger negotiating position because employers lost a great deal of money by letting their capital sit idle. Employers had a greater incentive to settle with their workers than employers in "labour-intensive" industries for whom idle capital was less of an issue. Capital-intensive employers were also, of course, able to produce more product per worker and were thus in a better position to buy labour peace than industries whose competitive advantage depended mainly upon cheap labour. Since the costs of entry into capital-intensive sectors were higher, there were often only a few companies in an industry and therefore a greater likelihood of success for both unions and management groupings to achieve a degree of co-operation.

Militant workers sometimes regarded the highly paid, well-groomed union leaders as labour bureaucrats in bed with management and uninterested in the views from the shop floor. While an agreement was in force, unions were required not to strike. Contracts generally dealt with a small range of issues affecting working conditions, leaving most areas of discretion regarding organization of the workplace and discipline of employees in the hands of owners and managers. Union leaders generally upheld their part of the bargain, insisting that workers use the grievance procedure when employers violated their rights under the agreement. Many workers found that this procedure was drawn out and that management's rights generally prevailed over workers' rights.[8]

The result was that many of the strikes of the late sixties and of the seventies were neither sanctioned nor led by the official union leadership. They were illegal industrial actions generally led by younger workers. Some of these rank-and-file leaders were Communists, or supporters of other left-wing groups such as the Waffle within the NDP; others were simply rebels with a cause: greater justice for workers. The younger members of the labour force of this period were more educated than their parents and less likely to hold managers and owners in awe. While most simply wanted to be treated with a degree of dignity, radicals regarded the hierarchical structure of industry itself to be a problem. They preached workers' control of industry, and since such control was incompatible with private ownership of industry, they called for public control of big companies. This "New Left" philosophy influenced, for example, the views of the Waffle group. Its overall importance among workers was hard to gauge, but it had considerable purchase with the rank-and-file leaders. Even for many non-radicals among younger workers, the arbitrary practices of management offended notions of fairness; they did not accept the views of many of their parents that it would be better to turn the other cheek. In 1965–6 alone, wildcat strikes accounted for twenty to thirty percent of all strikes. They left capitalists and trade union leaders alike shaking their heads about what was becoming of young people today (memories of the strikes of the wartime and early post-war period often having grown dim). But the wildcats sometimes forced trade union leaders to be more militant, and capitalists to make more concessions than they might have made if they were dealing only with the more pliable, established union leaders.[9]

Some companies chose not only to ignore the complaints that led to wildcats but to follow policies that would let workers know that the price of a wildcat would be even worse working conditions and more rigid supervision. Labour educator and former Ford assembly-line worker Don Wells noted that Ford in the sixties had a policy of refusing to carry on negotiations with union leaders during a big walk-out of workers until the workers returned to their jobs. The return to work was usually accompanied by announcements from management of "a large number of firings and suspensions following which union leaders negotiate lesser and less-numerous penalties." Characteristically, the return to work also meant that "supervision generally grew harsher, speedup accelerated, and there were long hours of compulsory overtime during which workers stayed on the job ten and twelve hours a day, six and sometimes even seven days a week."[10]

Militancy in the public sector, almost unknown in Canada after the general strikes of 1919, revived in the late sixties and became commonplace in the seventies. Groups such as nurses, teachers, civil servants, and postal workers, once seen as faithful servants of the public with no demands to make, began to insist that they too were workers who had families to support and rights to protect. The strikes by nurses and teachers announced, as we saw in Chapter Nine, that women workers were no longer willing to accept the public pretence that a woman worked only for extras and could (or wanted to) rely on a husband or a father for income.

Public-sector workers accounted for the growth in "union density," the percentage of workers in unions, in the sixties and seventies. In 1958, as the economy dipped into recession, 34.2 percent of Canadian employees belonged to a union, and most of these workers were in the private sector. In 1963, as the economy came out of recession, only 29.4 percent of workers still had unions, reflecting both job losses in unionized industries and the ability of owners to scare workers out of organizing during hard times. By 1982, just as the worst recession since the Great Depression began, thirty-nine percent of workers were organized.[11] But the percentage increase was largely the result of public service sector organizing, as attempts to organize the rest of the private sector faltered. That year, five of the ten largest unions in the country were public-sector unions. The biggest was the Canadian Union of Public Employees, which represented mainly municipal and hospital workers. With 275,000 members, CUPE had tripled its membership since the early sixties. This growth reflected the expansion of the municipal and hospital sectors in this period. By contrast the largest private-sector union, the United Steelworkers of America, though it had enjoyed growth since the early 1960s, had fallen from first place among unions to third, with about 180,000 members.[12]

While municipal employees had a long history of organizing, provincial government employees before the 1960s had largely been forbidden from organizing. Only in Saskatchewan, where the CCF government had granted its employees the right to unionize shortly after taking office in 1944, did provincial employees enjoy a civil right that all provincial governments granted to private-sector workers within their jurisdiction by the late forties. This changed in the 1960s, as provincial government employees' associations campaigned to have the same rights to negotiate for their members as any other workers' organization. Provincial governments, fearing wildcat strikes of their direct employees and of hospital workers, granted the principle of unionism while trying to hem in the rights of these public workers. "Essential services" legislation limited the right to strike to workers not deemed essential to the maintenance of public health and public order, leaving the state alone to decide without union input whose labour was essential. It often meant that provincial workers' strikes had minimal impact, since the managers who replaced strikers along with the essential workers could keep operations running at a minimally acceptable level for a period long enough to discourage strikers from continuing their industrial action.[13] Nonetheless, by 1982, the National Union of Provincial Government Employees, a loose coalition of provincial unions outside of Quebec, counted 230,000 members and successful provincial government employee strikes had occurred in several provinces.

Rounding out the five public service unions in the top ten were the Public Service Alliance, a union only formed in 1967 (and the largest organization of federal employees), and two Quebec unions: the Social Affairs Federation of the Confederation of National Trade Unions; and the Quebec Teachers' Congress. The PSA was the country's fourth largest union, while the two largest Quebec public service unions ranked ninth and tenth. Federal employees, like their provincial counterparts, had been denied the right to strike before the 1960s. A series of wildcats in 1965 and 1966, denounced by the union leaders, demonstrated the ineffectiveness of such a ban. The federal government therefore legalized strikes by its workers and established a Public Service Staff Relations Board to negotiate union contracts and attempt to head off strikes. Like provincial workers, the federal workers won only half a loaf, since the government gave itself the right to designate certain workers as essential. Non-essential workers, however, had the right to choose between striking and arbitration to settle disputes after 1967.

Among federal workers' unions, the most militant was the Canadian Union of Postal Workers. At that time, the organization comprised only inside postal workers. The Letter Carriers Union also had several strikes, but CUPW was the *bête noire* of Post Office management. Its members fought a protracted, but unsuccessful, battle to save jobs as mechanical sorting was introduced in the early seventies, and then fought equally bitter battles against management's efforts to wring every ounce out of the workers that went as far as using mechanical spying on sorters when they went to the washroom.[14] Led by militants like Presidents Joe Davidson and Jean-Claude Perrot, CUPW stood in contrast with many other unions where the leaders seemed more interested in presenting themselves as "labour statesmen" to impress management and government, than in fighting management on behalf of the workers.

Joe Morris, president of the CLC at the time the Trudeau government introduced wage controls in 1975, was one of these labour statesmen. Though he opposed the imposition of wage controls, particularly since, as Trudeau had earlier admitted, the accompanying price controls could not be implemented as effectively in a foreign-dominated economy, he opposed militant action to protest the controls. Eventually, the CLC did agree to a one-day general strike in October 1976 in which about a million Canadian workers participated.

Morris was mainly interested in pursuing a tripartite system of economic planning in Canada in which government, employers, and union officials would work together. While Trudeau expressed a brief, hazy interest in such an idea, it soon became apparent that the business community liked things pretty much as they were, and the government had no intention of imposing a straitjacket on the operations of business. Within the trade union movement, there was a general suspicion that labour would be treated as a rather junior partner in any tripartite system acceptable to government and business. Labour might then be blamed by its members for acquiescing in decisions that benefited capital at workers' expense. Radicals believed that an unfettered right to strike was workers' best defence against the assault on their rights by capital and the state, and suspected that Morris' target was as much the wildcat as the right of management to do as it pleased. In any case, by the end of the seventies, the tripartite idea had been blown away. Apart from support for the NDP, a party increasingly dominated by middle-class professionals, the labour movement lacked a political vision. The NDP's credibility, even with conservative labour officials, suffered when the three NDP provincial governments, though progressive in other respects, sided with Trudeau and imposed wage controls in the fall of 1975.[15]

Trade Unions and Nationalism

The growth of the public service unions tipped the balance in the Canadian Labour Congress away from the American unions that once had dominated the House of Labour in Canada. Also adding to the growing Canadianization of the union movement were breakaways from American unions. Complaints that the American headquarters were taking more money out of Canada than they were giving back in services had long been heard in many Canadian branches of American unions. In the nationalist environment of the early seventies, this often led to efforts to make the Canadian section of the union an independent union without formal ties to its American counterpart. In 1971, the Communications Workers of Canada; in 1974, the Canadian Papermakers' Union; and in 1975, the Canadian Brewery Workers Union were formed as breakaways from American unions. All remained active in the CLC.

But the impetus for breakaways had come from outside the CLC. A number of small breakaways had occurred during the sixties, particularly among moulders and machinists in Manitoba. Kept out of the CLC, the breakaways of the sixties united in 1969 to form a rival, if rather small, union central called the Congress of Canadian Unions. The CCU raided Steelworkers' locals in British Columbia and Moulders' and Machinists' locals in Manitoba, and was denounced by the CLC for splitting the ranks of labour. In practice, it may have kept established unions on their feet, and no doubt precipitated some decisions of unions to break away from their parent unions when the American headquarters proved hostile to demands for greater autonomy for Canadian union locals. For unions such as the Steelworkers and Autoworkers, which remained tied to American headquarters, it forced even conservative union leaders to insist on greater autonomy for the Canadian section within the international union as the price of preventing breakaways.

The construction trade unions, whose Washington headquarters were unwilling to yield to demands for Canadian locals to be treated

any differently than American locals, were unhappy with this nationalist trend. Canadian nationalism vis-à-vis the United States seemed
a particularly potent threat when it united with Quebec nationalism
to exclude the American construction unions from the Quebec scene
altogether. A royal commission in Quebec established that the international unions had used tactics of intimidation to prevent Quebec
workers from joining the construction worker wing of the Confederation of National Trade Unions. The Quebec Federation of Labour,
sensing that the construction unions affiliated with them might be
lost to the CNTU altogether as the Quebec government and the
workers reacted to the suggestion that the international unions were
behaving thuggishly, moved to assert its own control over the construction locals. When the independent Canadian unions in the CLC
supported this move, the international unions in construction pulled
their 200,000 Canadian members out of the Congress in 1981, and
formed their own conservative federation, the Canadian Federation
of Labour.

The spirited new Canadian unions made efforts to organize small,
labour-intensive manufacturers that the CLC unions had largely ignored because the costs of fighting manufacturers who depended
upon low wages and poor working conditions for their profits was
so much greater than the cost of organizing capital-intensive employers. CCU leaders Kent Rowley and Madeleine Parent, who had a
long history of leading workers' struggles — they had been jailed by
Duplessis for their work on behalf of the United Textile Workers —
had been Red-baited out of the mainstream labour movement, and
had helped to form the Canadian Textile and Chemical Union
(CTCU). In 1971, Rowley and Parent, who were ardent nationalists,
led a strike by workers at Texpack in Brantford. The 300 or so
strikers were production workers, many of them women, whose
American employer planned to phase out production work at their
Brantford facility and turn the Canadian operation into simply a
warehouse to distribute products from the American and Asian
branches of the firm. Rowley and Parent involved a variety of CCU
and CLC unions, the women's movement, the Waffle group, and
other left-wingers and nationalists in the struggle to maintain these
jobs. While the company attempted to keep production going with
replacement workers, the strikers and their supporters tried to prevent
this scab-operated company from breaking the strike, blocking entry
to the factory's gate with a huge line of picketers. But the company
had the state on its side, and the police battled the picketers, arresting

large numbers daily, often roughing up those whom they arrested. In the end, faced with negative publicity and disruption of production, the company relented and signed a contract that maintained the production jobs within Canada for the rest of the decade.[16]

Such a happy ending did not occur in other CCU-led strikes. In Toronto in 1973, the CTCU's attempts to win decent contract provisions for the immigrant labour force of Artistic Woodworkers, a picture-frame manufacturer, also featured police-labour confrontations and police brutality. Artistic eventually signed a contract with the union that promised the workers much of what they wanted. But when the picket lines were gone and the workers were back in the factory, management and foremen harassed union activists, called for an official decertification vote, and persuaded a majority of the workers, many of whom spoke little English and feared the loss of their jobs, to vote against the union. The company once again had complete control over workers' work conditions.[17]

A similar unhappy ending awaited the workers at Griffin Foundry in Winnipeg. Though many of the workers were well advanced in years, the company expected them to work compulsory overtime. The union, a CCU member called the Canadian Association of Industrial, Mechanical and Allied Workers (CAIMAW), called a strike in 1976 in which working conditions, including compulsory overtime, played a large role. To the chagrin of many who expected better from an NDP government, the Schreyer government refused either to legislate against the use of replacement workers by companies whose workers were on strike, or to legislate against compulsory overtime. We look now at how workers were treated by employers in this period.

On the Job

The incomes and the working conditions of Canadian workers varied from industry to industry and region to region and, as we have seen, race, ethnicity, and gender affected what sorts of jobs were available to individuals. For immigrant women, the conditions of employment and living that were available often resembled Third World conditions more than North American norms. Native workers were, like immigrants, often offered none of the protections that labour laws supposedly provided to all working Canadians. Unionized workers often earned far more than exploited immigrant women, Native, and African-Canadian workers, all of whom were under-represented

within the ranks of unionists. Many unionized workers lived in suburban homes, owned nice cars, and could afford such luxuries as
annual vacations, household gadgetry, and music lessons or enrol-
ment in sporting leagues for their children. If they remained with the
same employer for a long period, they could look forward to a
reasonably generous pension upon retirement. The "affluent worker,"
as some sociologists described these mainly male members of the
labour force, and the "middle-class worker," as some journalists
described him, defining class on the basis of consumer power rather
than the kind of work one performed, seemed to have it made.

But what was life like at the apex of the blue-collar economic
pyramid? The lives of metal miners suggested that, while the picture
of the affluent worker was not totally wrong, it was one-dimensional.
The average miner earned $9,298 in pay and $822 in employer-paid
benefits in 1972, compared to only $7,595 and $741 for the average
worker in manufacturing the year earlier.[18] Yet mining families did
not necessarily have greater purchasing power than households
where one worker was employed in manufacturing. Mining towns
were isolated, and many of the job ghettoes that provided urban
women with employment were simply unavailable to miners' wives.
In Thompson, Manitoba, in 1970, for example, 8.5 percent of the
labour force was composed of women against a national average of
over forty percent.[19] A miner's wife, whether she wished to work
outside the home or not, rarely had the option and had to accept the
economic dependence on a husband that many Canadian women
were anxious to escape. The remoteness of mining towns and their
domination by a single mining company often also meant a higher
cost of living than Canadians in bigger cities with a diversity of
industries experienced. This did not mean that a steadily employed
miner was deprived of many of the amenities that consumption-ori-
ented sociologists regarded as the trappings of middle-class life. It
simply meant that the metal miners were not as well off as the raw
statistics of their wages might suggest they were.

The work life of the metal miners, however, exposed the hollowness of the claim that these men were "middle class," living lives
somehow undifferentiated from those of university professors, doctors, and owners of small businesses. In fact, they faced constant
danger on the job. They faced ten times the likelihood of dying on
the job as workers in manufacturing. In Ontario from 1970 to 1975,
almost one in ten suffered an injury of significant enough proportions
to qualify them for workmen's compensation.[20] No wonder then that

single men often left mining jobs after a short period. In 1973, a mining industry study indicated that the turnover rate of skilled miners was a whopping 127.8 percent, five or six times the rate of other categories of employees of the industry. The turnover rate was four times greater for single miners than married ones, the latter proving more willing to face the dangers and discomforts of their jobs because mining employment yielded a reasonable family income. In Sudbury, where a large percentage of the miners were married men, the turnover rate was far below the national average for that industry.

The United Steelworkers described the conditions for underground workers that caused so many miners to give up high-paying jobs if they did not have families dependent upon their wages.

> ... underground rock that is frequently described as "solid" but which in fact is constantly in varying states of flux and change; total absence of natural light; working with heavy equipment which for the most part is designed for maximum efficiency, and not for the protection of the workers using it; the use of high explosives, high noise levels, air concussions, etc. ... hygienic, sanitary and health dangers arising from dusts, gases, fog, oils, deep holes, falling rock (loose), runs of muck (broken ores), slippery and unsure footing, and in some instances (as in Elliot Lake) ionizing radiation.[21]

An example of equipment designed for efficiency rather than worker protection was the scooptram. Operators of the scooptrams tended to develop back injuries within three or four years of operating the machine. Others developed respiratory diseases from the vehicles' diesel fumes. Though the cabs could be enclosed so that the operator was not bouncing around and had clean air, the cost would have been about $10,000 per scooptram and INCO resisted spending the money.[22]

The impact of mining companies was felt not only by the metal miner, but by his family and by community residents generally. In Sudbury, for example, a federal government study pinpointed the mining companies for sulphur dioxide emissions that cost the community mightily in damages to health, property, and vegetation. The study placed an annual figure of $465.9 million on the losses, though, obviously, deterioration of personal health and of the environment are not easy to measure in monetary terms. In 1970, the Ontario government ordered INCO to reduce its emissions by half, but INCO balked at the order, claiming that the clean-up would be too expensive, and the government relented.[23] In the 1970s environmentalist campaigns made the general public aware that sulphur dioxide emissions contributed to the creation of acid rain, which was destroying lakes. Eventually, such campaigns would force governments to compel industry to reduce emissions. But, significantly, the fact that such emissions were harmful to workers in mines and to residents of mining communities was not a good enough argument for forcing emission controls. The power of the companies was simply too great and that of working-class communities too weak.

The health of workers destroyed by industrial greed was hardly a hot news topic in the sixties and seventies, when the media were busily portraying unionized workers as affluent middle-class consumers whose work lives were somehow irrelevant even if half of their waking hours were spent on the job. Some academic accounts, however, painted a grimmer portrait. In 1975 for example, sociologist Elliott Leyton published a study of two Newfoundland fluorspar-mining company towns where miners were dying slow, painful deaths from silicosis or lung cancer. "One household in every three has a dead or dying miner in St. Lawrence and Lawn," noted Leyton.[24]

Once poor fishing villages, St. Lawrence and Lawn had welcomed the arrival of the American-owned St. Lawrence Corporation in 1933. But somewhere between five and ten years after they started working in the mines, the young men of these villages began to contract silicosis or lung cancer. For years the provincial workers' compensation board denied or minimized the relationship between their illnesses and the environmental conditions associated with the mine.

Such denials were hardly limited to Newfoundland. In 1974, the CBC radio program "As It Happens" carried several stories about a provincial health official in Ontario who was fired for going public about the damage that a lead plant in a poor area of eastern Toronto was inflicting, both upon the workers and upon children in a residential area near the plant. The official cited statistics that demonstrated the local children were lethargic and scored the lowest of any area in the city on IQ tests.

If workers in the mines and forests traded their health and safety for the trappings of a middle-class life, workers in other sectors often risked their health and safety for pittances because they had little option to do otherwise. In the late seventies, it was estimated that as many as a hundred thousand illegal immigrants toiled in Canada, mainly in sweatshops in Toronto and Montreal. For less than the minimum wage, immigrants, mainly women, worked in poorly ventilated firms with few pollution controls. These included, in addition to the traditionally exploitative textile and clothing sectors, chemical and plastics manufacturers, abattoirs, and restaurants.[25] Others worked by the piece in their own homes. Waged farmworkers, among whom immigrants, both legal and illegal, dominated the work force, also lived and worked in miserable conditions, and were specifically excluded from minimum wage laws in most provinces. In southern Ontario, about 50,000 farmworkers were employed each year, most of them being provided with work for only part of the year. Their working and living conditions were described by a federal task force as Dickensian.

For example, one Mexican family lived in "almost indescribable squalor." Noted the task force:

> A stove pipe led from the stove through the roof. Wrapped around the pipe at the roof intersection were layers of cardboards and newspaper to keep the rain out. The place was literally a death trap if a fire ever broke out ... and there is only one door.[26]

There were seven children in this family with an eighth on the way. All seven had at least one hernia.

Domestic workers, almost exclusively women and mainly Third World immigrants, were as unprotected by labour legislation as farmworkers. Immigrant women's organizations complained that the situation of domestics had changed little during the twentieth century. Many domestics were expected to be at the beck and call of their employers seven days a week, twenty-four hours a day, and to do virtually any house chore imaginable. In return, they received pay rates well below the legislated minimum wage for other workers, and often lived in dingy basement accommodations in spacious homes. For such women, the illusion of living in a society where almost everyone was middle-class and had similar abilities to consume was impossible to sustain. Indeed, beginning in 1973, the majority of immigrant domestics and farmworkers in Canada were provided only temporary work permits, a signal that the Canadian government regarded them as only temporary sojourners in Canada, to be avail-

Members of INTERCEDE, a Toronto-based advocacy group for domestic workers' rights, lobbying against proposed changes to the immigration program in 1991. INT.

able for exploitation by wealthy Canadians for a period, and then dismissed from the country.[27]

Class Identity

Though close study of the working and home lives of Canada's working people suggests that the view that most Canadians had become "middle class" is simplistic, there is little doubt that a combination of greater prosperity and media messages convinced many workers that they were indeed members of the middle class. Nonetheless, far more Canadians than Americans identified themselves readily as working class or poor when asked by a pollster in the early eighties to indicate to which social class they belonged: twenty-eight percent of all Canadians and only nine percent of Americans. The pollsters then provided a range of choices to those who could not provide an answer to this question on the first go-round. This pushed up the percentage of working-class and poor identifiers in the United States to twenty-eight percent and Canada's percentage to thirty-five percent.[28]

The greater readiness of Canadians to regard themselves as members of the working class or as members of the poverty class than Americans no doubt does much to explain why militancy has been more common here than in the United States. It has also provided a political space for the NDP, a party which has no counterpart in the

United States where only two parties, the Republicans and Democrats, both fairly conservative — though the Democrats are generally more liberal — have mattered much in electoral contests since World War I. The old-line parties, in turn, have been forced to be more liberal in Canada than in the United States, partly because they are dealing with an electorate in which a significant minority are self-consciously not middle class, and are unlikely to support political parties that do not embrace social programs.

Prosperity's Complaints

The growing militancy of working people, women, Native peoples, and ethnic (particularly visible) minorities in the 1960s and 1970s demonstrated that many Canadians felt a sense of grievance even if the nation's wealth was growing continuously. The distribution of that wealth, the environmental consequences of a "growth ethic," and the denial of involvement in economic and political decisions to certain groups became increasingly important issues in Canadian life. As Part Three demonstrates, such issues would create even more heated divisions within Canadian society in the eighties and nineties as the post-war period of continuous economic growth came decisively to an end.

Part Three

The Centre Cannot Hold:
Canada Since 1980

Twelve

Neo-Conservative Times

The period of post-war economic growth had come to an end by the late seventies. By 1980, "stagflation," with its combination of negligible economic growth, high unemployment, and high inflation seemed to have become a nearly permanent feature of the economies of Canada and most of the other Western nations. The Right proclaimed that Keynesian economic policies were a failure, and that the huge edifice of government programs meant to stimulate either the economy as a whole or specific industries, or to transfer monies to individuals as a matter of entitlement or because of need, was collapsing in on itself. Extensive government regulation of industry meant to assure fair practices for consumers, protection of the environment, safety for workers, and other such objectives had straitjacketed capitalists. The world economy was, therefore, slowing down, and the Canadian economy, suffering from allegedly excessive political interference, was performing less well than other industrial countries such as Japan, West Germany, or the United States.

The Left and the centre, which in 1980 might arguably include between them the NDP, a large section of the Liberal Party, trade unionists, and most government-employed professionals, was caught by surprise at the sudden re-emergence of respectability for *laissez-faire* ideas. Suddenly notions such as minimum wages, guaranteed pensions, social assistance and environmental controls were in disrepute as organized groups of businesspeople, accountants, professional managers, and corporate lawyers attacked government "red tape" as a fetter on the economic growth the country supposedly needed.

Though big business led the attack on state apparatuses that it lamented had grown too elephantine, state funds were often being spent mainly on behalf of private corporations. They would not willingly establish plants in poor regions, but they gladly accepted federal and provincial grants designed to lure them to such areas. Defence-related industries fought for and won federal subsidies de-

Parliament Hill in winter. NAC PA-168020.

signed to modernize and boost exports of their socially destructive products.[1] Large firms lined up for grants to enhance their technologies or to ease the terms of repayment of their debts. Multi-national oil companies welcomed governments as cash-rich partners in mega-projects. Huge financial companies saw nothing wrong with the federal government guaranteeing home loans that made these companies a large profit.

The voices of the precursors of the neo-conservatives in the sixties and seventies had fallen on deaf ears as they preached the dangers of state intervention in the marketplace and the taxation burden on industry of social programs. The economy overall seemed to be a success. Most Canadians were as little interested in the Right's presciptions for an open marketplace as they were in the Left's calls for a socialist transformation of the economy.

Most Canadians in the eighties and nineties also seemed to want to avoid polarization. But in an era of declining economic performance, the ideas of the Right attracted growing support, while the Left seemed generally in retreat — though, as we shall see, there were significant exceptions. The new right-wing ideology focussed on several inter-related themes. First, it spoke a great deal of "globalization" of capital and the limits this placed on national governments' abilities to control the pace and character of economic development.

Secondly, it decried the mounting debts that countries like Canada were accumulating in an effort to maintain social programs in an era of declining government revenues. Thirdly, it argued that capital, increasingly able to move where it wished, would favour countries and regions with low rates of inflation, minimal government debt, minimal government intervention, and low taxation.

The "global" character of capital was supposedly a contrast to an earlier era of "Fordism." In the Fordist world, companies located in a major industrial area, with a highly trained labour force and easy transportation access to major markets. Their labour force, usually unionized, enjoyed jobs for life as companies attempted to concentrate all their production in a small number of highly automated branches. In the post-Fordist era, companies, tired of labour demands and government regulation of everything from labour standards to environmental damage, established small, specialized plants in a variety of locations, including Third World countries where cheap labour and minimal governmental rules made up for increased transportation costs. Thanks to computers, communications within a company that had global operations were far easier to co-ordinate than they had ever been, and decentralization became an attractive means of reducing costs.

How could ordinary people and their governments in the First World react to the new cheap-labour, anti-regulation world that multi-national corporations were trying to create? The Right preached capitulation to the corporate agenda, promising that if governments and workers were less demanding of capitalists they would be more willing to keep their money at home. Margaret Thatcher, the Conservative leader whose party won the May 1979 election in Great Britain, slashed social spending and drastically reduced the money supply, thereby forcing up interest rates. Within a year, unemployment in Britain had increased from less than five percent of the labour force to over twelve percent.

Ronald Reagan, elected president of the United States in 1980, followed a similar course, and a year after his coming to office, the American unemployment rate had doubled to ten percent. Reagan, however, while he would continue to proclaim anti-statist policies, soon demonstrated that he was more interested in switching state priorities than in removing the state from the economy. His massive injection of funds into military expenditures beginning in 1982 helped to revive the economy that his earlier policies had harmed. Canadian politicians, particularly Conservatives, admired the British and American attack on the welfare state. But, as we shall see, the politics of protest that had forced legislative changes in the 1960s and 1970s remained strong in Canada. Though the Right would have its victories, workers, women's groups, Natives, and regional interests, among others, demanded with some success that their interests be accommodated as well.[2]

The Late Trudeau Period

Canada did not follow the British or American lead whole-heartedly, though right-wing perspectives gained considerable ground in government and business circles. Canada had, beginning in 1975, abandoned the Keynesian notion that monetary and fiscal policy should work hand in hand, that is, that greater state spending, for example, ought to be accompanied by low interest rates to promote economic recovery. The Bank of Canada that year, as we noted in Chapter Five, decided that it must pursue reduction in growth of the money supply as a means of containing inflation. But fiscal policy remained stimulatory with spending remaining static in per capita terms, despite declining overall revenues.

The result of this mismatch of fiscal and monetary policies was that both annual deficits and the national debt increased substantially from 1975, when the Bank of Canada's new policy was announced, to 1984, when the long-lived Liberal government was defeated by Brian Mulroney's Conservatives. Little would change during the nine years the Conservatives were in office. Under the Liberals before 1975, modest annual budgetary surpluses had become common and the national debt, well over 100 percent of GDP in 1945, had fallen to eighteen percent. But over the next nine years, annual deficits rose every year, reaching $30 billion the last year the Liberals were in office. Some of the increase was artificial, since figures once excluded from the national accounting were included. But there was little doubt that spending increases exceeded growth in the sluggish Canadian economy. Federal spending had accounted for 20.8 percent of GDP in 1975, but rose to twenty-four percent in 1984, while revenue fell from 18.5 to 17.2 percent. The federal debt by the latter date was equivalent in size to half of GDP, small relative to its level after the war but large relative to its position a few years earlier.[3]

Lack of potential sources of revenue was not the primary cause of the deficit. In November 1981, Finance Minister Allan MacEachen noted in his budget speech that "revenues lost through selective write-offs, exemptions and dividends are massive." He reported that $47 billion of personal income escaped tax in 1979, and many higher-income Canadians were paying little or no taxes at all.[4] But his government could hardly plead innocent in the creation of this state of affairs. Having rejected the thrust of the Carter Commission report on taxation, the Liberals had used tax credits for industries in a vain effort to create jobs. Employment tax credits, for example, rewarding employers who hired new full-time employees, were provided from 1978 through 1980. Tax shelters were created for investors in Canadian research, Canadian films, and urban apartment complexes.[5]

The government's high-interest policy contributed mightily to its deficit woes. As the nation's biggest borrower, the federal government had to pay a large premium for the money it borrowed when interest rates were high. It therefore had an incentive to keep rates low, particularly when its own revenues were below its expenditures and it was forced to borrow; but the Bank of Canada's tight-money policy, supported by the finance ministers of the period, caused the government to work against its own interests. Meanwhile, the government's revenue situation was worsened by high interest rates. With fewer individuals and companies in a position to take risks and borrow money, there were fewer jobs being created and fewer people able to pay taxes. The high interest rates ensured that the deficit, which might have been used to stimulate jobs, appeared to provide no benefits to Canadians at all.

But the Liberals were determined to "wrestle inflation to the ground," and apparently to do it on the backs of Canadian workers. Their wage and price controls in the late seventies had been unpopular because prices rose faster than wages, and the government received the blame. The Liberals even suffered the ignominy of a narrow electoral defeat in 1979 by Joe Clark's Conservatives. The Conservatives lost a vote of confidence seven months after their election, and the Liberals, once again led by Trudeau, returned to power in February 1980. They had no interest in using controls over wages and prices once again and taking the blame for declining standards of living. Instead, they favoured an intensification of the monetarist policies of the Bank of Canada. These would indirectly produce the results that wage controls had produced directly, but without political fallout since the government's heavy hand would not be visible. The argument was that tight money would produce high interest rates, which in turn would cause a slowdown of the economy; during a slowdown, unemployment would rise and workers, fearing job losses, would accept the redistribution of wealth from labour to capital that employers were increasingly demanding as their price for doing business in the country, rather than seeking friendlier climes elsewhere.

Interest rates exceeded twenty percent for much of 1980, though the rate of inflation was twelve percent. The "real interest rate," the gap between the rate of inflation and the cost of borrowing money, was higher than it had ever been since World War II. Indeed, for most of the fifties and sixties, the rate was about 1.5 percent. Suddenly it was five times as much. This was a great boon to lenders but of little help to anyone else. While large corporations with huge cash reserves could cut their borrowing and still maintain themselves or even expand, smaller companies were often forced to the wall, or compelled to make drastic cutbacks so that they would not have to borrow.

Similar tight-money or "monetarist" policies were being followed throughout the Western world with predictable consequences. "To bring inflation really under control" the Bank of Canada "jammed on the monetary brakes" in mid-1981. Interest rates shot up and economic activity slumped.[6] In the last quarter of 1981 the Canadian economy went into recession. The scale of the recession increased in the first three quarters of 1982 and unemployment reached a post-war high of 12.9 percent in the fall of that year.[7] But, to the delight of the Bank of Canada, the rate of inflation slipped from the double digits of the previous two years to about four percent. Bank governor Gerald Bouey, who had been responsible for the imposition of monetarism in 1975 and its implementation thereafter, now argued cheerfully that continuing "restraint" in monetary policy would lead to an era of economic stability. Right-wing economists, rather then lamenting high unemployment, emphasized the importance of the NAIRU, a concept we discussed in Chapter Five.[8]

During the recession of the early eighties, many corporations that were dismissing employees claimed that they were "downsizing." This word came to connote staff reductions which, even if they were induced by an economic downturn, were meant to be permanent. When the economy lifted again, the corporations wanted to be in a position where they could get by with less staff at all levels. The corporations were to be "restructured" to become "leaner and meaner." This would allow them to better compete in the new "globalized" economy. Such buzzwords would mark the corporate world's rhetoric in economic discussions for the rest of the century.

Apart from supporting the Bank of Canada's tight-money policy, the Trudeau government attempted to appease the better-off in June 1982, by reducing the highest margin for federal tax from forty-three percent to thirty-four percent.[9] But there was by no means a Thatcherite consistency to the Liberals' economic policies. Indeed, in the 1980 election, Trudeau lambasted Clark's Conservatives for their subservience to corporate interests. A Cabinet report entitled "Economic Development for Canada in the 1980s," tabled in November 1981, emphasized the limitations of leaving economic development purely to the private sector. The state, it argued, must "play an even more active role" in creating regional economic development and economic diversification among regions; it must also implement policies and programs in areas such as "industrial innovation and restructuring, manpower policy, regulatory policy and competition policy." In this state capitalist vision of economic development, the government was to move into investments that were "beyond the capacity of the private sector."[10] The Cabinet report caused consternation within the corporate community and suggested that the left wing in the Liberal party was exerting some influence on government policy. But the right wing eventually won the debate within the government ranks. Though some toughening of tax regulations was announced in November 1981, most of the changes were shelved in the next budget. New programs of government involvement in the economy, suggested by the 1981 Cabinet paper, never materialized.

Also, while the Trudeau government supported high interest rates and allowed unemployment to rise, they remained generally supportive of the social insurance programs and the Canada Assistance Policy, which between them defined a floor of income and of essential services for Canadians. Health Minister Monique Bégin successfully stared down the premiers of Ontario, Alberta, and British Columbia to end the increasing physician practice of extra-billing patients to top up what the doctors received from the provincial government for their medical services. Canadians were simply unwilling to part with their social programs or to let them be watered down, and, at least while Pierre Trudeau was prime minister, there was little suggestion on the part of the government that they should have to do so.

The Mulroney Era

Trudeau's Liberal successor, John Turner, during his brief period in office, suggested that Canada's deficit was too big and its debt load was too high. But he was vague about what should be done about either. Progressive Conservative leader Brian Mulroney was, if anything, vaguer. When he ran successfully for the Conservative leadership against then-leader Joe Clark in 1983, Mulroney denounced the Trudeau government for its "socialist" over-spending. During the election of 1984, Mulroney, a corporate lawyer and former president of Iron Ore of Canada, claimed that a Conservative government would get the deficit and debt under control. But he promised to protect Canada's social programs, which he said were a "sacred trust" between Canadians and their governments, and, during a nationally televised leaders' debate, he promised to add a national daycare program to the mix.

Mulroney won a landslide victory in the 1984 election after Turner proved unable to dissociate himself from a flurry of last-minute patronage appointments by the Trudeau government. Skeptics wondered which of Mulroney's contradictory promises he would break. In the end, he broke them all. Initially, Mulroney wished to focus squarely on the deficit, which, as a representative of big business, he regarded as particularly problematic. Unwilling to increase taxes, Mulroney focussed on cuts. His first target was the automatic indexing of old-age pensions and family allowances to the inflation rate. The Conservatives wanted to limit their increase to three percent per year, which at the time would have meant an annual erosion of one or two percent in the value of benefits. Mulroney argued that to break inflationary psychology, Canadians had to accept that their wages and their social benefits could not always rise to match the rate of inflation. Mulroney suggested that seniors understood the need for sacrifices, and were prepared to support him. They were not. "Grey power" asserted itself in a massive campaign that included a rally on Parliament Hill where one protester told the prime minister that if he did not reverse his stand on the pension issue, it would be "good-bye Charlie Brown" to his government at the next election. Mulroney castigated Canadians for wanting both to have allegedly rich social programs and to cut the deficit, ignoring the fact that he had pandered to such a view during the election. In the end, his government beat a retreat, recognizing that old-age pensioners simply had too great a clout as voters to become the target of a direct government attack.

Family allowances, however, were cut and in 1993, the federal government eliminated them altogether, rejecting a universal program in favour of a child tax credit which provided benefits only to mothers whose household income was modest.

But Mulroney had not given up on cutting government spending in his first term of office. He cut both military spending and foreign aid, to the chagrin of the Right and Left respectively. The daycare issue was shunted off to a government committee and no new funds were allocated. Annual cuts in the CBC budget and the privatization of Via Rail and Air Canada were denounced by nationalists who argued that the government was destroying institutions that had historically linked Canadians. Across-the-board cuts in department estimates and below-inflation salary increases for government employees helped the government to produce an operating surplus by the end of its first term in office. The biggest cuts, however, were in grants to the provinces. These cuts, since they did not involve the direct grant of federal funds to individuals, were less politically dangerous for the government than an attack on pensions might have been.

The Mulroney government, even more than its Liberal predecessor, wanted to encourage the wealthy through its taxation policies. While a temporary surtax on wealthier individuals and corporations was introduced in the 1985 budget, a lifetime capital gains tax exemption of $500,000 was also included.[11] A minimum income tax proposal announced by Finance Minister Michael Wilson in December 1985 was meant to fulfil a well-publicized Mulroney election promise to ensure that all Canadians paid their fair share of taxes. But it fell short of such an objective. In practice, high-income earners were still under-taxed on corporate income and capital gains, and retirement plan contributions were excluded from income as before.[12] It was a fitting commentary on the overall failure of seventies' and eighties' tax reforms to achieve equity that the Tories could congratulate themselves for forcing upper-income taxpayers to pay taxes that equalled in *dollar* amounts, rather than *percentage* amounts, the taxes paid by average Canadians. Michael Wilson rejected further tax reforms, telling the House: "We must not and we will not risk creating the kind of uncertainty and instability that could undermine the effort to get Canadians investing strongly in opportunities that will lead to growth and jobs."[13]

Taxes on corporate profits, which had fallen during the Trudeau years, continued to decline as a percentage of both total government revenues and gross domestic product during the Mulroney years. Between the fiscal years 1966–7 and 1990–1, revenues from corporate taxation declined from 2.7 percent to 1.8 percent of GDP. By contrast, revenue from personal income tax rose from 4.7 to 8.9 percent in the same period.[14]

The Attack on Government

As inflation eased thanks to the depression created by monetarist policies, interest rates declined and economic activity gradually began to pick up again. By the end of the 1980s, unemployment in Canada had fallen below eight percent. While right-wing newspaper columnists and publishers proclaimed that the rapid economic growth of this period demonstrated the correctness of the single-minded attack on inflation, those who remained unemployed questioned when the economic recovery would include them too. In the "downsized" world of the private sector, a recovery created jobs but still left many unemployed. In terms of unemployment, the recovery of the late eighties looked far less impressive than the recovery that followed the recession of 1957–62. The economic environment of the late eighties reflected the prescriptions of the New Right. Government regulations were eased or disappeared in many areas, and the marketplace became the arbiter of more decisions than had likely been the case since before World War II. Investors made fortunes from currency speculation, land deals, corporate mergers, and other unproductive enterprises. By 1990, the steam had largely gone out of this new era of capitalist greed. Worse, for workers, the Bank of Canada had a more extreme view than ever of the evils of inflation. Bank of Canada Governor John Crow, appointed by the Conservative government in 1987, was not content, as his predecessor Gerald Bouey had been, to maintain a low rate of inflation; he wanted to eliminate inflation altogether because he believed that price stability would encourage long-term economic development.

While the economy as a whole was to benefit from such development, many jobs would have to be sacrificed to maintain the "requisite" level of unemployment. Tight money was supposed to "discipline" the economy; but in reality, this meant the working class. The new economic discipline resulted in another recession by the middle of 1990. Indeed it ushered in a long period of double-digit unemployment in Canada and negligible economic growth. The Mulroney government, however, fretted mainly about the national deficit, which unsurprisingly grew as interest rates were forced up by the Bank of Canada and the costs of unemployment insurance and social assistance ballooned in the face of increasing unemployment. The government's policies had reduced the number of potential taxpayers and increased the numbers of those dependent on government aid. But the government did not conclude that its policies were at fault. Rather the many collectors of "handouts" were the problem.

The Right indeed tried to argue at one and the same time that a high NAIRU was required — the usual figure cited was about nine percent of the labour force — and that the army of the unemployed who had become the front line against inflation were the cause of economic problems, particularly alleged government over-spending. There were increasing complaints about individuals who did not want to work, who had the audacity to be unwilling to uproot themselves from regions where industry chose not to locate or chose to abandon, or who did not have the requisite skills to compete in the new global marketplace.

The view that the poor, whose numbers swelled during recessions, were the authors of their own misfortunes was pressed in particular by the new Reform Party, formed in 1987 by disgruntled Conservatives and other right-wingers in western Canada. Though the party wrapped itself in the cloak of western populism, its founders were four wealthy Westerners who believed the Conservative Party was moving too slowly to reduce the role of government in the economy. Their leader was Preston Manning, son and business partner of former Alberta Social Credit Premier Ernest C. Manning.[15] Reform called for a massive reduction in federal spending as part of a campaign to rid the country of its national deficit within a few years, and its debt over a few years more. It focussed on social programs as the root cause of national economic problems. Too many people allegedly were relying on the government rather than on themselves to put bread on the table.

Reform won no seats in the federal election of 1988, but it made an important breakthrough in the federal election of 1993, carrying 52 seats. This was 2 seats short of the separatist Bloc Québécois. The Liberals, who had campaigned on a moderately progressive platform emphasizing preservation of social programs and public spending on infrastructure to create jobs, won 178 seats, while the NDP tumbled from 42 seats in 1988 to a mere 9 seats. The governing Conservatives, dogged by the unpopularity of Brian Mulroney, had chosen a new leader, Kim Campbell, Canada's first woman prime minister, just months before the election. Campbell copied Reform in pledging to eliminate the deficit within her mandate, though she claimed it would take five years while Reform was prepared to do it in three. Campbell's right-wing platform alienated moderate Tories while often failing to convince right-wingers generally that the Tories, who had cut social programs, were truly prepared to give up the parish-pump electoral giveaways that Brian Mulroney favoured. The historic Conservative party elected only 2 MPs in 1993, raising questions about their future as a federal party.

With the NDP in disarray, the Liberals concluded that they need not worry about opposition on the left. They focussed on pleasing the business community and demonstrating to fiscal conservatives that they could address the concerns raised by the Reform Party. Prime Minister Jean Chrétien and his Finance Minister Paul Martin had important ties to the business community, and in office, they focussed on the deficit and cutting social programs. Though they joined with the provinces to spend some money on infrastructural improvements, their cuts in other areas greatly exceeded any new spending they undertook. They made it more difficult to collect unemployment insurance, which they renamed employment insurance, and they eliminated the Canada Assistance Plan, among other conservative measures. Though they compelled John Crow's resignation as governor of the Bank of Canada, as they had hinted they would before their election, the policies of the Bank favouring tight money and a high NAIRU did not change under the new governor Gordon Thiessen. In short, as political scientist Peter Leslie observed: "The Liberal government has moved to implement a vigorous deficit-reduction policy that confirms a decisive turn to the right in Canadian politics."[16]

The NAIRU, while it may be an elegant concept for the economists, has meant a great deal of human tragedy. The economic insecurity, the feelings of worthlessness, and sometimes the malnutrition of the unemployed exact a high toll in many lives and contribute to increased numbers of suicides, to increased rates of spousal and child abuse, and to higher rates of illness and hospitalization. There was also an impact on the nation's economic health. In 1996, the federal government's Human Resources Department carried out a careful study of the impact of unemployment in 1994, which averaged ten point four percent, on the economy. It estimated that the Canadian economy was at least $91 billion poorer than it would have been if there were no unemployment: $77 billion was lost in productivity and $14 billion lost as a result of health-related costs.[17]

The impact of neo-conservatism has been as evident at the provincial level as at the federal level. Sterling Lyon's Conservatives, in government in Manitoba from 1977 to 1981, embraced neo-conservatism and happily cut government jobs, meanwhile making it more difficult to collect social assistance and reducing the value of the grant made to those whom it still considered eligible. Bill Bennett Jr., after winning another polarized election contest in British Columbia in 1983 between Social Credit and the NDP, proceeded to slash public spending by firing about a quarter of the civil service, reducing social benefits, and substantially reducing grants to hospitals, school boards, and universities. Though there was a massive wave of protest from government workers and from users of public services, the government made only minor modifications in its program. Bennett privatized a variety of public services, setting off a trend that threatened the employment of many public employees since the private firms that competed for their jobs were generally non-unionized firms that paid low wages.

If Bennett's attack on the public service seemed unsurprising given British Columbia Social Credit's almost religious faith in the virtue of the private sector, the turnaround in Quebec's social policies surprised many. The Lévesque government had followed an essentially social democratic course during their first period in office, if only because they did not wish to alienate any section of the French-speaking community in the months before the referendum. When the referendum was lost in 1980 and the government won re-election in 1981 on a platform that said little about independence, its financial policies changed dramatically. Jacques Parizeau, still the Finance Minister, now focussed on cutting public-sector spending. The government unilaterally rolled back the wages of its employees in the public and parapublic sectors by eighteen percent for the first three months of 1982. This led to a bitter confrontation between the Parti Québécois government and a work force that had been largely supportive of the government's earlier social agenda and its campaign for sovereignty.

On the whole, however, Quebec governments in the 1980s, both Parti Québécois and Liberal, did not make drastic cuts to social services. In contrast, provincial governments generally were cutting social assistance rates and raising the minimum wage by less than the rate of inflation; these policies, added to rising unemployment, meant that the gap between wealthy and poor, always large in Canada, was becoming a chasm. There was some public backlash to neo-conservative agendas. In Ontario, which had forty-two years of unbroken Conservative government from 1943 to 1985, the voters, particularly in the urban areas, rejected the efforts of the Tories' new leader, Frank Miller, to shed Conservative pragmatism in favour of a neo-conservative program of spending cuts and privatization. Though the Tories narrowly won the most seats in the 1985 provincial election, the resurgent Liberals under David Peterson were able to govern after signing an accord with the third-placed New Democrats of Bob Rae. The accord simply called upon the Liberals to implement their promises to invest in public infrastructure in Ontario, including housing and childcare. Indeed, the Liberals spent freely, taking advantage of the economic upturn in the late eighties, and won a convincing majority in the 1987 provincial election. The NDP, this time, were second-ranked, with the Conservatives relegated to third position. When a large-scale election financing scandal discredited the Liberals, the voters of Ontario turned to Bob Rae's NDP in 1990, giving only one-quarter of their votes to the Tories led by Mike Harris.

The Rae government assumed power just as the Canadian economy entered the new recession, with Ontario's economy particularly hard hit because of the dramatic slump in manufacturing activity that occurred as interest rates soared. Some commentators also blamed the free trade agreement signed in 1988, which we will discuss in Chapter Thirteen, for the woes of Ontario manufacturing. Though the government was split on what direction to follow in the face of a recession, its initial decision, urged by Finance Minister Floyd Laughren, was to stimulate the economy with a large deficit. The spring 1991 budget increased public spending in most areas and included a deficit estimate of $12 billion for that year with smaller deficits to follow in subsequent years as the economy recovered. The economic stimulus of the Ontario budget was counteracted by the fiscal and monetary conservatism which the federal government practised in the late Mulroney years. Grants to provinces were cut again, defence spending was dramatically curtailed, and indeed, most government departments shed jobs.

Within a year, Bob Rae had had second thoughts about his first budget. He announced that spending cuts would be necessary to meet his government's deficit objectives, and though he remained committed to the view that government had the duty to help the less

Table One Poverty rates by type of family (in percentages)		
Year	Female single-parent	Two parents
1980	57.7	9.4
1986	58.8	10.8
1989	52.9	8.5
1990	60.6	9.6
1991	61.9	10.7
1992	58.4	10.1
Source: Figures reported by National Council of Welfare, 1994. Cited in Maureen Baker, "Elimating Child Poverty." 80.		

fortunate in society, his government implemented policies that raised rents for residents of subsidized housing, and squeezed hospitals, schools and universities a little more each year. In the summer of 1993, Rae suggested that all provincial and municipal employees earning over $30,000 per year take five percent pay cuts. This would save the provincial treasury several billion dollars annually, while limiting the number of positions governments would have to elimi-nate in the public service. The "social contract," an exchange of pay cuts for a degree of job security, enraged the public service trade unions and indeed most trade unions in the private sector. They had thought that they finally had a government in there working for them. In the end, the "social contract," which Rae had hoped to negotiate with the unions, was imposed on the large section of the labour force which drew all or part of its salary from the provincial government. That included workers in schools, hospitals, and universities as well as workers in provincial offices. Hated by the business community as alleged socialists, the Ontario NDP government had also disillu-sioned a large section of the labour movement as well as poverty activists.

The election of Mike Harris' Tories in the provincial election of 1995 seemed to suggest that many Ontario voters — Harris won forty-five percent of the vote — were prepared to accept a neo-con-servative agenda. Harris promised huge cuts in public services, par-ticularly in social assistance, and equally dramatic cuts in taxes, with the wealthy to benefit the most. He soon delivered on his promises, removing a hundred thousand people from the welfare rolls within a

Table Two Percentage of families living in poverty (various countries, 1987)		
Country	All families with children	One-parent families
Australia	18.59	53.19
Canada	17.67	48.83
Germany	8.82	32.09
Sweden	4.71	8.29
United Kingdom	16.63	25.00
United States	25.41	53.92

Source: Maureen Baker, "Eliminating Child Poverty," 81. These figures are based on the Luxembourg Income Study, which uses fifty percent of median income as the poverty line. This is the same poverty line that the Senate Task Force on Poverty adopted for Canada in 1970.

Table Three Percentage of all poor families with children lifted out of poverty by government intervention (mid-1980s)		
Country	Two-parent	Single-parent
Canada	17.6	19.3
France	58.7	47.0
West Germany	13.4	33.8
Netherlands	20.0	89.5
Sweden	47.4	81.1
United Kingdom	26.5	75.0
United States	-9.1*	4.6

Source: Maureen Baker, "Eliminating Child Poverty," 82. These figures are based on Luxembourg Income Study data.

* That is, the net effect of government policies was to increase poverty.

year and cutting the benefits of most of those who remained on social assistance. His government did not follow up to find out what had happened to those cut off welfare. Indeed in early 1997, they announced a large-scale devolution of powers that the province had gradually acquired in an effort to equalize services across municipal boundaries, regardless of local wealth. Municipalities would administer social assistance programs and raise half the costs (previously they paid twenty percent), and would be responsible for social housing, public transit, public health, and ambulance services, among others. In return, the province agreed to pick up the full tab for public education, removing education from the property tax. It then immediately reduced the number of school boards and limited their power. The Education Minister claimed that teachers were over-paid and schools too lavishly equipped.[18]

Harris was following in the footsteps of Alberta's Tory premier, Ralph Klein, who had made "downsizing" government his party's mantra, and thereby turned around the fortunes of a regime that seemed doomed. From late 1985 until late 1992, Don Getty, successor to Peter Lougheed, had served as a transitional figure in Alberta's Tory history. Getty indicated skepticism about the interventionism that had marked the Lougheed years, suggesting that it was a good thing if the legislature did not meet too much or pass too much legislation, since that would leave citizens to run more of their own lives. His government proved quite mean-spirited to the unemployed, whose ranks had swelled in the energy-producing province as international energy prices slumped throughout the mid- and late-eighties. But it was more than willing to provide loan guarantees to entrepreneurs, whose inability to get loans on their own from banks was held to be the result of the prejudice of eastern-controlled corporations against western-based capitalists. Billions of dollars were lost to the provincial treasury as bankers came calling on the provincial government for monies owing from failed ventures. The most spectacular failure saw the province's taxpayers pay over $600 million as the result of the failure of a cellular phone manufacturer that had persuaded the Cabinet that here was an opportunity to establish the high-technology future that Alberta, like all the other provinces, craved. Conservative popularity fell to about twelve percent in the polls in the dying days of the Getty administration and the Liberals, promising little more than an end to government loans to private companies, soared in the polls. Ralph Klein managed, however, to turn things around dramatically. Turning on the administration of which he was a member, he promised not only to end government intervention in business, but also to cut public spending in Alberta by twenty percent.

By the time of the June 1993 provincial election, Klein and Liberal leader Laurence Decore were vying with each other over who could cut spending faster and rid the province of an allegedly burdensome deficit estimated at between $2.3 and $3.2 billion, depending on how the counting was done. The NDP, largely defending the status quo, became irrelevant to a debate in which most provincial voters appeared to accept the logic of deficit reduction as the first priority.

Predictably, the cuts were generally unpopular in both provinces. Though demonstrations against the cuts in Alberta were modest and dispirited, polls showed a paradox. More than three voters in five opposed cuts to education and health and yet almost two-thirds claimed to support the Klein program as a whole, which, shorn of cuts to education and health, did not amount to very much. About the only cut that enjoyed massive popularity was the cut to social assistance. The cuts in this area were dramatic. Almost half of recipients were cut off in a two-year period beginning in mid-1993. A few found jobs; a few moved off the welfare rolls only nominally, receiving funds for enrolling in training programs that, more often than not, did not lead to jobs; many others were left destitute, with charitable agencies and relatives expected to look after their needs. The government did not follow up on those it cut from the welfare rolls, and so it could not report on how many people ended up in the various categories mentioned. The poor were increasingly to be treated as if they were invisible. Harris and Klein and their Cabinet ministers viciously criticized opponents of their cuts as "special interest groups" who had no concern about the general interest of citizens. The neo-conservatives, unlike their liberal predecessors, did not see the need for government to mediate the perspectives of big business, on the one hand, and the various groups that represented the majority of citizens, on the other. In their view, businesses alone created long-term, productive employment and the views of leading business people, therefore, reflected the general interest rather than narrow selfish interests. Other organized groups, such as trade unions, professional groupings, poverty organizations, and gender- and race-based organizations, were merely selfish pleaders for special interests.[19]

Whereas provincial governments in the fifties and sixties had competed to provide the best educational and health facilities to demonstrate to investors that they provided a stable climate for capital, now they competed to demonstrate that they provided the lowest taxes, the lowest minimum wages, and the weakest environmental and trade union movements. Alberta's Premier Klein, citing Alberta's claims in this regard, spoke of the "Alberta Advantage." But such tactics were hardly the preserve of those who professed to be right-wingers. New Brunswick's Premier Frank McKenna, a Liberal who defended federal programs to aid poor provinces, advertised internationally that New Brunswick offered low taxes, cheap labour, and a regulatory environment that was favourable to business, in a partially successful attempt to attract new head offices to his "under-developed" province. For disadvantaged provinces, competition to offer low taxes meant a climate of constant cutbacks in health and education spending, even if it was not accompanied by the strident right-wing rhetoric of ideological conservatives like Klein and Harris. Nova Scotia's Liberal government of the mid-nineties proved as conservative as its Conservative predecessor, and Roy Romanow's New Democrats closed rural hospitals to balance Saskatchewan's budget without having to introduce significant new taxes.

The New Poor

Poverty rates, as we have seen, fell in the 1960s as a result of the combination of a buoyant economy and an interventionist state. As the economy stalled in the 1970s, Statistics Canada reported little change from year to year in the number of Canadians who lived below the "low-income cutoff" line, Statscan's measure of the income below which an individual or a household could not reasonably be expected to afford a minimally acceptable level of shelter, food, and clothing. About fifteen percent of Canadians, or almost 3.5 million individuals in 1980, were poor, according to this measure. Perhaps another 1.5 million were also poor if one applied the Senate Poverty Committee's definition that those whose disposable income was less than one-half of the Canadian average should be considered poor. Using the Statscan definition, the poverty rate had risen to 17.8 percent in 1995; this translated into 5.2 million poverty-stricken Canadians.[20]

Concerned citizens, including church groups, social welfare agencies, and trade unions banded together in the 1980s to create "food banks," outlets that collected left-over perishables from supermarkets and restaurants, as well as donated non-perishables from individuals. Here the poor could pick up nutritional, if not generally fresh, food that social assistance or minimum-wage incomes made difficult for individuals and families to purchase. The food bank pioneers hoped that these outlets would be short-lived, and that goverment programs and higher minimum wages would intervene to make the food banks unnecessary. But during the recession of the early nineties, perhaps two million Canadians made use of a food bank at some point each year; many Canadians were dependent upon the food banks to avoid

starvation or at least malnutrition. Some food bank volunteers believed that the agencies they staffed represented the best means
through which more prosperous Canadians could help out the less
fortunate. Most, however, rejected this charitable philosophy as outdated and condemned governments for policies that compelled so
many people to line up for stale lettuce and tins of whatever someone
else had chosen to give them. The churches, and particularly the
Roman Catholic Church, increasingly argued that governments had
a moral duty to ensure that all citizens had adequate food, clothing,
and shelter to live in dignity. The Roman Catholic bishops, in several
statements, appeared to embrace a semi-socialist perspective, arguing that the rights of the poor ought to weigh more in the eyes of the
state than the profits of corporations. The churches themselves, however, had their right wing, who did not want to alienate their wealthier parishioners and argued that religion ought not to be mixed with
politics. The struggle between those who supported the "preferential
option for the poor" and those who claimed that the church should
be above mere temporal arguments raged into the nineties, the latter
group appeard to be more in the ascendant than they had been in the
eighties.[21]

Government policies made some effort to deal with poverty. The
well-organized pensioners were best at convincing governments to
increase social aid (almost never referred to as "welfare" when it
involved payments to the aged rather than to young mothers) during
the late Trudeau period. The Guaranteed Income Supplement was
raised. Poverty among persons aged sixty-five and over declined
from twenty-seven to nineteen percent between 1980 and 1985, according to Statistics Canada. The pensioners' lobby against the Mulroney cuts ensured that poverty rates for old people would not rise,
but, given the government's obsession with debt and maintaining low
tax rates for corporations, it was impossible to make further progress
for seniors. Older women fared worse than older men. Far more
likely to be solely dependent on government income, forty percent
of women aged seventy-five and over lived in poverty in 1995. Many
were in frail health but unable to afford the extra services that their
failing health meant they required.[22]

Some efforts were also made to deal with poverty for families with
children. In 1979, the Liberal government introduced a refundable
Child Tax Credit that amounted to a negative income tax for the
poorest Canadian families. The Mulroney government made a nominal effort to eliminate child poverty by the year 2000, and in 1989,

Parliament passed a motion that confirmed the country's resolve to achieve this goal. For most of the parliamentarians, it appeared that these were empty words. In 1993, when universal family allowance was abolished, some of the funds that had been used for the allowances were combined with child tax credit monies to create a Child Tax Benefit for low- and modest-income Canadian families. Counteracting such gains were the cuts made by the Liberals to unemployment benefits in 1994 and the continuing cuts in federal transfers for health, education, and social assistance.[23] As of 1995, the federal government also abolished the Canada Assistance Plan and began giving the provinces a lump sum for health, education, and social assistance rather than funding the latter separately. The Conservatives had weakened CAP in 1990, by modifying the dollar-for-dollar federal grant to provinces to limit increases in federal monies to the three richest provinces by five percent annually. At a time when unemployment was rising, this meant that the provincial share of growing social assistance expenses was increased significantly for these three provinces, an incentive to cut rates of assistance and make eligibility rules tougher. In British Columbia, for example, where an NDP government resisted the attack on social assistance recipients to a greater extent than other provincial governments, the federal share of social assistance payments dropped from fifty percent in 1990 to twenty-nine percent in the fiscal year 1994–5.[24]

Thanks to the combination of government policies and national economic performance, rates of family poverty were higher in the early nineties than they had been in 1980, though there had been a decline in poverty during the large eighties mini-boom. In 1995, 1.47 million children were being raised in poverty, an increase of thirty-nine percent since 1980.[25] As Table One suggests, families headed by female single parents were likely to be living in poverty. This highlighted continuing economic discrimination against women, continuing poor daycare policies in Canada (the Liberals in the nineties joined their Conservative predecessors in abandoning their childcare promises once in office), and the continuing inadequacy of social policies in Canada to make a dent on child poverty. Even during the buoyant late eighties, one Canadian family in six, families accounting for about twenty percent of all Canadian children, lived in poverty.

The degree of destitution suffered by families and by single, unemployed individuals varied from province to province. Singles on welfare in New Brunswick in 1993 received only twenty-four percent of Statscan's estimate of the minimum they needed to stay out of poverty; in Prince Edward Island, the most generous province, they received sixty-two percent. Couples with two children received seventy-three percent of the low-income cutoff income in Prince Edward Island and Ontario but only forty-five percent in New Brunswick.[26]

How did Canada's record of dealing with child poverty compare with that of other countries? If the comparison point was the United States, Canada fared reasonably well. In the United States, poverty levels for children in 1995 had regressed to the levels of 1965, before President Johnson's War on Povery had begun. The income of the poorest twenty percent of families in the United States had fallen by twenty-two percent, while the income of the richest twenty percent had increased by twenty-five percent. By contrast, in Canada, as sociologist John Myles reports: "To date rising labour market inequality in Canada has been offset by social transfers ... The final distribution of family income and child poverty has scarcely changed since the 1970s."[27] In 1993, the poverty rate, using an American definition, for single-parent families with two children was forty-one percent in the US, but only twenty-six percent in Canada. The gap between the income received by poor families and the income required to get them out of poverty was $2519 in Canada and $4172 in the United States. In 1990, the average total of public assistance for a destitute family of four in Canada was $14,932; in the US, it was $8684. Another contributing factor to lesser inequality in Canada than in its southern neighbour, suggests Myles, was that while unionization rates were in free fall and only about fifteen percent of the work force was unionized in the early nineties, Canadian unionization rates declined only slightly, from thirty-nine percent in 1980 to thirty-six percent in 1990. Union contracts were able to set the pace for wages in Canada far more than in the United States, and minimum wages levels increased more in Canada than the US.[28]

But, as Tables Two and Three demonstrate, the United States was the grinch among industrialized countries. Compared to industrialized countries other than the United States, Canada's success at reducing inequalities and aiding the poor is mediocre. In countries with long-standing socialist traditions, such as Sweden and Germany, the rates of poverty for families with children were substantially below Canadian rates (Table Two), and government policies played a large role in lifting families with children from poverty (Table Three). In Sweden, for example, sixty percent of all pre-school-age children were in public daycares in 1991, which cost a nominal rate, and thirteen percent were in private daycare. The youngest children were at home with their mothers, who received most of their regular job incomes while their babies were under the age of eighteen months. In France, ninety-four percent of three to six year olds attended *écoles maternelles*, which were operated by the state as part of the public school system. Rates of poverty for single mothers in these countries were quite low compared to Canada, where only fifteen percent of pre-schoolers were in licensed daycare.[29]

The Environmental Front

Just as Canada's politicians found it easy to pass a motion to end child poverty, only to find that it would be expensive to do so, they seemed to find it easy to promise major changes in environmental policy, only to turn around and suggest that the direct and indirect costs of cleanups were too great to consider. Some successes could, nevertheless, be recorded. An agreement was signed by the Mulroney government with the Bush administration in the early nineties to take steps to reduce acid rain. Leaded gasoline was banned after it became clear that lead in the atmosphere posed a danger to the mental development of children. Legislation forcing environmental assessments of major development projects was passed. But, from the point of view of the organized environmental movement, many such projects went ahead, even after large amounts of information assembled indicated that a project would be harmful to the environment. The Rafferty-Alameda dam in southern Saskatchewan, which flooded Native homelands, was almost completed before an assessment of the project was even done, and the Oldman River Dam in southern Alberta and the Alberta Pacific Pulp Mill in northern Alberta were built despite the demonstrated effects of these projects on local fishing and, in the pulp mill's case, farming. A report in the early nineties suggested most of British Columbia's pulp mills were dumping effluent into local waters, with injurious effects upon the province's fishery.

Yet, at least during the periods when the economy was expanding, particularly in the late eighties, opinion polls suggested that most Canadians were prepared to make some sacrifices to leave a greener world for future generations. Media reports had spread the message that carbon dioxide emissions were destroying the ozone layer that protected humans and animals from the harmful ultraviolet rays of the sun, contributing to skin cancers and at the same time warming the earth's temperature with potentially catastrophic environmental consequences. There was increasing awareness of the link between industrial pollution and acid rain as well as pollution and a variety of physical and mental disorders. Brian Mulroney, much as he did with daycare and child poverty, proved able to draw political advantage from environmental policy. His government, in its second term of office, unveiled a Green Plan with a great deal of fanfare. Political scientist Michael Howlett notes: "The results were a major expenditure initiative but one which ultimately had only symbolic value as successive federal Budgets repeatedly cut into budgeted allocations."[30]

The Liberals in opposition were critical of the Tories' willingness to sacrifice environmental promises on the altar of cost-cutting, to reduce the deficit. They pledged in their election manifesto of 1993, usually referred to as the "Red Book," to focus on sustainable development. Protection of the environment, whether in the form of the air we breathe or the national parks, was in the long-term economic interest even of industry, and could in any case create many short-term business opportunities for those with ideas about how to get the environment cleaned up. The Liberals promised, along with other planks in an ambitious environmental platform, to appoint an Environmental Auditor General who would investigate and publicize environmental malfeasance, and to set timetables for the banning of the worst of the toxic substances in the atmosphere. But, as Michael Howlett suggested, "the Liberals have lived up to few of their campaign promises on the environment, and have made little substantive change to Canadian environmental policy."[31] For the Liberals as for the Conservatives, cost-cutting had been the government priority, and the strategy for economic recovery had been to create a political environment in which businesses felt little reason to fear excessive government regulation or taxes.

This was also the strategy adopted by the United States, the country whose economic domination of Canada was, and continues to be, a constant challenge in the post-war period. The next chapter looks at the relationship between Canada and the United States in the period since 1980, with emphasis on the free trade agreement of 1988 that linked the economic and political fates of the two countries closer together than ever. We look at the effect of this close relationship between two countries of vastly different sizes on Canada's foreign policy-making and on its thinking about social issues.

Thirteen

Canada and the World in the Era of "Globalization"

Neo-conservatism in the eighties and nineties arose in a context where business leaders and mainstream politicians told Canadians daily that Canada had entered a new era of global competition. Companies could now move their operations relatively easily from one part of the globe to another if they did not like government policies where they had once operated. But neo-conservative ideas also found an audience in Canada because of perceived changes in the international economic environment and the success of neo-conservatives in gaining power both in Great Britain and the United States.

This chapter demonstrates the extent to which Canadian responses to the international marketplace and international politics were changing in the latter decades of the twentieth century. While the Trudeau government, in its last period in office (1980–4), remained moderately nationalist, its Mulroney successor was almost unabashedly continentalist. The National Energy Policy of 1980, the last major piece of economic nationalist legislation passed by a Canadian federal government in the twentieth century, gave way to the US-Canada Free Trade Agreement (FTA) of 1988 and the North American Free Trade Agreement (NAFTA) of 1992. Trudeau's denunciation of the American invasion of Grenada in 1983 gave way to Brian Mulroney's unequivocal endorsement of an American invasion of Panama and his commitment of Canadian troops to the American Gulf War effort (nominally, like Korea, a United Nations operation) in 1991. The path was not one way. In the mid-nineties the Liberal government was stoutly resisting American efforts to use threats of economic retaliation against countries that like Canada traded with Fidel Castro's Cuba. But free trade with the Americans, bitterly resisted by a majority of Canadians in 1988, had become a part of the political firmament, no longer contested by any of the parties with a major influence in Canadian federal politics. The 1960s fervour for an independent Canada was largely absent in the late 1990s. Most Canadians believed that their government had limited power to deal with multi-national corporations.

From the NEP to Free Trade

Finance Minister John Crosbie's December 1979 budget gave Canadians a Christmas present that, outside the energy-producing provinces, proved highly unpopular: a gradual rise in Canadian oil prices to world levels. Trudeau denounced this capitulation to marketplace economics. He defended his government's practice in the 1970s of using the National Energy Board to partially shield Canadians from the impact of rapidly rising energy costs, by limiting the price increases of domestic oil and subsidizing the costs of imported oil. He proposed that the Canadian government should move to replace the imported oil that fuelled much of eastern Canada with western oil. That oil should be kept at prices below world levels so as to provide a competitive advantage for Canadian industries. It was an argument that caused consternation in western Canada, which had little industry but a great deal of oil and gas, and did not appreciate what appeared to be a blatant effort to favour central Canadian manufacturers at the expense of western Canadian energy producers.

In October 1980, Trudeau unveiled his National Energy Program which made good on his election promises regarding energy. Not only would Canadian energy prices be kept below world levels, but the federal government would try to get increased revenues from the energy industry in order to deal with its growing deficit problem. The government was, however, prepared to invest billions in the energy industry in the form of incentives for the Canadianization of energy firms. In general, what was proposed was a policy that would replace American control over Canada's energy with Canadian (albeit still private) control, international pricing with Canadian pricing, and provincial benefits from oil riches with a sharing of these revenues between the federal government and the oil-producing provinces. The federal government also planned to spend hundreds of millions to find oil in territories that it directly controlled in the North, particularly in the Beaufort Sea.

The program was quite popular in Ontario and Quebec, though Quebec's separatist premier, René Lévesque, almost ritually attacked the federal government for making a grab at the resources of certain provinces, in this case, mainly Alberta and Saskatchewan. The premiers of Nova Scotia and Newfoundland, involved in their own battles with the Trudeau government over which level of government had control over offshore oil, opposed the NEP. In Alberta, the Liberal energy program lead to a nasty confrontation with the federal authorities. Peter Lougheed placed limits on the amount of oil that Alberta would ship to central Canada and denounced the federal government's policies as antithetical to the interests of Alberta. His ministers began referring to the federal government as "the Ottawa government," implying that it was a foreign state that had intervened in an area of Alberta's sovereign jurisdiction. By the end of 1981, both Lougheed and Trudeau had sufficiently compromised that the NEP was revised to increase oil prices and reduce federal expectations of revenues from the industry. The two leaders toasted their deal, but anger at Lougheed's "betrayal" gave temporary succour to right-wing separatist movements in Alberta, particularly the ephemeral Western Canada Concept which elected a member to the legislature in a by-election in early 1982.[1]

By the middle of 1982, it had become clear that the federal attempt to use domestic policy to shield Canadians from international economic forces was largely irrelevant. Much of the federal government's planning assumed that oil prices, which had risen from about two dollars a barrel before the OPEC-induced price increases in 1973 to almost forty dollars a barrel in 1981, would continue to rise and reach about eighty dollars a barrel by 2000. Instead, as consumers turned to alternative, cheaper sources of energy, and supposedly dwindling international oil supplies began to look more secure, oil prices began to drop. By April 1982, they had fallen to thirty dollars a barrel. Several multi-billion-dollar oil sands developments planned for Alberta and Saskatchewan by consortia that included the federal government, the provincial governments of Alberta and Saskatchewan, and the major oil companies, collapsed. Improvements in the technology to extract oil from tar sands made it economically feasible to look to the tar sands for both Canada's energy self-sufficiency and increased energy exports, when oil was selling at forty dollars a barrel and prices were still headed upwards. At thirty dollars a barrel it was too risky a proposition.

The reaction within western Canada, particularly Alberta, was shock. Many people blamed the federal government's NEP for scaring away investors in the petroleum industry, and for the failure of the mega-projects, which would have injected over 20 billion dollars into the western Canadian economy in the 1980s. The reaction was understandable given regional tensions. It was also ironic. Westerners had scolded the federal government for ignoring international market forces as the price of oil rose. Now, however, they were unwilling to accept that international market forces were more responsible than the "anti-American" federal government for the region's economic disappointments. Many suggested that had the federal government not attempted to expropriate the revenues from oil and gas in the three westernmost provinces, the mega-projects would have gone ahead before the international price of oil had fallen. Few noted that this might have been a worse disaster, since thousands of Canadians would have migrated to the West, particularly to Alberta, for jobs in an industry which international market forces would have virtually shut down by the late eighties. As conventional oil prices fell to as low as thirteen dollars a barrel by the end of the decade, the market for tar sands oil virtually disappeared, since this oil could not, at the time, be produced for that low a price. Only in the late nineties, as the technology for extracting heavy oil once more advanced and the price of oil recovered to over twenty dollars a barrel, did the prospects for oil from the tar sands seem to recover.

The western provinces were hardly the only ones affected by the decline in world oil prices. Newfoundland and Nova Scotia had both hoped, in the late seventies, to make billions from their offshore oil. Planned mega-projects in these provinces stalled and, as in the West, only revived in the mid-nineties, though in somewhat more modest form. Rather more dependent than Alberta on federal help in such areas as education, health, and social welfare, the Atlantic provinces attached less blame to the federal government for the dim prospects that faced the petroleum industry in the eighties. While Alberta complained about too much income from the province being drained by Ottawa, the Atlantic provinces, recipients of a goodly share of "transfer grants," had a different perspective.

Cheap oil and a degree of economic nationalism, the Trudeau government's prescription for strengthening the Canadian economy in the early eighties, seemed of little help during the recession that had begun in late 1981 and had become a virtual depression by mid-1982. With one Canadian in six who wanted to work unable to do so, the government was uncertain about which way to turn. It responded in the time-honoured Canadian government fashion when forced to make a decision: it appointed a royal commission to buy time. This one, set up in fall 1982, was called the Royal Commission on the Economic Union and Development Prospects for Canada. As its chair, Trudeau chose Donald Macdonald, a Trudeau Finance Minister in an earlier incarnation who had become a major figure in the corporate community afterwards. The Commission had a broad mandate to make recommendations regarding the best policies for Canada to follow to ensure economic development. It undertook a host of studies by economists and political scientists that produced an impressive guide to the distribution of income among Canadians, the strengths and weaknesses of the various provincial economies, and the ins and outs of federal-provincial wrangling in the early eighties. The Commission held hearings across the country. Social action groups, including poverty groups, and Church and labour organizations called on the Commission to recommend a strengthening of government economic planning in Canada. They observed that while post-war governments had implemented many social reforms and intervened in the economy in many ways, much of this intervention was aimed at aiding particular industries or companies. Too little was being done to guarantee that all Canadians lived above the poverty line, and that the views and interests of the poor were incorporated into key economic plans of industries and government.[2]

The majority of Macdonald Commission members, dominated by business people like Macdonald himself, came to the opposite conclusion. Canada did not need more government economic planning; it needed less. Nor should there be a repeat of efforts to establish a "Third Option" as an alternative to either autarchy or extensive trade with a single nation. Instead, the commissioners suggested that Canada take the initiative to secure a free trade agreement with the United States. This would shield Canada against growing protectionist sentiment in the Congress and, at the same time, force Canadian companies to be more competitive with their American counterparts. The commissioners noted the success that European economies had achieved as a result of the gradual removal of tariffs and other barriers to trade among members of the European Economic Community, and suggested that both Canada and the United States could benefit from ignoring their political borders when it came to trade.[3]

By the time the Macdonald Commission reported in 1985, the Mulroney Conservatives had replaced the Liberals in office. Support for free trade had been brewing within the Conservative party for some time, but Mulroney, recently the president of an American company in Canada, was anxious not to offend conservative nation-

alists, and dismissed the idea of a free trade agreement when he ran
for the party leadership in 1983. That issue had been decided by
Canadians in 1911, he said. No political party, including the Conservatives, advocated free trade during the federal election of 1984. But,
on free trade, as on existing social programs and childcare, Mulroney
did the opposite in office of what he had promised while Opposition
leader. In March 1985, the prime minister met with President Reagan
in Washington. The two agreed to take steps to reduce trade tensions
between the two countries. American forestry companies in the
northwest charged that low "stumpage fees," that is, rents charged
by the British Columbia government for lands that were being forested, constituted a subsidy for Canadian forestry producers selling
in American markets; American grain producers claimed — falsely
— that Canadian producers enjoyed greater state subsidies than they
did. In both cases, the congressional representatives for the states
where these industries were important argued for surcharges on the
Canadian product when it was imported to the US. Such arguments
reflected a general surliness in Congress about foreign competition
which, while primarily directed against Japan, threatened to produce
legislation on trade restrictions that would hurt Canada.

Even before the Macdonald Commission report was issued, Mulroney was under pressure from big business interests to deal with
trade issues with the Americans globally rather than on a piece-meal
basis. Free trade was the solution preferred by the Business Council
on National Issues, a forum that had been created in 1976 to represent
the interests of the 150 largest corporations in Canada. Over a third
of these companies were foreign controlled, and their owners and
managers resented regulations that forced them to carry out production in Canada that would be cheaper to do abroad. Indeed the BCNI
made quite clear that it did not like the extent of government involvement in the economy that had developed since the Great Depression.
If many business leaders of the thirties were willing to let the state
take over certain economic functions to produce a climate of greater
stability, their 1980s and 1990s counterparts felt that the opposite
remedy was in their interests. They wanted less government regulation, smaller government budgets in the social service areas, and
lower taxes on businesses and rich people. Owners of capital, rather
than the state, they argued, were in the best position to decide what
were fair wages, good working conditions, and safe environmental
practices. If the state would get off their backs, they could apply new
technologies, compete more vigorously in the international economy

of "lean and mean" mega-corporations, and increase Canada's national wealth.[4] As they recognized, however, the majority of Canadians continued to disagree with such an analysis, which its opponents generally called the "corporate agenda" to point out not only its point of origin, but also its likely principal beneficiaries.

The BCNI recognized that a free trade agreement might offer a backdoor solution for implementing an economic agenda unpopular with Canadians. Free trade, they could argue, would protect Canada from protectionist impulses in the US, preserving Canada's most important market. They need not argue about the side effects of a free trade deal. In practice, as opponents of a free trade agreement suggested, unless there were side deals on social policy, working conditions, wages, and environmental regulations, countries in a free trade pact were forced to fall to the lowest common denominator in order to preserve jobs. Companies would be able to relocate without penalty to the country which offered them the best deal on taxes, wages, regulations, and the like; in short, they did not have to balance such considerations with worries about tariffs or quotas against producers outside Canada.[5] There was little trouble persuading President Reagan, a virtual handmaiden of big corporations, to agree to such negotiations. Indeed, during his election campaign in 1980, he had promised to try to achieve free trade between the United States, Canada, and Mexico.

Mulroney proved equally easy to persuade. During his first year in office, he attempted to undo the modest nationalist efforts of the Liberals. The National Energy Program was abandoned, and plans to privatize Petro-Can, the government energy corporation, were announced. The government gave greater protection to American multi-national pharmaceutical firms for their products which Canadian companies were copying and offering to consumers at lower prices. The multi-nationals promised to do more research in Canada in return for the government's concessions, but consumer groups denounced a move that they regarded as likely to hurt individual consumers, as well as the burgeoning health budgets of provinces. Since drugs in hospitals and prescription drugs for seniors (and in Saskatchewan, for everybody) were paid for by provincial governments, forced use of brand names rather than generics for a variety of new drugs meant huge additional costs. The Foreign Investment Review Agency was disbanded and replaced by Investment Canada, a toothless regulator of foreign takeovers of Canadian companies. FIRA had turned down only a small number of applications from

American corporations planning takeovers of companies operating in Canada on the grounds that there was no net benefit to Canadians from the takeover. But the need to justify their takeover of firms infuriated American investors and the occasional rejection of an application produced exaggerated claims of FIRA's supposed malevolence towards American capitalists. Investment Canada moved to reassure non-resident investors. During its first six years of operation, the agency accepted more than 5000 applications and turned down none. For example, in 1990, it allowed Varta Batteries, which had plants in Winnipeg and St. Thomas, to be taken over by Johnson Controls Inc. of Milwaukee, even though this gave the latter firm a seventy-five percent share of the Canadian battery market. Two weeks later, Johnson closed Varta's Winnipeg plant, putting 192 workers out of a job. In 191, Johnson closed down another of its Canadian plants, dismissing 280 Canadian workers to move production to its Tennessee plant. Tennessee was a state known for its anti-union laws and low wages in the manufacturing sector.[6]

In September 1985, Brian Mulroney, the erstwhile opponent of free trade, announced that Canada and the United States were about to begin negotiating an accord on free trade. Soon after, a high-level negotiating team from Canada, headed by Simon Reisman, a veteran trade negotiator, began negotiations with the United States to produce a comprehensive trade agreement. On 4 October 1987, the Canadian and American governments reached agreement in principle on a bilateral free trade agreement. The agreement promised the removal of all tariff barriers to trade between the two countries within a five-year period of the signing of the FTA. Non-tariff barriers were also to be removed, though when an industry was threatened with total collapse in one country or the other, some provisions were made to allow the government of that country to defend its existence. "Unfair subsidies" of industries were to be eliminated, though the two countries would have five years to work out a clause that would define what sorts of subsidies were unfair, and which served legitimate social purposes to justify an exemption from free trade. Cultural industries were protected from the agreement's provisions for free trade. A panel of trade arbitrators, with equal participation from the two countries, would rule on disputes regarding violation of the FTA. Either country could abrogate the agreement after it had been in place for at least five years, by serving a year's notice of intent to end the deal.

While both houses of the American Congress passed the legislation without much debate, the agreement caused a great deal of controversy in Canada. The New Democrats had been opposed to the negotiations, arguing that any free trade deal would promote the corporate agenda by making it difficult for Canada to follow policies that differed from American policies. The Liberals were divided on the issue of free trade, as on most issues, but said little before the agreement was tabled before the House of Commons and the Senate. Under John Turner, the federal Liberal party seemed to be sinking into oblivion. Turner's lacklustre leadership resulted in a variety of plots to depose him that did not end with a decisive vote of confidence in his favour at a party convention in 1986. The historic party of government in twentieth-century Canada lacked direction, and it fell to third place in the opinion polls, as the New Democrats, lead by Ed Broadbent, soared to the top of the polls for much of 1987. The NDP seemed to benefit from the shock many Canadians felt because, while the economy was improving, unemployment remained high. Scandals involving government ministers and MPs also gave the Mulroney government an image of sleaze from which the affable Broadbent appeared to be the early beneficiary.

Turner tried to stage a comeback by placing his party on record as firmly opposing the deal negotiated by the Mulroney government. He vowed that a Liberal government would renegotiate the deal to provide greater protection for Canadian industries and workers. He was vague as to how this could be achieved within the framework of a "free trade" agreement, though he made frequent references to the 1965 Auto Pact. That agreement, with its guarantees that a certain percentage of North American automobile jobs would be reserved for Canadians, represented managed trade rather than free trade. But the two terms were easily confused, and though the FTA and the Auto Pact represented very different principles, Prime Minister Mulroney as well often pointed to the Auto Pact to demonstrate that "free trade" could be of great benefit to Canadians.

The Liberals and NDP lacked the votes in the House of Commons to defeat the FTA negotiated between the United States and Canada. But the Liberals still dominated the unelected Senate and they used their majority there to defeat the bill, indicating that they would only pass the FTA if a federal election produced a House majority in favour of the bill. Brian Mulroney had not mentioned free trade in the 1984 election, they noted, and he had no mandate to push through so momentous a piece of legislation without a vote of confidence from the Canadian people.

The 1988 Election

Mulroney obliged the Senate by calling an election for November 1988. The election was perhaps as close to a referendum on one issue as any in Canadian history, except for the 1917 "conscription" election. It was a referendum, however, in which the pro-free trade forces enjoyed an advantage: they were, for the most part, within one party, the governing Conservative Party. With both the Liberals and the New Democrats opposing the agreement, anti-free traders, a majority in most polls, were less clear about where to bestow their vote. As the election opened, the NDP remained the stronger contender of the two parties. But, although the NDP and its union allies had been opposing free trade over the previous three years, their electoral strategists had decided not to make free trade the issue of the election. An American public relations agency whom the NDP, supposedly a nationalist party, had hired to advise it on election strategy argued that Canadians did not rate the social democrats highly when asked which party could best manage the Canadian economy. Rather, what they liked about the NDP was its reliable defence of social programs from all suggestions of cutbacks, and the honesty of its leaders, most particularly national leader Ed Broadbent. So the NDP began its campaign with a focus on the avuncular Broadbent and his party's historic role as a defender of greater equality for Canadians.

But whatever the American publicists thought, it was free trade that the electors were concerned about. Turner seized momentum from Broadbent by using the election's only televised debate among the leaders to accuse Mulroney of having sold out the country. Though he remained ambivalent about free trade as a principle, Turner was able to project his party as an effective instrument for opposition to what the Liberal leader called the "Mulroney free trade plan." Both the Liberals and the NDP focussed their opposition on the agreement's blanket attacks on unfair subsidies, without defining such subsidies. As Turner indicated, the five-year stall in providing a definition of subsidies was irresponsible since, if the FTA was implemented, Canadian companies would do all their planning with it in mind and would be unwilling and probably unable to re-adjust if, in five years, the agreement was suddenly abrogated. So it was important to know from the word go if regional subsidies, medicare, or the Canadian Wheat Board and other agricultural commodity marketing boards were considered subsidies. Was this an agreement solely about trade or was it an attempt to remake Canada, which had developed very different institutions from the United States, along the American model?

Mulroney attempted to persuade Canadians to read the agreement literally. It had no provisions that required the elimination of medicare, the lowering of minimum wages, or the relaxing of environmental standards. Canadian governments would continue to remain sovereign. The opposition's arguments, he charged, were made up from whole cloth. The nonagenarian chair of the royal commission that had called upon Ottawa to institute medicare, Justice Emmett Hall, a lifelong Tory, also argued that nothing in the Free Trade Agreement required Canada to disband or weaken its social programs, including medicare. The business supporters of the agreement inundated Canadian homes with propaganda in favour of the agreement that also encouraged such a literal reading. The Council of Canadians, an organization of individuals opposed to the agreement, and the Pro-Canada Network (later the Action Canada Network), a coalition of trade unions, church groups, women's groups, and other social action groups, tried to counter this propaganda. But the funds available to them, as well as access to the media, paled against the resources accumulated by the supporters of the corporate agenda.

The November 1988 election gave the Conservatives forty-three percent of the vote. But this translated into a comfortable majority of House seats. The Liberals, with thirty-two percent of the vote, and the NDP with twenty percent had outpolled the free trade forces, but this counted for little in a first-past-the-post electoral system. Interestingly, the anti-free-trade vote was most likely to yield seats for the opposition in regions where one of the two parties opposing the deal was too weak to siphon many votes from the other. In the Atlantic provinces, though the Conservatives won forty-one percent of the vote, the Liberals, with forty-six percent, were able to win twenty of thirty-two seats.[7] In British Columbia, by contrast, the New Democrats became the magnet for free trade opponents, except in the Vancouver seat contested by Liberal leader Turner. Shortly after the election, the Senate agreed to ratify the agreement and it came into force on 1 January 1989.

The Effect of "Free Trade"

The election was no sooner over than the BCNI and other business organizations began to insist that Canadians must now adjust their wages, social programs, business taxes, and environmental standards to match the lowest common denominator available in certain regions of the United States, particularly in the South, where a long history of racism had allowed white corporate leaders to prevent any working-class political unity. In that region, trade unions had few members and state "right to work" laws banned compulsory union membership at any job site, making it difficult for unions to resist employer efforts to hire or retain only workers who agreed not to be union members. Minimum wages were half what they were in most Canadian provinces, social services were abysmal, environmental regulation was a joke, and taxation levels for the wealthy were low. Wages were even lower in the *maquiladoras*, the manufacturing centres on the Mexican side of the US-Mexican border, whose products could enter the US tariff-free, and via the FTA, then be shipped to Canada, again without tariff barriers. The message from the corporations was very different than what it had been in the election. They now seemed to admit that while the Free Trade Agreement did not spell out a neo-conservative agenda, such an agenda was implicit in the pact. "Companies need to use free trade as a catalyst to mobilize employees to cut costs," warned Ray Verdon of Nabisco Brands Ltd. "Nothing clears the mind so much as the spectre of being hung in the morning."[8]

Canadians had been told by the Tories during the election that their companies were not weaklings, and that they would be demonstrating lack of confidence in them if they voted against the FTA. But, after the election, thousands of companies, both foreign and Canadian controlled, demonstrated their lack of confidence in Canadians. Adam Zimmerman, chairman of Noranda Forest Inc., put the corporations' case bluntly: "If you are in a business that can move, why bother with the hassle of staying in Canada?"[9]

One company that did not want to bother with the hassle was Shellar Globe, an American-controlled automobile parts company. When 350 workers in its steering-wheel plant near Windsor, Ontario, went on strike, it moved this operation to Mexico.

With tariffs on US produce removed, US agri-business giant Hunt-Wesson closed its Tilbury, Ontario, ketchup plant, focussing its operations on its plants in Ohio and California. That left local farmers with no buyers for their tomatoes.[10] Nabisco's cost-cutting included forcing its Niagara Falls workers to accept a variety of concessions, while its Simcoe workers were "hung in the morning" as the plant closed for good. Indeed, in the early nineties hundreds of thousands of manufacturing jobs were lost in Canada in the wake of the FTA. Workers in many of the jobs that remained were forced to accept wage cuts and speedups to appease employers who knew that they could move jobs out of Canada without fear of retaliation in the Canadian market by the Canadian government, in the form of tariffs, quotas, or other measures. For example, 100 workers at the Electrowire plant in Owen Sound, Ontario, were told flatly by management that they would accept a wage freeze for three years and absorb the cost of living increase themselves, or the operation would be moved to Mexico. The company, which manufactures electrical harnesses for the automobile industry, is an American subsidiary. Management's letter to the workers enclosed a copy of a letter from a firm that helped companies relocate to the *maquiladora* zone. The advantages of relocation, noted the firm, included "co-operative workers that follow your instructions" and "hourly costs, including bonuses, space and utilities from $2.95 to $4.50 per hour compared with the Canadian average of $12.00 which does not include these costs." The Electrowire workers acceded to the company's demand.[11]

The damage went beyond the manufacturing sector. Canadian trucking firms shed 16,000 employees from 1989 to 1992, as American competitors invaded their market, free from any fears of regulation by provincial governments.[12] Part of the problem faced by the manufacturers and the truckers was that the Mulroney government oddly chose the time that the free trade agreement was introduced to pursue monetary policies that pushed the value of the Canadian dollar up from seventy-one cents to eighty-six cents within a year. The low dollar had stimulated Canadian exports, while the high dollar, unsurprisingly, attracted imports and priced many exporters out of their foreign markets. It sent Canadian shoppers who lived within a reasonable distance of the American border (easily a majority of Canadians) on shopping excursions to the south, where there were many bargains to be found with an eighty-six-cent Canadian dollar. During the free trade talks, the Americans had repeatedly charged that Canada had deliberately allowed its dollar to fall in value to compete unfairly with American producers. They demanded a higher dollar as part of the price of achieving an agreement on trade. Publicly, the Mulroney government never gave in to what seemed an outrageous effort to control Canadian monetary policy. But, the coincidence of the rise in the dollar and the implementation of the agreement caused many to question the government's motivation.[13]

Free trade, as its critics had predicted, not only cost Canadian jobs, but also shifted the patterns of Canadian trade away from inter-provincial trade towards greater north-south exchanges. Statistics Canada reported that interprovincial trade rose 6.6 percent from 1990 to 1995. In the same years, Canada's exports increased sixty-nine percent, and its imports by fifty-five percent. Quebec and Alberta, in particular, augmented their international trade at the expense of sales and purchases within Canada. In Quebec's case, a deficit of a billion dollars in its inter-provincial trade in 1995 was more than balanced by a $3.8 billion surplus in international trade. The Montreal *Gazette*, with an eye to the arguments of separatists, reported gloomily that "the province's fundamentally changed trade patterns could hold implications for its political future."[14]

While Canadians reeled from the job losses that coincided with the FTA's implementation, the Mulroney government denied any connection between the two. They blamed the recession for the losses and argued that, in the long term, the FTA would mean jobs. Before Canadians could catch their breath, their national government was joining with the Americans once again to launch a broader free trade deal, this time to include Mexico. The North American Free Trade Agreement, proclaimed in 1992, extended most of the provisions of the FTA to Mexico as well. Both the Americans and Mulroney viewed NAFTA as another step towards eventual free trade spanning all of the Americas.

Canadians were almost evenly divided regarding the benefits of NAFTA. While business organizations on the whole supported the idea of opening markets, the social activists of the Action Canada Network pointed out that the job losses and declining living standards ushered in by the FTA would only become worse if Canada was to compete with Third World countries where decades of oppression by military governments had given capitalists crushing power over workers and peasants, for whom unions were often out of the question, and state social programs non-existent.

But the business chorus was successful in convincing Canadians as a whole that "globalization," as supposedly represented by NAFTA, was inevitable and that there was no point in holding back the clock. Jean Chrétien suggested that there were a few problems with NAFTA, but called for re-negotiation rather than rejection. His party, attempting to appease NAFTA critics, wanted changes in the agreement's provisions regarding "the environment, energy, subsidies, cross-border dispute mechanisms, and anti-dumping codes."[15] NDP leader Audrey McLaughlin called for Canada to get out of both NAFTA and FTA. But her party was virtually decimated in the 1993 election. Nationalist Mel Hurtig formed a new party called the National Party, dedicated to providing Canadians with alternatives to the Americanization of their economy and cultural lives. But this party received fewer than two percent of ballots in the federal election. The reality was that neither the NDP nor Hurtig's party was able to make trade with the Americans a burning election issue in 1993, the way it had been in 1988. Chrétien, once in power, had discussions with the other NAFTA nation leaders regarding the agreement, but nothing of substance was changed. For good or evil, the Canadian economy seemed to have become more than ever a regional variant within the American economy. Where did this leave Canada within the world?

Foreign Policy

Having angered the Americans with some of its economic policies directed at foreign investors, such as NEP and FIRA, the Trudeau government continued in the early eighties to avoid taking foreign policy stances that would also irk the Americans. The exception was the US invasion of Grenada, a tiny Caribbean country, in the fall of 1983. The Americans, backed by other Caribbean governments, had decided to intervene in Grenada after hard-line Marxists ousted the more moderate, though also unelected, left-wing regime headed by Maurice Bishop. The new regime was certainly unpopular in Grenada, but both Trudeau and Margaret Thatcher pointed out that it was up to the people of Grenada to establish their governments, and wrong of the Americans to invade and install a new government.

Canada was not defiant, by contrast, as the Americans stepped up the nuclear arms race. In July 1983, Canada answered affirmatively to an American request to test the CRUISE missile over northern Canada. The CRUISE was an intermediate-range weapon, whose beauty to military planners was that it could fly unmanned at low altitudes and subsonic speeds, making it unlikely that the air and sea sensors of "the enemy" could detect its presence. Peace activists considered weapons of this kind particularly dangerous because their very existence would provoke paranoia about possible attack, even when there was no physical evidence that an attack was under way. This made an accidental nuclear war ever more likely.[16]

Trudeau agreed to CRUISE testing at the same time that he advocated a policy of "nuclear suffocation," the limitation and eventual end to the production of new strategic nuclear weapon systems. The NDP's foreign affairs critic, Pauline Jewett, scathingly dismissed this concept, an alternative to disarmament, as "the strategy of nuclear weapons components production, cruise missile testing and sycophantic support for Ronald Reagan's nuclear war-fighting scenarios."[17]

Jewett's reference to nuclear weapons components production was hardly facetious. Not only nuclear weapons, but weapons generally proved a lucrative export item for Canada during both the Trudeau and Mulroney years. Canada's military exports were only $336 million in 1970, but climbed to $721 million in 1980, and $1.9 billion in 1985. Most of that weaponry went to the United States, with about ten percent going to western Europe. Some of the rest found its way into war zones. Canada, via third parties, cheerfully supplied both sides in the Iran-Iraq war that raged through most of the eighties. Engines for military aircraft produced by Brazil and Italy and sold to the two combatants were made in Canada. Government permits were issued for these sales, which were not examined very closely because part of the government's industrial policy was to promote arms sales. Between 1969 and 1985, the government gave subsidies for modernizing, upgrading, and marketing military hardware that ranged from 9.3 to 38.3 percent of each year's military sales to the Americans.[18]

In 1985, government officials described their goals regarding the Defence Production Sharing Agreement of 1959 to be "greater integration of military production, greater standardizaton of military equipment, wider dispersal of production facilities, establishment of supplemental sources of supply."[19] Such "integration" between Canadian and American defence production was largely incompatible with establishing Canadian foreign policies at variance with American policies, and occasional clashes between Canada and the United States did occur. They were not in the area of human rights. Though Canada maintained that protection of human rights everywhere was important to this country, human rights considerations were, in practice, "marginal" to policy-makers.[20] They were also applied selectively and hypocritically so as not to offend American sensitivities. Because the Americans had vital interests in Saudi Arabia and Indonesia, for example, Canada ignored human rights violations in these nations while happily denouncing similar violations in the Soviet Union and its satellites.[21]

Despite such constraints, Pierre Trudeau tried to stake out some independent ground for Canada in world affairs. Apart from promoting limitations on development of nuclear weapons, Trudeau joined many Third World leaders in the early eighties in calling for a better distribution of wealth among the world's nations. Canada, however, with its economy in recesson, was not willing to increase its meagre foreign aid budget. Much of the aid offered by the Canadian International Development Agency (CIDA) was "tied aid," that is, aid dollars were dependent on the recipient nation using that money to buy goods produced in Canada. This was clearly meant to benefit Canadian industries rather than to recognize economic independence for recipient nations.

The Mulroney government set out its foreign policy objectives in a 1985 document entitled "Competitiveness and Security," which highlighted trade as the paramount objective of Canada's dealings with other nations and linked Canada's security to its alliance with other Western nations, especially the United States.[22] The Mulroney government spent little time decrying increases in nuclear weaponry or in worrying about the distribution of wealth between industrialized and Third World countries. When Ronald Reagan announced in 1985 that his government intended to spend billions to produce a nuclear shield around the US, the peace movement in both the United States and Canada denounced the idea as sheer folly and a waste of monies that could be used to feed the world's hungry people. Indeed, it was argued, nuclear tensions could only increase if one of the two superpowers appeared to be on the verge of making itself invulnerable at the same time that it continued to harbour nuclear weapons; the other country was bound to become dangerously fearful about what would happen once the "enemy" was able to launch a nuclear attack without fear of retaliation. Mulroney sidestepped the issues of morality and prudence surrounding Reagan's so-called "Star Wars" initiative to announce that Canadian companies could accept Star Wars research contracts, but that the Canadian government would have no direct involvement in the project. The government then announced a $12 billion program of nuclear submarines for surveillance of the Canadian North. His government would prove a reliable ally of its FTA and then NAFTA partner.

The Mulroney government also made Canada one of twenty-eight countries to participate in an American plan in 1991, to make war on Iraq in retaliation for its invasion of oil-rich Kuwait the previous year. Neither the Americans nor the Canadians had paid much attention as Iraq invaded Iran in 1979; indeed, both countries supplied weapons to Iraq during that long war. But Iran, after the 1979 overthrow of the Shah, who had been propped up by the United States, was governed by Muslim fundamentalists who, while as undemocratic as the Shah, were also hostile to most foreigners, and particularly the Americans. Neither Canada nor the United States was perturbed that a country with such a government should face unprovoked aggression from another country. Kuwait, by contrast, run by an authoritarian monarchy, was a huge source of profits for American oil companies, and an important source for oil for the US, as well as several western European countries. Iraq could not be allowed to conquer such a country and threaten American dominance over Middle Eastern oil. Nor were the Americans willing to wait to see if UN-ordered sanctions against Iraq would work.[23] With the Cold War effectively over, there was a huge clamour in the US for a "peace dividend," that is, for either new domestic spending or tax cuts resulting from cutting a bloated military budget that had grown in the name of a cause that no longer existed. By going to war in the Gulf, American President George Bush and his congressional supporters who represented the still-thriving "military-industrial complex" in the US could justify maintaining military spending at high levels for a bit longer. Canada, which stood to lose trade if the Americans required less of the military hardware produced in Canada, did not wish to demur from President Bush's approach. During the Gulf War, Secretary of State for External Affairs Joe Clark had nonetheless suggested that after the war the UN should work to achieve a global embargo on arms to the Middle East.But George Bush's administration opposed such an embargo vehemently, and indeed, at the end of the war, provided almost $20 billion in arms to their Middle Eastern allies against Iraq. Canada did not protest and did not take its embargo plan to the UN.

But the Tories did have some skirmishes with the Americans. A costly one involved Canada's sovereignty in its northern waters. When the American icebreaker *Polar Sea* passed through Canadian waters without warning or permission in August 1985, Joe Clark presented to Parliament a Canadian Laws Offshore Application Act and beefed up Canadian air and sea surveillance of the Arctic. The

Mulroney Conservatives also continued and extended cautious efforts by the Trudeau government to boycott trade with racist South Africa, though the Americans were hostile to such efforts until Congress joined the international boycott in 1986. Mulroney also proved willing to recognize the Palestinian Liberation Organization as the legitimate leaders of the Palestinians after the PLO agreed to recognize the state of Israel in return for the latter's recognition of the right of the Palestinians to statehood.

The Tories' plan to equip Canada with expensive nuclear subs would become an embarrassment as the Cold War wound down after the accession to power in the Soviet Union of Mikhail Gorbachev in 1985. Gorbachev, anxious to focus Soviet attention on the domestic economy rather than continue the ruinous competition with the Americans for military superiority, carried out a "peace offensive" with the West. He led the way in negotiating agreements with the Americans for massive reductions in nuclear armaments. He also attempted to reform both the Soviet economy and the Soviet political system.

By the end of 1991, the Soviet Union had collapsed and the successor states in the now-independent republics went capitalist for the most part, and had no interest in continuing an ideological struggle with the West. With the Soviet nuclear threat gone, the Tories had difficulty explaining why the subs were still needed. The Liberal defeat of the Tories put an end to the plans for the nuclear submarines.

Otherwise, the change of government in 1993 made as little difference in foreign policy as in trade policy. Indeed, the Chrétien government stressed the linkage between the two every bit as much as the Mulroney government. While the Liberals in opposition had been critical of the Tories' disregard for human rights issues — a significant exception was Mulroney's earlier-mentioned willingness to enforce a partial trade boycott against South Africa, in solidarity with Commonwealth countries in the Third World — they changed their tune when they were in office. The People's Republic of China had snuffed out a pro-democracy movement in 1989 by slaughtering about 4000 demonstrators in Peking's Tiananmen Square, and China continued to repress pro-democracy activities through the 1990s. For the Tories and the Liberals alike, what was more important was that despite the continued rule of the Communist Party in China, the economy of the country had taken on a capitalist character. Trade and investment from the West were welcome. The prime minister and the premiers together visited the People's Republic in 1994, to drum up trade. They kept their thoughts regarding the government's human rights record to themselves. In light of the Liberals' unwillingness to denounce even more murderous right-wing governments in the Third World during earlier periods of power, this openness towards a repressive, nominally Communist regime is hardly surprising. Also, in the light of their earlier record, it comes as little shock that they proved willing to allow the export of fighter aircraft to Turkey, helicopters to Colombia, and a variety of weapons systems to Thailand, all countries with repressive regimes.[24] Such sales violated the spirit of the promises the Liberals made in their campaign "Red Book" in 1993, but the "Red Book" had also promised the renegotiation of NAFTA, the maintenance of social program funding, and the abolition of the Goods and Services Tax (GST) imposed by the Mulroney government. None of these promises were fulfilled.

Though the Chrétien government attempted to avoid conflict with the Americans, one festering sore, at least from the viewpoint of right-wing Republicans, was Canada's continuing trade with Communist Cuba. Canada had never broken off trade relations with Cuba, and when the Soviet Union collapsed, leaving Cuba bereft of its principal investment and trade partner, the investment possibilities in Cuba expanded greatly. Cuba was particularly anxious to have Canadian mining companies as co-partners in developing its minerals, so they would have exports that would bring foreign currency into a country that had only survived the American embargo imposed in 1959 because of Soviet aid. American Senator Jesse Helms, well-known both for his opposition to civil rights for African-Americans and for his anti-Communism, co-sponsored a bill, known as the Helms-Burton bill, which created American trade penalties for countries that traded with Cuba, and held the officers of foreign companies which traded with Cuba liable for prosecution under American law. This would effectively bar these individuals from entering the United States. It was a particularly offensive bill coming from a country which had allowed its corporations to conduct trade with Nazi Germany during the early years of World War II. Canada and the countries of western Europe protested the bill, which passed Congress and received President Bill Clinton's support. The Clinton administration delayed the bill's promulgation, but would not withdraw from the principle that the Americans had the right to punish nations that traded with countries that the US deemed its "enemies," to prosecute non-resident officers of companies incorporated abroad, or to seize the US properties of such companies.

Canada continued to play an important role in international peacekeeping efforts during both the Mulroney and Chrétien periods. Though the defence budget was reduced, and Canada had reduced the number of theatres in which it was willing to play a peacekeeping role, it remained in Cyprus and in a number of new hot spots. For example, as the Yugoslav republic collapsed in the nineties in the wake of the fall of Communism in Eastern Europe, Canada played a role in keeping the various ethnic factions apart, as Serbs and Croats clashed, and then Bosnia became a killing ground where Serb forces proved particularly vicious in their efforts at "ethnic cleansing" of areas where Moslems or Croats lived side by side with Serbs. Canada was also involved in trying to restore order to Somalia, a country which had received arms first from the Soviets and then the West, as a result of the complicated politics of the Cold War, only to disintegrate in the 1990s. Canada's participation, while first applauded at home as well as by many Somalis, was quickly tainted when members of the Canadian Airborne regiment killed a Somali teenager whom they suspected of trying to loot their compound. While the military attempted a cover-up, it soon became clear that organized racists with Nazi connections had infiltrated the regiment, and that the young Somali had been murdered in cold blood. He had been tortured, and several members of the regiment had participated in the torture while others had looked on without attempting to stop this inhuman behaviour. Subsequent trials and a government investigation raised serious questions about the professionalism of the Canadian military and the soundness of its recruiting practices.

At the end of the century, Canada's role in the world community was probably less important than it had been at any point in the post-war period. Having tied its trade and its foreign policy closely to the Americans, Canada gave itself a margin of manoeuvre on the international stage that was quite restricted. In an era of deficit-cutting, Canada was also anxious to cut both its military budget and its foreign aid. Much of its foreign aid, indeed, was no longer going to the world's poorest countries, but instead to the nations that formed from the remains of the former Soviet empire. None of these nations were as desperately poor as Third World countries, but many of them had large emigré groups in Canada willing to pressure Canadian governments for aid. In general, Canada contented itself with a declining presence in peacekeeping, and with efforts to increase Cana-

dian trade in various countries. Talk of supporting movements for
democracy and of redistributing wealth among the nations of the
world still occurred, but there was little concrete evidence that such
concerns were being converted into actions. Of course, the Cold War
had distorted whatever efforts Canada had made in such directions
before 1990. The end of the Cold War seemed to bring little positive
change in Canadian foreign policy directions. Perhaps the country
was too small to affect international events. Or perhaps its leaders
were too small-minded. In either case, it seems fair to say that at the
end of the century, Canada, though a prosperous industrial nation,
played a peripheral role in world affairs. Its internal divisions,
focussed on the ever-present "national unity" debate, have made a
greater role seem unrealistic.

Brian Mulroney, 1983. NAC PA-146485

Fourteen

Quebec Nationalism and Globalism

On 30 October 1995, the people of Quebec, for a second time, voted in a referendum that asked them, more or less directly, whether they wished Quebec to remain within Canada. The result was fairly close to a dead heat. While 2,362,355 people casting valid ballots, accounting for 50.6 percent of the voters, voted "non," 2,308,504 voters marked their ballots "oui." This meant that 49.4 percent of the Quebec electorate had expressed a preference for Quebec becoming a sovereign nation. There were some voting irregularities that inflated support for the sovereignist option, and there were accusations that the question on the ballot was dishonestly phrased. Nonetheless, it was clear that just about half of the Quebec population, and about sixty percent of its francophones, were prepared for Quebec either to leave Canada or, at a minimum, to have Quebec recognized as a virtually autonomous entity within Canada. This chapter traces the ups and downs of Quebec nationalism from the defeat of the 1980 referendum to the near-victory of the 1995 referendum and the aftermath of the second referendum. As we shall see, the political and economic changes of the eighties and nineties changed the character of Quebec nationalism, while limiting the ability of the federal government to appear as a necessary element in the lives of the Québécois.

The New Constitution of 1982

During the 1980 referendum, Pierre Trudeau had promised Québécois voters that a defeat of the sovereignist option would be rewarded by constitutional changes. He was vague, however, about what changes he envisioned. Provincial Liberal leader Claude Ryan, as leader of the "non" forces in the provincial referendum, had called, in his "Livre Beige," for a massive decentralization of power in

Canada, but there could be little doubt that Pierre Trudeau, a defender of a strong central government, did not support Ryan. Trudeau had always made clear his view that Canada was already one of the world's most decentralized nations. He believed that the federal government had a duty to ensure that Canadians felt at home when they moved from one part of the nation to the other, whether with regard to the social programs available to them or with regard to language rights. The federal government, in his view, was the major instrument for achieving some degree of uniformity of living conditions across the country.

René Lévesque, humble in defeat, announced that he accepted the verdict of the Quebec electorate and would try to protect Quebec's interests within Confederation, attempting to win provincial control over as many jurisdictions as possible. His government was re-elected in 1981 with just short of half the votes cast, their significantly better showing than the "oui" vote in the referendum result a clear indication that the Québécois liked the reformist orientation of the PQ, and the apparent honesty and efficiency of its administration. He was no sooner re-elected than he had to cope with what appeared to Quebec separatists as a dangerous gambit on Trudeau's part: Trudeau intended to repatriate the Canadian constitution and, if necessary, he would approach the Queen directly to end British control over the Canadian constitution. Trudeau's strategy broke with federal attempts over two decades to win support of all provinces for constitutional changes. British Prime Minister Margaret Thatcher indicated publicly that she would accede to a request from the Canadian government to repatriate the constitution. Whether the provincial governments joined in such a request was a domestic matter, rather than a matter of concern for the British government.

The provinces, but especially Quebec, hoped to use repatriation to redefine the relative powers of the provinces and the federal government. Only Ontario and New Brunswick agreed to Trudeau's original proposal, which included several features not discussed in previous rounds of federal-provincial constitutional discussions. First, Trudeau included a Charter of Rights and Freedoms which was similar to the American Bill of Rights. This would assert federal control in an area previously reserved under the British North America Act for the provinces: civil rights. Secondly, Trudeau's amending formula would not give provincial governments the right to veto constitutional changes. While governments alone would be involved in ratifying changes, provided they were in agreement, the people of the provinces whose governments opposed constitutional changes would have the final say via a referendum. Either Ontario, Quebec, or a majority of the western or Atlantic provinces could force such a referendum by refusing to ratify a constitutional change approved by Ottawa. Again, the provincial governments regarded such appeals to the people over their provincial leaders as a federal attempt to weaken provinces in areas under their jurisdiction. The eight provinces that disagreed with Trudeau's proposals formed a common front to oppose the prime minister. They called for a repatriation without the Charter, and with an amending formula that gave no province a veto, but required the approval of seven provinces with fifty percent of the population, before a constitutional change could occur.

René Lévesque joined the common front, although, ironically, the separatist premier was the first Quebec premier to agree to a proposal that would remove Quebec's right to a veto over constitutional changes. Later, when the new constitution was ratified without Quebec's support, Pierre Trudeau would claim that Lévesque had given up Quebec's veto when he joined the "group of eight" in a common front. This was misleading. Earlier Quebec premiers, who had clung tenaciously to a veto for Quebec, were not negotiating with a prime minister determined to force repatriation no matter what the provinces thought. They did not face the choice that Lévesque faced. As a sovereignist, he bitterly resented Trudeau's suggestion that the civil liberties of Québécois needed to be protected by what he regarded as a foreign government, its Supreme Court to have precedence over the legislative assembly of Quebec. Nor did he recognize the right of such a government to force votes in Quebec on questions of jurisdiction, where the Quebec government was unwilling to cede powers. Several provinces were taking the federal government to court to stop unilateral patriation and argued that their prospects for victory in the courts and their prospects for winning favour in the court of public opinion would be strengthened if they put forth constructive proposals. So, reluctantly, Lévesque, who would have liked to use the obstructionist tactics that non-sovereignist provincial governments in Quebec had used in the past, threw in his lot with the other premiers who were opposing Trudeau. While his main goal in the area of constitutional change was to win more powers for Quebec now that sovereignty had been put on the back burner for a while, he felt that in the short term, it was more important not to let Trudeau erode those powers Quebec already enjoyed. He had the support of the Quebec provincial Liberals, most of whom felt that Trudeau had misled the province's voters during the referendum. His promises of constitutional change, while vague, had been interpreted to mean changes that would strengthen Quebec's powers, not those of the federal government.

The Supreme Court ruled in September 1981 that the federal government did not require the unanimous consent of the provinces to repatriate the constitution, though it did need the support of several provinces representing a substantial percentage of the Canadian population. This was not especially helpful to the provinces, since Trudeau indicated that, in his view, this allowed him to go to the Queen with the support of the two provinces he had already brought onside. With Margaret Thatcher unwavering in her disinterest regarding provincial views, Trudeau was assured of success. A last-ditch effort to achieve a federal-provincial agreement before Trudeau went to London occurred in early November 1981. The provinces were negotiating from a weak position. All the polls indicated that Canadians generally liked the idea of the Charter of Rights and Freedoms and had little interest in the arcane debates about amending the constitution. Manitoba Premier Sterling Lyon, a right-winger facing defeat in an election to be held within days of the federal-provincial meeting, felt that he had to compromise with the federal government so that his voters did not blame him for causing the stillbirth of a constitution that included the Charter. In the end, the seven premiers other than Lévesque in the "group of eight" met with Trudeau and the two premiers who already supported him and hammered out a compromise. They conceded the Charter to Trudeau and he conceded their amending formula. The reach of the Charter, however, was reduced by allowing the provinces the right to attach a "notwithstanding" clause to override pieces of legislation to which they did not wish the Charter to apply.

René Lévesque was left in the dark as his supposed colleagues worked out a deal with his nemesis. A constitutional deal was worked out without the participation of a province where one-quarter of Canada's population and five-sixths of its francophones lived. Lévesque drew as much political advantage from this turn of events as possible. He complained of the stab in the back by the English-speaking premiers, and of the centralizing constitution with which Quebec had been saddled. His personal humiliation by the premiers and Trudeau, he argued, was really a humiliation of Québécois generally. Trudeau responded sharply that he and many of his leading ministers were Québécois as well and that, while Lévesque claimed to want to participate in the constitution-making process, his separatist goals caused him to attempt to wreck the process. This accusation seemed somewhat hollow considering that Lévesque had surrendered Quebec's right to a veto in order to make common cause with other premiers. It also did not change the fact that Trudeau and the premiers had shut Lévesque out of the last-minute negotiations rather than allowing him to participate, for better or worse.[1]

The Quebec Liberals agreed with the Parti Québécois that the process had been flawed and the result injurious to Quebec interests. The Quebec National Assembly unanimously condemned the federal government for planning to proceed to Britain without Quebec's support, undermining Trudeau's claim that the split in Quebec over the new constitution was simply a measure of the federalist-separatist divide. Quebec nationalism was not limited to the sovereignist movement, as Trudeau was well aware. His efforts to raise the stature of the federal government in the province were bound to be opposed by nationalists of all stripes.

During the last several weeks of 1981, the debate on the constitution within English Canada, on the one hand, and Quebec, on the other, reflected the "two solitudes" that had marked Canada since the Conquest of 1760. Outside of Quebec, the media focus was on the efforts of women and Natives to win some concessions before the final wording of the new constitution was determined. English-Canadian women, led by the National Action Committee on the Status of Women, had pressured the federal government to include two sections in the new constitution that would win for Canadian women the equivalent of the "equal rights amendment" for which American feminists were carrying out a long, and eventually unsuccessful, struggle. Particularly important was Section 28, which stated that "notwithstanding anything in this Charter, the rights and freedoms referred to in it are guaranteed equally to male and female persons." NAC's campaign for this section had cost it the membership of the Fédération des femmes du Québec, which joined the provincial politicians in rejecting unilateral repatriation and resented NAC's assumption that dealing solely with the federal government was acceptable. After the deal had been struck between the nine premiers, all male, and Trudeau, the women's movement in English Canada went into full gear to force the political leaders to exempt Section 28 from the "notwithstanding" clause.[2] Natives proved less successful than women in winning their demands for constitutional guarantees, though promises were included for several federal-provincial conferences to discuss entrenchment of constitutional guarantees of Native rights.

In Quebec, there was little discussion of whether the constitution would enhance the rights of women or Native peoples. Instead, the focus was on the supposed "ganging-up" by English-Canadians to impose upon Quebec a constitution it did not want, and about which it had not been consulted. The Parti Québécois argued that Quebec's provincial charter of rights included stronger guarantees for the rights of women than the proposed federal constitution. René Lévesque angrily announced that his government would introduce legislation to make the "notwithstanding" clause apply to all Quebec laws. He could do little, however, about a clause that Trudeau and the premiers had included which gave the right to education in the language of their choice to all Canadian-born individuals, regardless of the province in which they were born. This would nullify the clause in Quebec's Charter of the French Language, or Bill 101, which gave the right to education in English in the province solely to Quebec-born anglophones.

Neo-Conservative Sovereignists

But the people of Quebec were generally becoming tired of the endless constitutional debate. The constitutional repatriation, which finally occurred in 1982, provoked little reaction outside of government circles. While many were disappointed that the federal government was trying to win more powers for itself rather than devolving more responsibilities to Quebec City, there were accusations that Lévesque, in his own way, had joined Trudeau in singing a different tune after the referendum than before. Before the Québécois had voted, the Lévesque government had gone out of its way to demonstrate the crucial role that the Quebec government could play in delivering social and educational services to the people, and establishing the rules for economic players. Quebec, in the late seventies, had the highest minimum wage in North America and the only anti-scab law on the continent. The provincial government was expanding health and educational services, and generously supporting cultural endeavours.

But with the referendum behind it and endowed with a comfortable second-term majority, the Lévesque government seemed to have caught the neo-conservative bug that was infecting the industrialized

Queen Elizabeth II and Pierre Elliot Trudeau, Canadian prime minister from 1968–79 and 1980–84, signing the Canadian constitution document in Ottawa, April 1982. NAC PA-140705

world. It could hardly ignore the effect of the 1982 recession on the Quebec treasury, which already bore the costs of Quebec's efforts from the Quiet Revolution, to present Quebec as a nation-in-the-making: embassies abroad, unemployment exchanges that paralleled Canada Manpower, and, since 1977, the Office de la langue française, which administered the province's language legislation. No longer mainly concerned with showcasing the Quebec government's progressive social legislation, the second-term PQ government focussed instead on Quebec's debts, high taxes, and the need to reduce both. This meant cutbacks in the public sector. It also meant salary cuts for Quebec civil servants and state employees, who had won handsome concessions from the PQ in the pre-referendum period. Indeed, the Quebec government ignored the contracts it had signed with workers to force wage cutbacks of 19.5 percent across the public service for the first three months of 1983.

Increasingly, the government looked to the private sector, with which it had formed important economic partnerships, to steer the Quebec economy and to produce the prosperity which the PQ had once suggested would come from the efforts of an activist state. One of the key proponents of greater emphasis on private entrepreneurship was Pierre Laurin, brother of Camille Laurin, the major force behind Bill 101. As director of the École des hautes études commerciales in Montreal from 1975 to 1981, Pierre Laurin's objective was "to demonstrate that entrepreneurial values are no longer suspect among French-speaking Quebecers."[3] The H.E.C., founded in 1907, had focussed, until the 1970s, on accounting and economics. Laurin expanded its programs to include marketing, finance, quantitative methods, and human resource management. He sent bright graduates to Harvard for postgraduate studies in an effort to ensure that highly trained French-speaking managers were available for Quebec-based corporations. By the early 1980s, the H.E.C. had 1800 degree program students and 6000 part-timers.[4]

H.E.C. graduates, as well as well-trained francophone graduates in business and engineering, were in demand not only in the public sector, as they had been during the Quiet Revolution, but also in the private sector. Bill 101, however much anglophones may have resented it, caused many corporations operating in Quebec to see the writing on the wall: the working language of the province of Quebec, whether or not it remained in Canada, was to be French. It therefore made eminent good sense to search out well-qualified, bilingual francophones for management and professional positions.

The number of large francophone-owned firms was also on the rise. In 1978, firms controlled by francophones employed 27.8 percent of the manufacturing labour force, compared to only 21.7 percent in 1961. In construction, the figures were 74.4 percent versus 50.7 percent; in the financial sector, 44.8 percent against 25.8 percent; and in services, 75 percent versus 71.4 percent.[5] Among the giant companies under francophone control were the grocery chain Provigo, formerly anglophone-controlled, Gaz Métropolitain, also formerly in anglophone hands, Bombardier, and Sodarcan, an insurance brokerage firm. Sodarcan was owned by the father and brother of Jacques Parizeau, and, like the H.E.C., provided a family linkage between the PQ government and the private-sector architects of a class of francophone capitalists whose purview was international rather than simply domestic.[6] The government played an important role in fostering the growth of the francophone bourgeoisie. Investments by the government's investment fund, the Caisse de dépôts et de placements, in Quebec firms tended to favour francophone investors. In 1977, the Caisse acquired a large block of shares in Provigo to ward off an attempt by a Nova Scotia-based firm to win control; later the government sold its shares to a francophone conglomerate.[7]

The francophone bourgeoisie, while it supported the close linkage between the state and the private sector that some commentators referred to as "Quebec Inc.," otherwise shared the neo-conservative perspectives that had become the common fare of multi-national corporations anxious to increase their own autonomy and profits, at the expense of state authority. They wanted freedom to invest at home and abroad, without having to worry about taxes, regulations, and trade unions. On most issues, the francophone and anglophone bourgeoisie in Quebec spoke with one voice. In the 1980s, the leaders of the PQ seemed anxious to adjust their policies to meet the demands of the bourgeoisie. Minimum wages and social assistance rates were frozen while inflation ate away at their value, regulation of industry became more lax, and promises of additional public daycare and housing were suspended indefinitely. The size of the civil service was cut, and government dealings with the unions demonstrated a determination to cut wage increases granted in the past. Rather than bargain with the unions, the government used legislation to reduce wages, nullify already signed contracts, and ban strikes by those affected by such changes.[8]

The new neo-conservative agenda caused some commentators to claim that the PQ had become the political expression of the new francophone bourgeoisie. This seemed simplistic because, while the wealthy private-sector francophones supported greater decentralization within the Canadian federation to give more jurisdictions to the Quebec government, most of its members were completely opposed to the sovereignty project. Above all, they wanted political stability and they were unconvinced by the PQ scenario in which separatism would occur with no political or economic fallout.[9]

But, if the PQ, as a sovereignist party, could not become the direct representative of the province's bourgeoisie, it had certainly strayed far from its social democratic roots. Well-heeled members of Cabinet such as Parizeau and Laurin were hardly representative of the party's grass-roots, though Lévesque, a former television news celebrity, was reasonably representative. The PQ had a membership in the late 1970s estimated as high as 300,000. Middle-class state employees were particularly prominent within the membership: teachers, professors, social workers, and medical professionals were over-represented relative to their proportion of the provincial population. Francophone students provided a large group of adherents, while a large element of the private-sector membership came from cultural workers who benefited from the PQ's generous support in the late seventies of cultural endeavours, the product of the party's desire to promote a vibrant Quebec culture clearly distinct from the rest of

North American culture. Though the PQ was not a workers' party, many trade unionists who supported sovereignty for Quebec participated in the organization and worked with its social-democratic wing to press for a continued commitment on the part of the government and the party to a social-reform agenda. All of these groups were alienated, to some degree, by the PQ's partial retreat from social democracy in the eighties. PQ membership fell to below 60,000 by the time Lévesque stepped down as premier and party leader in 1985.

René Lévesque was disheartened by decreasing interest in the party and what he regarded as the unrealistic desire of many Québécois to cling to a social-reform agenda that he no longer believed Quebec could afford. PQ support began to decline in the polls and with it, support for sovereignty seemed to sink like a stone. Lévesque, having persuaded the party faithful in 1981 that the PQ could not carry out a second referendum during its second term in office, now declared that it could not do so if it won a third election victory. Several Cabinet ministers, including Parizeau, responded by leaving the Cabinet, while others declared that they would not seek re-election. Though Lévesque would be lionized by the PQ after his death in late 1987, he doubted the political popularity of any discussion of constitutional issues during his last years in office, and wished to focus on the economy.

Unfortunately for Lévesque and his party, their ideas began to sound very much like those of the provincial Liberal Party. The Liberals had turned on Claude Ryan for his uninspiring leadership, after he had failed to win the 1981 provincial election on the heels of the successful "non" campaign. In one of the surprising political comebacks of the century in Canada, the Liberals chose Robert Bourassa as Ryan's successor. Bourassa had spent his time after his electoral debacle of 1976 studying European political and economic developments. His calm lectures about economic policy made him a more credible proponent of the new neo-conservative economics than the divided, and seemingly directionless, PQ.

When Lévesque, who later admitted that he lost much of his interest in political life after the defeat of the referendum in 1980, retired in 1985, his party was searching desperately for a way to revive its sagging fortunes. In an imaginative effort to rekindle interest in the sovereignist party, the PQ decided against a delegate convention of the party faithful to choose the new leader. Instead, there would be a vote in which the entire membership could participate. Québécois who wished to participate in this democratic exercise had only to purchase a membership in the party. Only about 40,000 non-members took advantage of this chance to choose the new premier, reflecting the disenchantment at the time of many former Péquistes. Still, this was the first time that a governing party in Canada had allowed all citizens agreeing to join the party the opportunity to choose a premier. It was an example that would be picked up by other governing parties seeking to revive flagging fortunes, for example, by the Alberta Conservatives in 1993 when Ralph Klein was elected to succeed Don Getty.

The PQ electoral contest in the fall of 1985 was won by Pierre-Marc Johnson, son of the former Union Nationale Premier Daniel Johnson, and brother of the prominent Liberal politician, Daniel Johnson Junior. Johnson was a soft-liner on the separatist issue and a conservative on economic issues. His election demonstrated how far the PQ had moved on both social and constitutional issues. Johnson not only promised that he would keep Lévesque's pledge not to have a referendum during a third PQ mandate, but also indicated that he was unsure how he himself would vote in a referendum should Quebec suddenly hold another one. He called an election quickly after winning the leadership and pledged to cut public spending and to make Quebec a more attractive place to invest.

For many former PQ voters, Johnson and Bourassa were two peas in a pod. The PQ record during its second term seemed unimpressive to those who had identified the PQ during its first term in office with efforts to create greater equality among Quebec's citizens. The electorate in 1985 decided to give the supposedly discredited Robert Bourassa a second political life. The PQ won thirty-eight percent of the vote, but this was an even smaller percentage of Quebec voters than the "oui" side had claimed in the 1980 referendum.

Quebec Society in the 1980s and 90s

The publicity given to Quebec's new entrepreneurs and the embracing of neo-conservatism, to a certain extent, by both major provincial parties, seemed to suggest a change in popular thinking in Quebec. So did the declining interest in the sovereignty issue. But, changing fashions among the elite are not always reliable guides to the popular mood. In fact, opinion surveys suggested that the people of Quebec were the most social democratic and civil libertarian on the continent. While Canadians generally were more liberal than Americans, the Québécois were far more liberal, taken together, than their anglophone compatriots. An opinion poll in 1987 suggested that forty-eight percent of the Québécois were preparing to vote for the NDP in the next federal election. The free trade issue, and the simple reality of the NDP having virtually no organization in that province, demonstrated a year later that such a poll was chimerical. But, as the pollsters discovered, whether or not Québécois were planning to vote for the NDP, more of them than residents of any other province shared that party's perspective on issues ranging from social spending to Canadian participation in NATO. This was particularly the case among francophones.

This was no rogue poll. Seymour Martin Lipset, in his book, *Contintental Divide*, demonstrates first that Canadians are more secular and more socialist in their outlook than Americans, while francophone Canadians are the most secular and socialist of the Canadians. For example, when asked in the early 1980s whether they believed in the devil, only twenty-two percent of francophones answered affirmatively as opposed to forty-six percent of Canadian anglophones and sixty-seven percent of Americans. While eighty-four percent of Americans and seventy-three percent of English-speaking Canadians believed that there is a heaven, a more modest fifty-eight percent of francophone Canadians shared this belief. While fifty-one percent of Americans and forty-nine percent of English-Canadians would leave sexual activity entirely to individual choice, sixty-six percent of francophones were willing to let the individual decide on sexual matters. More French-Canadians than anglophones would choose equality over liberty; and thirty-eight percent of French-Canadians, but only twenty-nine percent of anglophone Canadians and twenty percent of Americans thought that reducing class differences was of greater importance than freedom.[10]

Certainly, the employees of the Quebec state affected by the PQ government's wage rollbacks for 1983 chose equality over order. About 300,000 workers defied the government's legislation that forbade strikes over the wage rollbacks, only returning to work when the government passed even more draconian legislation that, according to labour historian Bryan Palmer,

> provided for fines, imprisonment, and the decertification of bargaining agents, overriding the federal Charter of Rights and Freedoms and the provincial Charter of Human Rights. Those targeted were refused the right of trial and denied the

opportunity to present evidence or secure legal protection. To be absent from work was to be guilty.[11]

The trade union movement, while it fought the retrograde legislation of the PQ's second term, was not willing to make a complete break with the government. Happy to have won anti-scab legislation and various reforms regarding health and safety in workplaces, many unionists were unprepared to accept radical leadership. In the Centrale de l'enseignement du Québec (CEQ), the teachers' union, a radical wing failed miserably before the 1980 referendum in its effort to win popular support among the membership for a socialist, sovereignist Quebec. While a majority of Quebec's teachers supported independence, many were PQ activists and were happy with what they regarded as the PQ's social democratic orientation. Efforts within the Confederation of National Trade Unions to kick-start a labour party for Quebec in 1978 also came to nothing, because of the objections of those who wanted to avoid a division among nationalist forces. By the time the PQ turned on the labour movement, particularly public-sector workers, socialist forces within the union movement were too weak for a serious alternative party to be created. In any case, what most union members appeared to want was not a Marxist revolutionary alternative, but a genuine social democracy of the sort the PQ appeared to be abandoning in the face of the capitalist collapse in 1982.[12]

Women figured largely among the victims of the PQ's job and salary cuts. Nurses, teachers, social workers, government secretaries, clerks, and cleaners, many of whom had regarded the PQ as an ally in their struggles for better wages and working conditions in the 1970s, were embittered as the government wiped away many of the benefits that strikes and threats of strikes had brought during that decade. The women's movement had made gains during the first PQ administration, as the government tried to appeal to the various social movements and persuade them that a Quebec nation-state would provide them with the social justice that Canadian federalism did not. In the early eighties, as the government tried to appease investors during rough economic times, women once again were told that they had to be willing to make sacrifices.

Beginning in the seventies, as the trend towards fewer babies became clear to Quebec's conservative, and largely male, demographers grouped in the Association des démographes du Québec, this group of academics sounded alarm bells and called for pro-natalist policies. They argued that such policies were necessary to ensure that Quebec remained a vibrant society with an important weight within Canada or, if Quebec left Canada, within the Quebec-Canada partnership that would supposedly succeed it. Natalist policies were often termed "family policies," but, in fact, they were directed at the behaviour of women, who would, of course, have to bear the extra babies that the state increasingly demanded.

Beneath the surface, there was another dimension to the pro-natalist discourse. It had strong racial overtones. The former PQ minister and feminist, Lise Payette, a television celebrity before and after her political career, revealed this dimension forcefully in her 1988 television production, *Disparaître* ("To Disappear"). Payette, using questionable figures and racist stereotypes, argued that the combination of below-replacement birth rates by old-stock francophones in Quebec and the high birth rates of non-white immigrants would produce a Quebec in which the descendants of the original immigrants would lose their political control. Worse, following the pattern of British inner cities, there would be crime and poverty among the new immigrants that would undermine the stability of Quebec society. Quebec feminists, who had linked nationalism with feminism, were generally uncomfortable with Payette's views. While some were strongly anti-racist, others simply rejected the assumption of nationalists that white Quebec francophone women had a responsibility to become "baby machines" once again to serve the ends of the nationalist cause.

Feminists and conservative nationalists disagreed both about the cause and the solution to lower birth rates in Quebec. Feminists argued that women in Quebec still bore most of the responsibility for housework and raising children, and that both men and the state would have to change their attitudes if they expected women to bear more children. Women did not want to forego careers and economic independence to become mothers. State policies in such areas as maternity insurance and daycare would have to become more attractive if the state wanted to lure more women into having babies. The conservative nationalists argued, by contrast, that women seeking careers reflected a new selfishness on the part of women and that state policies, therefore, had to be aimed at making it appear more attractive for Quebec women to have children and then stay at home with them. The conservatives won the debate as far as the second Bourassa government was concerned. In 1988, they introduced a baby bonus: mothers received $500 upon the birth of each of their first two children, and $3000 for all subsequent children they bore. By 1991, the government had raised its payout to $1000 for the second child, and $7000 for all children beyond the second.[13] However the baby bonus may have contributed to a conservative "family policy" agenda, it sat poorly with the neo-conservative economic agenda for paring government social spending. The Bourassa government partly made this up by cutting social spending in most other areas, and ignoring demands of daycare advocates for substantial increases in government subsidies.

Despite the hysteria created by some nationalists that the old-stock francophones and their language were about to disappear, the French language in the eighties and nineties was stronger than ever in Quebec. Bill 101, and the determination of the francophone majority, had broken down the resistance of many anglophones and allophones. Those least comfortable with having to work in the French language left the province. Indeed many young anglophones, even if they were bilingual, left Quebec because they assumed, rightly or wrongly, that better-paying jobs would increasingly be reserved for bilingual Québécois who were of francophone old-stock descent. Most of those who remained became functionally bilingual. While anti-French bigots could certainly be found in the anglophone community, most anglophones accepted that French was now the working language of Quebec. They pressed, however, for greater respect for languages other than French, and for the government to stop eroding the rights of anglophones to schools and hospitals in districts where the English language predominated. Alliance Quebec, the major organization of anglophones in the eighties, represented this moderate approach of the anglophone community, though for the supporters of a unilingual French Quebec, there was no difference between anglophone extremists and moderates since they all supported the right of individuals to speak and, in some circumstances, work in the English language.

Visible minorities, and particularly the African-Canadian communities of Quebec, centred in Montreal, bore the brunt of racism in Quebec along with Native people. African-Canadians faced discrimination in employment and housing. Young African-Canadians complained that they were roughed up by the police for hanging out in certain places and kept out of bars by bouncers employed by racist publicans. The large number of Haitian cab drivers received fewer customers than other cabbies because the cab companies allowed customers to specify if they did not want black drivers. Several police

Les Ballets Jazz de Montréal, La Compagnie.

killings of African-Canadian suspects in minor crimes particularly drew the ire of the disparate African-Canadian community of Montreal. While similar charges of police racism were common in Toronto, many English-speaking African-Canadians felt, rightly or wrongly, that they were treated as particularly loathsome by police and toughs in Montreal because they were both black and anglophone.

The international success of Quebec films, particularly Denys Arcand's *Decline of the American Empire*, singers such as Celine Dion and Michel Rivard, and dance troupes such as Les Ballets Jazz de Montréal, spoke to the vibrancy of Quebec francophone culture. Unlike English Canada, where there was no language barrier to limit the popularity of American imports, French Canada continued to produce its own cultural artifacts. These ranged from TV soaps and serials, often based on Quebec history or, in the case of the much-watched *Lance et compte*, on popular cultural pursuits such as hockey; classical and jazz music; film; theatre; and popular novels and non-fiction works. There were signs of popular weariness with Quebec-produced works: sales of locally written books dropped during the eighties, and francophone popular-music radio stations demanded that the CRTC let them play more English tunes so that they could fend off competition both from anglophone Montreal and American stations. But, on the whole, francophone Quebec artists received a great deal of acclaim at home, and increasingly in France and other francophone countries.

Little had changed, however, in how either federalists or sovereignists viewed such cultural successes. Federalists believed that they demonstrated that Quebec could preserve its culture intact within the Canadian federation, while sovereignists believed that they showed that Quebec had no need of Canada with its diluted American anglophone culture. Though constitutional issues seemed of decreasing interest to most Québécois, the Bourassa government was determined to win concessions from Ottawa that they hoped would prevent the eruption of another round of nationalism from which the PQ would be the inevitable political winner in Quebec.

The Meech Lake Debacle

By 1986, Robert Bourassa and Brian Mulroney were determined to win constitutional changes that would allow Quebec to sign the 1982 constitutional agreement. Such a signature would be purely symbolic, since the Constitution Act of 1982 already applied in Quebec. But both leaders believed that the achievement of some changes, however cosmetic, that would recognize Quebec's particular status within Confederation, would strengthen federalist forces in the province. For Robert Bourassa, this would translate into an advantage for his party over the PQ, while also reassuring jittery investors that there was little chance of Quebec leaving Confederation. For Brian Mulroney, whose party had won a majority of Quebec seats in 1984 despite its historic weakness in the province, it would give the federal Conservatives the image of the party that had righted the wrong committed against Quebec by Trudeau's federal Liberals in 1981.

Robert Bourassa set forth a list of five minimum demands for Quebec's acceptance of the constitution: restoration of Quebec's veto over constitutional changes; recognition of Quebec as a distinct society; limits on federal spending in areas of provincial jurisdiction; Quebec involvement in nominations to the Supreme Court; and constitutional entrenchment of Quebec's *de facto* control over immigration to the province. Brian Mulroney assembled the first ministers at a luxury resort in Meech Lake in April 1987, and the eleven men, behind closed doors, worked out an agreement that became known as the Meech Lake Accord. This granted Quebec's demands. Quebec received a veto, but so did every other province. A "distinct society" clause was included that indicated that courts were to take into consideration that "the role of the Legislature and Government of Quebec is to preserve and promote the distinct identity of Quebec." But this was tempered with a recognition that linguistic duality within provinces was a "fundamental characteristic" of Canada. Provinces received the right to opt out of new federal shared-cost programs provided that they established comparable programs that met national objectives. The three Supreme Court justices from Quebec would have to be agreeable to both federal and Quebec governments. Finally, the existing arrangements for immigration, implemented during the Trudeau era, which gave Quebec a large say over immigration policy, would receive constitutional protection.[14]

The Meech Lake Accord received the stamp of approval from all three federal parties as well as the first ministers. But the unity of the political elites did not prevent opposition from other sources. Some of the opposition was simply anti-Quebec. From the Quiet Revolution onwards, right-wing bigots in other provinces had claimed that there was a Quebec conspiracy to take over the country and make everyone speak French. Organizations such as the Alliance for the Preservation of English Canada and Western Canada Concept subscribed to this conspiracy theory, and a number of books by the theory's devotees became Canadian best-sellers. Generally, the extremists claimed that Trudeau was the leader of a "French socialist conspiracy" whose purpose was to remould Canada into a French-speaking socialist police state. They cited as evidence the French on cereal boxes, the metric system, and the socialist conspiracy to deprive Canadians of civil rights supposedly behind the Trudeau government's unwillingness to entrench property rights in the 1982 constitution. While such extremists were a small but noisy minority of anglophone Canadians, they were able to convince many more English-Canadians that "distinct society" meant "superior society," and that the Meech Lake Accord was, therefore, a slap in the face for English Canadians.

Many Meech Lake opponents, however, were not opposed to French Canadian aspirations. Instead, they were supporters of a strong central state: Trudeau Liberals, Diefenbaker Tories, and Douglas New Democrats. How, for example, asked feminists, could a national daycare program be introduced if provinces could opt out, and how would the federal government ensure that they established a comparable program? How, asked Native peoples, could their attempts to get self-government entrenched in the constitution ever succeed if the support of all ten provinces were required? Two attempts to win entrenchment under the formula requiring support of seven provinces with fifty percent of the population had failed by one province. With Alberta determined to prevent Natives from gaining control over oil-rich territories, would Native self-government have to be shelved forever?

Not all Meech Lake opponents regarded the "distinct society" issue in the same manner. The trade union movement generally supported Quebec's right to special status within Confederation as the homeland of the French language in North America. They objected, however, to all provinces receiving the powers that Quebec had been demanding for several generations, on the grounds that this would weaken the federal government and eventually cause the provinces to compete with one another to cut social programs. Some academic specialists in Canadian and Quebec history and politics also agreed that what came to be known as "asymmetrical federalism" might be appropriate for Canada, since a majority of Québécois wanted a stronger provincial state while a majority of Canadians outside Quebec wanted to preserve a strong federal state. Surveys suggested, however, that most anglophones outside Quebec obstinately clung to the view that all provinces must be treated equally. The ten-province veto obviously suggested that their premiers believed the same.

Other opponents of Meech Lake, led by Pierre Trudeau, argued that the Accord gave constitutional assent to the view that the French language and culture were seriously threatened in Quebec and that this might justify some erosion of individual rights to achieve a greater good. Trudeau claimed that this simply catered to separatist propaganda and reinforced the mythology that a strong, welfare-oriented federal government was a conspiracy against Quebec francophones, rather than a means of uniting Canadians of all provinces and languages. Brian Mulroney sometimes suggested that the "distinct society" clause was largely symbolic while the Quebec Liberal leaders argued that it would give courts in Quebec a great deal of leeway in allowing Quebec to tread on former federal prerogatives. If the former argument were true, Trudeau opined, the "distinct society" clause would eventually be rejected as a fraud by the Québécois; if the latter interpretation were true, then courts rather than Canada's legislators would be deciding what the limits of the distinct society clause really were. In either case, argued Trudeau, the entrenchment of the vague phrase "distinct society" in the constitution was unacceptable.[15]

The Meech Accord required the approval of the federal Parliament and the ten provincial legislatures by the end of June 1990. While Parliament and several provinces quickly voted the assent needed, there were problems in other provinces. The first holdout was New Brunswick, where a new Liberal administration under Frank McKenna took power in 1987 before the provincial Tories had voted on the Accord. McKenna's Liberals won every New Brunswick seat, and McKenna demanded a number of changes before he would ask his legislature to approve the Accord. Brian Mulroney, confident that he could pressure one small province to buckle under, was unwilling to discuss changes.

By the end of 1988, Mulroney had another small province to contend with: Manitoba. At the time of the accord's initial announcement, only Sharon Carstairs, the lone Liberal in the provincial legislature, rejected the Accord in principle. Carstairs believed the Accord would weaken the role of the federal government in providing relatively similar social programs and benefits across the country. The June 1988 election in Manitoba, however, changed the party arithmetic. Carstairs now had twenty of the fifty-seven seats in the legislature, and the new Conservative Premier, Gary Filmon, governing with a minority of legislative seats, did not want to confront backbenchers in his party who opposed the Accord.

As 1988 came to a close, Filmon had an issue that allowed him to withdraw the Manitoba Conservatives' support of Meech Lake. The Supreme Court had ruled that Quebec's *loi d'affichage* or sign law, a component of Bill 101, violated constitutional guarantees for the two official languages. The law required, among other things, that stores post signs in French only, both inside and outside. During the 1985 provincial election, when nationalism seemed at a low ebb, Bourassa had promised to allow English on signs as long as French was also included, and was the more prominent language. After his election, he did nothing, claiming that he was awaiting the courts' verdict of the legality of the PQ sign legislation. But by the time the Supreme Court had spoken, a new wave of nationalism had emerged in Quebec. It seemed to be sparked by the death of René Lévesque in late 1987. Opponents of the soft line on sovereignty of which Lévesque himself ironically was the major proponent, particularly in the post-referendum period, forced the resignation of Pierre-Marc Johnson as PQ leader and put Jacques Parizeau, a hard-liner who believed that Quebec should declare its sovereignty first and not worry whether or not Canada offered an association, in his place. Language was the volatile issue for nationalists, and Bourassa decided to ignore his promises to the English community and to pacify the nationalists by using the "notwithstanding" provision of the constitution to override the Supreme Court decision. He put forth legislation that allowed some English on inside signs in certain places. This pleased no one. Proponents of unilingualism, and sovereignists more generally, objected to any alteration of Bill 101. Anglophones objected to the implication that their language was something filthy that had to be hidden away behind closed doors and to be seen only in small letters.

Filmon, whose party had vehemently opposed NDP attempts to recognize linguistic dualism in Manitoba, now demanded that Quebec show more tolerance of its linguistic minorities, particularly the anglophones. He withdrew his support from Meech Lake. Within months, he was one of three premiers opposing Meech, after Clyde Wells' Liberals defeated the Newfoundland Conservatives. Wells' opposition to Meech was more fundamental than Filmon's or McKenna's. Like Trudeau, he objected to any special deals for Quebec within Confederation, proclaiming that all provinces must be treated as complete equals. Though Newfoundland had already voted in favour of Meech, Wells' Liberals removed that support.

As the deadline for Meech approached, it became clear that Canadians were divided about the desirability of the Accord along anglophone/francophone lines. Most anglophones opposed Meech, while most francophones supported it. What both shared in common was that most had no real notion of its contents, as they freely admitted to pollsters. Meech had become a symbol. For many French-Canadians, failure to pass Meech would signify yet another rejection of Quebec. But, for many anglophones, passing Meech meant giving in to Quebec demands and giving Quebec a superior position within Confederation. Brian Mulroney gathered the premiers together at the eleventh hour and a shaky deal, which preserved all the principles of Meech, was achieved. Insistence by Mulroney and Bourassa that the chief beneficiaries of a breakdown of Meech would be the separatists partly shook the resolve of Wells and the three Manitoba party leaders who had decided to work together on the constitutional issue; Frank McKenna was completely persuaded by the doomsayers and had largely dropped his demands for changes in Meech. Wells agreed to have his provincial legislature take a free vote on the amended Meech, while the Manitoba leaders agreed to recommend the passage of Meech II to their parties. Their support for its passage was, however, dispirited. The legislation had to be passed by Manitoba by the end of June 1990. There were only a few days left before this could happen. Certain procedures of the legislature would have to be waived so that the members could vote on Meech right away. These required the support of all members of the legislature. But one member, Elijah Harper, a northern Manitoba Cree and NDP member of the legislature, refused to support Meech. Reflecting the view of Native peoples in Canada generally that their interests would be harmed if Native self-government were not granted before the provinces all received a constitutional veto, Harper simply said "no" as the Speaker of the Legislature asked members whether they woud waive the various readings of a new bill. It was possible for the Manitoba political leaders to override an individual member's rights and force the passage of Meech. But, recognizing that public opinion was against them, they allowed Harper to kill the bill. Clyde Wells then announced that there was no need for Newfoundland to have a free vote in its legislature since Manitoba's failure to vote meant the Accord could not be approved in time. Meech was dead.[16]

From Meech to the Revival of the Sovereignty Movement

The sovereignists had derided Meech Lake from the moment that Mulroney revealed its contents. But they had had little impact on popular attitudes to the Accord in Quebec before its demise in the Manitoba legislature. Although the Accord was no more than one page in length, had been printed in every major newspaper and discussed on news shows frequently over three years, four out of five Québécois polled in early 1990 freely admitted to knowing little about the Accord's provisions. Uninterested in the never-ending constitutional debates, most were inclined to trust Bourassa over Parizeau in such matters at the time.

The defeat of Meech, however, was a made-to-order present for the sovereignists. Quebec, they claimed, had been humiliated. The modest demands of Premier Bourassa, more moderate than the demands of other Quebec governments since the war, had been rejected. Quebec, it appeared, could never sign the constitution of Canada. In such circumstances, asked the sovereignists, why should Quebec want to remain part of Canada? Polls indicated that a comfortable majority of the population shared this view in the aftermath of Meech's death. The defeat of Meech was linked in the public mind with a number of recent anti-francophone and anti-Quebec incidents in Ontario and other provinces, including an incident where the Quebec flag was stomped on in Brockville, and a refusal by some Ontario cities with medium-sized French-speaking communities to provide services in the language of the minority. The *Fête nationale* of Quebec occurred within days of the fateful legislative manoeuvres in Manitoba, and it proved to be an emotional outpouring of Quebec nationalism on a scale unseen since the defeat of the referendum a decade earlier.

Robert Bourassa was shattered by the defeat of Meech as well. But his reaction was more tactical than emotional. He appeared to make common cause with the separatists for a period to put pressure on the rest of the country to revisit Meech. He appointed a commission to propose constitutional alternatives for Quebec and made a separatist its co-chair. His party set forth a new constitutional agenda that would give Quebec control over most jurisdictions, leaving Ottawa with control over little more than foreign policy and defence policy. This was sovereignty-association but without the word sovereignty being mentioned. Bourassa suggested that the model arrangement for Quebec in Canada might be along the lines of the European Economic Community, in which sovereign states surrendered jurisdiction over a fixed number of areas, but otherwise retained control over matters affecting the lives of their citizens. For decentralizers, this harkened back to the original Confederation agreement in any case, in which there had been no hint of support for shared-cost programs initiated by the federal government to control responsibilities normally under provincial jurisdiction. Bourassa also refused to participate in negotiations with any other level of government than the federal government, arguing that federal-provincial conferences were of no interest to Quebec before it had become a full-fledged member once again of the Canadian constitutional club. Most importantly, Bourassa pledged a referendum in Quebec on the province's constitutional future, though he was vague about what alternatives might be placed before the voters.

The federal government also initiated consultations with Canadians about how to reshape the new constitution to meet Quebec's demands without alienating anglophones. Neither the Mulroney government nor many of the provincial governments were pleased, however, when these consultations gave a forum to feminist, Native, anti-racist, and poverty groups who demanded a variety of changes to meet the needs of their constituencies. In the end, another meeting of Mulroney and the premiers came up with a new agreement in the summer of 1992 in Charlottetown. Though the Meech concessions to Quebec remained intact, this round of constitution-making also included the "Triple-E Senate" — elected, equal, effective — demanded by several western and Atlantic premiers as a counter-weight to central Canadian control of the population-based House of Commons. Each province would have an equal number of members in an elected Senate, just as American states did. The agreement conceded Native self-government and transferred some jurisdictions to the provinces, such as forestry and housing. Several provincial governments, including Quebec's, had promised their voters that any future constitutional package would be submitted to a referendum before being submitted to the legislature. In the end, the Mulroney government decided that a national referendum was the best strategy. A majority of voters in every province would have to support the Charlottetown Agreement before Parliament could ratify it. But they didn't. In Quebec, a majority, still upset by the defeat of Meech, turned down what sovereignists told them was an agreement giving Quebec very little. In British Columbia and Alberta, even larger majorities turned down an agreement that opponents of Charlottetown claimed gave Quebec too much. Only Atlantic Canada gave a clear majority of votes in favour of the agreement while Ontario, in a virtual dead heat, was also marginally in favour of Charlottetown.

The federalists in Quebec increasingly had little to offer. While Trudeau suggested that the moderate nationalists such as Bourassa, who remained federalists, unfairly characterized Ottawa's powers within Quebec as too great, the dominant belief in Quebec was that there was too much federal interference in Quebec, and as a result, too much duplication of effort. While "soft nationalists" were still hesitant to support the complete rupture of Quebec from Canada with all the economic instability this might bring, there was increasing disenchantment with the provincial Liberal Party and with the Quebec wing of the federal Liberal Party. In the dying days of the Meech Lake Accord, Lucien Bouchard, Minister of the Environment in the Mulroney government, quit the government and the Conservative Party in anger over English Canada's unwillingness to concede the modest demands of Meech. Bouchard was a long-time sovereignist who had played an important role in the Lake Saguenay region as a regional organizer for the "oui" side during the PQ's 1980 referendum. Mulroney, trying to build up a new Conservative coalition in Quebec, had lured a variety of sometime sovereignists to Ottawa in an effort to consolidate and increase his party's support among Quebec nationalists. Bouchard was an old law school buddy of Mulroney's and Mulroney named him ambassador to France in 1985, later luring him into electoral politics and the federal Cabinet.

Not long after leaving the Conservative caucus, Bouchard announced the creation of the Bloc Québécois, an unusual federal party whose major purpose would be to defend the right of Quebec to become autonomous from Canada should a referendum in the province produce a majority in favour of sovereignty. In the meantime, the party's goal would be to argue for Quebec's interests in the federal Parliament rather than submerge Quebec's interests to partisan interests, as the BQ charged the Quebec Liberal and Conservative caucuses had done. His small caucus of mainly Conservative defectors was considerably enlarged after the 1993 federal election when the BQ captured forty-nine percent of the vote in Quebec and a large majority of the seats.

A year later, the Quebec Liberals, led by Bourassa's successor, Daniel Johnson, were defeated in a provincial election by the PQ under Parizeau. But the PQ and Liberals each won about forty-four percent of the vote, with the Liberals winning most of the anglophone and allophone vote, and the PQ winning a majority of francophone ballots. Parizeau soft-pedalled sovereignty during the provincial election. Recognizing that many soft nationalists, four years after the defeat of Meech, were unprepared to elect a government purely on the basis of its constitutional position, Parizeau focussed on the economy. Much like Jean Chrétien in the federal election in 1993, Parizeau promised to cut the deficit without trimming social spending or increasing anyone's taxes. Indeed, the PQ promised to make full employment its goal, a reassuring prospect for the unemployed of Quebec, officially about twelve percent of the labour force, but certainly more when those who had given up job searching because of discouragement and the part-timers who wanted full-time work were factored in.

About ten percent of francophone voters in 1994 cast their ballot for a new party, the Parti Action Démocratique du Québec. Led by Mario Dumont, the twenty-four-year-old former head of the Quebec Young Liberals, the PADQ supported continued negotiations with Ottawa to create the EEC-type arrangement which Dumont's former mentor, Robert Bourassa, had once proposed. Neither sovereignist nor truly federalist, the PADQ appealed to soft nationalists who did not believe PQ promises that sovereignty would not dominate their political agenda, but who wanted a change from the Liberals.

During the early months of the new PQ regime, it became clear that Parizeau and Bouchard shared somewhat different visions of an independent Quebec. Bouchard largely accepted René Lévesque's view of the importance of achieving a partnership with Canada that would assure the post-separation economic stability of a sovereign Quebec. Parizeau did not think the rest of Canada would want to negotiate such a partnership and saw no reason why an independent Quebec should not set out immediately to chart its own course. Gradually, however, Parizeau conceded the obvious: the Québécois wished to have their cake and eat it. There was no point consulting them about a sovereignty which some studies suggested would reduce their standard of living substantially. Whether or not a new partnership with Canada was possible for a Quebec that left the country, it was important for sovereignists of all stripes to work together. Bouchard was more popular than Parizeau and better able to influence young Dumont, whose fence-sitting voters would be crucial in a close contest on sovereignty.

In June 1995, the three nationalist political leaders announced the principles that would govern a sovereignty referendum to be held later that year. The people of Quebec would be asked whether they wanted Quebec to declare sovereignty and then spend a year trying to get Canada to negotiate the specifics of their new relationship. The call for negotiations met the demands of Bouchard and Dumont, while the declaration of sovereignty before such negotiations occurred satisfied Parizeau, who still assumed that Canada probably would not negotiate at all.

The second referendum campaign on sovereignty opened sleepily in September with all polls suggesting merely a rerun of the May 1980 referendum. A majority of Québécois remained unconvinced that leaving Canada was desirable even if Canada was unwilling to grant the Quebec government more powers. The unpopular Jacques Parizeau proved inept throughout the early weeks of the campaign in persuading "non" voters to switch to his side. Three weeks before the vote, the "oui" side announced that Bouchard, not Parizeau, would lead the Quebec-Canada negotiations that would follow a "oui" vote. Bouchard, rather than Parizeau, became the *de facto* leader of the rest of the campaign. His appeals to Quebec pride convinced many "non" and undecided voters to support the "oui" side. Many Quebec voters were upset that the federal government offered Quebec nothing during the campaign. Bouchard's insistence that the only two options before voters were sovereignty or the status quo came to have the ring of truth to it. Bouchard lambasted the federal government for its cuts to provinces for social programs, promising that an independent Quebec would be a more socially just place than Canada.

In the end, the sovereignists lost only narrowly. Federalists claimed that Quebec would plunge into an economic abyss if sovereignty occurred. But that was certainly debatable. As we saw in Chapter Thirteen, Quebec's exports were increasingly going to American markets in the years following the Free Trade Agreement. The rest of Canada exported more to Quebec than it imported from that province, and Ontario, in particular, benefited handsomely from trade with Quebec. Indeed, the sovereignists in Quebec had supported the Free Trade Agreement precisely because they recognized that free trade would increase north-south trade at the expense of east-west economic links. This would reduce Canada's ability to punish Quebec if it separated from Canada. Opponents of sovereignty warned that Quebec would be banished from the FTA and its NAFTA successor if Quebec left Confederation. Few Québécois, however, seemed to believe that at a time when the Americans were working to bring South American countries into their free trade zone they would allow Canada to shut Quebec out. Some federalists pointed out that the Americans regarded "Quebec Inc." with its enmeshing of state bodies and private companies as riddled with anti-free trade practices. The Americans were powerless to deal with "Quebec Inc." while Quebec was part of Canada, since the federal government claimed powerlessness regarding practices by provincial governments within areas of provincial jurisdiction; but a sovereign Quebec could be forced to play by the rules as the Americans wished to interpret them.

In any case, the interprovincial links within the Canadian economy had been greatly weakened by free trade. While dairy farmers in Quebec stood to lose their Ontario market if Canada's supply-management system for farm products, which had partly survived free trade, was removed for Quebec, the reality was that Quebec was trading less and less with other Canadian provinces.

That hardly made the economics of sovereignty easy to figure out. Sovereignists decried the Canadian federal debt, which had grown exponentially since the 1980 referendum, when it had not been an issue in the campaign. But, as even most economists who supported Quebec independence admitted, Quebec could not repudiate its share of the debt without shaking the confidence of international investors in the economies of both Quebec and Canada. Sovereignists and federalists wrangled about what share of the debt Quebec should pay. Should it be in proportion to Quebec's population relative to Canada's? Or should it reflect the size of the Quebec economy relative to that of Canada? Should the people who left Quebec or were likely to leave Quebec after independence be counted as Canadians or Québécois? How would federal property in Quebec be dealt with? What would happen to the equalization payments that Quebec received as one of the poorer provinces in Canada? There were no definitive answers to any of these questions. Yet, advocates of sovereignty recognized that economic fears prevented many soft nationalists from voting for sovereignty, and therefore emphasized that the federal system meant a great deal of duplication in the expenses of the two levels of government and a great deal of unproductive infighting.[17]

On referendum night, Jacques Parizeau, his dream shattered, lashed out selectively at those who had supported the "non" side in the referendum. He told supporters that they had been defeated only by "money and the ethnic vote." This conveniently ignored the forty percent of francophone voters who had also opposed a leap into the unknown. But it reflected an increasingly nasty intolerance on the part of the sovereignists. Parizeau's defeat speech asked his audience to "never forget that three-fifths of who we are voted yes." The suggestion was that anglophones and allophones who voted no, unlike the two-fifths of francophones who also voted no, were not part of "who we are," were not real Québécois.[18]

Whether because of the close result in the referendum or because of the remarks of Parizeau and others, anglophones in Quebec became quite militant in their opposition to the sovereignist movement in the months that followed the referendum. A partition movement in Montreal, once regarded as a fringe element, gained a great deal of respectability within the anglophone and allophone communities with its call to allow various areas of Quebec, such as the west island of Montreal, to vote on whether they wished to join an independent Quebec or to remain within Canada. Advertising executive Howard Galganov led a boycott campaign to force businesses to post bilingual signs where they were legally allowed to do so, rather than leaving their signs only in French in order to avoid retaliation from a hooligan element within nationalist circles.[19] As they had been doing since 1976, non-francophones continued their exodus from Quebec. Native people, also longstanding opponents of Quebec independence, threatened to take their territories out of Quebec altogether rather than have their treaty rights at the mercy of a government with which their relations for some time had been tense.

Meanwhile, the Quebec economy performed less well than the Canadian economy as a whole in the year following the referendum. Sovereignists and federalists debated the extent to which this was the result of investor jitteriness about Quebec's political future. For example, shortly after the referendum, David Caplan, chairman and chief executive of Pratt and Whitney Canada, complained that fears about Quebec separation were making it difficult for the company to hire engineers and technicians willing to move to Quebec. The company employed 6300 people at its plant in Longueuil, which manufactured gas turbine engines for aircraft. Quebec Federation of Labour spokesperson Claude Vincent accused the company of using the sovereignty debate as a smokescreen for moving jobs to the company's Toronto plant. Smokescreen or not, many companies were transferring jobs out of Montreal, and the city, which had long since fallen behind Toronto as the headquarters for Canadian firms, fell behind Calgary as well in 1996. Of course, sovereignty or not, it was difficult to compete with the "Alberta advantage" of low taxes, low minimum wages, and anti-union legislation.

But, was an independent Quebec going to simply compete with the Calgarys and Torontos for investors' favour? Would Quebec independence mean more than a seat in the United Nations and the recognition of Quebec's flag as a national flag? Sometimes, particularly when they were out of office, the PQ suggested that what Quebec sought was genuine independence, economic as well as political. In office, however, the PQ seemed mainly interested in reducing Quebec's debt and in avoiding any further increases in corporate taxation. It cut social services and called on all Québécois to put the province's economic house in order so that Quebec could be in a better position to start life as an independent nation. Jacques Parizeau left the premiership shortly after the referendum and Lucien Bouchard was drafted to become the new Quebec premier. This former Mulroney Cabinet minister demonstrated in office that it was no fluke that he had been in a Conservative Cabinet during his short spell as a federalist. Focussing on debt reduction above all else, he alienated many socially minded sovereignists who believed the purpose of sovereignty was to create a more equal society rather than simply one in which the preservation of the French language became the sole area of government intervention against the rights of corporations to do as they wished. Nevertheless, Bouchard seemed to be the only Quebec leader who could rally the sovereignty vote in the promised third referendum.

Francophones Outside Quebec

Whatever anglophones in Quebec might have thought of their position, they were, as sovereignists reminded them time and again, in far better shape than the francophones outside Quebec. In the run-up to the 1995 referendum, political scientist and *Le Devoir* editorial columnist Josée Legault presented forcefully the Quebec nationalist view of the fate of francophones who lived outside the boundaries of Quebec and Acadian New Brunswick:

> If there remain a million Canadians outside Quebec whose maternal language is French, just 600,000 use the language. Add to this an insufficient birth rate, a completely anglicized environment, sociocultural infrastructures that are often laughable, an amorphous leadership, and the heavy heritage of a century of anti-French legislation with the complicit silence of Ottawa. The sad reality is that the vitality of franco-

phones outside Quebec — outside the Acadian nation — only exists in the imagination of federalist strategists.

From Saint Boniface to Saint John, with Sudbury along the way, an alarming proportion of young francophones are becoming anglicized for one simple reason: their language has become a dead language in English Canada.[20]

This sort of analysis was hotly contested by many people outside Quebec. The billions that had been spent making the federal civil service bilingual, educating hundreds of thousands of young anglophones in French immersion classes, and supporting francophone cultural institutions outside Quebec surely suggested that the French language outside Quebec was not dead. Yet, as we have seen earlier, a thorough study in 1978 by francophone organizations did indeed suggest galloping anglicization, despite the changes of the Trudeau years. The 1991 census suggested a continuing decline in the number of Canadians outside Quebec with French as their maternal language who still spoke French at home. By this measure of assimilation, forty-three percent of Ontario francophones, sixty-three percent of Manitoba francophones, and more than seventy-five percent of francophones in all other provinces except Quebec and New Brunswick were lost to the French-Canadian nation. French was the language of work for only a small percentage of those who used French as a home language. Yet, in New Brunswick, the rate of assimilation was only eleven percent, suggesting that French remained a viable language in an area like Acadia where a high concentration of French-Canadians compensated for anglicizing influences.

Francophones outside Quebec have attempted to improve the legal position of their language with varying results. New Brunswick became Canada's only officially bilingual province when the Constitution Act was proclaimed in April 1982, and its government has made substantial efforts to ensure that services are available equally to anglophones and francophones in a province where almost two in five residents have French as their mother tongue. Ontario also became officially bilingual in the late eighties, though the provision of services in French occurs only in areas where there is a large concentration of francophones. In British Columbia and the Atlantic region outside New Brunswick, little has been done to promote the French language.

In the Prairie provinces, the status of the French language became a political issue in the 1980s, with the results largely negative for francophones. This was particularly the case in Manitoba, where a failed attempt was made by the NDP government in the early 1980s to guarantee services in French. The government only acted after the Supreme Court had nullified legislation in the province dating from 1890 that declared French no longer an official language in the province. This violated the provisions of the Manitoba Act of 1870, the federal legislation that gave Manitoba provincehood. The Court ordered translations into French of all legislation passed in Manitoba from 1890 onwards. Rather than spend $100 million on such a symbolic, and useless, token of Manitoba's bilingualism, the government worked with the francophone community to determine what services should be available in both French and English as a compensation for not translating the legislation. The francophone association and the government came to such an agreement, with the former agreeing not to ask the Court to enforce its translation order. But popular anger with the deal between the francophones and the government, fanned by the Conservatives in the legislature, forced the NDP eventually to withdraw the legislation.

Alberta and Saskatchewan, technically officially bilingual under the unenforced language sections of the North West Territories Act, were given the right in the Constitution Act of 1982 to declare themselves unilingual within a set period. Both took advantage of this right in 1988. A few years earlier, however, francophones won the right in both provinces to a trial in their own language.[21]

Francophones outside Quebec generally supported efforts made by Quebec to strengthen the French language in Quebec, arguing that without a vibrant francophone Quebec, the French culture in North America was doomed. But most of them opposed the Quebec sovereignty project because they believed that a Canada without Quebec would renounce bilingualism or at least treat it as a matter of indifference.

Conclusion

The forces of sovereignty and federalism remained in equal balance at the end of 1996, and Quebec's political future remained as uncertain as ever. Federalists in the province could only decry the continued rigidity of the rest of the country, which refused to accept notions of asymmetrical federalism. To the chagrin, however, of many anglophone liberals and socialists, there were signs that the federal government was caving in to demands for a decentralized Confederation in which the federal government conceded most of the new powers it had carved out for itself since the Depression. This would strengthen the Quebec government's powers, but without giving Quebec more powers than other provincial governments enjoyed. The "Quebec question" and the associated question of national unity seemed more elusive than ever as the twentieth century came close to an end.

Fifteen

Other Voices in a Neo-Conservative Age

Most Canadians did not buy wholly into the neo-conservative ideology that shaped the late 1980s and 1990s. Many rejected it completely. It was no accident that neither Brian Mulroney nor Jean Chrétien admitted in 1984 and 1993 respectively that they intended to cut spending on social programs and national institutions such as the CBC. Even Mike Harris, announcing his "Common-Sense Revolution" to the Ontario electorate in 1995, felt the need to claim disingenuously that public spending would be drastically cut along with taxes, without cutting monies from the province's health system. Neo-conservatives benefited, however, from voter cynicism, the belief that, in the final analysis, all politicians and political parties were much the same and interested mainly in lining their own pockets. From this viewpoint, the major conflict in Canadian life was not between social classes or among social visions, but between politicians on the one hand, and citizens on the other. Neo-conservatives could argue that while they were politicians too, they were dedicated to the reduction of government rather than to its increase, and that they could therefore be relied upon to reduce bureaucracy and restore power to ordinary people. (That most power was in the hands of big corporations rather than workaday people was deliberately obscured in this analysis.)

While increasingly jaundiced views of politicians contributed to political passivity, oppositional movements remained strong in Canadian political life. Neo-conservatism threatened the gains made since World War II by trade unions, women, Natives, and visible minorities. Environmentalists and gays were also threatened by the desire of neo-conservatives to reduce the state's role in economic life, on the one hand, and to increase state control over individuals' sex lives, on the other. Of course, not every economic conservative was a social conservative or vice versa, but the political alliance between the two in the 1990s was a close one. Though neo-conservatives were not always openly sexist, racist, or elitist, their economic philosophy, with its assumption of the fairness of market forces, rejected protection for trade union members, affirmative action programs, state-subsidized childcare policies, and the like. The potential victims of neo-conservatism fought back with varying degrees of success. In this chapter, we look at the successes and setbacks experienced by the groups that composed the majority of members of society but who were increasingly called "special interest groups" by the neo-conservatives for whom only corporate interests among organized groups were spared this label.

Neo-Conservatism and the Women's Movement

"A stinging U of A political science department paper titled *Road Kill: Women in Alberta's Drive Toward Deficit Elimination* attacks this government as being antifeminist and patriarchal," bristled rural Alberta Conservative MLA Judy Gordon in the Alberta legislature in March 1995. "Were taxpayer dollars used either directly or indirectly to fund the writing of this overly biased and poorly researched paper?" asked the shocked Tory.[1] In fact, what *Road Kill* illustrated with facts and figures was that women suffered disproportionately from the implementation of the neo-conservative agenda. A far larger percentage of working women than men worked in the public service, with women dominant in several "helping professions" such as nursing and social work, as well as public education. Secretarial and clerical employees of governments were overwhelmingly women. Cutting public service jobs hurt more women employees than men.

Women were also disproportionately hurt as the users of services. Women with dependent children figured prominently in the welfare rolls. They required daycare subsidies to make it financially feasible for them to work outside the home, but neo-conservatives were cutting such subsidies. Many wished to remain at home with young children, but government decisions favouring "workfare," as in Ontario in 1996, often deprived them of this option. On the whole, neo-conservatives stigmatized single moms, whether they held paid jobs or not. Conservative discourse in the eighties and nineties called for "the family" and not the state to care for children. But the family ideal that public policy tended to favour was the male-headed, single-income family. This was a shrinking proportion of the total number of family units. More than ten percent of children were being raised by one parent, usually their mother, and most two-parent families were also families where both parents worked outside the home.

When women's paid "caring" jobs were cut, the politicians' rhetoric suggested that "the family" should take over the chores for which paid workers, usually women, were no longer to be available. In practice, it was women, not the family as a whole, who were expected to look after old or sick people to whom hospital services or old-age homes were no longer available. It was also mothers, not fathers, who were expected to come into schools to help out as class sizes grew bigger and teaching assistant and secretarial positions in the schools dried up. There was a certain logic to all this, though it was rarely made explicit. Women were expected to give up their paid jobs and to stay home to look after various needs that in the previous period had been socialized. While the women's movement fought to end gender typing, a backlash against women's gains was emerging to demand a return to a former era where women were confined to unpaid caring in the home and the community.

But the women's movement in Canada remained resilient and it did have gains to celebrate in the 1980s and 1990s. The inclusion of an equal rights clause in the 1982 Constitution Act was the result of a concerted campaign by women's organizations. The Supreme Court's first woman justice, Bertha Wilson, proved to have a feminist outlook and played an important role in shaping some significant decisions by the Court in the late eighties. In 1988, the Court ruled unconstitutional Canada's existing abortion law on the grounds that it interfered with the new constitution's guarantee of women's security of person. An attempt by the government to recriminalize abortion in certain circumstances failed to win approval in the Senate, where even a number of Conservative women appointees made clear their belief that a woman's ability to control her body represented a fundamental right that the state had no right to take away.[2] Women legislators in Parliament of all three parties worked together in 1985 to end the loss of treaty rights by Native women who married non-treaty men. The long campaign of Native women for an end to this sexist discrimination in the Indian Act had borne little fruit before there was a contingent of women in Parliament to press the case.

Violence against women was an important concern for the women's movement in the late twentieth century. Surveys suggested that a large percentage of Canadian women had been victims of sexual assaults, while many had endured beatings by husbands or boyfriends. The pathological anger that some men directed towards women was made particularly evident on 6 December 1989, when a misognynist gunman, who said he wanted to kill feminists, burst into the École polytechnique of the Université de Montréal and murdered 14 women engineering students in cold blood. Women such as Geneviève Bergeron and Barbara Maria Klueznick, who did not even know their assailant, were gunned down because the deranged young man had been unable to gain entrance to the engineering school and blamed the minority of women in the program for his failure.[3] Parents and fellow students of the murdered women campaigned to make access to guns in Canada more difficult, and their demands were partly met by the Liberal government in 1995.

A variety of women's groups, ranging from feminist lawyers to prostitutes, worked together to produce legislation in 1993 that strengthened women's rights in sexual assault cases. Both partners to sexual activity had to give explicit consent whereas before, a woman had to demonstrate that she had struggled to prevent unwanted sex occurring. Still, a Supreme Court decision in 1994 that allowed extreme drunkenness as a pretext for a rapist claiming that he was not criminally responsible for his actions demonstrated that women's legal protection against sexual assault was by no means total in Canada.[4]

Women made gains in education as well. By the 1990s, women were more likely than men to get university degrees. But they remained overwhelmingly within traditional programs for women such as nursing, social work, and education, and arts. Overall, women's undergraduate enrolments increased from 36.7 percent of the full-time total in the 1970–1 academic year to 53.6 percent in 1992–3. The increase in graduate enrolments was even more impressive, from 22.3 to forty-two percent. Women formed the majority of part-time students in both undergraduate and graduate categories by 1992–3. Ironically, given the rationalization of the Montreal murderer, women were dramatically under-represented in engineering and applied sciences, accounting for only seventeen percent of all students in 1992.[5]

As suggested above, some of the gains that occurred reflected the fact that there were more women in political life than ever before, though men still held an overwhelming percentage of legislative seats and Cabinet posts both federally and provincially. Kim Campbell became prime minister briefly in 1993 as the demoralized Conservatives sought to revitalize their party before the federal election

that decimated their parliamentary representation. The NDP chose
Audrey McLaughlin as its federal leader in 1989, and her successor
was Alexa McDonough. Several women led provincial governments
in the 1990s as well, while others led the Official Opposition in
various provinces. Still, there was nowhere near gender balance in
political life at the senior levels. Only in city council and school
board elections did something close to gender parity occur in a
variety of cities and towns.

The National Action Committee on the Status of Women continued to play a co-ordinating role for women's struggles in Canada in
the 1980s and 1990s. Or, at least, it did so in English Canada. The
Fédération des femmes du Québec, as noted in Chapter Fourteen,
pulled out of NAC to protest its support for the Constitution Act of
1982, and NAC and some Quebec women's groups clashed over the
Meech Lake Accord as well. While NAC indicated concerns that the
"distinct society" clause could be used to detract from women's
rights in Quebec, a province where the Catholic Church's influence
had long limited the choices available to women, Quebec women
bristled at this suggestion. They accused English-Canadian women
of being unaware of the progress that Quebec women had made, and
were insistent that Quebec francophone women, as supporters of
Quebec's nationalist aspirations, did not wish to participate in a
campaign that could work against Quebec being granted greater
recognition as a distinct society within Canada.

By the early nineties, however, there had been a greater rapproche-
ment between the Quebec women's organizations and NAC as the
latter, under the leadership of Judy Rebick, a socialist feminist, came
to accept the notion of asymmetrical federalism. NAC made use of
the constitutional discussions after the failure of the Meech Lake
Accord to press an agenda that would give women greater political
representation (for example, by having half of the Senate seats allocated to women), and to guarantee a decent standard of living for all
women and children. Though some liberal feminists embraced neo-
conservatism in whole or in part, the organized women's movement
was focussing increasingly on the plight of less-privileged women,
for whom recession and government cutbacks were particularly disastrous. During the constitutional talks, NAC worked closely with
the Action Canada Network, a coalition of trade union, church, and
community organizations that had broadened their scope from opposing the free trade agreement to pressing more generally for policies that redistributed wealth and power. NAC and other women's

organizations had opposed the free trade agreement and NAFTA because many of the low-wage manufacturing jobs that free trade threatened were held by women. Women in clerical positions in many service industries were also affected by the opening up of all services to free trade, from computer reservation systems used by airlines and railway companies, to mail-order catalogues, to information providers such as credit bureaus and personnel firms.[6]

Visible minority women increasingly demanded that the larger women's movement recognize their particularly vulnerable position within Canadian society. While women's movement campaigns for more public funds for breast cancer research or for abortion rights could unite women of all classes and races, visible minority women argued that they faced more immediate problems of racism and poverty that the women's movement had tended to ignore. In the 1990s, NAC tried to address demands from minority women by including more of them in leadership positions in the organization and by making anti-racist campaigns an integral part of women's movement political campaigns. In 1992, Sunera Thobani, an articulate Indo-Canadian political activist, single mother, and immigrant from Tanzania, became NAC president, much to the chagrin of conservative feminists who felt it was inappropriate for someone who had lived in Canada for only four years to head a national organization. African-Canadian activist Beverly Bain had earlier been named NAC's executive director. The ability of the women's movement in Canada to maintain a coalition, however brittle, of women of many different backgrounds and ideological perspectives, contrasted sharply with the experience of the United States, where no equivalent of NAC had emerged. While most feminist activists in Canada agreed on the importance of using the state to achieve women's objectives, American activists, reflecting the different American political tradition, had always been more divided on the issue of whether women could gain anything by putting pressure on a state apparatus that reflected the interests of patriarchy and imperialism. Canadian women, like European women, tended to see the state as an arena of contest rather than a fixed set of perspectives.

The Canadian women's movement, confronted by the neo-conservative assault of Canada's elites, asserted more than ever the need for government programs that compensated women for the poverty traps that gender roles often dumped them in. Low social assistance rates, the lack of adequate supplementary income for older women who had never had an attachment to the labour force and therefore did not receive Canada Pension Plan cheques, and the limited nature of government programs that recognized women's responsibility for the care of children were all targets of NAC and other groups.[7]

For all the victories of the Canadian women's movement, its main disappointments in the eighties and nineties came from governments' failures to deliver on promises that would have improved women's position in the paid labour force. The federal government's own Canadian Advisory Council on the Status of Women, discussing proposed changes to the Unemployment Insurance Act in 1989 that made it more difficult to collect UI, summarized the programs that were needed:

> Affordable, quality child care, comprehensive maternity and paternal leave policies, job creation, affirmative action programs, pay equity, flexible work arrangements, and adequate pensions, together with training programs and unemployment insurance, are parts of the whole position of women's employment status; they interrelate, but are not interchangeable.[8]

Increasingly, however, the federal government was only willing to spend money on job-training programs, which often did not prepare women for available jobs or increase the number of jobs available. Both Brian Mulroney and Jean Chrétien lied to women about their intentions regarding daycare, the former promising a national daycare program in 1984 and 1988, and the latter, promising 100,000 new, publicly subsidized daycare spaces.

Lynette Pike, a St. John's social worker and single mom of a six-year-old daughter, described the results of the failure of Canada to develop a national daycare policy when she appeared before the House of Commons Special Committee on Child Care in March 1986. Her daughter had been in seventeen care arrangements since her birth in April 1979. These ranged from having both parents at home to using relatives and neighbours, hiring strangers, and paying privately operated daycares. Both mother and daughter were exhausted as individual providers turned out to be child-beaters, the wives of alcoholics, or simply between jobs while daycares closed down for the summer, or were too far away to make sense as long-term care providers.[9]

Experiences of this kind caused fewer women than men in Canada to buy the arguments of neo-conservatives that the country could not afford to have the rich social programs that it did, never mind to expand its programs. A "gender gap" in political preferences and in political perspectives became noticeable in the polls during the nineties. For example, while nineteen percent of men in Canada indicated before the federal election in 1993 that they intended to vote Reform, only twelve percent of women intended to vote for this right-wing party. Similarly, there was a huge gap between the percentage of women and men intending to vote for Mike Harris in the 1995 provincial election in Ontario, and in the number of women and men who supported Premier Klein's cutbacks program in Alberta.

Native People at Century's End

> They said they wouldn't log Lyell Island at first and now I hear they are going to go ahead. So today I am here because pretty soon all we are going to be fighting for is stumps. When Frank Beban and his crew are through and there are stumps left on Lyell Island, they got a place to go. We, the Haida people, will be on the Island. I don't want my children and my future grandchildren to inherit stumps.[10]

Explaining her people's close connection with nature, Gwaganad's presentation to the British Columbia Supreme Court explained why the Haida opposed indiscriminate logging of South Moresby. Along with many environmentalists, the Haida were unimpressed by the companies' claims that they were reforesting and that there would be second growth to replace the trees cut down for commercial purposes. Gwaganad noted that the twenty-year-old second growth trees near Salt Lagoon were placed so close together that growth of the trees was thwarted. Her emphasis on the fact that Lyell Island was her ancestral home, while the loggers were transients who would not have to live with the consequences of their actions, is important in understanding Native insistence in the late twentieth century on recognition of their territorial rights.

The 1980s had begun with some hope for progress on the issues of Native land claims and self-government within their lands. As we saw in Chapter Fourteen, the Constitution Act of 1982 called on the provinces and the federal government to have several conferences on Native demands for self-government. But the First Nations required the support of seven provinces with fifty percent of the population to win an amendment that granted self-government. The three westernmost provinces along with Quebec, which was boycotting all constitutional discussions, did not give consent to such an amendment. The western premiers argued disingenuously that the term "self-determination" was unclear, but public opinion generally was mixed as to whether Canada's first inhabitants had a right to apply their own laws and run their own schools, social services, and courts, funded by taxes collected from all Canadians. Though Native people as a whole were unquestionably poor, many Canadians seemed to focus on the "special" rights that they enjoyed and believed that they were too well treated. While Natives blamed discrimination, poor education, and limited resources on reserves for the massive rates of unemployment among Natives, unsympathetic Euro-Canadians blamed social welfare and alcoholism. In the era of neo-conservatism, blaming victims of the free-market system for their own misfortunes certainly had a new lease on life.

In northern Canada, in the wake of the Berger Commission, the federal government proved relatively open to negotiations. The 2500 Inuvialuit of the Mackenzie River delta area agreed in 1984 to a deal that gave them title to only a fifth of the area they once called their own, but gave them $152 million over thirteen years, which they have subsequently invested in businesses throughout the country. On the lands that they did get to keep, they retained sole rights to hunt fur-bearing animals and musk ox, and they were given an advisory role to the government in wildlife management.[11] The Yukon First Nations signed an agreement in principle in 1990 that will give them full aboriginal rights within a territory of 41,000 square kilometres. The Inuit Tapirisat signed an agreement with the government in 1992, after eleven years of negotiations, that builds on the precedents of the James Bay Agreement and the Inuvialuit Agreement. The Inuit agreement calls for the creation of Nunavut Territory, a territorial unit in which the Inuit will form the overwhelming majority of the population. The division of the Northwest Territories had little support from the Dene, who have failed, as yet, to arrive at a territorial agreement with the federal government. Court decisions have caused the Dene to believe that the federal offers, which include consultation with Natives regarding wildlife management, are weak because they neither require First Nations consent nor force compensation by the government when an aboriginal right is affected by government actions. Like all the other northern groups, the Dene want to control the pace and character of economic development within the territories where they live, but they are less convinced than others that the land concessions made by the government go far enough to assure such local control.[12]

Land claims south of the sixtieth parallel, unlike those in the North, have progressed with glacial speed. Outside of the North, the federal government has not only the usual corporate interests with which to contend, but also the provinces, who rarely place the interests of the First People above those of companies which promise job creation. The Lubicon Cree, who have been waiting since 1939 for the federal government to make good on its promises of a reserve, have faced six decades of provincial and federal duplicity. The federal government arbitrarily removed members from the band list in 1942 and then tried to compel the Lubicon to accept a smaller reserve. The province allowed petroleum drillers onto Lubicon territory in the 1970s, without Lubicon permission. When the exploration for energy caused game and fur-bearing animals to leave the area, the province tried to argue that the Natives could no longer support a traditional economy and, therefore, had no reason to oppose further industrial development. Chief Bernard Ominayak took the Lubicon plight to the United Nations and won the endorsation of the World Council of Churches. Though Alberta Premier Don Getty proved amenable to a solution in the late eighties, the federal government insisted that it owed the Lubicon far less compensation than the band claimed and that it need not grant the Cree the control over economic development that the Lubicon demanded in the wake of the desructive impact of the petroleum industry. The government tried to weaken the unity of northern Alberta Cree by granting smaller reserves in the region to several groups of Natives that included some members of the Lubicon band. After more than sixty years of waiting, some Natives, whether or not they agreed with Ominayak's defence of the traditional Lubicon demands, were tempted by Indian Affairs to accept half or less of a loaf.[13]

Like the Lubicon, the Mohawk of Kanesatake in Quebec had never signed away their rights to what they had regarded as their ancestral lands. The largely French-Canadian town of Oka ignored their claims, and in 1988, announced plans to allow the expansion of a local golf course into the Oka forest. The Mohawk denounced a plan that would cut them off from their ancient cemetery and make a mockery of their land claim. While Mohawk protest caused the province and municipality initially to agree to a moratorium on the golf course expansion, the municipality unilaterally suspended the moratorium in March 1989. With the federal and provincial governments apparently uninterested in intervening, the Mohawk decided to erect barricades to prevent the municipality from entering territories claimed by the Mohawk. A Quebec provincial police effort to force the Mohawk to retreat ended with the death of a policeman on 11 July 1990. A seventy-eight-day stand-off followed before the Mohawk Warriors surrendered to the Canadian armed forces. The federal government had been forced to purchase the disputed golf course lands from the municipality and to negotiate their transfer to the Mohawk. But control over the rest of the Oka forest also remained in dispute. During the stand-off, Native people across the country set up barricades on roads and railways in solidarity with the Mohawk.[14]

Kahn-Tineta Horn, a Mohawk activist who was arrested for her role in the defence of Oka, summarized the feeling of many First Nations peoples about their position within Canada.

> We tried to negotiate for hundreds of years, and where did it get us? We're losing more and more, and finally when it came to that piece of land at Kanesatake for a damn golf course and they wanted that too, we finally said no, you're not taking any more. And we stood up. So it's symbolic of something in the Indian people that's changed. We aren't afraid anymore. We're willing to negotiate, but not willing to allow the Canadian government to take advantage of us any longer.[15]

The Mohawk were not alone among Native people in the 1990s who felt the need to resort to force to protect their lands for future generations. Apart from the conflicts on South Moresby mentioned above, there were armed confrontations between Blackfoot nations and the government of Alberta over the impact of the Oldman River Dam on local wildlife, and between the Chippewa and the Ontario government over a provincial park at Ipperwash situated over a burial site, among others. In British Columbia, a group of Natives occupied a ranch near Ferguson Lake, claiming that the rancher was an illegal occupant on Native land.

Sometimes First Nations were able to win a victory over unbending governments without resorting to violence. The Cree of northern Quebec, for example, outwitted Robert Bourassa and Jacques Parizeau, both of whom were committed to the development of Great Whale River as part of a massive James Bay II hydroelectric power expansion. Most of the additional power to be generated would be

A ceremony to return medicine pipe bundles from the Provincial Museum of Alberta to the Sarcee. GAIA NA-4890-5.

exported to the United States. The Quebec government was largely unwilling to discuss with the Cree the impact of this project on northern Quebec's wildlife, given Quebec's dream of an economic empire built on hydroelectric power. So the Cree, unable to persuade the people of Quebec that their government's project was immoral, appealed in a slick campaign to the people of New York State not to accept Quebec power. The utilities in the state, caving in to public pressure, agreed not to buy power from Quebec until proper impact-assessment hearings were held on Great Whale. The Quebec government was forced to shelve the project, and the Cree hoped that the shelving was indefinite.[16]

There were some settlements that satisfied both First Nations and the federal government. The British Columbia government, which had maintained for over a century that it had extinguished Native land claims before entering Confederation, had finally agreed in the 1990s to allow Native groups to file land claims. The combination of Native militancy and the election of an NDP provincial government in 1991 produced a change in climate in a province where Native rights had traditionally been trampled upon by the state. The British Columbia Treaty Commission was established, with federal and provincial participation, to deal with claims. In the spring of 1996 the Nishga reached an agreement with both levels of government that gave them $200 million, 2000 square kilometres of land, and a high degree of self-government.[17] The settlement gave some hope to the thirty-seven Native groups that had filed claims with the Treaty Commission that governments might finally be serious in dealing with Native demands for control over at least some part of their historic land base, and over self-determination for Native people.

Such hopes seemed distant just a few years earlier when the Chief Justice of the British Columbia Supreme Court, Allan McEachern, delivered his rejection of the claim by the Gitksan and Wet'suwet'en people that they had a right to title and joint jurisdiction of their 57,000-square-kilometre ancestral home in the Skeena region. After a three-year trial, during which the Native nations had presented both oral evidence and academic experts to back up their claim that they had had a continuous presence over many centuries in the area, they were treated to a judge's account that rejected oral evidence altogether. Relying purely on the documentary record and reading that quite selectively, McEachern presented a view both of Native pre-contact history and of early contact history that most historians and anthropologists have long rejected. He presented the Gitksan and Wet'suwet'en people as nomads who had no real claim to any territory. Ignoring the partnership of Natives and Europeans that characterized the fur trade, McEachern suggested that Natives had been unable to adapt to the European presence. He did not believe that there was a Native culture or economy worth preserving. "Indian dependence upon the white society was one of their greatest problems," wrote the judge, apparently unaware that fur-trader dependence upon the Natives vastly exceeded Native dependence upon the fur traders.[18] Essentially, McEachern accepted the old imperialist view that Natives were savages and that, therefore, they had no rights but those that the imperial power granted them. Ruling that the Proclamation of 1763, which granted rights to various Native groups, did not apply to British Columbia, McEachern told the Natives that the British government had acted quite correctly in asserting its sovereignty over the territory of British Columbia in the 1800s, and that Canada had acquired total control over all Crown lands in BC when the province entered Confederation in 1871.

McEachern's views confirmed what many Canadians wanted to believe: they owed Natives nothing. But the five-member panel of the British Columbia Court of Appeals rejected McEachern's claim that aboriginal rights had been extinguished before 1871. Only two members, however, ruled in favour of the Gitksan claim, with the majority favouring another trial to determine "the scope, content and consequences of such non-exclusive Aboriginal rights of use and occupation."[19] The Gitksan and Wet'suwet'en people, though they considered an appeal to the Supreme Court, decided first to try the route of the British Columbia Treaty Commission.

Many issues divided First Nations people as they struggled to gain self-determination and control over a viable land base. Was violence justified in certain instances to gain Native objectives? Did the establishment of casinos on reserves, which created jobs, conflict with Native social/spiritual values? Was a Native elite developing that looked after its own and ignored rank-and-file Native people? What rights should off-reserve Natives enjoy? Should reserves welcome back the Native women and their children who had been expelled because they married non-treaty husbands? The latter issue seemed clear enough to most non-Natives. It was the law of the land after 1985 that the Native women could return to their reserves and ask for housing. Chiefs who protested that these women and their kids had lost their Native language and culture could be seen as sexists who continued to defend their own right to marry whomever they chose, but to deny this right to Native women. But, the reserves were not given extra money or extra land to accommodate the increased population that removal of the century-old injustice against Native women should have made possible. The result was that many Native women were to find that their efforts to rejoin their reserves were opposed by many, perhaps most, members of their band. They demanded that the question of their inclusion on reserves be settled before the issue of self-determination for Native peoples could be resolved.

Native women and children often bore the brunt of alcoholism and despair on reserves. Native men had few employment prospects either on or off the reserve, and spent much of their time drinking. The result was a cycle of drinking and family violence, in which assaults, including rapes, of wives and children were not uncommon. Unsurprisingly, many women were less than keen on the devolution of social services to reserves where the reserves remained solely under men's control. They fought with their own leaders and with governments to have the problems of spousal and child abuse dealt with openly, so that healing on the reserves could begin. Anti-alcohol campaigners on many reserves were also generally led by women, concerned with rehabilitating social units that had been degraded by marginalization within the larger society, followed by a cycle of alcoholism and violence.[20]

Native women were regaining their traditional pre-contact power in many First Nations societies, the problems of the off-reserve women and of men's violence against women notwithstanding. Wherever efforts to revive traditional practices occurred, and women were often instrumental in campaigns for such revivals, the crucial role of women in most First Nations' power structures was rediscovered. This was particularly true among the Mohawk. Kahn-Tineta Horn recalled that during the Oka crisis,

> when [Quebec Native Affairs Minister] John Ciaccia went to Kanesatake after that shooting broke out, he was met by a man, and then taken to meet with the women. He said, well, where are your leaders? All these women were sitting around, and they said, you're talking to the leaders, the women. He was surprised. He was uncomfortable. I believe he didn't take them seriously.[21]

Immigrants and Racism

The character of Canadian immigration had changed by the 1980s, thanks to the removal in 1962 and 1967 of regulations that were meant to keep the country white. Visible-minority Canadians, including both immigrants and Natives, were estimated in the mid-1990s to comprise about thirteen percent of the Canadian population. By 2016, it was forecast, they would make up twenty percent of the population. The 1991 census noted that almost 600,000 Canadians were of Chinese descent, while more than 400,000 Canadians were of South Asian background. There were over 200,000 Canadians of West Indian descent, 200,000 Arab-Canadians, 200,000 Latinos, and 90,000 Filipino-Canadians. During the 1990s, new immigration from Hong Kong, on the verge of returning to control by China in 1997, and war-torn Somalia, and Ethiopia, as well as "family class" immigrants related to previous immigrants, had boosted the numbers of Canadian immigrants from Asia, Africa, and Latin America. Europe and the United States, the source of ninety-six percent of immigrants to Canada from 1945 to 1962, were the source of less than half of new Canadians in the 1980s and 1990s. For citizens of poorer and war-afflicted countries, Canada's high rates of unemployment proved less a deterrent than they did for citizens of other wealthy, industrialized nations.

Many immigrants prospered in Canada. Most had marketable skills and many, such as the Hong Kong businessmen who received preferential treatment by the Immigration authorities, brought large amounts of capital into the country. Most visible-minority immigrants, like immigrants generally, migrated to Canada's big cities where not only were jobs more likely to be available, but their communities were likely to be large enough to allow for a continuation of some of the cultural life of their home countries. Community organizations served a cultural purpose as well as providing aid in finding accommodation and employment, and otherwise ensuring that new arrivals were not lost among the skyscrapers and four-lane-highways of their adopted home. Like European immigrant groups before them, immigrants from other continents established their own restaurants, newspapers, churches, and community centres.

Regrettably, however, like past visible-minority immigrants to Canada, many of the new immigrants learned from experience that many Canadians were racist. Human rights legislation, including the protections in the Constitution Act of 1982, ensured that the overt racism practised before World War II in hiring and in accommodation was rare. But unspoken discrimination was common. An advertised apartment for rent was suddenly not available when an African-Canadian showed up to look it over; a Chinese-Canadian secretarial applicant did not have the right personality for the job; a taxi dispatcher in Montreal or Edmonton allowed customers to specify that they wanted a white cabbie. There were attacks on South Asian–Canadians and African-Canadians in Toronto's subway; Edmonton nightclubs imposed an informal rule of excluding some groups of non-whites; there were clashes between white and black students in Nova Scotia.

Sikhs, who wore their turbans when entering certain Canadian Legion halls, as their religion demanded they do, were asked to leave, even if they were decorated war veterans. The fledgling Reform Party called for an immigration policy that would preserve Canada's character, only altering the policy to focus on economic criteria for immigrants after extensive criticism from the media and from groups representing immigrants. While their party denied that the old policy had been an attempt to re-impose the colour bar, many active Reformers were unabashed in opposing a colour-blind policy, suggesting that Canadian culture, as they saw it, depended upon having a country overwhelmingly composed of white Christians. Even more egregious than the xenophobic wing of the Reform Party were the right-wing extremist groups composed of troubled young white men, resentful about limited employment prospects and somewhat lost in the anomic society that characterized many of Canada's cities. Though the numbers of the population enrolled in such organizations was insignificant, their violent orientation made them a threat to minority groups, including visible minorities, Jews, and gays. Apart from the Nazis and the Ku Klux Klan, who had maintained a slimy but shadowy existence in the country throughout the post-war period, American imports such as the Aryan Nations entered the fray using violence to produce a Canada composed exclusively of white, Christian heterosexual people, with fixed male and female gender roles.

Immigrants of African and South Asian descent often had little choice but to accept low-paying, non-unionized jobs in factories where working conditions were degrading, or to work as farm labourers. South Asians working on farms in British Columbia, notes sociologist Tania Das Gupta, picked pesticide-sprayed crops without any protective masks or clothing. Living in makeshift homes, usually converted barns and sheds, without electricity or toilets, these workers, mainly women, were provided no childcare facilities, and several child drownings had resulted while mothers of young children were working. In the factories, claims Das Gupta, "one common managerial practice with South Asian women workers is to ghettoize them in the worst and least-paid tasks and in specific shifts or areas of the shop floor."[22]

Many immigrant women found that during periods of high unemployment, such as the 1990s, they had few options but to do homework, either sewing, typing at piece rates for an employer, or babysitting in wealthy homes. The "Filipino nanny" allowed to immigrate to Canada to look after children of two-income professional or business families became common in many high-income urban neighbourhoods. Low wages and working hours that went beyond legislated maximums were typical of home-work employments. Beyond the reach of unions or even factory inspectors, home-workers' exploitation was often invisible to the larger public. Many kept their spirits up by focussing on their children, whom they hoped would have a better life as a result of their hard work. Ming Lai, a Chinese-Canadian seamstress in Toronto, told researchers:

I support my children with my money, so I cannot afford not to work ... I'm very stingy on myself. But in terms of the children, I try and get them as much as they need. My husband, once in a while, he gives them a little bit of money ... 98 percent of the time I pay for everything. I feel that with my two children, I have to try my best to support them until they become mature, until they become independent. I would also like them to go to university.[23]

African-Canadians seemed to be particular targets of racism, along with First Nations people. Harassed by police officers even when there was no evidence that they had committed or were about to commit a crime, Canadian blacks, particularly young males, felt threatened rather than protected by those charged with protecting citizens. Several were killed in suspicious circumstances, or when trying to flee arrest for relatively minor charges. Black men in Canada, as in the United States, often seemed to be the last hired and first fired in the labour force. While black women fared somewhat better, their earnings were below those of white women in the labour force. Many, including African-Canadian nurses, complained that they were supervised more closely than white employees and subjected to racial stereotyping, while black women in dominantly male work environments were particularly vulnerable to sexual harassment since many of their superiors accepted stereotypes of the undifferentiated sexual availability of black women.[24] The extensive discrimination against Canadian blacks, and particularly black youths, was revealed by Stephen Lewis, Canada's former ambassador to the United Nations, in a report prepared for the Ontario government after a riot in Toronto in 1991. The riot began as a demonstration of solidarity with rioters in Los Angeles angry over the acquittal of two policemen caught on a well-publicized videotape while involved in the savage beating of Rodney King. Lewis painted a portrait of a community where young people felt that they were forced to be outsiders within society. But while the NDP government in Ontario practised affirmative action in its hirings, it was reluctant, like most Canadian governments, to free vast amounts of money for either programs of anti-racism or programs to impose affirmative action on the private sector. In any case, the backlash against the NDP's supposed generosity in providing social assistance to new arrivals from Africa and the West Indies was an important factor in defeating the province's first social democratic government in 1995.

Several studies in 1996 indicated that even Canadian-born members of visible-minority groups earned less than their white Canadian-born counterparts. Using 1991 census data, two University of Toronto economists concluded that African-Canadian men earned twenty percent less than whites, while South Asians earned sixteen percent less. The gap was much smaller, however, for Chinese and Southeast Asian men, and there was no gap overall for Canadian-born visible-minority women compared to white women, despite the low wages of most African-Canadian women. The researchers were hesitant to explain the gaps their research had identified. While it might be due to discrimination against certain visible-minority groups, in whole or in part, they said, it might also be explained by cultural factors. Education, age, experience, and language ability, however, did not seem to explain the phenomenon. York University anthropology professor Carol Tator noted: "There is a large body of knowledge that says if your skin is black or brown, as opposed to white, you experience a whole set of discriminatory barriers."[25]

Many Canadians were unaware or skeptical of the accusations by visible minorities of racism in Canada. Complacency about Canadian racism, however, dissolved temporarily when the armed forces, after first attempting to cover up the evidence, were forced to admit that organized racist extremists had penetrated the Canadian Airborne Regiment which had been assigned to peacekeeping duties in Somalia (see Chapter Thirteen).

The vulnerable economic situation of some visible-minority groups was particularly evident duirng the 1980s and 1990s, because high unemployment meant that even menial jobs were not available for young people from stigmatized groups. African-Canadians and Vietnamese-Canadians were particularly hard hit by youth unemployment, and the strains upon their communities were palpable. Youth "gangs" among the Vietnamese, while small relative to the total Canadian Vietnamese population, were involved in a variety of crimes, including violent crimes. Visible minority and immigrants' rights groups called not only for greater opportunities for education and jobs for non-whites in Canada, but for greater willingness on the part of the police and the authorities generally to learn more about other cultures, and to work with community groups to achieve better understanding and a measure of social justice.

Visible-minority Canadians figured prominently in the country's cultural life in the 1980s and 1990s. Some of Canada's best-known writers, nationally and internationally, were either Third World immigrants or Canadian-born writers of colour. Michael Ondaatje, who had established himself as an important Canadian poet in the 1970s with *The Collected Works of Billy the Kid*, winner of a Governor-General's Award, went on to produce the best-selling *The English Patient* in 1992. *The English Patient* won Ondaatje, who was born in Sri Lanka, the first Booker Prize to be awarded to a Canadian, and was turned into an acclaimed movie in 1996. Rohinton Mistry, who was born in India, wrote vivid novels about his home country that won international audiences. M.G. Vassanji, an East Indian of Kenyan origin, wrote about the experiences of being a minority person both in Africa and in Canada. Joy Kogawa fictionalized the Japanese-Canadian history of discrimination and resistance, while Dionne Brand, a Trinidadian immigrant, produced both fictional and biographical accounts of the struggles of African-Canadians.

Novelists, poets, and dramatists of visible-minority background differed on the question of whether an artist could or should act as a spokesperson for a cultural group or focus on universal themes. Neil Bissoondath and Evelyn Lau, respectively of East Indian–Caribbean and Chinese-Canadian background, saw their art primarily as individual expression, while both Brand and Marlene Nourbese Philip believed that their experiences as black women in Canada, and in Brand's case, as a black lesbian, were the primary forces that shaped their art. Bissoondath, somewhat iconoclastically, risked criticism from immigrant groups generally by opposing multi-cultural grants, arguing that cultural endeavours should be judged on artistic merits rather than on their role in preserving the alleged characteristics of a particular national culture.[26]

Gay Rights and Sexual Politics

Discrimination against homosexuals, like discrimination against non-whites, increasingly lost its legal underpinnings in the 1980s and 1990s. It persisted nonetheless. Reform MP Bob Ringma spoke for many "redneck" Canadians in May 1996 when, during a parliamentary debate on adding sexual orientation to the constitution's list of grounds upon which discrimination could not be based, he defended discrimination in certain circumstances against both homosexuals and non-whites. If it would cost an employer business to do otherwise, Ringma thought it wholly defensible to move a black or homosexual employee to the back of the shop.[27] Though disciplined by party leader Preston Manning, Ringma had a great deal of support in his party for these views.

There was other evidence of homophobia in Canada. Raids on gay bath houses in Toronto and Vancouver in the early eighties, grisly murders of gays in Montreal in the 1980s and 1990s, and a "Christian" college's firing of a lab assistant in Edmonton in 1993 on the grounds that he was gay provided some glimpses into the popular antipathy to gays. "Fag" became the primary insult heard in elementary school yards. Gays and lesbians were increasingly coming out of the closet, but they often met with such a chilly reception on the outside that they preferred to build their own institutions until such time as the larger society could accept that sexual orientation was a private matter. Conservative clerics denounced the "gay lifestyle," conflating sexual orientation with promiscuity and pedophilia. Defenders of "the family" defined the term in such a way that single parents (except perhaps widows and widowers) and gay couples were outside its framework. They opposed the inclusion of gay partners in family benefits plans, though court decisions, based on Charter protections, largely undercut them. More successfully, they fought efforts to allow gay couples to adopt children. An effort by the NDP government in Ontario to allow such adoptions collapsed when both Opposition parties denounced the measure and some members of the government caucus took advantage of a free vote on the issue to vote against their own government.

Censorship policies in Canada continued to treat depictions of homosexual coupling differently than heterosexual sex acts. The gay magazine *The Body Politic* was forced out of print as objectionable to community standards, though its defenders noted that it was no more explicit in its portrayal of sex acts than many men's magazines. In general, customs officials and law enforcement authorities seemed to believe that the line between erotic and obscene which was drawn — also sometimes with contention — for heterosexual publications need not be drawn at all for homosexuals: any depiction of two men or two women performing sex acts was obscene.

The spread of AIDS, beginning in the early eighties, within the gay male community carved a deadly path. But it also mobilized thousands of gays to work together and openly for public funds to research the causes and possible cures for this dreaded disease, and for widespread availability of the resulting, and often expensive, drugs needed to resist the disease. Conservatives, especially in the churches, labelled AIDS the "gay plague," even though many heterosexual men and women were contracting the disease, and preached sexual abstinence outside lawful heterosexual marriages as the solution to AIDS.

As the century was drawing to a close, gays and lesbians had made considerable progress. It was no longer illegal for persons of the same sex to have consensual sexual relations, and no longer considered a sign of pathology if they did. Explicit discrimination against homosexuals was no longer allowed, and gays and lesbians had a number of large organizations to speak for them. Still, there was little doubt that discrimination against homosexuals was very much alive in Canada and that gays and lesbians, outside, perhaps, of certain progressive coalitions, remained outsiders in Canadian life, treated with contempt or pity by the majority.[28]

Trade Unions on the Defensive

While the women's, gay, and visible-minority movements had always been movements of outsiders looking in on the power structure, the trade union movement, or at least its leaders, superficially had become part of the Establishment in the three decades following World War II. Media accounts talked about a society in which three "bigs" — big business, big government, and big labour — worked together to create an economy that functioned relatively smoothly, but which stifled most private initiative. As we have suggested in earlier chapters, it is simply wrong to claim that organized labour in Canada ever enjoyed the informal power that big corporations could exercise. They could not determine the location of firms, make decisions on whether firms would expand or contract their work force, or decide how the labour process would be organized. Yet, on the surface, it seemed to be true that many big corporations, particularly in capital-intensive sectors, relied on good relations with their unions to ensure continuous production and to stem revolts on the factory floor. The militancy of workers employed by the state in the 1960s and 1970s seemed to give a great deal of power to unions whose members were thought to have lifetime jobs.

By the 1990s, it was clearer to what extent management held the upper hand in its dealings with trade unions collectively, and with individual workers, unionized or not. As we have seen, the free trade agreement became a bludgeon used by many corporations in their negotiations with workers regarding wages and working conditions. This inevitably weakened private-sector unions. The public sector proved not to be as immune to layoffs as it had been in an earlier period. So-called "downsizing" of government occurred largely through shrinkage of the public labour force, with remaining workers finding themselves subject to speed-ups and increased work loads. Public-sector workers often found their jobs privatized. The Mulroney government sold off publicly owned airplane manufacturing firms, Petro-Canada, VIA Rail, and Air Canada, while provincial governments also sold off public assets, often at bargain basement prices. Many unionized service jobs both in government and the private sector were removed from the government or company payroll, only to be contracted out to the lowest private bidder. Laundry workers in hospitals, cleaning staff and cafeteria workers in government buildings, and other groups composed mainly of immigrant women lost modest-paying union jobs and often found work again by working for the non-union private sub-contractor for a wage that was a fraction of their former union wages. Better-paid, "skilled" male workers were also sometimes victimized by the new anti-unionism of government and employers. During the recession of the early eighties, Alberta had passed legislation that allowed construction companies locked into union contracts to form "spinoff companies" to which such contracts would not apply. The result was a massive decline in the number of unionized construction sites in the province.

Still, the union movement in Canada fared far better than the American union movement. In the early seventies, about a third of all workers in both countries were unionized. Yet by the early 1990s, only about sixteen percent of American workers held union membership cards, while thirty-six percent of Canadian workers were unionists. This was about three percent down from the peak reached about 1980, but suggested, nonetheless, that the union movement in Canada remained robust. In the United States, so-called "right to work" legislation destroyed the "closed" union shop and allowed employers, particularly in the South, to warn workers that they could find their plant relocated if they chose to join a union. While some Canadian legislation, such as the spinoff legislation in Alberta mentioned above, was also intended to weaken unions' ability to recruit and hold members, no "right to work" legislation emerged, and trade unions were generally able to persuade their members that unions made more sense than ever when times were hard and employers were less likely to concede much to the workers.[29]

The movement towards independent Canadian unionism, which had gained momentum in the 1970s, continued into the 1980s. In 1985 the Canadian Automobile Workers (CAW) held their founding convention, after the leaders of the over 100,000 Canadian members of the United Automobile Workers worked out the terms of separation of the Canadians from the American-based UAW. In 1986, it was the turn of the Canadian members of the International Woodworkers of America to announce that they had established a union independent of their American counterparts. By 1986, six of every ten unionists in Canada belonged to independent Canadian unions, compared to only three in ten just twenty years earlier. The conservative, American-controlled construction unions, angry at what they saw as the CLC's increasing nationalism, left the labour central and formed their own union central, the Canadian Federation of Labour.[30]

The character of the trade union leadership was changing in the 1980s and 1990s in Canada. As late as 1985, fully two-thirds of Canada's "labour elite" — the leading officials of the biggest forty unions in Canada — were of British descent. One-sixth were French-Canadian. In 1990, the British-origin leaders had fallen to just below half of all the leaders, while the French-Canadians had increased to 29.3 percent. More than two in ten of the leaders were of ethnic origins other than English or French.[31]

Women had also made important gains in representation in the trade union movement. In 1985, Grace Hartman, a typist and longtime union activist, became president of Canada's largest union, the Canadian Union of Public Employees. The next year, Shirley Carr, also from CUPE, became the Canadian Labour Congress's first woman president. In 1987, lab technologist Gwen Wolfe became the first woman to head a provincial labour federation when she was elected president by the Nova Scotia Federation of Labour.[32] In the mid-1990s, women headed the provincial federations of labour in all three Prairie provinces, and held more of the key positions in individual unions than ever before. Judy Darcy became president of CUPE in 1991, and in 1996 Cheryl Kryzaniwsky was elected president of the national council of the Canadian Autoworkers Union. A former Air Canada reservations clerk, Kryzaniwsky became president of her union local in the late eighties. At that time, only ten percent of union officers in CAW were women, whereas by the time Kryzaniwsky became council president, about half of the officers were women. Nonetheless Kryzaniwsky observed that women, apart from the difficulties they found as mothers in finding time for union activities, still faced a degree of gender discrimination within the union movement.

> There is absolutely no question in our organization today, a man can say something and automatically be taken much more seriously than if a woman were to say the same thing. The difference is a woman has to build up credibility. You have to prove yourself first to be listened to.[33]

Women trade unionists played an important role in some of the key confrontations between employers and workers in the 1980s and 1990s, notably in Operation Solidarity in British Columbia in 1983, labour's response to Social Credit premier W.A.C. Bennett Junior's attack on the public service. Women also played prominent roles in Ontario in the fight against the huge cutbacks in education, health, and social services which Mike Harris' Conservatives implemented after their election in 1995. Immigrant women played a major role in the movement to organize British Columbia's farmworkers; in a successful struggle for reinstatement of Toronto pizza workers who were unjustly fired; and in a strike by Superplastics workers in Mississauga, Ontario, for better wages and working conditions. The latter struggle achieved some success in part because the larger feminist movement joined the picket line, placing additional pressure on management to compromise.[34]

Labour's relationship with the NDP soured somewhat after the Rae government imposed its "social contract" on Ontario workers in 1993 (see Chapter Twelve). Increasingly, labour formed coalitions with feminists, gays, environmentalists, and poverty activists on specific issues. Internally, however, the labour movement was divided between radicals and mainstream elements who believed that labour should avoid civil disobedience and focus politically on election of the NDP. The radicals argued that the bureaucratic unionism practiced by the labour movement in the past would no longer work, because owners and managers had become far more hard-line in opposing workers' demands. They called for mobilization of workers in demonstrations, sit-ins, and other indications of unrest, to embarrass and cause the downfall of governments that followed an anti-labour agenda. The radicals argued that the Ontario NDP government had gotten away with implementing almost none of its platform because Bob Rae and the other party leaders took labour, which seemed demobilized and dispirited, for granted. Workers would have to show militancy if they intended to be taken seriously by any administration, regardless of party affiliation.

Environmentalism Versus Employment

If the workers' movement seemed largely on the defensive as the century ended, the environmental movement was fairly militant, though not always successful in its campaigns. The large corporations and the media presented Canadians with a stark choice: environment or employment. From this perspective, efforts to regulate the environment would prevent the economic growth necessary to deal with Canada's high rates of unemployment. In any case, argued the corporations, they were cleaning up their act. Development as such was not a problem, as the Cassandras of the environmentalist movement seemed to believe; rather, "sustainable development" was the issue and corporate moguls had even more interest in ensuring that it occurred than state regulators. The market, rather than rigid state bureaucrats enforcing uninformed rules, should determine the pace and character of economic development and of conservation measures. This strategy seems to have worked quite well. In the late eighties, as unemployment eased, Canadians generally indicated a willingness to put environmental issues at or near the top of the national agenda. But in the nineties, as unemployment soared again, many Canadians seemed to think that they had to choose between the environment and jobs. Media images of British Columbia and New Brunswick loggers and environmentalists at loggerheads, of the Lubicon Cree arguing with oil-rig workers in Alberta, and of Newfoundland and northern First Nations sealers debating sealing practices in international forums, told much of the conventional story. Forest logging roads throughout the country seemed to be blocked by activists in the 1990s. From the Christmas Mountains in New Brunswick, to Pukatawagan in the Porcupines of Manitoba, to the Slocan Valley in British Columbia, those concerned with conservation of Canada's great forests, with aboriginal people often in the lead, were increasingly saying no to new logging developments.

But many environmentalists rejected the view that conservation of resources such as forests and fish was at odds with maintaining jobs. Logging in Canada doubled from 1950 to the mid-nineties. But the number of jobs in the industry fell by half and the methods being used to cut trees, particularly clear-cutting, were more devastating than earlier practices. Clearly, increases in logging had not produced more jobs. In fact, argued environmentalists, the move away from small logging companies using traditional methods, to mega-corporations such as British Columbia's MacMillan-Bloedel and the Japanese giants, Mitsubishi and Daishowa, had resulted both in fewer jobs and in less conservation.[35] Greg Mitchell, a logging contractor for a sawmill in Corner Brook, might have seemed at first blush to be an unlikely candidate for the role of an environmental activist. But Mitchell's Humber Environmental Action Group had campaigned throughout the country and at the United Nations to denounce overcutting of Newfoundland's forests. Mitchell, who opposed clear-cutting and had joined forces with Forest Allies, a movement that pointed out the habitat loss of the pine marten thanks to overcutting, believed that small contractors, if they were given tenure in the forest, would have the incentive to conserve that big trans-nationals did not. While the former had only a small area to cut and nowhere to go if it was denuded, the latter could and did scour the world for new forests to rape. Similarly, Native activists argued that their desire to continue to live off the land made them natural conservationists. In northern Quebec, the Cree argued that the extension of logging roads had almost rid certain areas of wildlife.[36]

In both the inshore and offshore fisheries as well, big companies with little interest in local communities were responsible for destroying more jobs than they created with their emphasis on increasing their catch. The offshore cod fishery was ruined by the draggers from a variety of countries scooping up the cod along the Grand Banks. An indefinite moratorium on the cod fishery in 1995 put thousands of Newfoundland fishers out of work, forcing them to look for another line of work in a province with a rate of unemployment almost twice the national average. Ironically, while the small fishers could no longer catch cod, the draggers continued to catch millions of pounds of cod as bycatch as they fished for other species.

Lori Vitale Cox, a fisher in Bay St. Lawrence, in northern Cape Breton, described the changes that occurred in her community after the federal government began, via subsidies in the 1970s, to encourage inshore fishers to buy bigger boats with high-technology gear. Like many fishing villages, Bay St. Lawrence was characterized by a lack of class distinctions among its citizens before the 1970s. Almost everyone fished from spring till late fall "in small boats with wooden traps, hooks, harpoons and small nets," and supplemented their fishing income by growing a few crops and hunting. Most houses were heated by wood. "The economy was embedded in the social life of the community in such a way that people worked together and depended upon each other." But after a handful of locals with big boats captured the government's licences for the crab fishery, a few prospered while the rest of the community grew poorer. The result, wrote Cox, was that

> a few people in The Bay now vacation in the Caribbean and need to hire financial advisers to help them invest money, while others don't even have enough money to buy their kids winter boots or a decent pair of running shoes. A few have become owners, and their neighbours and relations have become their hired help. Fifteen years is not a very long time for such drastic changes in economic and social patterns. This kind of disparity is starting to rip the fabric of the community to shreds.[37]

Women in Bay St. Lawrence staged a blockade of the harbour and demanded that the government share the existing crab quota among all full-time fishing families in the village. This would have provided a respectable income for all families in the community and removed the need for unemployment insurance for the fishers. Injunctions were used to break the blockade, but there were many other similar protests throughout the Atlantic region as communities struggled for their lives, while the draggers destroyed the resource that had kept these communities alive for centuries.

Despite many victories for environmentalists, particularly those of Native communities mentioned earlier, the 1990s was a bleak period for the Canadian environment. The growth ethic that had been present in industrial societies from their inception had been somewhat modified in the 1970s and 1980s as governments, pressured by environmentalists, began to accept the need for greater environmental regulation. By the 1990s, the neo-conservative view that corporations could better protect the environment than governments, and could do so without stalling job creation, had taken hold.

In Alberta, the government decided to ignore the findings of a federal-provincial Review Board assessing the environmental effect of the proposed Alberta-Pacific pulp mill on the Athabasca River, a river already badly polluted by a number of pulp mills. The independent review board accepted the evidence of environmentalists and

Native groups that the new mill would harm the fishery on the river and that Native peoples in northern Alberta depended upon fish for a nutritious diet. But the government claimed that Alberta-Pacific was modifying its plans to meet the review board's concerns, and saw no reason to have the board itself determine whether this was the case.[38]

In Ontario, the right-wing government of Mike Harris, rejecting the perspective of the previous NDP and Liberal governments that the old-growth red and white pine forests in Temagami deserved protection, simply handed out licences to logging and mining firms that wanted to "develop" the Temagami region.

The federal government had little reason to be complacent, having signed an international agreement to restrict greenhouse gas emissions to 1989 levels, only to allow emission levels to rise by five percent in the next six years.[39]

Nonetheless, while the logic of the market seemed to prevail in Canada in the 1990s to a degree unseen since the 1930s, the strength of the various movements discussed in this chapter suggested that neo-conservatism was not nearly as hegemonic in its control over people's thinking as its supporters might like to think. Opponents of neo-conservatism were, however, not always clear about what they wanted to replace it with. Should Canada simply revert to the policies of the fifties through the seventies, even though a considerable degree of poverty marked these "golden years" for Canada? Was some form of socialism credible to Canadians or had the failure of the Soviet-style dictatorships discredited all ideas of socialism and Communism? Could Canada leave the free trade agreements and plan its own economic destiny or did the "new globalism" force opponents of the control trans-national corporations exercised over the world's citizens to use international forums to assert popular control over economic development? Did the answers to Canada's economic problems lie in the federal government's assumption of responsibilities to provide a decent livelihood for citizens and environmental regulations to ensure that they breathed clean air and drank clean water? Or was it up to local governments and popular organizations to seize the initiative? The answers to such questions were unclear as the end of the twentieth century beckoned. How they are answered will determine much about how Canadians will live together and with the other nations of the world in the twenty-first century.

Sixteen

Canada in the Twenty-First Century

On January 1, 2012, the world in which Canadians lived was in many ways the same as it had been on January 1, 2000. It was still a world dominated by the United States, its giant corporations, and its imperial-minded government. But that dominance was somewhat offset by the dramatic growth in the economic power of China and, to a lesser extent, by the rise of other economies including those of India, Brazil, and Russia. Governments were still more interested in economic growth as a solution to problems of wealth distribution than in the redistribution of wealth. The environment still seemed to take a back seat to economic growth as well. Within Canada, the debates that dominated the twentieth century continued without any knockdown winners or clear changes in direction.

Yet, a series of interrelated global events and phenomena had changed the context of those debates. First, there were the attacks on New York and Washington, D.C., on September 11, 2001, by self-styled Muslim freedom fighters, mostly from Saudi Arabia, who hijacked planes and crashed them into the World Trade Towers in New York and the Pentagon in Washington, killing 3,000 people. The Americans, led by President George W. Bush, whose entourage was dominated by individuals connected to the international petroleum industry, responded with a war against Afghanistan, whose Muslim extremist government gave shelter to Osama Bin Laden, head of Al-Qaeda, which later claimed responsibility for the so-called 9/11 attacks. Afghanistan's actual participation in planning the attacks was rather minimal, since all the intelligence gathered suggested that they were planned within the United States under the nose of quarrelling and ineffective national security bodies rather than in Afghanistan itself. For good measure, Bush used the 9/11 attacks to create sufficient American anxiety about all Muslims that he was able to persuade Congress and a number of pliable governments around the world to wage war in 2003 against Iraq, though its dictator, Saddam Hussein, was secular and had suppressed political movements in his country that claimed Islam as their inspiration. Many critics suspected that the politics of oil was more important in the invasions of Afghanistan and Iraq than either revenge for 9/11 or a concern that these countries were led by ruthless dictators. The Americans, after all, had a long history of empowering dictators friendly to American capital.[1]

The Americans, though able to crush the governments of both Afghanistan and Iraq, proved unable to establish viable alternative regimes. It didn't stop them from interfering elsewhere, though—for example, in Libya in 2011. But with increasing anger at home about unending and expensive wars in the Middle East, the American government had few answers to those who questioned why their taxes seemed to be going towards warfare while state funds for urban infrastructure, education systems, and medical care were increasingly hard to find. In practice, as it did during the Vietnam War, the American government simply used debt rather than taxation to fight wars that the "silent majority" might otherwise turn against. With a significant minority of Americans opposed to these wars even at their inception, it was too dangerous to tax citizens to pay for all the expensive weaponry and expanded military payroll.

The growth in debt occurred at a time when the United States had increasingly lost its competitive edge in the world. American banks, huge computer networks, and entertainment companies sucked in a great deal of wealth from the rest of the world, but that did not prevent the loss of jobs and government revenues that resulted from American-based manufacturers increasingly locating their production in countries with cheap labour and eventually offshoring many other types of economic activity, including call centres, accounting, printing, and advertising.

The *CIA Factbook* for 2011 told a sobering story of a country where "since 1975, practically all the gains in household income have gone to the top 20 per cent of households."[2] Somehow, the neo-liberal prescription that handing over more power to markets would raise all had failed four out of five Americans. A tragicomedy emerged in the early 2000s in which an increasingly unregulated financial sector seeking quick profits made mortgage loans to working-class and poor Americans whose incomes were too low to repay them. These poor households then made further loans against the inflated value of their properties in an artificially hot housing market.

This amounted to a huge pyramid scheme, which the underlying maldistribution of wealth could not support. It began to unravel when the housing market and mortgage repayments stalled. Lehman Brothers, a long-established leading investment banking firm, collapsed in 2008. Instead of helping out the destitute who were being removed from their homes for failure to pay their mortgages, the American government gave in to demands from the banks that they, unlike individual Americans who got into financial difficulties, not be allowed to fail.[3]

With their money tied up in coddling bankers and feeding a self-serving and often inefficient war machine, the American government seemed to have little money left over for programs for its citizens. Meanwhile, well-funded corporate campaigns gave many Americans, perhaps a majority, the idea that somehow the billionaires and multi-millionaires among them could not spare any more money for the public purse.

Welfare liberalism in the thirty years after World War Two had attempted to prevent the inevitable redistribution of wealth by uncontrolled monopoly capitalism in favour of the wealthy. It attempted instead, through a variety of programs, to freeze social class differences rather than allow the income gap between rich and poor to grow. Its proponents argued that there was no need to redistribute wealth because private control of most of the economy would ensure that the pie would get bigger and that even if its division remained vastly unequal, those at the bottom would constantly have a few more material goods and therefore a reason to support the capitalist economic system. Neo-liberals, by contrast, suggested that weaker state protections of individuals and control over corporate operations would allow the pie to grow much faster. That did not happen, and the United States, already a very unequal country in 1997, with a Gini coefficient of 40.8—a measure from one to one hundred of relative income shares of the richest and poorest tenths of the population in which the higher the number, the more unequal the population—had reached 45 in 2008, without much economic growth occurring to shield the poor from the consequences of a growing income gap.[4]

Environmental knowledge in the early twentieth century blew holes in theories of economic growth as the saviour that would allow the rich to live luxuriously while the poor could hope to get a few more crumbs at some point. Economic growth was literally destroying the planet. It was no longer simply vague issues of pollution that the public had to confront. It was now clear that "global warming," created by industrial activity, threatened the ecology of the planet.

Big corporations and conservative governments organized campaigns to counter growing evidence regarding the impacts of global warming. But the evidence was overwhelming. The Intergovernmental Panel on Climate Change (IPCC), a global body of scientists under United Nations auspices, had filed reports in 1990, 1995, and 2001, suggesting that disturbing annual increases in global temperatures on land, sea, and permafrost were escalating. Their fourth report in February 2007 reported that the Greenland glaciers were likely beyond saving from melting, and that would hike sea levels by seven metres, sinking many coastal areas. Increased human production of greenhouse gases was confirmed to be the culprit. The burning of fossil fuels, agricultural practices, and deforestation all had contributed to global warming. The concentration of carbon dioxide in 2005 was 379 parts per million. It had been 280 parts per million 150 years earlier. Global temperatures would rise 1.9 to 4.6 degrees by 2100 if humans made no changes in how they conducted themselves. Scientists concluded that global emissions had to fall by 90 per cent within a few decades to prevent the massive danger to life on Earth that such fast increases in average temperatures represented.[5]

Canada's Economy in the Brave New World

How did Canada fare in a world where elected governments acting on behalf of all citizens became increasingly irrelevant as large multinational corporations were left to focus on profits?

For ordinary Canadians, the first decade of the twenty-first century was not a prosperous time. As in the United States, the distribution of wealth became less equal. The Gini coefficient climbed from 28 in 1989 to 32 in 2005. Although this figure is respectable when compared to the United States, it is a reflection of great inequality when compared to Sweden at 23, Hungary at 24.6, Norway at 25, and the Czech Republic at 26, among others. The Conference Board of Canada, a conservative business organization, noted that between 1976 and 2009 the gap in real average incomes between the richest and poorest 20 per cent of Canadians, after tax and adjusted for inflation, rose from $92,300 to $117,500. Observing that both the lower and middle classes lost considerable shares of overall income, the Board concluded that "Most gains have gone to a very small group of 'super-rich.'"[6] Still, it did note that during that third of a century there had been a modest gain of about $3,000 per household in median income.

An earlier report for the Canadian Centre for Policy Alternatives demonstrated that on an hourly basis there was, in fact, a loss of net household income for both the poor and middle-income households. The average Canadian family was putting in almost 200 hours more per year in paid work in 2004 than in 1976. As the two-income household had become the norm, that also meant increased daycare costs sufficient to more than swallow up whatever small gains the extra hours of work were providing relative to family incomes three decades earlier. Proportionately higher costs of housing and rent also reduced the standard of living. That might have been bearable if the sacrifice that all Canadians were making was equal. But the richest 10 per cent of families raising children had average earnings 82 times those of the poorest 10 per cent of families, and alone among income groups they were working fewer hours than their counterparts a generation earlier. Chief executive officers of corporations saw their remuneration increase from $3.5 million in 1998 to $9.1 million in 2005. The average Canadian worker during the same period experienced an increase from $33,000 to $38,000, which, after inflation was factored in, actually represented a decline in income of almost 3 per cent. In 1998 the CEO had been worth 106 times the average worker; by 2005 that figure had increased to 240. Unions and social justice organizations proved no match for corporate political lobbies in persuading governments to implement their agendas. The corporate agenda focused on lower rates of taxation for the super-rich and reduced government regulation of the economy. Only "Canada's tax and transfer system stopped the freefall of incomes for about half the population raising children."[7]

For those involved in the exploitation of oil and gas, Canada seemed to be doing rather well. The concerns about fossil fuels and the environment notwithstanding, both demand for oil and international prices soared after an apparent glut pushed prices downwards throughout the 1990s. While the average international spot price for oil fell to US$9.76 per barrel in January 1999, it reached $147 in July 2008, before recession in the West pulled it down all the way to $34.57 in January 2009, a temporary setback. By September 2011 it had reached $110.56. This elevenfold increase in price from 1999 to 2010 was augmented by an increase in production of better than one-third. Canada's national production of oil was 2.8 million barrels a day in 2010 and was predicted to reach 4.7 million barrels a day in 2025. Natural gas production and prices had also soared during the first decade of the twenty-first century.[8]

The fate of Canada's economy seemed increasingly to lie in the production of fossil fuels along with other energy resources. The revival of demand for oil and gas restoked the Alberta economy, which had fallen into hard times for much of the 1980s and 1990s. But it also turned two formerly have-not provinces, Saskatchewan and Newfoundland, into at least temporarily wealthy ones. In 2008 Saskatchewan followed Alberta as the province with the country's highest GDP per capita while Newfoundland was third. Newfoundland's new wealth, however, has to be seen in perspective because it also continued to have the country's highest unemployment rate (13.5 per cent against a national average of 7.1 per cent in September 2011) and its outports remained devastated by the destruction of the cod fishery that took place in the 1990s. With Nova Scotia also enjoying a modest oil boom, total crude oil production in the Atlantic provinces increased 250 per cent from 1999 to 2010 and accounted for over 9 per cent of all oil by the latter date.[9]

Canada reached "peak oil," the point after which sources of conventional oil are in decline, in the early twenty-first century. Increasingly, the major source of Canada's oil came from the bitumen

Tailing pond north of Syncrude processing facility and upgrader.

sands—called the tar sands throughout most of the twentieth century—of the Fort McMurray area. The oil within these sands was far harder to extract than conventional oil and required large quantities of water to convert the tarlike substance into the same product that conventional oil represented. By the 1990s an international environmental movement, critical in general of the huge amounts of carbon released into the atmosphere in the production of fossil fuels, took special aim at the tar sands for their higher than average production of carbon.[10] In an effort to minimize the issue of tar sands oil versus conventional oil, the petroleum companies, abetted by the government of Alberta and the media, rebranded the "tar sands" as the "oil sands." Soon the corporate-controlled media in Alberta banished the term "tar sands," and that practice quickly spread nationally, even to the CBC.

The "sands" companies did spend some money attempting to improve the fossil fuel impact of their product. But they also spent much more attempting to discredit claims by scientists and the environmental movement that the viscous oil from the sands was much dirtier and produced more greenhouse gas than conventional oil. The companies, with the support of the Alberta and Canadian governments, advertised their efforts to reduce "carbon intensity," that is, the amount of carbon emitted into the planet's atmosphere for each barrel of oil extracted. In most years, however, the total carbon produced by the tar sands rose dramatically anyway for the simple reason that far more bitumen was being produced.[11]

In the early 2000s environmentalists in Canada attempted to inform the public about the harmful effects of the tar sands on human health and the environment and called for a moratorium on new projects. When this alarm failed to have an impact on the full-steam-ahead policies of the Alberta and federal governments, they called for a slowdown of the breakneck pace of extraction of bitumen. Much of the organized opposition to the tar sands came from outside the country. Despite the multimillion dollar campaigns of the oil companies and the Alberta government as they attempted to "greenwash" the tar sands, the European Union ruled in 2011 that oil from the sands required 107 grams of carbon per megajoule of extraction and processing versus 87.5 grams for conventional oil. This was part of an overall classification by the EU of non-conventional sources of fuel, and other fuels received even worse rankings. The rankings were determined by scientists, yet the Canadian and Alberta governments claimed that they were produced by politicians and were uniquely aimed at the Athabasca tar sands.

Although Canada had no markets for bitumen in the EU at the time, it worried that the bad publicity from European scientists would hurt its existing and potential markets in the United States and Asia. When the EU made its ruling, Canada was in negotiations with the United States to build a $7 billion pipeline, called Keystone, to carry raw bitumen from Fort McMurray to refineries in Illinois and Oklahoma and then on to the Gulf Coast. The pipeline met opposition from many Democratic Party senators and congressmen, as well as from a broad base of citizens and politicians in Nebraska, where people feared potential oil leaks into an aquifer that supplied much of the state's supply of water for drinking and irrigation. A huge civil society campaign, which publicized its cause via civil disobedience and signed up many celebrities, united both residents along the path of the pipeline and opponents of the tar sands. In November 2011 the State Department, recognizing the potential dangers to President Barack Obama's re-election, announced that the route for the pipeline would be reconsidered.

Another controversial pipeline in 2011, called Northern Gateway, proposed to move bitumen and other sources of oil from Edmonton to Kitimat, from where these products would be shipped to Asia. That created concerns within Canada about potential leaks along the route as well as the negative environmental impacts of increasing bitumen production and tanker traffic to get it to its new markets, of which China was the biggest. Chief Jackie Thomas of the Sai'kuz First Nation in north-central British Columbia commented on a pipeline that would pass through his people's territory by saying "We won't trade the safety of our rivers, lands, and fish that are our lifeblood."[12] The labour movement protested that both pipelines would be piping away Canadian jobs that could be created by refining the bitumen in Canada and then shipping it to various markets.

Environmentalists supported moving away from a reliance on fossil fuels in favour of the development of energy sources such as wind, sun, and biomass that produce little in the way of greenhouse gases. Labour proposed a more modest solution. Canada could reduce its bitumen production but create as many jobs from this resource by both extracting and processing it rather than simply extracting and exporting bitumen. Keeping most of the processed bitumen within Canada could also allow the country to stop its importation of most of central and eastern Canada's oil from the Middle East, they argued.

Both environmentalists and labour urged Canadian governments to follow Norway's example of setting aside a large percentage of the monies earned by selling oil to subsidize the development of less polluting fuels as well as putting more public funds into public transportation, cycling paths, and the redesign of buildings and cities to make them more environmentally sustainable.

According to *The Economist*, in January 2011 the sands contained 173 billion barrels of recoverable oil with a potential value of $15.7 trillion. That meant that, making use of the Athabasca River region oil alone, Canada could continue to produce as much oil as it was producing in 2011 for another 150 years.[13] By 2010 53 per cent of the oil produced in all of Canada came from the tar sands, and the forecast was that by 2025 that figure would reach 80 per cent. The "sands" provided employment for tens of thousands of construction workers, many of whom were flown in from other provinces to work fourteen days in a row, for twelve hours a day, before being flown back home for a week and then starting the grind of travel and gruelling workdays again. While in the Fort McMurray area, these workers, almost exclusively male outside of the workers in canteens, lived in company camps. Their employers provided them with meals and accommodation so they would not spend money on necessities during their work weeks. But, separated from families and friends, a very large number of these workers sought escape via cocaine, alcohol, and the purchase of sex from prostitutes. Although Fort McMurray became home to a growing number of professionals and retailers, it was simply a waystation for the construction workers, who included not only workers from across Canada but also many "TFWs" (temporary foreign workers), an acronym for people who were regarded as good enough to risk their lives in dangerous jobs in cold places but not good enough to become permanent Canadian citizens.

TFW numbers were rising quickly across the country before the recession began in the last quarter of 2008. There were 125,367 in 2004 and 251,235 in 2008, working not only in the tar sands but also on farms, as caregivers in homes, as cooks and waiters in restaurants, and in a variety of other occupations, mainly at the low end of the skill scale. An Alberta study suggested that a majority were poorly treated. The numbers of TFWs had jumped fourfold in that province between 2004 and 2008, from 13,167 to 57,707. A study by Edmonton lawyer Yessy Byl, sponsored by the Alberta Federation of

Labour, demonstrated that 60 per cent of employers with TFWs were breaching either the Employment Standards Code or the Occupational Health and Safety Act. But penalties against such employers were rare, and their vulnerable employees feared deportation if they raised their voices.[14]

Human rights advocates challenged the notion that there were people who were good enough to work for Canada, often for many years, but not good enough to ever become citizens. The state authorities responsible for this program argued in response that Canada's commodities-fuelled prosperity was susceptible to the vagaries of the international economy. It was hardly new for Canada to be dependent on global commodities markets. But Canadian manufacturing, its progress stalled in the last quarter of the twentieth century, was increasingly becoming an endangered sector. The rush of manufacturers to the cheap labour markets of poor countries had been clear in the 1980s and 1990s, and increasing free trade removed possible penalties from companies that tried to produce their products cheaply abroad and then export those products to wealthy countries.

The commodities boom of the early twenty-first century speeded up the demise of manufacturing. It pushed up the value of the Canadian dollar in currency markets, making Canadian products more expensive when priced against their competitors. Between 2002 and 2007 about one in ten manufacturing jobs disappeared in Canada, with Ontario and Quebec proving the big losers, losing between them 266,000 jobs. The automobile and automobile parts, steel, electronics, and shipbuilding sectors all shed workers. Then came the recession in 2008, and within a year industrial production had fallen 15 per cent, net unemployment had increased by 400,000, and GDP had fallen 3 per cent. Though the Canadian government, along with the American government, pumped billions into the flagging automobile sector, employment in the Ontario-based industry continued to decline precipitously. As a new recession began in late 2011, manufacturing employment tumbled further. In September and October alone 72,000 manufacturing jobs evaporated in factories big and small, including the shutdown of Ford's large car assembly plant outside St. Thomas, Ontario. It was no surprise then that by the end of 2011 manufacturing, which accounted for more Canadian jobs from 1976 to 1990 than any other sector, had fallen into third place behind both trade and the combination of health care and social assistance.[15]

Even the oil-producing provinces, despite their growing consumer power, lost manufacturing firms and gained few replacements. In Alberta, for example, most of the meatpacking industry disappeared along with the large multinational chemical company, Celanese, and the clothing giant, GWG. The oil companies, at least when markets were buoyant, could not find all the labour they needed, and so they offered relatively high wages that encouraged many blue-collar workers to move into construction and oil rig work rather than leave for greener pastures in another industry. Manufacturers generally could not compete with the energy giants and therefore had an incentive to locate outside oil-producing regions unless they were producing equipment or parts specifically for the energy industry. And with the high dollar that the fossil fuel industry created, the manufacturers had little incentive to simply relocate in the provinces without oil and gas. The overall phenomenon was sometimes referred to as the "Dutch disease" because the Netherlands had experienced a hollowing-out of its manufacturing base in the 1960s and 1970s after the discovery of large quantities of natural gas in 1959 pushed up the value of its currency relative to other European countries.

Outsourcing of Canadian jobs was not limited to manufacturing. Service jobs also went offshore, including many call centre jobs that had been created in the 1990s. Telus, which employed 29,000 people in Canada, had outsourced about 750 call centre jobs to the Philippines by 2007. In 2009 they outsourced 3,000 more call centre jobs, as well as their hardware and software server operation, payment and processing for Ontario customers, and much else.

The Last Years of Liberal Dominance, 1997–2005

Jean Chrétien won re-election in 1997 and 2000, but with support from barely more than four in ten Canadian voters on either occasion. The regional divisions evident in the 1993 election persisted, with western Canada sticking with Reform and a large section of Quebec seats staying with the sovereignist Bloc Québécois, although the Liberals regained many seats from the latter in both elections. Liberal cuts to unemployment insurance and other social programs turned many Atlantic Canadians towards the NDP and Progressive Conservatives in 1997.

In the 2000 election, the Liberals prepared to outdo the Reform Party at its own game, promising massive income tax cuts that particularly benefited the wealthy, as well as corporate income tax reductions. In response to complaints that his government's under-funding of social programs was continuing the precedent set by the Mulroney and Campbell PCs, Chrétien gave the provinces a pre-election gift by restoring medicare funding to the level reached before the Liberals first took office in 1993. That opened the government up to criticism both from those on the Right who claimed that publicly administered and delivered medical care would bankrupt Canada and from those on the Left who accused the Liberals of having not only broken their promises to restore PC funding cuts, but also of having implemented deep cuts of their own. For the latter group, the restoration of funding only to the level of the Mulroney years still left the provinces with too little federal money to deal adequately with medical needs. In contrast, the Right, led by the major business organizations in the country, claimed that two-tier medicare was the answer: private medical insurance for those who had the means to pay for it, with state medicare for those who did not. In April 2001 Chrétien announced that Roy Romanow, the former NDP premier of Saskatchewan, would serve as a one-man commissioner to research and report on the Future of Health Care in Canada. Romanow sponsored a large number of studies of Canadian and international medical practices to answer the question of whether public or private medical services were more efficient and cost-effective.

The Romanow report, released in November 2002, rejected neo-liberal claims that Canadian health spending was rising too rapidly and that privatization of some or all of health delivery would prevent government deficits. Health spending was rising as a proportion of GDP in all industrialized countries, whether they relied mainly on private or public health care, partly because of the aging of populations and the additional health spending that a segment of people in their last years required and partly because of a growing reliance of citizens of all ages on medical systems to solve health issues. While Canada was spending 9.1 per cent of its GDP on health care in 2000, the comparable figure for the United States, where public health care was available only to seniors and the destitute, was 13.3 per cent. Canada had significantly better health outcomes than the Americans as evidenced by longer life expectancy and lower infant mortality. Its public debt per capita was lower than in the United States. While supporters of greater privatization, recognizing that the American model was almost an embarrassment to their argument, pointed to various services that were privately provided in western European countries, Romanow observed that in almost all of those countries over 80 per cent of health services were paid for by the state. In Canada, where pharmaceuticals outside of hospitals as well as dental care were paid by individuals, governments were paying only 67 per cent of the health bill. Scandinavian countries, which had the highest percentage of health bills paid by the state, also reported the best health outcomes. Two-tier medical care, the Romanow Report reminded Canadians, had existed before universal medicare was introduced and meant an inferior service for those who had to rely on non-profit services provided by charitable agencies. As long as the middle and upper classes had to rely on state services, they would press for their improvement; once they could pay for better services privately, they would lead the effort to remake the remaining state-provided services so that they were cheap and shoddy.[16]

In 2004 the federal government pledged an additional $35 billion for health care over a five-year period, a figure that would suppos-edly compensate for increasing demands on the provincial health systems. After the election that year, a new federal-provincial deal promised continued federal increases in health spending until 2014. But some provinces, particularly Alberta, continued to champ at the bit to expand private health care, and the federal agreement to provide extra financing did not prevent this. The public was largely hostile to privatization because its supporters could not demonstrate how allowing doctors to practise in both the public and private sectors would improve service to patients when a shortage of doctors and other practitioners had created many of the problems of medical services in the first place.[17]

Critics of simply increasing spending on health services based on the medical model did not all come from the Right. There was growing skepticism about a focus solely on increasing the numbers of doctors, nurses, and hospitals. Many health practitioners, particu-larly those outside conventional medicine, pointed to better nutrition, exercise, and reduced stress as well as natural remedies as being as useful as the chemical medications and surgeries of the mainstream medical system. In turn, however, supporters of greater social equal-ity sometimes criticized the importance that proponents of more holistic medicine placed on individual behaviour. They suggested that consideration of the impact of poverty and inequality needed to be front and centre in discussions of health. Residents in poor urban neighbourhoods often lived considerably shorter lives than residents in the wealthiest neighbourhoods. Working-class people generally had less time and money to spend on exercise and to purchase organic food than solidly middle-class exponents of back-to-nature philosophies. Indeed the middle class, along with the wealthy, were often responsible in their day jobs for poisoning the atmosphere, reducing the quality of the food supply, and shutting down public recreational facilities. In short, the cuts in public services that included reducing the numbers of environmental and public health inspectors, as well as public gymnasia and swimming pools, contributed to illnesses of many kinds and increased the needs for health practitioners. Restoring funding for such services should be viewed as contributing to public health.[18]

The focus of public policy, however, continued to be on hospitals and doctors. This provided a lifeboat to the Liberals in the 2004 federal election. They had been riding high for some time thanks to divisions among the parties to their right and to their left, in both cases based on regional factors. On the Left, the sovereignist Bloc and the NDP operated within different provinces and probably had little impact on each other's fortunes. Together they enjoyed considerably less than one-quarter of the national vote in the elections during the 1990s and early 2000s. The Right had a larger vote, but its divisions made it appear no less able to defeat the Liberals. The Reform Party, with a solid base in western Canada, remained the dominant force and formed the Official Opposition in 1997 with sixty seats. The PCs, bloodied by their reduction to just two seats in 1993, increased their strength to twenty seats in 1997, demonstrating strength in the Atlantic provinces and Quebec. But the split on the Right in Ontario once again delivered almost all of that province's seats to the federal Liberals. The PCs' national popular vote was only slightly smaller than the popular vote for Reform, and the two parties together enjoyed the support of about 37 per cent of Canadians, within striking distance of the Liberals.

Efforts were made by pro-business forces to unite the two parties, but there were lingering differences between them. The PCs were certainly fiscal conservatives but not to the extent that the Reform Party was; while the latter called for drastic cuts to federal social, environmental, and economic regulatory programs, the PCs still saw the need for a regulatory regime and were only slightly to the right of the governing Liberals. The PCs were also generally not as socially conservative as Reform. While the latter wanted to bring back legal limits to abortion in Canada and to resist efforts to legislate rights for homosexuals, including same-sex marriage, the PCs were willing, at least to some degree, to accommodate feminist and gay rights demands, particularly during the period from 1998 to 2003 when Joe Clark again became party leader.

The Reform Party changed its name to the Canadian Alliance in 2000 and invited PCs to join with them in a "unite the right" campaign. The PCs spurned the invitation, and the Right entered the 2000 campaign still divided into two parties. Stockwell Day became the leader of the Canadian Alliance after defeating Preston Manning, Reform's national leader, for leadership of the new party. Day was even more socially conservative than Manning. He had once been principal of a Christian school in which creationism was presented as science. A CBC report during the election revealed that Day told his students that the earth was only 6,000 years old and that humans and dinosaurs had coexisted. While none of this hurt Day in western Canada, where Reform's support easily transferred to the Canadian Alliance, it prevented his party from making more than minor gains in Ontario, which it needed to penetrate in order to form a national government.[19]

Many voters, however, were disillusioned with the Liberals because of suggestions of influence peddling on the part of Prime Minister Chrétien during the 2000 election. The optic was that the Liberals believed themselves to be Canada's natural governing party and felt that they could do pretty much as they wanted. A fight between Chrétien and his fiscally conservative finance minister, Paul Martin, had become rather public and this further eroded confidence in the Liberal government. Chrétien forced Martin out of the Cabinet in 2002 but subsequently resigned as party leader and prime minister, allowing his rival to achieve a virtual coronation as party leader in late 2003. The Liberals soared to new heights in the polls.[20]

The business community was generally comfortable with Martin's accession to the prime ministership since he was a wealthy businessman who had cut social programs and taxes on the wealthy when finance minister.[21] But it was important to them to have an alternative government in the wings that was committed to even more pro-business policies than the Liberals. This was impossible while the Reformers and PCs continued to divide the right-wing vote and to denounce each other's policies. Consequently, the business community decided to play hardball to unite Canada's conservatives. They made clear to the two party leaders that they would provide no further money to either party unless the PCs and the Canadian Alliance united. The Canadian Alliance had dumped the hapless Day in 2002 and replaced him with Stephen Harper, a former Reform MP for Calgary from 1993 to 1997, who had then become national vice-president of the Canadian Citizens Coalition. That organization was a creation of right-wing businessmen opposed to virtually all taxation of businesses and the wealthy, and Harper did not initially prove popular with Canadians. The PCs meanwhile replaced Joe Clark with Peter MacKay, a fiscal and social conservative from Nova Scotia, in 2003.

Though MacKay had promised when he won the PC leadership not to merge the historic party with the Canadian Alliance, he relented as it became clear that the PCs would not be able to raise money if they maintained their independence and that the electoral rewards for conservatives from a merger were potentially immense. By the end of 2003 the two parties agreed to merge to create the Conservative Party of Canada. In March 2004 Harper defeated Belinda Stronach, the daughter and protegé of business icon Frank Stronach, to become party leader.[22]

Nevertheless, the united Right might have stood little chance of defeating Paul Martin's Liberals except for the eruption of a government scandal just a month before Harper's leadership victory. In 1996 the Chrétien government had launched the federal Sponsorship Program through which federal monies were given to help organizers of various public events across the country. Unsurprisingly, patronage played an important role in the awarding of grants. Auditor General Sheila Fraser revealed in February 2004 that about $100 million had been awarded to cronies of the Liberals in Quebec for virtually no work and with much of the money finding its way back to the Liberal Party itself. Prime Minister Martin hoped to defuse the issue by appointing a Commission of Inquiry under Justice John H. Gomery and denied any involvement of his own in the granting of phony sponsorship grants. But the opposition successfully convinced Canadians that the entire Liberal Party was involved in this scam and that Martin, as the second most powerful Cabinet minister for much of the Chrétien period, must have known what was going on.

Martin nonetheless called an election for June 2004. Although he had been the major right-wing force in the Chrétien government, and was one of Canada's wealthiest businessmen, he tried to prevent the united Conservatives from taking office on a wave of anger against alleged Liberal corruption by focusing on the Liberals social welfare credentials. A defence of publicly administered and delivered medicare was front and centre in his campaign. Harper, as part of a bland campaign focused on Liberal corruption rather than Conservative policies, downplayed his past support for private medicare and for provinces to be able to do what they wanted with federal medicare monies handed over to them. Harper was regarded suspiciously in central and eastern Canada for his signing of the "Alberta Accord"—a right-wing open letter to Ralph Klein—that praised the Alberta premier for his defence of Alberta's health policies during the 2000 federal election. The letter urged Klein to take measures that would lead to Alberta "resuming control of the powers that we possess under the constitution of Canada but that we have allowed the federal government to exercise." That meant building "firewalls" around the province that would protect it from federal meddling in areas that the Constitution reserved for the provinces.[23] "Firewall Steve" was therefore blindsided and unable to respond when Klein, in the closing days of the 2004 election, again revived his plans for two-tier medicare in violation of the Canada Health Act. The Liberals made hay out of Harper's silence, warning citizens across the country that they would no longer have a federal government willing to protect them from provincial experiments with two-tier medicine.[24]

Despite qualms about Harper, Canadians gave Paul Martin's Liberals only 135 seats out of 308 in the 2004 election, a drop of 37 seats for the governing party compared to 2000. The Conservatives won 99 seats, while the Bloc carried 54 seats and the NDP 19, and an Independent from British Columbia, Chuck Cadman, also won. Martin attempted to govern alone and to provide what he considered moderate social spending and tax cut policies, but he needed an ally if he was to remain in power. The NDP's new leader, Jack Layton, became that ally temporarily. Layton was a former Toronto city councillor who had been president of the Federation of Canadian Municipalities. Following in the footsteps of former national NDP leaders Tommy Douglas and David Lewis, who had taken advantage of Liberal minority governments to promote their party's social agenda, Layton called on Martin to cancel the $4.6 billion in corporate tax cuts that he had announced in his budget and use the money for social spending.

Martin, clinging to office, agreed to change his budget. As a result, the federal government was once again back in the business of building homes for the poor, providing funding for cooperatives, and spending more money on the environment and foreign aid. His government won a slim vote of confidence on the revised budget in spring 2005, with Cadman joining the NDP to provide the majority needed. That summer the Liberal–NDP alliance, in light of Supreme Court decisions that regarded same-sex marriage as a right under the equality provisions of the Charter of Rights and Freedoms, voted to make gay marriage legal in Canada. Canada was only the fifth country in the world to recognize same-sex marriages as having the same legal status as opposite-sex marriages.

Martin, still dogged by the Sponsorship Program in which he insisted he had played no part, attempted to build on his reformist credentials in the months that followed. He met with the provinces and came up with a deal for a national daycare program. A similar meeting in November 2005 with the provinces and the major Aboriginal organizations produced the so-called Kelowna Accord, which pledged $5 billion over five years for education, housing, health services, and economic development for Canada's Aboriginal peoples, a majority of whom lived in poverty. What percentage of the funds would come from Ottawa, however, was put off to a later meeting. Martin also pledged that Canada would take measures to ensure that it complied with the Kyoto Accord, which it signed in 1997 to indicate its willingness to cut its carbon emissions and help in the effort to reduce global warming. Canada had committed to reducing its emissions to a level 6 per cent below its 1990 production of greenhouse gases. In fact, by 2004, it had increased emissions by 20 per cent.

Though the Gomery Commission would ultimately exonerate Martin from any wrongdoing in the sponsorship scandal, Canadian public opinion was slipping away from the Liberals towards both the Conservatives and the NDP. Legislation proposed by Martin in 2005 was clearly meant to shore up his alliance with the latter. The NDP, however, was afraid to look like it was in bed with a government it viewed as corrupt at its core. It was also suspicious that the Liberals' sudden liberalism after so many years of cutting social spending was a ploy to steal NDP votes in an eventual election. For these reasons, it joined with the other parties to defeat the Conservatives in November 2005. The NDP suggested that the Liberals remained as much a pro-corporate party as the Conservatives, pointing to the government's decision that month not to tax the controversial investment instruments called income trusts, which the party viewed as a form of corporate tax evasion. The Kelowna, Kyoto, and daycare accords would have to wait until after an election was held in January 2006.

Domestic Political Developments from 2006

The Liberals campaigned on promises to deliver on their environmental, Aboriginal rights, and daycare pledges, while also promising to go ahead with the corporate tax cuts that they had withdrawn to get NDP support. By contrast, the Conservatives supported increased tax write-offs for parents as an alternative to help with daycare, claiming that support of the latter discriminated against stay-at-home mothers. They rejected both the Kelowna and Kyoto accords, the former as too expensive and the latter as interfering with economic growth. Harper was on record as a skeptic about climate change science, regarding it as a "socialist scheme designed to suck money out of rich countries,"[25] but he was careful about what he said during the campaign. While he had persuaded his party to drop all efforts to make abortion an election issue, Harper did promise a free vote on same-sex marriage if he formed a government. The major carrot that he dangled before the electorate was a cut in the GST from 7 per cent to 6 per cent and then gradually to 5 per cent. He gave no indication of how the lost revenue would be replaced, but he promised to cut unidentified wasteful government spending.

The Bloc campaigned, as it always did, on a mix of nationalist and social promises, insisting that federal monies for specific policy areas had to be handed to Quebec for its provincial government to determine priorities without questions asked. The NDP platform was similar to that of the Liberals on social and environmental issues, but the party questioned the sincerity of the government regarding those issues, noting that the decision not to tax income trusts and promises of corporate tax reduction would remove the likely funding sources for desired programs.

Early polling during the election suggested that the new Parliament would look similar to the old one, and the Liberals showed an early lead in the polls. But that changed when the RCMP, in mid-election, announced a criminal investigation into alleged leaks to some large investors of the government's plans about the non-taxation of income trusts. Such an announcement in mid-election was strange enough, but even more peculiar was the decision by RCMP Commissioner Giuliano Zaccardelli to announce that Finance Minister Ralph

Goodale was being investigated as part of the overall probe. While Goodale was later completely vindicated, the RCMP's gambit, for which no proper explanation has ever been provided, caused many Canadians who had been clinging to the Liberals to decide that they had to go.

When the votes were counted, the Conservatives had emerged as the largest party in the House with 124 seats, while the Liberals were reduced to 103. The Bloc retained 51 seats, and the NDP jumped to 29 seats. While the Conservatives were the only party that openly supported a neo-liberal agenda, the three parties of the Centre and Left appeared to give little thought to the idea of creating a coalition to take steps to implement Kyoto, Kelowna, and the daycare accords. For the Bloc, a coalition with the corrupt and federalist Liberals was unthinkable, just as a coalition with sovereignists was a non-start for the Liberals. The Conservatives, nominally as federalist as the Liberals but in practice a party that opposed an activist agenda for the federal government, proved able to establish a working arrangement with the Bloc, despite the very different views of the two parties on social, environmental, and international issues. The Conservatives, having elected no one in Quebec in 2004, had taken 10 seats in 2006 and were anxious to build a Quebec base. They promised to re-examine the national equalization grants with a view to giving more money to Quebec and supported Bloc views that the federal government should not interfere in provincial health and social service programs. Though Harper's western members were in many cases francophobic, he was responsible for having Parliament pass a purely symbolic resolution in November 2006 that recognized Quebec as a "nation" within Canada.[26]

As his unlikely alliance with the Bloc suggested, Harper proved to be a shrewd prime minister. After the election, he kept his ministers and caucus, which included a number of individuals with extreme views on social issues, on short leashes just as he had done during the election; for instance, all their public statements had to be vetted by the Prime Minister's Office. Harper did not make the big cuts in federal expenditures that the former Reform Party might have wished for, if only because with just a minority he could not risk offending all the parties at the same time. But even in a minority situation the government had sufficient power to prevent the other parties from forcing it to take measures to reduce greenhouse gas emissions or to introduce a national daycare program. The Kelowna Accord gave way to a modest increase in spending on programs to improve the dismal conditions of life on Aboriginal reserves. The government cut staffing in regulatory programs, including those dealing with environmental regulation, and cut funds for the CBC. Overall, though, the new government's cuts to the GST and to corporate taxes depleted the surpluses that had been accumulated under the Liberals, leaving little cushion for harder times to come.[27]

Meanwhile, the federal Liberals, in some disarray after their defeat, held a national convention in December 2006 and, by a narrow margin, chose Stéphane Dion as leader. Dion was a professor of public administration and one-time sovereignist who had served in the Cabinets of both Jean Chrétien and Paul Martin. Most notably, he was minister of intergovernmental affairs in the late 1990s and responsible for referring several questions to the Supreme Court regarding Quebec's right to declare independence unilaterally—it had no such right, according to the Court, but the federal government would be expected to negotiate independence if a majority of Québécois expressed a clear preference to leave the federation. Once the Court had ruled, Dion introduced the Clarity Act, which was passed in 2000 and which specified that any future referendum on sovereignty in Quebec had to pose an unambiguous question, unlike those posed in 1980 and 1995. If a referendum with a clear question produced a majority in favour of sovereignty, Quebec could not leave until it had negotiated with the federal government the terms of its parting from Canada to the satisfaction of both parties. Dion raised the ire of Quebec nationalists by declaring that if Canada's boundaries were not indivisible, neither were Quebec's and that Aboriginal people in Quebec's North and English-speaking districts of Montreal Island could vote not to become part of an independent Quebec.

Dion had great difficulty establishing his leadership within a party that was held together less by ideology than by a long history of having the spoils of office at its disposal. In opposition, Liberals were fractious both on a personal and ideological level. A committed environmentalist, Dion tried to end the drift in his party by giving it a strong identification with ecological issues, lifting ideas from Canada's Green Party, which in polls conducted between elections sometimes had the support of 10 to 12 per cent of all voters. In June 2008 Dion announced the party's Green Shift, an effort to implement Kyoto with concrete policies in which a carbon tax—that is, a tax on the use of fossil fuels—was the key element. Dion promised that

Liberal leader Stéphane Dion speaks at a breakfast meeting on September 15, 2008, during the federal election campaign.

other taxes would be reduced so that the carbon tax would not be a money grab but instead a means of inducing consumers to consider driving less, building more fuel-efficient homes, and using alternative sources of energy rather than fossil fuels. Quebec and British Columbia had already introduced such a tax at the provincial level. The Québécois generally were more environmentally conscious than other Canadians, and Dion may have hoped that he would receive a better audience with Quebec voters as Captain Green than as Captain Canada.[28]

Dion no doubt believed that he had a great deal of time to persuade Canadians of the need for a carbon tax. In 2007 Harper had introduced legislation that fixed the date of Canada's elections, short of an opposition vote of confidence forcing an early election. The date for the next election was set for October 19, 2009. But the legislation was not binding on the government. Harper, aware that the economies of Western nations were about to go into an economic tailspin, wanted an election before that happened, hoping to win a majority. Watching the public's initial antipathy to the Liberals' Green Shift, he approached the governor general to dissolve Parliament and force an election one year and five days earlier than it was supposed to occur.

Harper promised that any government led by him would never introduce a carbon tax but that it would legislate maximum emissions on big polluters, something that it had not done to date. The NDP proposed a cap-and-trade system that would put a carbon tax on companies that produced emissions over specified limits, though allowing companies to trade "carbon credits" with others that produced emissions below their government-specified targets. The Conservatives rightly pointed out that both the carbon tax and the cap-and-trade system were aimed at the fossil fuel industry and were simply different routes to the same end: higher prices at the pump meant to dissuade consumption and push people towards use of greener energies.

Polls indicated that Harper might gain a majority, partly by increasing his Quebec support. While Québécois, as polls suggested, were more social democratic than other Canadians, and Bloc policies generally reflected their thinking, they feared being left with little representation in a new majority government. But Harper's campaign in 2008 emphasized a get-tough approach to crime, including teenage crime, rather than support for rehabilitation, as well as cuts to funding for the arts, both of which alienated Quebec voters.

The Conservatives also made clear that they intended, if they had a majority, to scrap the long-gun registry, which continued to be popular in Quebec where memories of the massacre of women engineering students in 1989 remained vivid. The Québécois decided to cling to the Bloc rather than vote to be part of a majority government that ignored their values.

In the latter part of the election, Stéphane Dion, recognizing that he had championed a losing issue, attempted to shift electoral focus to the looming global recession, the inevitability of which the financial crisis emerging in the United States was making clear. The collapse of Lehman Brothers in mid-September and subsequent revelations that most of the United States' banking system was resting on an ocean of sand was obviously going to have international consequences. But the would-be prime minister offered few solutions other than a national conference of business leaders and all levels of government to deal with the coming crisis. Harper chided him for his prophecies of doom and suggested that the Canadian economy was strong and could withstand all possible challenges.

The hold of neo-liberalism over all Canadian political parties—a phenomenon they shared with most capitalist democracies—was revealed during the English-language leaders' debate in which Dion made his pitch for a concerted effort led by the government of Canada to plan for the expected recession. Asked if they were willing to go into debt to create jobs during the upcoming recession, all five party leaders replied in the negative. Keynesianism, it seemed, was dead in Canadian political life.[29]

It revived rather quickly, however, if not in a particularly robust manner, after the election, which returned 143 Conservatives, 77 Liberals, 51 Bloquistes, 37 NDP, and 2 Independents. The Conservatives had gained 19 seats since 2006 but remained 12 seats short of a majority. The Liberals were in shock, their vote having fallen to its lowest level nationally since the party had formed in the 1870s.

It was soon plain to everyone that the American financial chaos was not short term and that a recession was on its way. But the Harper government's fiscal update on November 27, 2008, focused on debt reduction rather than economic stimulus and, for good measure, mentioned its intention of ending the per-vote subsidies that all political parties received. The Conservative Party had devised a winning strategy to reach right-wing Canadians and get them to contribute to the party's operations, but the opposition parties, especially the Liberals, seemed incapable of expanding their funding base. The government having declared war on the other parties' main source of funding, the three other parties met and decided not only to vote a lack of confidence in the Harper government but to suggest an alternative coalition government of Liberals and New Democrats, with the Bloc guaranteeing support for a minimum of two years in non-confidence votes but having no direct participation within the government.

Harper withdrew the threat of defunding the political parties, but the opposition parties persisted in their efforts to form a coalition government and wrote to Governor General Michaëlle Jean to ask her to replace the Harper government with the parties that held the majority in the House of Commons. Harper, though he had won only 38 per cent of the vote and lacked a parliamentary majority, described the efforts of the remaining parties in the House to overthrow him as an attack on democracy. He suggested that his party, because it was the largest party in the House, had the right to govern, though nothing in British constitutional practice guaranteed any such right to a party that lacked a majority. The prime minister, whose first term had mainly been made possible by the cooperation he received from the Bloc, now declared that any government dependent on Bloc votes was cozying up to separatists. Harper asked Jean to prorogue the House immediately for six weeks so that he could avoid the vote of non-confidence that would either precipitate a coalition government or a new election. She acceded to his request.

By the time Parliament met early in 2009, the Liberals had a new leader, Michael Ignatieff. Ignatieff was a celebrated international academic who had lived most of his adult life abroad but had returned to Canada to run for the Martin Liberals in 2004. A one-time socialist, he had gradually moved rightwards in his political thinking and had supported the United States' invasion of Iraq in 2003. Representing, at least at first, a more moderate liberalism than Stéphane Dion, Ignatieff was uninterested in supporting the coalition with the other two opposition parties. The coalition had always been hazy about how much stimulus was necessary to help reduce recession-created unemployment. Ignatieff was relatively satisfied with the $40 billion of stimulus over two years with a $60 billion deficit that Harper promised in the 2009 budget, although it was proportionately much less than the United States and most European countries promised to spend.

As noted above, Canada shed many jobs during the 2008–09 recession, but it suffered less economic pain than many other Western countries. This was attributed to the relatively modest participation of its financial institutions in the hedge funds and derivatives that had proved to be wildly speculative financial instruments. In turn, the conservative behaviour of the Canadian banks was the result of long-established government rules of financial regulation. As the Americans had loosened their state regulation of the financial sector, the Conservatives, in opposition, had demanded that the Canadian government show more confidence in its private sector and had promised to untie the strings of government control should it take office. When it took office as a minority government, however, it was in no position to win parliamentary support for such an endeavour. Instead, as the American and European banks had to be shored up with government money, the Conservatives took credit for the solvency of Canada's banks.

The Harper stimulus plan included funding the Canadian share of a joint bailout with the United States of the automobile industry, which nonetheless shrank and shed many employees. The stimulus plan also included subsidies for home renovations and energy-efficiency improvements, as well as federal aid for "shovel-ready" projects across the country. Most of these projects only got off the ground after the recession had passed, but the Conservatives used state funds for a partisan advertising campaign of billboards and television ads for "Canada's Economic Action Plan." The government spent $53.2 million advertising the program in 2009–10 and then budgeted $26 million for television ads in 2011. Every building that had a window or door replaced with some federal monies bore testimony to that government's involvement. The government insisted that Canada's economic performance during the recession was a model for the rest of the world, and the media, which suffered its own downsizing in staff, especially reporters, did not challenge this narrative much. But, in fact, Canada's performance was middling. Economist Jim Stanford noted that the change in Canada's GDP in 2009 gave its performance only a ranking of 61 of 107 nations for whom this could be calculated, while the improvement in its employment rate the following year ranked twenty-eighth out of seventy-four countries.[30]

Although they had been elected in part because many Canadians viewed the Liberals as too arrogant in power, there was abundant evidence that the Conservatives, though a minority, also had come rather quickly to see themselves as having the right to rule without informing Canadians of what they were doing. Their economic goals were also contradictory. By early 2011 the Conservatives had declared that their priority was the reduction of debts and deficits. The deficit in 2009–10 reached $55.6 billion but dropped to $36.2 billion in 2010–11. While proclaiming the need for government cutbacks to reduce the deficit further, Harper was also continuing to cut corporate tax rates, as had the Liberal government before him. The Liberals cut corporate taxes from 28 to 21 per cent between 2000 and 2004, and the Conservatives had made further cuts that would reduce the corporate tax to only 15 per cent on January 1, 2012. That would mean that the federal government share of 2010 corporate profits would yield $23 billion less than that tax provided in 2000.[31]

At the same time as Harper planned to reduce Canada's corporate tax to the lowest level among the G7 countries—the major world economic powers—he continued to pursue his tough-on-crime policies, modelled on policies that had proved to be both expensive and ineffective in the United States and were increasingly questioned even by the Right in that country. Harper wanted to stiffen sentences and to remove the authority of judges to waive minimum penalties. Though homicide and other crime rates were at their lowest levels in Canada since the 1960s, the Conservatives believed that the light sentences that were being handed out to minors convicted of serious crimes and to both minors and adults convicted on drug charges were unacceptable in a law-abiding nation. The Liberals had prepared legislation to legalize possession, though not the sale, of marijuana in 2003 but had failed to move it outside of the consideration of a parliamentary committee. The Conservatives dropped the idea entirely and emphasized their opposition to the use of any illegal drug. They even attempted to close down Insite, a successful Vancouver effort to apply a "harm reduction" philosophy to drug addiction by providing clean needles and supervision for addicts, a population among whom HIV and hepatitis, among other diseases, was rampant. Only a Supreme Court decision prevented Insite's closing.

Some experts calculated that the additional costs for the justice system as a result of the Conservatives' proposed reforms would be several billion dollars. Meanwhile, the government claimed that its planned purchase of Stealth fighter jets would cost about $15 billion over the following twenty years, although the parliamentary budget officer, backed by American defence experts, calculated the costs at double that figure. The opposition parties demanded that the federal government provide them with detailed calculations of the costs of the justice reforms, the fighter jets, and the corporate tax cuts. When the government provided only partial responses to these requests, in March 2011 the three opposition parties took the unusual step of passing a motion that accused the government of being in contempt of Parliament. The government, after all, was responsible to Parliament, they argued, and had no right to turn down repeated requests from MPs for accurate information.

The opposition introduced a motion of non-confidence against the government and won, precipitating another federal election in 2011, the fourth since 2004. Stephen Harper asked Canadians to give him a majority to end the succession of minority governments and to prevent a coalition of the other parties that he insisted was planned if the Conservatives won only a minority. The issues had been defined by the battles in Parliament before the non-confidence motion was passed: prisons, jets, corporate taxes, and whether and how to reduce Canada's greenhouse gas emissions (with a focus on the tar sands/oil sands). Some commentators noted however that, given the severity of the recession that had ended in 2010 but whose underlying causes and consequences had scarcely been addressed, the opposition emphases were not especially radical. There was little discussion during the election of the distribution of wealth in Canada—particularly the growth of poverty and unemployment—and the environment, which had been a focus of discussion in the 2008 election, rarely came up as a topic. No party discussed implementing a more ambitious stimulus program should another recession occur. Neither control over Canada's financial institutions nor trade policy became an issue. Apart from corporate taxes, fiscal policy was not discussed. Nor was foreign policy. In short, while there were tangible differences between the opposition parties and the clearly right-wing Conservatives, all the parties had, to some degree, embraced neo-liberal ideas with their emphasis on the private marketplace as the fundamental economic decision maker with governments playing only a supporting role.

Differences among the opposition parties were less clear than differences between these four parties and the governing party. The Liberals seemed, as they had in the past, to have stolen NDP ideas, and given how centrist the latter had become, the Liberals found less need than ever to reject at least some NDP policies. The major difference seemed to be that the NDP wanted to raise corporate taxes a tad while the Liberals were content simply not to cut them. Several strategic voting websites, such as Project Democracy and Catch 22 Harper Conservatives emerged, focusing on defeating vulnerable Conservatives by urging all anti-Conservative voters to cast their ballot for the opposition candidate with the best chance of winning in a particular riding.

When the election campaign began, polls suggested that no party could defeat the Conservatives for first place but that a fourth minority Parliament was the most likely result and that the Liberals, Bloc, and NDP would finish in the same order as in the 2008 election. But campaigns do matter, and everything had changed by the time voting day arrived in May 2011. The dynamics within Quebec produced a shift that had repercussions throughout Canada. The Québécois were more disenchanted than Canadians generally with the jails and jets promised by the Conservatives. Also unhappy with their provincial Liberal regime, still angry that the federal Liberals in Quebec had disgraced their province with their sleazy sponsorship scams, and unimpressed by Liberal leader Michael Ignatieff, they were unwilling to return to the federal Liberal fold. While many sovereignists were content to continue to support the Bloc, soft nationalists were disillusioned by the party's seeming irrelevance in Ottawa. A bash celebrating the party's twenty years of representation in Ottawa caused many former supporters to question what use there was to keep electing representatives of a party that pointedly did not want to form a federal government. Unfortunately for the Bloc, the Parti Québécois had made plans for a convention before the federal election had been called, and PQ leader Pauline Marois, facing a revolt from passionate sovereignists, used it to emphasize that the next PQ government would hold another referendum on sovereignty. Bloc leader Gilles Duceppe was at her side at the convention. Most Québécois, regardless of their views on the national question, opposed another referendum, which was sure to be divisive and to draw their provincial government away from a focus on an economy plagued with unemployment and poverty.

Into this stew dropped Jack Layton, the NDP leader, a man well-liked by the Québécois although they had viewed his party as hopelessly anglophone and federalist in the past and given it little attention. Layton made use of media appearances, and particularly the French language leaders' debate, to emphasize that his party's stances on social issues were much the same as those of the Bloc.

He also pledged to support the Bloc's call for all federal services in Quebec to fall under Bill 101, the provincial Charter of the French Language, which made French the language of work in the province instead of requiring civil servants to be bilingual. Layton argued that, unlike the Bloc, which ran no candidates outside Quebec, his party was a national party with prospects of forming a federal government.

Overnight, Quebec support moved in the direction of Jack Layton, despite the fact that his party had few members in the province and most of its candidates were running desultory campaigns. As NDP numbers shot up in Quebec, Michael Ignatieff's arguments that a vote for the NDP was a wasted vote in a two-party contest between Conservatives and Liberals collapsed. Polls showed the NDP displacing the Liberals as the number two party almost everywhere in the country. But the NDP's sudden rise seemed to scare some right-wing Liberal voters into switching to the Conservatives. On election night the Conservatives won a slightly higher popular vote than polls had predicted, taking 167 seats, an absolute majority of Parliament's 308 seats. The NDP won 102 seats, 59 of them in Quebec, and formed the Official Opposition for the first time in federal election history. The Liberals dropped to only 34 seats and the Bloc to a mere 4 members, an insufficient number to retain their position as an official party in Parliament. Green leader Elizabeth May won a seat in British Columbia, giving that party its first elected member in any federal or provincial election in Canada. By contrast, both Michael Ignatieff and Gilles Duceppe lost their seats and immediately gave up their positions as leaders of their parties.

If the main story of the election was the emergence of a Conservative majority, the rise of the NDP to second spot seemed almost equally important. While the NDP had become a centrist party that no longer talked about nationalizing banks and taxing the rich, its ties with labour and progressive civil society movements made its reformist credentials appear more genuine than those of the Liberals, who seemed aloof from left-wing groups and closer to corporate Canada, even when the party espoused similar policies to the NDP. Jack Layton had become Canada's best-liked politician, and polls suggested that if they had to choose between Stephen Harper and Jack Layton as prime minister, Canadians preferred the latter. Unfortunately, Layton, who had earlier successfully survived a bout of prostate cancer, was soon stricken again, this time by a deadlier

NDP leader Jack Layton at a town hall meeting in 2008.

cancer. His death in August 2011 was followed by a national outpouring of grief that caused Harper to make the offer of a state funeral to
his family.

His majority in hand, Harper began to reshape the nation's politics
in ways that had been beyond his reach with a minority government.
Before the end of 2011 he had announced the end of the Canadian
Wheat Board, the gun registry, and federal per-vote financing for
parties. His government proceeded with its crime agenda and, for
good measure, seemed to criminalize strikes within areas under
federal jurisdiction. Both a strike at Canada Post and a planned strike
at Air Canada were scuttled by the Harper government as not being
in the national interest.

Canada and the World in the Twenty-First Century

If the neo-liberalism of the 1990s still dominated Canada's domestic policies in the early twenty-first century, the trade issues of
the 1980s and 1990s still dominated the country's foreign policy.
Trade considerations pervaded everything, and since Canada's trade
remained largely with the United States, keeping on the right side of
the Americans was still fundamental in the determination of foreign
policy. In any case, Canada shared with the Americans the view that

governments should be judged by how open they were to free trade and free investment.

While the promotion of democracy and human rights remained the rhetorical goal of the foreign policy of both Canada and the United States, their practices on the ground reflected mainly the goal of assuring profits for their country's investors. That was particularly true in the Caribbean and Latin America where Canada's long-established investments in minerals and banking remained important. About a quarter of Canada's foreign direct investment, amounting to $117 billion in 2007, was in that region, and Canada had become the leading foreign investor in Latin American mining. The Canadian-dominated mining companies, like mining companies in the region generally, took advantage of capital-friendly governments to exploit local workers, peasants, and Aboriginal peoples. In 2005, for example, the International Labour Organization condemned Skye Resources for removing six Mayan groups from their traditional lands without consultation. Meanwhile, Canada was supplying arms to the Colombian military, whose frequent violations of civil liberties of their people were well documented. Within the United Nations, Canada continued its campaign to prevent asbestos, whose industrial use within Canada had long been banned because of its considerable health hazards, from being labelled a hazardous substance. The remaining asbestos mines in Canada could only sell their product abroad, and the Canadian government was determined to help them do it regardless of the health consequences for the people in countries that bought the product.[32]

Canada countenanced the overthrow of elected governments when these governments, working in the interests of their own people, were hostile to the interests of Canadian investors. While Canada had supported the brutal dictatorships friendly to foreign capital that ruled Haiti for decades, it proved quite hostile to the governments led by Jean-Baptiste Aristide that were elected in 1994 and then 2000. The Canadian government joined the United States and France in demonizing Aristide, whose government established a variety of social programs that required redistribution of wealth in one of the world's most inegalitarian countries. Ignoring his government's solid record of aiding the Haitian people, they trumped up charges of Aristide's violations of human rights and then aided rebels, whose roots lay in earlier ruthlessly authoritarian and inegalitarian regimes, to create chaos. Eventually the rebels kidnapped the elected president and imposed their own man. All the social progress made under Aristide evaporated.[33] Canada was less directly involved in an ultimately unsuccessful American-backed effort to overthrow Hugo Chávez, the elected president of Venezuela, in 2003, but its officials and media helped to spread claims that Chávez's socialist rhetoric was a cover-up for corruption, human rights abuses, and a failure to redistribute wealth. The CIA's own figures demonstrated that Chávez was indeed responsible for a fairly large redistribution of wealth and for a dramatic reduction in poverty in the country.[34]

Canada had less reason to get involved in the war in Afghanistan that the Americans launched after the 9/11 attacks ostensibly to seek revenge for that country's refusal to hand over Osama bin Laden. Canada wanted to remain on good terms with its American ally and so, right from the start, offered to play a subordinate role. Initially that involved simply sending a special forces unit to aid the Americans, but that role grew as it became clear that the lightning victory of the United States over the Taliban government of Afghanistan had not secured that country for the West. Rather, the Taliban proved able to recruit supporters both within Afghanistan and Pakistan and to fight a war of attrition against the Americans and their allies. Regular Canadian troops entered the country early in 2002 and remained there until July 2011, when they were replaced by personnel allegedly involved only in the country's rebuilding efforts but not in combat. From August 2003 to October 2005, 6,000 Canadian soldiers were part of NATO's "international security assistance force" whose goal was to protect the newly elected Afghan government. But beginning in late 2005 the main work of Canada's forces in Afghanistan was to fight a counter-insurgency in Kandahar province. By July 2011, 161 Canadians had died in Afghanistan.[35]

As it became clear during 2002 that the Americans also intended to invade Iraq, Canadians opposed to such an invasion began to demonstrate in large numbers against Canadian participation. The government of Jean Chrétien wavered, but ultimately, when the Americans invaded and called for a "Coalition of the Willing" to support them, Canada announced it was unwilling. Huge demonstrations across the country, far larger than any demonstrations in the 1960s against the Vietnam War, confirmed the pollsters' claim that Canadians wanted nothing to do with another Middle Eastern war. With 200,000 people protesting Canadian participation in any Iraq war on a freezing winter day in Montreal and with Quebec in the

Peace in Iraq demonstration in Montreal, March 15, 2003.

midst of a provincial election that Chrétien hoped would dislodge the PQ government that was firmly anti-war, the federalist prime minister was not anxious to hand his separatist enemies an election gift. But Stephen Harper, as leader of the Opposition, denounced this failure on the part of the Canadian government to play its usual follow-the-leader role when the Americans declared a war. Canada's increased role in the Afghanistan war that year appeared to be a peace offering by Chrétien to a furious American President George W. Bush, who made plain that contracts for rebuilding Iraq after the bombings of the Coalition of the Willing would go only to members of that coalition.[36]

Canadian opinion on continued participation in the Afghan War was always divided, with opponents appearing to outnumber supporters as the war dragged on. There was little substance in the government's advertised goal of ensuring that Afghan women be freed from the tyranny that the patriarchal Taliban had imposed upon them before the Western powers threw them out. Most of the country was under the control of powerful warlords allied with the new Afghan government, men with disdain for Western democratic norms and any notions of women's rights. There were also questions raised about Canada's practice of raiding Afghan homes in search of weapons and information about possible Taliban insurgents. NATO bombings, in which Canada participated and which resulted in many civilian deaths, were criticized even by the Afghan government. Questions were also raised about Canada's showcase efforts to build a national police force in the country. Afghanistan had historically been governed fairly effectively via local power structures, and there was little evidence the wish for a strong central government came from the Afghan people as opposed to the West.[37]

The NDP echoed popular anti-war sentiment throughout most of the Afghan War. However, no political party appeared willing to question Canada's decision to follow the United States and several European countries when they provided air support, often to over-whelming degrees, for rebels of unknown background and goals in an uprising with regional overtones against long-time Libyan dictator Muammar Gaddafi in the summer of 2011. Canada's military involvement was intense during the federal election that year, but no party was willing to discuss the matter.

The Harper government's positions on foreign policy issues did not represent a sharp break with those of its Liberal predecessor. But, as on domestic policy, there were important nuances. Liberal governments, while certainly friendly to the State of Israel, attempted to demonstrate support as well for the right of Palestinians to have their own state. Harper chose to become Israel's most strident ally, unwilling to criticize Israel when it expanded its illegal settlements in the West Bank or started a war with the rulers of the Gaza Strip in 2008. There were many reasons for Canada's one-sided Middle East policy: Harper's own convictions, the desire to court the traditionally Liberal Jewish communities in Canada, and the importance to Conservative fundraising of evangelical Christians who support Israel because of their beliefs related to the Second Coming of Jesus Christ.[38] After Barack Obama became president of the United States in early 2009 and attempted to encourage Israel to be more reasonable in its dealings with the Palestinians, Harper's government was alone in the world in its total agreement with Israeli policies.

Involvement in foreign wars as well as spending on internal security, which allegedly needed to be beefed up to deal with possible attacks by Islamic terrorists, did not come cheap. Between 2001 and 2011, according to one economist's estimate, Canada added $69 billion in inflation-adjusted national security spending relative to its previous expenditures. For 2011–12, the country planned to spend a full $13 billion more, again in inflation-adjusted figures, on national security than it had spent in the year before 9/11.[39]

Social Movements in the New Millennium

The neo-liberal focus on the market as the ethical distributor of goods and on reining in the role of governments outside of protection of property within and without the country limited the successes of social movements, including the women's movement, the Aboriginal rights and anti-racist movements, and the environmental movement. The labour movement and the anti-poverty movement, which also looked to the state to create rules that focused on social justice, were similarly on the defensive. The corporate-controlled media gave little attention to their struggles, and while the Internet gave them an opportunity to reach new audiences, its patterns of usage also suggested that moneyed interests could indeed establish control within cyberspace.

Many in the union movement came increasingly to believe that it was fighting for its life. The shrinking of both manufacturing jobs and the state apparatus deprived the labour movement of members: only 30 per cent of Canadian workers were still trade union members in 2010, about one-quarter fewer than the high-water mark in the early 1980s. Women had become a majority of trade unionists, if only because unionism was now so heavily concentrated within the state sector where women workers outnumbered men, and women gradually came to hold a larger share of the leadership positions within unions. Under threat from anti-labour laws and a dominant individualist ideology that questioned the continuing need for collective bargaining, trade unions sought closer alliances with other social movements to seek social change or at least prevent governments from eroding acquired rights. As employers insisted on scrapping defined benefits pensions in favour of defined contributions pensions that tied workers' retirement incomes to the performance of the stock and bond markets, Canada's unions called for the Canada Pension Plan to be enriched since its defined benefits were too small to allow people to live above the poverty line once their working lives were over.

The unions also worked with the anti-poverty movement, led by Canadians Against Poverty (formerly the National Anti-Poverty Organization), to push for a guaranteed annual income for Canadians, one that would be above the poverty level and that would guarantee all Canadians the right to adequate food, shelter, medical care, and opportunities for recreation.[40] The environmental movements, often at odds with the unions because the latter still regarded economic growth as key to providing their members with a decent living, were also supportive of efforts to establish guaranteed incomes. While green movements sometimes seemed to avoid the issue of distribution of income, they increasingly came to see that issues of how much should be produced and who had the right to how much were related.

All of these movements came together, at least to some degree, in various actions in favour of a social order based on ideas of national and international social justice. They united against the leading forces of a globalization based on freedom of action for multinational corporations. The World Trade Organization (WTO), formed in 1995 by the wealthy nations to serve as the major institutional enforcer of rules against governments placing the interests of their citizens above the interests of investors and traders, became an early focus of protesters. On November 30, 1999, as trade ministers met in Seattle to plan further curbs against trade restrictions, social activists from across the United States and from other countries gathered in the streets of the city to protest these secret meetings and their assumption that the interests of big capital would create wealth that would ultimately trickle down to benefit many. While the protesters ranged from anarchists calling for the revolutionary overthrow of international capitalism to trade union leaders calling for tariff protection of jobs at home, and their actions ranged from peaceful marches to attempts to storm through police lines protecting the privileged world leaders, all were united in the belief that the assumptions and actions of the WTO were illegitimate.

Afterwards, for many years, most meetings of the major political and economic players in the world were greeted by huge demonstrations similar to those in Seattle. While the corporate media barely concerned themselves with the issues raised by the protesters, focusing mainly on whether or not they were well-behaved and whether clashes with police occurred, such gatherings provided a sense of empowerment to opponents of the emerging neo-liberal global order. Canada hosted a number of international meetings that attracted huge protests. In April 2001 the leaders of the countries of North and South America met in Quebec City to discuss an American proposal for free trade throughout the Americas. About 70,000 demonstrators marched, demonstrated, and sometimes engaged in civil disobedience, and "...a new generation of activists stood in solidarity with trade unions against the oppressive powers of the state—as the 'wall of shame' and an overwhelming police presence were used to curtail democratic rights of assembly and protest."[41] The "wall of shame" referred to a huge security perimeter that the government erected to insure that the assembled world leaders never had to see, much less confront, those unhappy with the neo-liberal restructuring of the world.

In 2007, when the North American leaders met at Montebello to discuss economic policies, there was another set of protest events. This time, protesters provided irrefutable evidence that members of the Quebec Provincial Police (QPP) had infiltrated their ranks. They claimed the QPP was responsible for the violent actions that the media covered, while neglecting their demands for economic policies subordinated to social justice goals. The federal and provincial governments eventually admitted the presence of the QPP in demonstrators' ranks but continued to deny that government agents provoked the violence.[42]

The role of agents provocateurs and of the police more generally was similarly debated in June 2010 when the Canadian government chose to hold the G20 economic summit—the meeting of the leaders

Toronto police forming a blockade against protesters, June 26, 2010.

of the twenty richest countries—in downtown Toronto, temporarily turning the centre of Canada's largest city into a police state where people had to pass checkpoints to get anywhere. Demonstrators were cornered and manhandled, and 560 were arrested, the police claiming that they were stopping a riot while the protesters argued that they were simply exercising their rights as citizens to engage in lawful protest. The Harper government, while proclaiming its desire to reduce the costs of government, spent about $858 million to hold this meeting in Toronto and, along with the G8 meetings that were held in Huntsville immediately preceding the G20 meetings, spent over a billion to fete national leaders in an age when such a meeting could have been carried out for free in the virtual universe.[43]

Not all of the energy of social activists who opposed the capitalist globalization agenda focused on international meetings of the power elite. *Adbusters*, an anti-consumption magazine, called, via a Twitter posting in the summer of 2011, for an occupation of Wall Street. That year several popular uprisings had occurred in Arab countries, and the example of people living under dictatorships risking their lives to occupy public squares inspired many people in Western countries to wonder why they did not take the lower risk opportunity to express their demands publicly and pointedly. A series of daily protest marches by anti-capitalist and mainly unemployed *Indignados* (indignant people) throughout Spain, making use of the main civic squares, began in May. In September 2011 a group of social activists, fed up that their government had bailed out Wall Street in 2008 rather than its victims and then allowed the American financial system to continue operating as it had operated before the scam of 2008, decided to "Occupy Wall Street," as *Adbusters* had suggested. In practice, that simply meant taking over a park in the heart of Manhattan near the opulent bank towers of that city and creating a cooperative, leaderless tent city community of opponents of American financial capitalism of various origins and ideologies. Ignored at first by the media, their persistence caused clashes with the civic authorities and police, who regarded them as a public eyesore and charged 700 of them with traffic and other violations for marching across the Brooklyn Bridge roadway rather than using the pedestrian crossing. Publicity from the efforts to repress this movement caused social activists elsewhere to establish their own movements to claim public space and make demands for a radical change in the distribution of power and wealth. "We Are The 99 Per Cent" became a popular slogan of the "Occupy" movement, focusing its attack on the super-rich who were running economies and taking most of the increased wealth of the past several decades for themselves.

Montreal area students paint messages on placards at the Occupy Montreal protest site in Victoria Square on October 15, 2011.

On October 15, 2011, Occupy demonstrations occurred in 951 cities in 82 countries. In Canada, there were 22 demonstrations; some of the demonstrators occupied land in the heart of their cities to establish tent cities that featured cooperative economic relations, educational activities related to social change, and plans for more public actions. For a few days the media gave some attention to the maldistribution of wealth that had led to the protests and to the especially dismal prospects for Canadian youth as Canada approached the beginning of a new recession with the previous one barely over. But attention once again soon turned to law and order, and every infraction and tragedy that occurred in an Occupy encampment received special notice such as stories of death or hospitalization resulting from drug overdoses or hypothermia. By contrast, the many more stories of such tragedies occurring in poverty-stricken areas across the country received no attention at all. Even with the bad publicity in the media, a poll in November by *The Globe and Mail* showed that 58 per cent of Canadians had a favourable or somewhat favourable view of the Occupy movement, a figure that rose to 73 per cent for Canadians aged 18 to 29. Support for the protests was strongest in Quebec and British Columbia, where unemployment was high, and weakest in the Prairie provinces, where resource-fuelled employment also fuelled conservative politics.[44]

Canada's Future

The Occupy movement, with its vision of a Canada marked by economic equality, no hierarchy in decision-making, and deep environmentalism, stood sharply at the other end of an ideological spectrum from Steven Harper's government, which extolled the ethics of an uncontrolled marketplace, social and economic power based on successes in the marketplace, and a conviction that industrialists and financiers, based on their own long-term interests, would clean up their previous messes. Most Canadians stood somewhere in between. Canada remained one of the world's wealthiest countries and a beacon to immigrants from poorer nations. Its social statistics—life expectancy, infant mortality rates, crime rates, obesity rates, rates of reported mental health problems, reported rates of happiness—were all better than those in the United States, its wealthier but far less equal neighbour. By contrast, both wealthier and less wealthy countries with greater income equality enjoyed better social statistics than

Canada, a reminder that while some measure of wealth was important to well-being, smaller income gaps and a sense of social inclusion contributed a great deal to overall happiness.[45] At no point during the post-war period could Canada claim to offer equality of opportunity to all its citizens, much less a rough equality of condition. Though it was a political democracy, it offered less democracy within its economic and social arrangements, though its citizens took advantage of the former to try to deepen the latter. For the first thirty years or so after World War Two, there seemed to be many encouraging results of activist efforts: less racism, sexism, and class exploitation, and the beginnings of a recognition of the need to stop despoiling the environment. But, arguably, over the last thirty years and more these efforts have stalled. Whether there is another historical cycle around the corner that will focus more on social justice than economic growth is unclear, but certainly there is much in Canada's story from 1945 onwards to suggest that movements for social and economic justice are as much embedded in the nation's fabric as the hegemonic interests of big business and its ideal of unfettered economic growth as the saviour of the nation.

Notes

Chapter One

1. A brief but succinct picture of Canada as the war ended is found in Desmond Morton, *1945: When Canada Won the War* (Ottawa: Canadian Historical Association, 1995).

2. For example, a poll of 7,000 Canadians done for the Canadian Chamber of Commerce in 1944 indicated that a small majority of those with opinions on the subject either favoured outright public ownership of Canada's major industries or public-private competition as an option to private enterprise alone. The results showed forty-five per cent of Canadians were in favour of private ownership, thirty-seven per cent were in favour of government ownership, ten per cent favoured mixed enterprise, and eight per cent had no opinion. Similar surveys conducted over the next four years indicated a huge shift towards private enterprise in 1947 and 1948. National Archives of Canada (NA), MG 28, 3, Box 62, Vol. 1, Canadian Chamber of Commerce Papers, 19th Annual Meeting, *Addresses*, 1948.

3. Malcolm G. Taylor, *Health Insurance and Canadian Public Policy: The Seven Decisions That Created the Canadian Health Insurance System* (Montreal: McGill-Queen's University Press, 1987), 166.

4. NA, National Liberal Federation Papers, Vol. 961, MG 28 IV-3. By October 1945, the support for government ownership and management in the Gallup had fallen to twenty-one per cent and support for private ownership and management had risen to sixty-four per cent.

5. NA, MG 28, 3, Canadian Chamber of Commerce Papers, 29th Annual Meeting, *Addresses*, October 1958.

6. *Economic Council of Canada, Fifth Annual Review: The Challenge of Growth and Change* (Ottawa: 1968).

7. *Star Weekly* [Toronto], 11 January 1947.

8. NA, National Council of Women of Canada Papers, MG 28, I 25, Vol. 101, Gwendolyn Shand, National Committee on Laws, to Mrs. F. F. Worthington, corresponding secretary, NCWC, 12 August 1955, "The Social Status of Women in Nova Scotia."

9. Kathryn McPherson, *Bedside Matters: The Transformation of Canadian Nursing, 1900–1990* (Toronto: Oxford University Press, 1996), 211–12.

10. E. A. (Nora) Cebotarev, "From Domesticity to the Public Sphere: Farm Women, 1945-86," in Joy Parr, ed., *A Diversity of Women: Ontario, 1945–*

1980 (Toronto: University of Toronto Press, 1995), 203.

11. On wartime and early post-war thinking on social welfare issues see: Alvin Finkel, "Paradise Postponed: A Re-examination of the Green Book Propos-als of 1945," *Journal of the Canadian Historical Association*, 1993: 120–142; Alvin Finkel, "Origins of the Welfare State in Canada," in Leo Panitch, ed., *The Canadian State: Political Economy and Political Power* (Toronto: University of Toronto Press, 1977); Dennis Guest, *The Emergence of Social Security in Canada* (Vancouver: University of British Columbia Press, 1980); and James Struthers, *The Limits of Affluence: Welfare in Ontario, 1920–1970* (Toronto: University of Toronto Press, 1994).

On the early implementation of unemployment insurance, see: Gary Dingledine, *A Chronology of Response: The Evolution of Unemployment Insurance from 1940 to 1980* (Ottawa: Employment and Immigration Canada, 1981). Opposing views on which groups carried the day in the struggle for unemployment insurance are found in Alvin Finkel, *Business and Social Reform in the Thirties* (Toronto: James Lorimer & Co., 1979); Carl Cuneo, "State Mediation of Class Contradictions in Canadian Unemployment Insurance, 1930–1935," *Studies in Political Economy*, 3 (1980); James Struthers, *No Fault of Their Own: Unemployment and the Canadian Welfare State, 1914–1941* (Toronto: University of Toronto Press, 1981); and Leslie Pal, *State, Class and Bureaucracy: Canadian Unemployment Insurance and Public Policy* (Montreal: McGill-Queen's University Press, 1988).

12. Jane Lewis, "Towards a Framework for Analyzing the Position of Women Under Income Security Policies," Diane Pask, Kathleen E. Mahoney, Catherine A. Brown, eds., *Women, the Law, and the Economy* (Toronto: 1985), 145–59.

13. Dominique Jean, "Family Allowances and Family Autonomy: Quebec Fami-lies Encounter the Welfare State, 1945–1955," in Bettina Bradbury, ed. *Canadian Family History: Selected Readings* (Toronto: Copp Clark, 1992), 401-37; Raymond B. Blake, "Mackenzie King and the Genesis of Family Allowances in Canada, 1939–1944," in Raymond B. Blake and Jeff Keshen, *Social Welfare Policy in Canada: Historical Readings* (Toronto: Copp Clark, 1995), 244–54.

14. Quoted in Alvin Finkel, "Paradise Postponed: A Re-examination of the Green Book Proposals of 1945," 128.

15. James Snell, *The Citizen's Wage: The State and the Elderly in Canada, 1900–1951* (Toronto: University of Toronto Press, 1996); Kenneth Bryden, *Old Age Pensions and Policy-Making in Canada* (Montreal: McGill-Queen's University Press, 1974).

16. Paul-André Linteau, René Durocher, Jean-Claude Robert, and Francois

Ricard, *Quebec Since 1930* (Toronto: James Lorimer & Co., 1991), 281.

17. Penny E. Bryden, "Liberal Politics and Social Policy in the Pearson Era, 1957–1968," Chapter One (Ph.D. thesis, York University, 1994).

18. Harold Chorney, "The Economic and Political Consequences of Canadian Monetarism," paper Presented to the British Association of Canadian Studies Annual Meeting, University of Nottingham, 12 April 1991.

19. Mitchell made his views on the subject known to King. NA, MG 26, J1, William Lyon Mackenzie King Papers, Vol. 347, 299, 492–9, Mitchell to King, 20 November 1943.

20. Kari Levitt, *Silent Surrender: The Multinational Corporation in Canada* (Toronto: Gage, 1971); and Mel Watkins et al., *Foreign Ownership and the Structure of Canadian Industry, Report of the Task Force on the Structure of Canadian Industry* (Ottawa: Ministry of Supply and Services, 1968).

21. Quoted in Philip Resnick, *The Land of Cain: Class and Nationalism in English Canada, 1945–1975* (Vancouver: New Star, 1977), 90.

22. D. Cuff and J. L. Granatstein, *American Dollars—Canadian Prosperity: Canadian-American Economic Relations, 1945-50* (Toronto: Samuel Stevens, 1978), 199–200.

23. Jack Granatstein et al., *Twentieth Century Canada* (Toronto: McGraw-Hill, Ryerson, 1983), 301. This statement remained intact in revisions of this text, for example, in Nation, by the same publisher, in 1990, 406.

24. *Nation*, 401.

25. For a comprehensive account of the government's "security" policies, see Reg Whitaker and Gary Marcuse, *Cold War Canada: The Making of a National Insecurity State, 1945–1957* (Toronto: University of Toronto Press, 1995).

26. Reginald Whitaker, "Origins of the Canadian Government's Internal Security System, 1946–1952," *Canadian Historical Review*, 65, 2 (June 1984): 154–183.

27. Daniel J. Robinson and David Kimmel, "The Queer Career of Homosexual Security Vetting in Cold War Canada," *Canadian Historical Review*, 75, 3 (September 1994): 319–345; Gary Kinsman, "'Character Weakness' and 'Fruit Machines': Towards an Analysis of the Anti-Homosexual Security Campaign in the Canadian Civil Service," *Labour/Le Travail* 35 (Spring 1995): 133–62.

28. The impact of Cold War thinking on Canadian immigration policy is explored in Reginald Whitaker, *Double Standard: The Secret History of Canadian Immigration* (Toronto: Lester and Orpen Dennys, 1987); and

Alvin Finkel, "Canadian Immigration Policy and the Cold War, 1945–1980," *Journal of Canadian Studies*, 21, 3 (Autumn 1986): 53–70.

29. NA, *Cabinet Conclusions*, Vol. 8, 5 March 1947.

30. Phillip Girard, "From Subversion to Liberation: Homosexuals and the Immigration Act, 1952–1977," *Canadian Journal of Law and Society*, 2 (1987): 1-27.

31. Charles Lipton, *The Trade Union Movement of Canada, 1827–1959*, 3rd ed. (Toronto: NC Press, 1973), 284–85.

32. John Stanton, *Life and Death of a Union: The History of the Canadian Seamen's Union, 1936–1949* (Toronto: Steel Rail, 1978); William Kaplan, *Everything That Floats: Pat Sullivan, Hal Banks, and the Seamen's Unions of Canada* (Toronto: University of Toronto Press, 1987).

33. Alvin Finkel, "Canadian Immigration Policy," 56.

34. *Ibid.*, 62–64.

35. See, for example, the testimony of individuals in Len Sher, *The Un-Canadians: True Stories of the Blacklist Era* (Toronto: Lester, 1992).

36. See Irving Abella, *Nationalism, Communism and Canadian Labour* (Toronto: University of Toronto Press, 1973).

37. Susan Prentice, "Workers, Mothers, Reds: Toronto's Postwar Daycare Fight," *Studies in Political Economy*, 30 (1989): 130.

38. Alvin Finkel, "Even the Little Children Cooperated: Family Strategies, Childcare Discourse, and Social Welfare Debates, 1945-1975," *Labour/Le Travail* 36 (Fall 1995): 104–5.

Chapter Two

1. Canada. Advisory Committee on Reconstruction, *Final Report 4: Housing and Community Planning,* Final Report of the Subcommittee, C. A. Curtis, chairman (Ottawa, 1944).

2. Humphrey Carver, *Compassionate Landscape* (Toronto: University of Toronto Press, 1975); Jill Wade, *Houses for All: The Struggle for Social Housing in Vancouver, 1919–1950* (Vancouver: University of British Columbia Press, 1994).

3. John C. Bacher, *Keeping to the Marketplace: The Evolution of Canadian Housing Policy* (Montreal: McGill-Queen's University Press, 1993), 174–6; Donald G. Wetherell and Irene R. Kmet, *Homes in Alberta: Building, Trends, and Design, 1870–1967* (Edmonton: University of Alberta Press, 1991), 222–225.

4. John C. Bacher, *Keeping to the Marketplace: The Evolution of Canadian Housing Policy*, 183; Albert Rose, *Canadian Housing Policies, 1935–1980*

(Scarborough: Butterworth, 1980); Michael Doucet and John Weaver, *Housing* the North American City (Montreal: McGill-Queen's University Press, 1991).

5. Albert Rose, *Regent Park: A Study in Slum Clearance* (Toronto: University of Toronto Press, 1958).

6. Veronica Strong-Boag, "'Their Side of the Story': Women's Voices from Ontario Suburbs, 1945–60," Joy Parr, ed., *A Diversity of Women: Ontario, 1945–1980* (Toronto: University of Toronto Press, 1995), 46.

7. Veronica Strong-Boag, "Home Dreams: Women and the Suburban Experiment in Canada, 1945–60," *Canadian Historical Review*, 72, 4 (1991): 471–504.

8. On post-war sexuality and sex roles, see Mariana Valverde, "Building Anti-Delinquent Communities: Morality, Gender, and Generation in the City," in Joy Parr, ed., *A Diversity of Women: Ontario, 1945–1980*, 19–45.

9. Alvin Finkel, "Canadian Immigration Policy and the Cold War, 1945–1980," *Journal of Canadian Studies*, 21, 3 (Autumn 1986), 66.

10. Agnes Calliste, "Canada's Immigration Policy and Domestics from the Caribbean: The Second Domestic Scheme," in Jesse Vorst et al., eds., *Race, Class and Gender: Bonds and Barriers* (Toronto: Between the Lines, 1989): 133–165.

11. Alvin Finkel, "Canadian Immigration Policy," 66.

12. Franca Iacovetta, *Such Hardworking People: Italian Immigrants in Postwar Toronto* (Montreal: McGill-Queen's University Press, 1993), Chapter 6.

13. Franca Iacovetta, *Such Hardworking People*, Chapter 7.

14. *Ibid.*, 98–99.

15. *The Globe and Mail*, 28 May 1947, 6.

16. Gerald E. Dirks, *Canada's Refugee Policy: Indifference or Opportunism?* (Montreal: McGill-Queen's University Press, 1977), 157.

17. Franca Iacovetta, *Such Hardworking People*, ix.

18. NA, MG 28, 3, Canadian Chamber of Commerce Papers, 29th Annual Meeting, *Addresses*, "Address by K. A. Ross," 7 October 1958.

19. A detailed history of the residential school experience is found in J. R. Miller, *Shingwauk's Vision: A History of Native Residential Schools* (Toronto: University of Toronto Press, 1996).

20. Anastasia M. Shkilnyk, *A Poison Stronger Than Love: The Destruction of an Ojibwa Community* (New Haven: Yale University Press, 1985), 117.

21. Frank James Tester and Peter Kulchyski, *Tammarniit (Mistakes): Inuit*

Relocation in the Eastern Arctic, 1939–63, 1.

22. *Ibid.*, 45.

23. On changing views regarding the rights of the elderly, see James Snell, *The Citizen's Wage: The State and the Elderly in Canada, 1900–1951* (Toronto: University of Toronto Press, 1996).

24. NA, Department of National Health and Welfare, RG 29, Vol. 918, "Interdepartmental Committee on the Federal-Provincial Conference," 1955, "Information Re Provincial Legislation, Unemployment Assistance."

25. Robert Rutherdale, "Fatherhood and the Social Construction of Memory: Breadwinning and Male Parenting on a Job Frontier, 1945–1966," in Joy Parr and Mark Rosenfeld, eds., *Gender and History in Canada* (Toronto: Copp Clark, 1996), 357–375; Mark Rosenfeld, "'It Was a Hard Life': Class and Gender in the Work and Family Rhythms of a Railway Town, 1920–1950," Canadian Historical Association, *Historical Papers* (1988): 237–79.

26. A recent review of the abundant literature on this question is found in Anne Forrest, "Securing the Male Breadwinner: A Feminist Interpretation of PC 1003," in Cy Gonick, Paul Phillips, and Jesse Vorst, eds., *Labour Gains, Labour Pains: Fifty Years of PC 1003: Socialist Studies*, 10 (Winnipeg/Halifax: Society for Socialist Studies/Fernwood Publishing, 1995), 140–142.

27. Ann Porter, "Women and Income Security in the Post-War Period: The Case of Unemployment Insurance, 1945–1962," *Labour/Le Travail*, 31: 111–144.

28. Pamela H. Sugiman, *Labour's Dilemma: The Gender Politics of Auto Workers in Canada, 1937–1979* (Toronto: University of Toronto Press, 1994); Julie Guard, "Fair Play or Fair Pay? Gender Relations, Class Consciousness, and Union Solidarity in the Canadian UE," *Labour/Le Travail*, 37 (Spring 1996): 149–177; Alvin Finkel, "Trade Unions and the Welfare State in Can-ada, 1945–90," in Cy Gonick, Paul Phillips, and Jesse Vorst, eds., *Labour Gains, Labour Pains: Fifty Years of PC 1003: Socialist Studies*, 10 (Winnipeg/Halifax: Society for Socialist Studies/Fernwood Publishing, 1995): 59–77.

29. Veronica Strong-Boag, "Canada's Wage-Earning Wives and the Construction of the Middle Class, 1945–60," *Journal of Canadian Studies*, 29 (Fall 1994): 5–25.

30. *The Star Weekly*, 4 January 1947.

31. *Saturday Night*, 5 May 1945.

32. Joan Sangster, *Earning Respect: The Lives of Working Women in Small Town Ontario, 1920–1960* (Toronto: University of Toronto Press, 1995);

Joan Sangster, "Doing Two Jobs: The Wage-Earning Mother, 1945–70," in Joy Parr, ed., *A Diversity of Women: Ontario, 1945–1980* (Toronto: University of Toronto Press, 1995): 98–134; Strong-Boag, "Canada's Wage-Earning Wives and the Construction of the Middle Class, 1945–1960."

33. Alvin Finkel, "Even the Little Children Cooperated: Family Strategies, Childcare Discourse, and Social Welfare Debates, 1945–1975," *Labour/Le Travail*, 36 (Fall 1995): 91–118.

34. Bryan D. Palmer, *Working Class Experience: Rethinking the History of Canadian Labour, 1800–1991*, 2nd ed. (Toronto: McClelland and Stewart, 1992), 281.

35. Various Gallup polls as reported in NA, National Liberal Federation, MG 28 IV-3, Vol. 961, "Gallup Poll 1957–68."

36. I. D. Thompson, "The Myth of Integrated Wildlife/Forestry Management," in Chad and Pam Gaffield, eds., *Consuming Canada: Readings in Environmental History* (Toronto: Copp Clark, 1995), 214.

37. David A. Gauthier and J. David Henry, "Misunderstanding the Prairies," in Monte Hummel, ed., *Endangered Species* (Toronto: Key Porter, 1989), 183–93.

38. Michel F. Girard, "The Oka Crisis from an Environmental History Perspective, 1870–1990," in Chad and Pam Gaffield, *Consuming Canada*, 298–315.

39. *Maclean's*, 1 August 1945.

Chapter Three

1. Paul-André Linteau, René Durocher, Jean-Claude Robert, and Francois Ricard, *Quebec Since 1930* (Toronto: James Lorimer & Co., 1991), 265–66; Kenneth McRoberts, *Quebec: Social Change and Political Crisis,* Third Edition (Toronto: McClelland and Stewart, 1988), 170.

2. Linteau et al., *Quebec Since 1930*, 477.

3. Much of the analysis here of relations between church and state in the Duplessis period and of conflicting views within the state apparatus is based on the work of Dominique Marshall, "Aux Origines Sociales de l'Etat providence: families Québécoises, obligation scolaire et allocations familiales, 1940–1960," unpublished Ph.D. thesis, Universite de Montreal, 1989.

4. Kenneth McRoberts, *Quebec: Social Change and Political Crisis*, 11.

5. Clio Collective, *Quebec Women: A History* (Toronto: Women's Press, 1987), 297–300. The classical colleges provided the academic training required for students who intended to go on to universities after graduating from school.

6. Clio Collective, *Quebec Women: A History*, 283–4; Alvin Finkel, "Even the Little Children Cooperated: Family Strategies, Childcare Discourse, and Social Welfare Debates, 1945–1975," *Labour/Le Travail*, 36 (Fall 1995): 94–95; Ruth Roach Pierson, "'They're Still Women After All': The Second World War and Canadian Womanhood," (Toronto: McClelland and Stewart, 1986), 55.

7. Monique Begin, "The Royal Commission on the Status of Women in Canada: Twenty Years Later," in Constance Backhouse and David H. Flaherty, eds., *Challenging Times: The Women's Movement in Canada and the United States* (Montreal: McGill-Queen's Press, 1992), 28.

8. Micheline Dumont, "Origins of the Women's Movement in Quebec," in Constance Backhouse and David H. Flaherty, eds, *Challenging Times: The Women's Movement in Canada and the United States* (Montreal: McGill-Queen's Press, 1992), 83–84.

9. Simon Lapointe, "L'influence de la gauche catholique française sur l'ideologie politique de la CTCC-CSN de 1948 a 1964," *Revue d'histoire de l'Amerique française*, 49, 3 (Hiver 1996): 331–356.

10. Paul-André Linteau et al., *Quebec Since 1930* (Toronto: James Lorimer & Co., 1991), 252.

11. Serge Gagnon, *Quebec and its Historians: The Twentieth Century* (Montreal: Harvest House, 1985), 53–89.

12. Joan Sangster, "Doing Two Jobs: The Wage-Earning Mother," in Joy Parr, ed., *A Diversity of Women: Ontario 1945–1980* (Toronto: University of Toronto Press, 1995), 99–100.

13. Franca Iacovetta, "Remaking Their Lives: Women Immigrants, Survivors, and Refugees," in Joy Parr, ed., *A Diversity of Women: Ontario 1945–1980* (Toronto: University of Toronto Press, 1995), 153–4.

14. Margaret Little, "The Blurring of Boundaries: Private and Public Welfare for Single Mothers in Ontario," *Studies in Political Economy*, 47 (Summer 1995): 89–110.

15. Susan Prentice, "Workers, Mothers, Reds: Toronto's Postwar Daycare Fight," *Studies in Political Economy*, 30 (1989): 115–141.

16. James Struthers, *The Limits of Affluence: Welfare in Ontario, 1920–1970* (Toronto: University of Toronto Press, 1994), 138–141.

17. Gale Wills, *A Marriage of Convenience: Business and Social Work in Toronto 1918–1957* (Toronto: University of Toronto Press, 1995), 137–38.

18. James Struthers, *The Limits of Affluence*, 180.

19. Margaret Conrad, "The 1950s: The Decade of Development," in E. R. Forbes and D. A. Muise, eds., *The Atlantic Provinces in Confederation*

(Toronto/Fredericton: 1993), 382–420.

20. James L. Kenny, "'We Must Speculate to Accumulate!' Mineral Development and the Limits of State Intervention, New Brunswick, 1952–1960," *Acadiensis*, 23, 2 (Spring 1994): 94–123.

21. Margaret Conrad, "The Politics of Place: Regionalism and Community in Atlantic Canada," in James N. McCrorie and Martha L. MacDonald, *The Constitutional Future of the Prairie and Atlantic Regions of Canada* (Regina: Canadian Plains Research Center, 1992), 29.

22. Raymond B. Blake, *Canadians At Last: Canada Integrates Newfoundland as a Province* (Toronto: University of Toronto Press, 1992); L. Richard Lund, "'Fishing for Stamps:' The Origins and Development of Unemployment Insurance for Canada's Commercial Fisheries, 1941–71," paper presented at the 74th Annual Meeting of the Canadian Historical Association (Montreal, 1995).

23. On British Columbia in the early post-war period, see Jean Barman, The *West Beyond the West: A History of British Columbia*, Second Edition (Toronto: University of Toronto Press, 1996).

24. Walter D. Young, *Democracy and Discontent: Progressivism, Socialism, and Social Credit in the Canadian West*, Second Edition (Toronto: McGraw-Hill Ryerson, 1978), 103–105.

25. On the Ernest Manning years, see Alvin Finkel, *The Social Credit Phenomenon in Alberta* (Toronto: University of Toronto Press, 1989); and Howard Palmer with Tamara Palmer, *Alberta: A History* (Edmonton: Hurtig, 1990).

26. On Saskatchewan political developments, see John Archer, *Saskatchewan: A History* (Saskatoon: Western Producer Prairie Books, 1980). On the development of medicare, see Robin F. Badgley and Samuel Wolfe, *Doctor's Strike: Medical Care and Conflict in Saskatchewan* (Toronto: Macmillan, 1967). On community clinics, see Stan Rand, *Privilege and Policy: A History of Community Clinics in Saskatchewan* (Saskatoon: Community Health Co-operative Federation, 1994).

27. Gerald Friesen, *The Canadian Prairies: A History* (Toronto: University of Toronto Press, 1987), 419–421; Cy Gonick, "The Manitoba Economy Since World War II," in Jim Silver and Jeremy Hull, eds., *The Political Economy of Manitoba* (Regina: Canadian Plains Research Center, 1990).

Chapter Four

1. The liberal-internationalist literature, which stresses Canada's middle-power role, dominates published foreign-policy materials. Among good recent overviews are: Norman Hillmer, *Empire to Umpire: Canada and*

the World to the 1990s (Toronto: Copp Clark, 1994); and J. L. Granatstein and Norman Hillmer, *For Better or For Worse: Canada and the U.S. to the 1990s* (Toronto: Copp Clark, 1991). Among works that explore the arguments for the counter-viewpoint that Canada largely subordinates its foreign policy to the wishes of the Americans, see Michael K. Hawes, *Principal Power, Middle Power, or Satellite? Competing Perspectives in the Study of Canadian Foreign Policy* (Toronto: York University Research Programs in Strategic Studies, 1984); and the overview essays by Steven Langdon, Stephen Randall, and Garth Stevenson in Norman Hillmer and Garth Stevenson, eds., *A Foremost Nation: Canadian Foreign Policy and a Changing World* (Toronto: McClelland and Stewart, 1977).

2. Edelgard E. Mahant and Graeme S. Mount, *An Introduction to Canadian-American Relations* (Toronto: Methuen, 1984), 160–3; James Eayrs, *In Defence of Canada, Volume 3: Peacemaking and Deterrence* (Toronto: University of Toronto Press, 1972), 265, 268.

3. Writes political scientist Peter Calvocoressi: the Soviets were aware that "the United States could not destroy its advanced technological knowledge and it would therefore retain a huge advantage over the USSR which, by accepting the Baruch Plan, would inhibit its own advances in nuclear physics." Peter Calvocoressi, *World Politics Since 1945*, 5th ed. (London: Longman, 1987), 6.

4. Mahant and Mount, 164; Robert W. Malcolmson, *Nuclear Fallacies: How We Have Been Misguided Since Hiroshima* (Montreal: McGill-Queen's University Press, 1985), 36.

5. Joseph Levitt, *Pearson and Canada's Role in Nuclear Disarmament and Arms Control Negotiations, 1945–1957* (Montreal: McGill-Queen's University Press, 1993).

6. James Eayrs, *In Defence of Canada, Volume 5: Growing Up Allied* (Toronto: University of Toronto Press, 1980), 267, 234; David Lilienthal, *The Journals of David E. Lilienthal: Volume 2: The Atomic Energy Years, 1945–1950* (New York: Harper and Row, 1964), 584–85.

7. Ernie Regehr and Simon Rosenblum, "The Changing Nature of the Arms Race," in Ernie Regehr and Simon Rosenblum, eds., *Canada and the Nuclear Arms Race* (Toronto: James Lorimer & Co., 1983), 22.

8. John Lewis Gaddis, *The Long Peace: Inquiries Into the History of the Cold War* (New York: Oxford University Press, 1987), 132; Malcolmson, *Nuclear Fallacies*, 48.

9. Peter Goodwin, *Nuclear War: The Facts on Our Survival* (New York: Routledge, 1981), 121.

10. Peter Calvocoressi, *World Politics Since 1945*, 307–08; I. F. Stone, *The Hidden History of the Korean War, 1950–1951 (A Nonconformist*

History of Our Times) (Toronto: Little, Brown and Company, 1988), 116, 133–34, 270.

11. Denis Stairs, *The Diplomacy of Constraint: Canada, the Korean War and the United States* (Toronto: University of Toronto Press, 1974); John W. Holmes, *Life with Uncle: The Canadian-American Relationship* (Toronto: University of Toronto Press, 1981), 35–36.

12. David B. Dewitt and John J. Kirton, *Canada as a Principal Power: A Study in Foreign Policy and International Relations* (Toronto: John Wiley and Sons, 1983), 54.

13. On the American involvement in Indochina, see: George C. Herring, *America's Longest War: The United States and Vietnam, 1950–1975*, 2nd ed. (Philadelphia: Temple University Press, 1986); Stanley Karnow, *Vietnam: A History* (New York: Viking, 1983); and *The Pentagon Papers: The Defense Department History of United States Decision-making in Vietnam: The Senator Gravel Edition*, 4 vols. (New York: Beacon Press, 1971).

14. James Eayrs, *In Defence of Canada: Indochina: Roots of Complicity*, Vol. 5 (Toronto: University of Toronto Press, 1983), 68–9.

15. Douglas A. Ross, *In the Interests of Peace: Canada and Vietnam 1954–1973* (Toronto: University of Toronto Press, 1984), 122, 141.

16. Victor Levant, *Quiet Complicity: Canadian Involvement in the Vietnam War* (Toronto: Between the Lines, 1986), 141–172.

17. Dennis J. Duncanson, *Government and Revolution in Vietnam* (London: Oxford University Press, 1968), 10.

18. Douglas Ross, *In the Interests of Peace*, 6.

19. Denis Smith, *Rogue Tory: The Life and Legend of John G. Diefenbaker* (Toronto: Macfarlane Walter and Ross, 1995), 264.

20. Joseph T. Jockel, "The Canada-United States Military Co-operation Committee and Continental Air Defence, 1946," *Canadian Historical Review*, 64, 3 (September 1983): 352–377; John Swettenham, *McNaughton, Volume 3: 1944–1966* (Toronto: Ryerson, 1969), 171; Leonard V. Johnson, *A General for Peace* (Toronto: James Lorimer & Co., 1987), 33.

21. Douglas Bland, *The Administration of Defence Policy in Canada, 1947–1985* (Kingston: Ronald P. Frye, 1987), 199.

22. George Ignatieff, *The Making of a Peacemonger: The Memoirs of George Ignatieff* (Toronto: University of Toronto Press, 1985), 186–87.

23. On the Arrow controversy, see Denis Smith, *Rogue Tory*, 307–25; Palmiro Campagna, *Storms of Controversy: The Secret Arrow Files*

Revealed (Toronto: Stoddart, 1992); and James Dow, *The Arrow* (Toronto: James Lorimer & Co., 1979).

24. Mahant and Mount, 200.

25. Michael Tucker, "Canada and the Test-Ban Negotiations 1955–71," in Kim Richard Nossal, ed., *An Acceptance of Paradox: Essays on Canadian Diplomacy in honour of John W. Holmes* (Toronto: Canadian Institute of International Affairs, 1982), 116–17.

26. George Ignatieff, *The Making of a Peacemonger*, 186–88, 203.

27. Typical is John F. Hilliker, "The Politicians and the 'Pearsonalities': The Diefenbaker Government and the Conduct of Canadian External Relations," in J. L. Granatstein, ed., *Canadian Foreign Policy: Historical Readings*, revised edition (Copp Clark Pitman 1993): 223–239.

28. John G. Diefenbaker, *One Canada: Memoirs of the Right Honourable John G. Diefenbaker: The Tumultuous Years, 1962–1967* (Toronto: Macmillan, 1977), 122.

29. J. L. Granatstein, *Canadian Foreign Policy Since 1945: Middle Power or Satellite?* (Toronto: Copp Clark, 1973), 116.

30. Paul Martin, *A Very Public Life, Volume 2: So Many Worlds* (Toronto: Deneau, 1985), 365–66.

31. Peyton V. Lyon, *Canada in World Affairs, 1961–1963* (Toronto: Oxford University Press, Canadian Institute of International Affairs, 1968), 81.

32. Jocelyn Maynard Ghent, "Canada, the United States, and the Cuban Missile Crisis," *Pacific Historical Review*, 58 (1979): 159–184.

33. Peyton V. Lyon, *Canada in World Affairs, 1961–1963*, 37–59; Denis Smith, *Rogue Tory*, 453–62.

34. Candace Loewen, "Mike Hears Voices: Voice of Women and Lester Pearson, 1960–1963," *Atlantis*, 12, 2 (Spring 1987): 29. On Canada and the Cuban crisis, more generally, see Jocelyn Maynard Ghent, "Canada, the United States, and the Cuban Missile Crisis," 159–184.

35. Denis Smith, *Rogue Tory*, 462–488.

36. J. L. Granatstein, *Canadian Foreign Policy Since 1945: Middle Power or Satellite?* (Toronto: Copp Clark, 1973), 126–27.

37. Candace Loewen, "Mike Hears Voices"; Kay Macpherson, "Persistent Voices: Twenty-Five Years with Voice of Women," *Atlantis* 12, 2 (Spring 1987): 60–71.

38. On Canadian attitudes to the creation of Israel see David Bercuson, *Canada and the Birth of Israel: A Study in Canadian Foreign Policy* (Toronto: University of Toronto Press, 1985). A rather different view of

Canada's behaviour is presented in Tareq Y. Ismael, "Canadian Foreign Policy in the Arab World," in Tareq Y. Ismael, ed., *Canada and the Arab World* (Edmonton: University of Alberta Press, 1985).

39. J. L. Granatstein, "Canada and Peacekeeping: Image and Reality," *Canadian Foreign Policy: Historical Readings*, revised edition, (Toronto: Copp Clark Pitman, 1993), 276–285.

40. Brian Tennyson, *Canadian Relations with South Africa: A Diplomatic History* (Washington, D.C.: University Press of America, 1982), 120.

41. *Ibid.*, 179.

42. Denis Smith, *Rogue Tory*, 359.

43. *Ibid.*, 365.

44. Peyton Lyon, *Canada in World Affairs, 1961–1963*, 296.

45. John G. Diefenbaker, *One Canada: The Memoirs of the Right Honourable John G. Diefenbaker: The Years of Achievement, 1957–1962* (Toronto: Macmillan, 1976), 182.

Chapter Five

1. All figures are from F. H. Leacey, ed., *Historical Statistics of Canada, Volume Two* (Ottawa: Queen's Printer, 1983); and *Canada Year Book*, 1994.

2. OECD Bulletin, No. 146 (Jan. 1984), reprinted in Andrew Armitage, *Social Welfare in Canada: Ideas, Realities and Future Paths*, 2nd ed. (Toronto: McClelland and Stewart, 1988), 22.

3. On the debates within the Liberal Party after 1957 see Penny E. Bryden, "The Liberal Party of Canada: Organizing for Social Reform, 1957–1966," in Gustav Schmidt and Jack L. Granatstein, *Canada at the Crossroads? The Critical 1960s* (Bochum: Universitatsverlag D.N. Brockmeyer, 1994), 25–45; and Penny E. Bryden, "Liberal Politics and Social Policy in the Pearson Era, 1957–1968," unpublished Ph.D. dissertation, York University, 1994.

4. NA, MG 28, 3, 62, Vol. 4, Canadian Chamber of Commerce Papers, 36th Annual Meeting, *Addresses*, address by J. M. Keith, 29 September 1965.

5. NA, MG 28, 3, 62, Vol. 9, Canadian Chamber of Commerce Papers, Minutes of the Health and Welfare Committee, "Committee Minutes, Health and Welfare Committee, 1964–1966," 9 March 1966.

6. Commission evidence is found in NA, RG 33, Series 78, "Royal Commission on Health Services."

7. On the battle for medicare, see Penny Bryden, "Liberal Politics and Social Policy in the Pearson Era, 1957–1968," and Malcolm G. Taylor, *Health Insurance and Canadian Public Policy: The Seven Decisions That Created the Canadian Health Insurance System* (Montreal: McGill-Queen's University Press, 1978).

8. Penny Bryden, "Liberal Politics and Social Policy in the Pearson Era, 1957–1968," Chapter 7 and Epilogue.

9. Leslie Bella, "The Provincial Role in the Canadian Welfare State: The Influence of Provincial Social Policy Initiatives on the Design of the Canada Assistance Plan," *Canadian Public Administration*, 22, 3 (Fall 1977): 439–452.

10. Stephen Clarkson and Christina McCall, *Trudeau and Our Times, Vol. 1: The Magnificent Obsession* (Toronto: McClelland and Stewart, 1990), discusses Trudeau's early life.

11. Leslie Pal, *State, Class, and Bureaucracy: Canadian Unemployment Insurance and Public Policy* (Montreal: McGill-Queen's University Press, 1988), 43–44.

12. On labour in the 1960s, see Bryan D. Palmer, *Working Class Experience: Rethinking the History of Canadian Labour, 1800–1991*, 2nd ed., (Toronto: McClelland and Stewart, 1992), 313–25.

13. Kenneth Norrie and Douglas Owram, *A History of the Canadian Economy* (Toronto: Harcourt Brace Jovanovich, 1991), 576.

14. Harold Chorney, "The Economic and Political Consequences of Monetarism," Paper Presented to the British Association of Canadian Studies Annual Meeting, University of Nottingham, 12 April 1991.

15. Canada, *Report of the Royal Commission on Taxation, Volumes 1 and 2* (Ottawa: Queen's Printer, 1966).

16. *Ibid.*, Volume 2, 246.

17. J. Harvey Perry, *Canadian Tax Reform #68: Background of Current Fiscal Problems* (Toronto: Canadian Tax Foundation, 1982), 99; Robin W. Boadway and Harry M. Kitchen, *Canadian Tax Policy: Canadian Tax Papers #63* (Toronto: Canadian Tax Foundation, 1980), 82.

18. Stephen McBride, *Not Working: State, Unemployment, and Neo-Conservatism in Canada* (Toronto: University of Toronto Press, 1992), Chapters 2–4.

19. Harold Chorney, *The Deficit: Hysteria and the Current Economic Crisis* (Ottawa: Canadian Centre for Policy Alternatives, 1984); Harold Chorney, *The Deficit and Debt Management: An Alternative to Monetarism* (Ottawa: Canadian Centre for Policy Alternatives, 1989); Robert Campbell, *Grand Illusions: The Politics of the Keynesian Experience in Canada,*

1945–1975 (Peterborough: Broadview Press, 1987).

20. Stephen McBride, *Not Working*, 85.

21. Kenneth Norrie and Douglas Owram, *A History of the Canadian Economy*, 602–3.

22. Stephen McBride, "Coercion and Consent: The Recurring Corporatist Temptation in Canadian Labour Relations," in Cy Gonick, Paul Phillips, and Jesse Vorst, eds., Labour Gains, Labour Pains: Fifty Years of PC 1003 (Winnipeg/Halifax: Society for Socialist Studies/Fernwood Publishing, 1995), 86–87.

23. Cy Gonick, *The Great Economic Debate: Failed Economics and a Future for Canada* (Toronto: James Lorimer & Co., 1987), 184–5.

24. Stephen McBride, *Not Working*, 75.

25. Robin Boadway and Harry Kitchen, *Canadian Tax Policy*, 115–117.

26. Clarence L. Barber and John C. P. McCallum, *Unemployment and Inflation: The Canadian Experience* (Toronto: James Lorimer & Co., 1980).

27. Harold Chorney, "The Economic and Political Consequences of Canadian Monetarism." Paper presented to the British Association of Canadian Studies Annual Meeting, University of Nottingham, 12 April 1991.

28. Harold Chorney, "Perverse policy: Monetarist policies lurk behind high unemployment," *Winnipeg Free Press*, 4 December 1994.

29. Stephen McBride, *Not Working*, 75.

30. Derek P. J. Hum, *Federalism and the Poor: A Review of the Canada Assistance Plan* (Toronto: Ontario Economic Council, 1983), 19–26.

31. John Myles, *When Markets Fail: Social Welfare in Canada and the United States* (New York: United Nations Institute for Social Development, June 1995), 8.

32. Kenneth Norrie and Douglas Owram, *A History of the Canadian Economy*, 608.

33. See, for example, Jill Quadagno, *The Color of Welfare: How Racism Undermined the War on Poverty* (New York: Oxford University Press, 1994).

34. George C. Herring, *America's Longest War: The United States and Vietnam, 1950–1975*, 2nd ed., (Philadelphia: Temple University Press, 1986), 86, 151.

35. The agreement was the Heeney-Merchant Report of 1965, named for the Canadian and American diplomats who produced it. It is reprinted in

J. L. Granatstein, *Canadian Foreign Policy: Historical Readings*, Revised Edition (Toronto: Copp Clark Pitman, 1993), 38–54.

36. Canada's support for the South Vietnamese and Americans is carefully detailed in Victor Levant, *Quiet Complicity: Canadian Involvement in the Vietnam War* (Toronto: Between the Lines, 1986).

37. Gareth Porter, *A Peace Denied: The United States, Vietnam, and the Paris Agreement* (Bloomington, Indiana: Indiana University Press, 1975), 221–9; Victor Levant, *Quiet Complicity*, 213–254.

38. *Saturday Night*, June 1970.

39. John Kirton and Don Munton, "The Manhattan Voyages and Their Aftermath," in Franklyn Griffiths, ed., *Politics of the Northwest Passage* (Montreal: McGill-Queen's University Press, 1987), 70.

40. Franklyn Griffiths and John C. Polanyi, eds., *The Dangers of Nuclear War: A Pugwash Symposium* (Toronto: University of Toronto Press, 1979), ix–x.

41. Michael Tucker, "Canada and the Non-Proliferation of Nuclear Weapons," in Michael Tucker, ed., *Canadian Foreign Policy: Contemporary Issues and Themes* (Toronto: McGraw-Hill Ryerson, 1980), 210.

42. Stephen J. Randall, "Canadian Policy and the Development of Latin America," in Norman Hillmer and Garth Stevenson, eds., *A Foremost Nation: Canadian Foreign Policy and a Changing World* (Toronto: McClelland and Stewart, 1977), 224–25.

Chapter Six

1. William Lyon Mackenzie King, *The Mackenzie King Diaries: 1932–47* (Toronto: University of Toronto Press, 1978), 8 November 1935.

2. Wallace Clement, *Continental Corporate Power: Economic Elite Linkages Between Canada and the United States* (Toronto: McClelland and Stewart, 1984), 85.

3. Daniel Drache and Arthur Kroker, "The Labyrinth of Dependency," *Canadian Journal of Political and Social Theory*, 7, 3 (Fall 1983): 14.

4. "Uncle Sam Moves to Canada," *The Star Weekly*, 11 January 1947.

5. Jorge Niosi, "The Canadian Bourgeoisie: Towards a Synthetical Approach," *Canadian Journal of Political and Social Theory*, 7, 3 (Fall 1983): 143.

6. Kari Levitt, *Silent Surrender: The Multinational Corporation in Canada* (Toronto: Macmillan, 1970), 137.

7. Paul Martin, *A Very Public Life, Volume 2: So Many Worlds* (Toronto: Deneau, 1985), 389.

8. *Ibid.*, 387.

9. Kari Levitt, *Silent Surrender*, 2–3.

10. Arthur Blanchette, ed., *Canadian Foreign Policy, 1966–1976: Selected Speeches and Documents* (Agincourt: Gage Publishers, 1980), 130.

11. Edelgard E. Mahant and Graeme S. Mount, *An Introduction to Canadian-American Relations* (Toronto: Methuen, 1984), 206; Denis Smith, *Gentle Patriot: A Political Biography of Walter Gordon* (Edmonton: Hurtig, 1973), 153–163.

12. John N. McDougall, *The Politics and Economics of Eric Kierans: A Man for all Canadians* (Montreal: McGill-Queen's University Press, 1993), 43–47.

13. Robert Bothwell, *Canada and the United States: The Politics of Partnership* (Toronto: University of Toronto Press, 1992), 93.

14. Canada, Privy Council Office, *Foreign Ownership and the Structure of Canadian Industry* (Ottawa: Queen's Printer, 1968).

15. Robert Bothwell, *Canada and the United States*, 104.

16. Edelgard E. Mahant and Graeme S. Mount, *An Introduction to Canadian-American Relations*, 225–26.

17. Robert Bothwell, *Canada and the United States*, 105.

18. Mahant and Mount, *An Introduction to Canadian-American Relations*, 220.

19. Robert Bothwell, *Canada and the United States*, 110.

20. Bryan D. Palmer, *Working Class Experience: Rethinking the History of Canadian Labour, 1800–1991* (Toronto: McClelland and Stewart, 1992), 318–20.

21. Edelgard E. Mahant and Graeme S. Mount, *An Introduction to Canadian-American Relations*, 189.

Chapter Seven

1. Gerard Bouchard, "Une nation, deux cultures: Continuites et ruptures dans la pen see quebecoise traditionelle (1840–1960)," in Gerard Bouchard and Serge Courville, eds., *La construction d'une culture: Le Quebec et l'Amerique française* (Quebec: Les Presses de l'Universite Laval, 1993), 3–47.

2. Paul-André Linteau, René Durocher, Jean-Claude Robert, and Francois Ricard, *Quebec Since 1930* (Toronto: James Lorimer & Co., 1991), 477.

3. *Ibid.*; Denis Moniere, *Le Developpement des ideologies au Quebec: des origines a nos jours* (Montreal: Quebec/Amerique, 1977), 257.

4. William D. Coleman, *The Independence Movement in Quebec, 1945–1980* (Toronto: University of Toronto Press, 1984), 101.

5. Linteau et al., *Quebec Since 1930*, 479; Tony Clarke, *Behind the Mitre: The Moral Leadership Crisis in the Canadian Catholic Church* (Toronto: HarperCollins, 1995), 4–5.

6. Linteau et al., *Quebec Since 1930*, 476, 478.

7. Tony Clarke, *Behind the Mitre*, 5–15.

8. Xavier Gelinas, "La droite intellectuelle et la Revolution tranquille: Le cas de la revue Tradition et progres, 1957–62," *Canadian Historical Review*, 77, 3 (September 1996): 353–87.

9. Clio Collective, *Quebec Women: A History* (Toronto: Women's Press, 1987), 314.

10. Angus McLaren and Arlene Tigar McLaren, *The Bedroom and the State* (Toronto: McClelland and Stewart, 1986), 14.

11. Micheline Dumont, *Girls' Schooling in Quebec, 1639–1960* (Ottawa: Canadian Historical Association, 1990), 24–5; Clio Collective, *Quebec Women*, 297–300.

12. Clio Collective, *Quebec Women*, 336–41.

13. NA, RG 33/89, Canada, Royal Commission on the Status of Women in Canada, *Briefs*, Vol. 13, Brief 155, "Memoire présente a la Commission royale d'enquete sur la situation de la femme au Canada," par la Federation des femmes du Quebec, March 1968.

14. NA, RG 33/89, Vol. 15, Brief 303, 14 June 1968.

15. NA, MG 32, C 25, Thérèse Casgrain papers, Vol. 6, "Federation des femmes du Quebec 1966–71," "Memoire presente a l'Honorable Robert Bourassa, Premier Ministre du Quebec par la Federation des femmes du Quebec."

16. RG 33/89, Vol. 12, Brief 102.

17. RG 33/89, Vol. 12, Brief 129.

18. Mona-Josee Gagnon, "Les Centrales Syndicates et la Condition Feminine," *Maintenant*, 140 (November): 25–27.

19. Kenneth McRoberts, *Quebec: Social Change and Political Crisis*, Third Edition (Toronto: McClelland and Stewart, 1988), 132.

20. Denis Moniere, *Le developpement des ideologies*, 255.

21. Linteau et al., *Quebec Since 1930*, 482–86.

22. Kenneth McRoberts, *Quebec*, 200–02; Pierre Vallieres, *Negres Blancs de l'Amerique* (Montreal: Parti pris, 1969).

23. Paul W. Fox, *Politics: Canada*, 2nd ed. (Toronto: McGraw-Hill

Ryerson, 1966), 70–71.

24. Kenneth McRoberts, *Quebec*, 170–72.

25. Maurice Pinard, *The Rise of a Third Party: A Study in Crisis Politics*, enlarged ed. (Montreal: McGill-Queen's, 1975), 246–47.

26. Kenneth McRoberts, *Quebec*, 201.

27. Richard Jones, *Community in Crisis: French-Canadian Nationalism in Perspective* (Toronto: McClelland and Stewart, 1972), 61.

28. Montreal Star, 27 March–6 April 1974. Excerpts from the series are found in Irving Abella and David Millar, eds., *The Canadian Worker in the Twentieth Century* (Toronto: Oxford University Press, 1978).

29. Joseph Smucker, "The Labour Movement in Quebec," in Joseph Smucker, *Industrialization in Canada*, 217–39.

30. Ramsay Cook, "Quebec's New Quiet Revolutionaries," in Ramsay Cook, *Canada, Quebec and the Uses of Nationalism* (Toronto: McClelland and Stewart, 1986), 101–2.

31. Francois Vaillancourt and Pierre Saint-Laurent, "Les determinants de revolu-tion de l'ecart de revenu entre Canadien anglais et Canadien frangais," *Journal of Canadian Studies*, 15, 4 (Winter 1980–81): 69–74.

32. Linteau et al., *Quebec Since 1930*, 538–39.

33. Kenneth McRoberts, *Quebec*, 332.

34. Jorge Niosi, "The Rise of French-Canadian Capitalism," in Alain Gagnon, ed., *Quebec: State and Society in Crisis* (Toronto: Methuen, 1984), 186–200.

35. Kenneth McRoberts, *Quebec*, 186–87.

Chapter Eight

1. The most spectacular "giveaway" debacles in Canada are discussed in detail in Philip Mathias, *Forced Growth: Five Studies of Government Involvement in the Development of Canada* (Toronto: Lewis and Samuel, 1971).

2. Delia Stanley, "The Illusions and Realities of Progress," in E. R. Forbes and D. A. Muise, eds., *The Atlantic Provinces in Confederation* (Toronto: University of Toronto Press, 1993), 421.

3. As Bruce Smardon notes, Atlantic Canadians tended to regard the various policies that redistributed funds to their region as compensation for federal economic policies that were biased in favour of central Canada. Bruce Smardon, "The Federal Welfare State and the Politics of Retrenchment in Canada," in Raymond B. Blake and Jeff Keshen, *Social*

Welfare Policy in Canada: Historical Readings (Toronto: Copp Clark, 1995), 349.

4. *Ibid.*, 426–28.

5. *Ibid.*, 429–30; 4345; John Reid, "The 1970s: Sharpening the Sceptical Edge," in E. R. Forbes and D. A. Muise, eds., *The Atlantic Provinces in Confederation* (Toronto: University of Toronto Press, 1993), 466–69.

6. *Ibid.*, 466–67.

7. Bryan D. Palmer, *Working Class Experience: Rethinking the History of Canadian Labour*, 1800–1991 (Toronto: McClelland and Stewart, 1992), 396–97.

8. John Reid, "The 1970s," 454–55.

9. Noel Iverson and D. Ralph Matthews, *Communities in Decline: An Examination of Household Resettlement in Newfoundland*, Newfoundland Social and Economic Studies, No. 6 (St. John's: Memorial University, 1968).

10. William E. Schrank, Noel Roy, Rosemary Ommer, and Blanca Skoda, "The Future of the Newfoundland Fishery," in James N. McCrorie and Martha L. MacDonald, eds., *The Constitutional Future of the Prairie and Atlantic Regions of Canada* (Regina: Canadian Plains Research Center, 1992), 126.

11. David Milne, "Challenging Constitutional Dependency: A Revisionist View of Atlantic Canada," in James N. McCrorie and Martha L. MacDonald, eds., *The Constitutional Future of the Prairie and Atlantic Regions of Canada* (Regina: Canadian Plains Research Center, 1992), 312.

12. Rick Williams, in Robert J. Brym and R. James Sacouman, ed., *Underdevelopment and Social Movements in Atlantic Canada* (Toronto: New Hogtown Press, 1979).

13. Schrank et al., "The Future of the Newfoundland Fishery," 132.

14. *Ibid.*, 143; Delia Stanley, "The 1970s," 460.

15. Donald H. Clairmont, *Africville: The Life and Death of a Canadian Black Community*, revised ed. (Toronto: Canadian Scholars' Press, 1987).

16. John Reid, "The 1970s," 478–83.

17. Stephen G. Tomblin, "The Struggle for Regional Integration: Atlantic-Maritime Canada," in James N. McCrorie and Martha L. MacDonald, eds., *The Constitutional Future of the Prairie and Atlantic Regions of Canada* (Regina: Canadian Plains Research Center, 1992), 181–208.

18. Cy Gonick, "The Manitoba Economy Since World War II," in Jim Silver and Jeremy Hull, eds., *The Political Economy of Manitoba* (Regina: Canadian Plains Research Center, 1990).

19. Phil Mathias, *Forced Growth*, 178.

20. The present author was editor of The Manitoban at the time. The principal researcher and writer of the articles was Harold Chorney.

21. That is, a company that is involved in all aspects of an operation, from the provision of the capital equipment, to the processing, to wholesaling, and final retail sale of the end product.

22. The best source of information on Saskatchewan's economic development in the 1960s and 1970s is John Richards and Larry Pratt, *Prairie Capitalism: Power and Influence in the New West* (Toronto: McClelland and Stewart, 1979), especially Chapter 10. See also Ken Collier, "Social Democracy and Underdevelopment: The Case of Northern Saskatchewan," in Jim Harding, ed., *Social Policy and Social Justice: The NDP Government in Saskatchewan During the Blakeney Years* (Waterloo: Wilfrid Laurier University Press, 1995), 325.

23. Bill Harding, "The Two Faces of Public Ownership: From the Regina Manifesto to Uranium Mining," in Jim Harding, ed., *Social Policy and Social Justice*, 289.

24. For example, in 1961, when the price of wheat was low, per capita income in Saskatchewan was seventy-eight per cent of the national average, while in the following year, with wheat prices significantly higher, Saskatchewan's per capita income jumped to 102 per cent of the Canadian average. T. N. Brewis, "The Problem of Regional Disparities," in T. N. Brewis, ed., *Growth and the Canadian Economy* (Toronto: McClelland and Stewart, 1968), 91.

25. Judith Martin, "The Continuing Struggle for Universal Day Care," in Jim Harding, ed., *Social Policy and Social Justice: The NDP Government in Saskatchewan During the Blakeney Years* (Waterloo: Wilfrid Laurier University Press, 1995): 17–51.

26. Robert Sass, "The Work Environment Board and the Limits of Social Democracy," in Jim Harding, ed., *Social Policy and Social Justice: The NDP Government in Saskatchewan During the Blakeney Years* (Waterloo: Wilfrid Laurier University Press, 1995), 53–83.

27. Background on the relationship between the labour movement and the NDP is found in several articles in Errol Black and Jim Silver, *Hard Bargains: The Manitoba Labour Movement Confronts the 1990s*. Manitoba Labour History Series (Winnipeg: Manitoba Labour Education Centre, 1991).

28. Bill Harding, "The Two Faces of Public Ownership."

29. Harold Chorney and Phillip Hansen, "Neo-Conservatism, Social Democracy and 'Province Building': The Experience of Manitoba,"

Canadian Review of Sociology and Anthropology, 22, 1 (February 1985): 1–29.

30. Ed Shaffer, "Oil and Class in Alberta," *Canadian Dimension*, 13, 8 (June 1979), 43.

31. John Richards and Larry Pratt, *Prairie Capitalism*, 66.

32. Larry Pratt, *The Tar Sands: Syncrude and the Politics of Oil* (Edmonton: Hurtig, 1976), 27.

33. Howard Palmer with Tamara Palmer, *Alberta: A New History* (Edmonton:Hurtig, 1990), 351.

34. This was indicated in a variety of reports in the *Edmonton Journal* and *Calgary Herald* at the time.

35. Howard Palmer with Tamara Palmer, *Alberta*, 342–43.

36. Martin Robin, *Pillars of Profit: The Company Province, 1934–1972* (Toronto: McClelland and Stewart, 1973), 293.

37. *Ibid.*, 294.

38. *Ibid.*, 283.

Chapter Nine

1. Thérèse F. Casgrain, *Une femme chez les hommes* (Montreal: Editions du jour, 1971).

2. Pat Armstrong and Hugh Armstrong, *The Double Ghetto: Canadian Women and Their Segregated Work* (Toronto: McClelland and Stewart, 1978).

3. S. June Menzies for Canadian Advisory Council on the Status of Women, *New Directions for Public Policy: A Position Paper on the One-Parent Family* (Ottawa: Information Canada, 1976), 1.

4. Carole Swan, "Women in the Canadian Labour Force: The Present Reality," in Naomi Herson and Dorothy E. Smith, eds., *Women and the Canadian Labour Force: Proceedings and Papers from a Workshop Held at the University of British Columbia in January 1981* (Ottawa: Social Sciences and Humanities Research Council of Canada, 1982), 35, 54.

5. *Ibid.*, 54.

6. *Ibid.*, 84.

7. Alvin Finkel, "Populism and Gender: The UFA and Social Credit Experiences," *Journal of Canadian Studies*, 27, 4 (Winter 1992–93): 80–86.

8. Alvin Finkel, "Even the Little Children Cooperated: Family Strategies, Childcare Discourse, and Social Welfare Debates, 1945–1975," *Labour/Le Travail*, 36 (Fall 1995): 103–6.

9. NA Therese Casgrain Papers, MG 32, Vol. 1, "Correspondence 1967–1968," Grace MacInnis, MP, Vancouver-Kingsway to Casgrain, 29 November 1967.

10. NA Royal Commission on the Status of Women, RG 33/89, Vol. 11, Brief 28, Sherrill Jackson, Montreal, 12 June 1968.

11. NA Royal Commission on the Status of Women, Vol. 11, Brief 2, Nancy Bryan, Fredericton, brief prepared, 26 July 1967.

12. NA Royal Commission on the Status of Women, Vol.16, Brief 318, Manitoba Volunteer Committee on the Status of Women, 29–31 May, 1968.

13. *Ibid.*

14. NA Royal Commission on the Status of Women, Vol. 11, Brief 52.

15. NA Royal Commission on the Status of Women, Vol. 12, Briefs 88 and 89.

16. NA Royal Commission on the Status of Women, Vol. 16, Brief 318, Manitoba Volunteer Committee on the Status of Women.

17. *Report of the Royal Commission on the Status of Women in Canada* (Ottawa: Information Canada, 1970), xii.

18. Jill Vickers, "The Intellectual Origins of the Women's Movement in Canada," in Constance Backhouse and David H. Flaherty, eds., *Challenging Times: The Women's Movement in Canada and the United States* (Montreal: McGill-Queen's, 1992), 45, 40.

19. John Myles, *When Markets Fail: Social Welfare in Canada and the United States* (New York: United Nations Research Institute for Social Development, 1995), 8–9.

20. Maureen Baker, "Eliminating Child Poverty: How Does Canada Compare?" *American Review of Canadian Studies* (Spring 1995): 80.

21. Graham S. Lowe, "Problems and Issues in the Unionization of Female Workers: Some Reflections on the Case of Canadian Employees," in Herson and Smith, *Women and the Canadian Labour Force*, 309; Carole Swan, "Women in the Canadian Labour Force," 89; Paul Phillips and Erin Phillips, *Women and Work: Inequality in the Labour Market* (Toronto: James Lorimer & Co., 1983), 131.

22. Paul and Erin Phillips, *Women and Work*, 148–49.

23. Graham Lowe, "Problems and Issues in the Unionization of Female Workers," 321, 326.

24. Heather Menzies, *Computers on the Job: Surviving Canada's Microcomputers Revolution* (Toronto: James Lorimer & Co., 1983), 56.

25. Alison Prentice et al., *Canadian Women: A History*, 2nd ed., (Toronto: Harcourt Brace, 1996), 390.

Chapter Ten

1. *The Globe and Mail*, 21 October 1996.

2. J. R. Miller, *Skyscrapers Hide the Heavens: A History of Indian-White Relations in Canada*, revised ed. (Toronto: University of Toronto Press, 1989), 252.

3. Olive Patricia Dickason, *Canada's First Nations: A History of Founding Peoples from Earliest Times* (Toronto: McClelland and Stewart, 1992), 401.

4. Anastasia M. Shkilnyk, "The Destruction of an Ojibwa Community: Relations with the Outside Society," in Ken S. Coates and Robin Fisher, *Out of the Background: Readings on Canadian Native History*, second edition (Toronto: Copp Clark, 1996), 231.

5. J. R. Miller, *Skyscrapers Hide the Heavens*, 252.

6. In Jeanne Perreault and Sylvia Vance, *Writing the Circle: Native Women of Western Canada* (Edmonton: NeWest, 1993), 142–44.

7. Sally M. Weaver, *Making Canadian Indian Policy: The Hidden Agenda 1968–1970* (Toronto: University of Toronto Press, 1981).

8. Arthur J. Ray, *I Have Lived Here Since the World Began: An Illustrated History of Canada's Native People* (Toronto: Lester and Key Porter, 1996), 334–35.

9. *Ibid.*, 336–37.

10. Boyce Richardson, *Strangers Devour the Land: A Chronicle of the Assault Upon the Last Coherent Hunting Culture in North America, the Cree Indians of Northern Quebec, and Their Vast Primeval Homelands* (Toronto: Macmillan, 1975); Olive Patricia Dickason, *Canada's First Nations*, 405.

11. Thomas R. Berger, *Northern Frontier, Northern Homeland*, 2 vols. (Ottawa: Supply and Services Canada, 1977).

12. J. R. Miller, *Skyscrapers Hide the Heavens*, 259–60.

13. R. Quinn Duffy, *The Road to Nunavut: The Progress of the Eastern Arctic Inuit since the Second World War* (Kingston: McGill-Queen's, 1988), 236–37.

14. Robert Davis, *The Genocide Machine in Canada: The Pacification of the North* (Montreal: Black Rose, 1973).

15. Alison Prentice et al., *Canadian Women: A History*, 2nd ed. (Toronto: Harcourt Brace, 1996), 429, 430

16. James Burke, *Paper Tomahawks: From Red Tape to Red Power* (Winnipeg: Queenston House, 1976).

17. Harold Cardinal, *The Unjust Society: The Tragedy of Canada's Indians* (Edmonton: Hurtig, 1969).

18. George Manuel and Michael Posluns, *The Fourth World: An Indian Reality* (Toronto: Collier Macmillan, 1974).

19. Maria Campbell, *Halfbreed* (Toronto; McClelland and Stewart, 1973).

Chapter Eleven

1. Wallace Clement, *The Struggle to Organize: Resistance in Canada's Fishery* (Toronto: McClelland and Stewart, 1986), 73.

2. Alberta Labour, *Union Membership in Alberta*, 1980; Statistics Canada, *The Labour Force*, January, 1980.

3. Alvin Finkel, "The Cold War, Alberta Labour, and the Social Credit Regime," *Labour/Le Travail*, 21 (Spring 1988): 138–40.

4. This, of course, can easily be overstated. The strike wave of the early post-war period, and, indeed, the Depression and wartime militancy, demonstrate that the 1950s was, in many respects, an atypical period in Canadian industrial relations. Even the 1950s, as we have seen, witnessed a number of large-scale strikes, some featuring violent encounters between workers and the combination of management and the state.

5. Restrictive monetary policy, according to economists Clarence Barber and John McCallum, "added an estimated 1.5 percentage points to Canada's unemployment rate between 1975 and 1978." Clarence L. Barber and John C. P. McCallum, *Unemployment and Inflation: The Canadian Experience* (Toronto: James Lorimer & Co., 1980), 128.

6. Bryan Palmer, *Working Class Experience*, 2nd ed. (Toronto: McClelland and Stewart, 1992), 272–73.

7. Stuart M. Jamieson, "Labour Relations," *The Canadian Encyclopedia*, Vol. 2 (Edmonton: Hurtig, 1985), 961.

8. Larry Haiven, "Past Practice and Custom and Practice: 'Adjustment' and Industrial Conflict in North America and the United Kingdom," *Comparative Labor Law Journal*, 12, 3 (Spring 1991): 300–34.

9. Bryan Palmer, *Working Class Experience*, 273.

10. Don Wells, "Autoworkers on the Firing Line," in Craig Heron and Robert Storey, *On the Job: Confronting the Labour Process in Canada* (Montreal: McGill-Queen's, 1986), 337.

11. *Directory of Labour Organizations in Canada* (Ottawa: Canadian

Government Publishing Centre, 1982), 18.

12. *Ibid.*, 16–17.

13. Robert Laxer, *Canada's Unions* (Toronto: James Lorimer & Co., 1976), 226–33, 234–39.

14. Bryan Palmer, *Working Class Experience*, 355–58

15. *Ibid.*, 336, 344.

16. *Ibid.*, 318–19.

17. *Ibid.*, 319.

18. Wallace Clement, *Hardrock Mining: Industrial Relations and Technological Change at INCO* (Toronto: McClelland and Stewart, 1981), 367.

19. *Ibid.*, 59.

20. *Ibid.*, 221–22.

21. *Ibid.*, 227–28. From a statement prepared by the United Steelworkers for the Ham Commission, as reported in the *Financial Post*, 9 December 1978, 16.

22. *Ibid.*, 233–36.

23. *Ibid.*, 249.

24. Elliott Leyton, *Dying Hard: The Ravages of Industrial Carnage* (Toronto: McClelland and Stewart, 1975), 11.

25. Sheila Arnopolous, "Immigrants and Women: Sweatshops of the 1970s," in Irving Abella and David Millar, eds., *The Canadian Worker in the Twentieth Century* (Toronto: Oxford University Press, 1978), 204.

26. Bob Ward, *Harvest of Concern* (Toronto: Ontario Federation of Labour, 1974), 9.

27. Agnes Calliste, "Canada's Immigration Policy and Domestics from the Caribbean: The Second Domestic Scheme," in Wendy Mitchinson et al., eds., *Canadian Women: A Reader* (Toronto: Harcourt Brace, 1996), 398.

28. Seymour Martin Lipset, *Continental Divide: The Values and Institutions of the United States and Canada* (New York: Routledge, 1990), 154.

Chapter Twelve

1. Between 1969 and 1985, defence productivity subsidies for modernizing, upgrading, and marketing military hardware accounted, on an annual basis, for between 9.3 and 38.3 per cent of Canada's military sales to the Americans. See Chapter 13, endnote 18.

2. For the tenor of international debates about economic performance in this period, see Eric Hobsbawm, *The Age of Extremes: A History of the World, 1914–1991* (New York: Pantheon, 1994), Chapter 14, "The Crisis Decades."

3. Peter Leslie, "The Economic Framework: Fiscal and Monetary Policy," in Andrew F. Johnson and Andrew Stritch, eds., *Canadian Public Policy: Globalization and Political Parties* (Toronto: Copp Clark, 1996), 28.

4. Canada, House of Commons, *Debates*, 12 November 1981, 12, 722.

5. Robin W. Boadway and Harry M. Kitchen, *Canadian Tax Policy: Canadian Tax Papers #63* (Toronto 1980), 115–17.

6. Kenneth Norrie and Douglas Owram, *A History of the Canadian Economy* (Toronto: Harcourt, Brace, Jovanovich), 603.

7. The average rate of unemployment for 1982 was 11 per cent. David A. Wolfe, "The Rise and Demise of the Keynesian Era in Canada: Economic Policy, 1930–1982," in Michael S. Cross and Gregory S. Kealey, eds., *Modern Canada 1930–1980s* (Toronto: McClelland and Stewart, 1984), 51.

8. The NAIRU is explained in more detail in Kenneth Norrie and Douglas Owram, *A History of the Canadian Economy*, 602.

9. Canada, House of Commons, *Debates*, 28 June 1982, 18, 880.

10. Government of Canada, *Economic Development for Canada in the 1980s* (Ottawa, 1981), 11.

11. Canada, House of Commons, *Debates*, 23 May 1985, 5014–15.

12. *The Globe and Mail*, 5 December 1985.

13. Canada, House of Commons, *Debates*, 23 May 1985, 5019.

14. Maureen Baker, "Eliminating Child Poverty: How Does Canada Compare?," *American Review of Canadian Studies* (Spring 1995), 99.

15. On the early development of the Reform Party, see Trevor Harrison, *Of Passionate Intensity: Right Wing Populism and the Reform Party of Canada* (Toronto: University of Toronto Press, 1995).

16. Peter Leslie, "The Economic Framework: Fiscal and Monetary Policy," in Andrew F. Johnson and Andrew Stritch, *Canadian Public Policy: Globalization and Political Parties* (Toronto: Copp Clark, 1997), 42.

17. *Edmonton Journal*, 9 December 1996.

18. *The Globe and Mail*, 18 January 1997.

19. On the Klein cuts, see the essays in Trevor Harrison and Gordon Laxer, *The Trojan Horse: Alberta and the Future of Canada* (Montreal: Black Rose, 1995).

20. *Edmonton Journal*, 12 December 1996.

21. Tony Clarke, *Behind the Mitre: The Moral Leadership Crisis in the Canadian Catholic Church* (Toronto: HarperCollins, 1995).

22. *The Globe and Mail*, 6 December 1996.

23. John Myles, *When Markets Fail: Social Welfare in Canada and the United States* (New York: United Nations Research Institute for Social Development, 1995), 3, 8, 11.

24. Maureen Baker, "Eliminating Child Poverty," 84.

25. *Edmonton Journal*, 12 December 1996.

26. Maureen Baker, "Eliminating Child Poverty," 95.

27. John Myles, *When Markets Fail: Social Welfare in Canada and the United States*, 2.

28. *Ibid.*, 7, 12.

29. Maureen Baker, "Eliminating Child Poverty," 92–93.

30. *Ibid.*, 81.

31. *Ibid.*, 82.

32. Michael Howlett, "Sustainable Development: Environmental Policy," in Andrew F. Johnson and Andrew Stritch, eds., *Canadian Public Policy: Globalization and Political Parties* (Toronto: Copp Clark, 1996), 105.

33. *Ibid.*, 112.

Chapter Thirteen

1. Kenneth Norrie and Douglas Owram, *A History of the Canadian Economy* (Toronto: Harcourt Brace Jovanovich, 1991), 612–13; Howard Palmer with Tamara Palmer, *Alberta: A New History* (Edmonton: Hurtig, 1990), 350–54; G. Bruce Doern and Glen Toner, *The Politics of Energy: The Development and Implementation of the NEP* (Toronto: Methuen, 1985).

2. Daniel Drache and Duncan Cameron, eds., *The Other Macdonald Report: The Consensus on Canada's Future that the Macdonald Commission Left Out* (Toronto: James Lorimer and Co., 1985).

3 .*Report of the Royal Commission on Economic Union and Development Prospects for Canada* (Ottawa: Minister of Supply and Services Canada, 1985); Richard Simeon, "Inside the Macdonald Commission," *Studies in Political Economy*, 22 (Spring 1987): 167–79.

4. David Langille, "The Business Council on National Issues and the Canadian State," *Studies in Political Economy*, 24 (Autumn 1987): 41–85. Langille points out that the BCNI was not entirely "neo-liberal.

" It favoured a partnership between business and the state in programs of economic adjustment; in other words, while it wanted government spending to be slashed, it did not want to abandon state programs of direct benefit to business.

5. On the evolution of the free trade negotiations, see Mel Hurtig, *The Betrayal of Canada* (Toronto: Stoddart, 1991), 10–15; and Maude Barlow and Bruce Campbell, *Take Back the Nation 2: Meeting the Threat of NAFTA* (Toronto: Key Porter, 1993), 1–17.

6. Barlow and Campbell, 26–27.

7. "Epilogue: The 1980s," in E. R. Forbes and D. A. Muise, *The Atlantic Provinces in Confederation* (Toronto: University of Toronto Press, 1994), 511.

8. Mel Hurtig, *The Betrayal of Canada*, 180.

9. *Ibid.*, 31.

10. Barlow and Campbell, 23.

11. Richard Martin, "Canadian Labour and North American Integration," in Stephen Randall, ed., *North America Without Borders? Integrating Canada, the United States, and Mexico* (Calgary: University of Calgary Press, 1992), 184.

12. Barlow and Campbell, 28.

13. Barlow and Campbell, 11–15.

14. Montreal Gazette, 24 December 1996.

15. W. Andy Knight, 'Foreign Policy: Coping with a Post-Cold War Environment," in Andrew F. Johnson and Andrew Stritch, *Canadian Public Policy: Globalization and Political Parties* (Toronto: Copp Clark, 1997), 226.

16. John Barrett, "Canada's Arms Control and Disarmament Policy: Redefining the Achievable," in Ernie Regehr and Simon Rosenblum, eds., *The Road to Peace* (Toronto: James Lorimer & Co., 1988), 82; Peter Goodwin, *Nuclear War: The Facts on Our Survival* (New York: Routledge, 1981), 118.

17. Pauline Jewett, "'Suffocation' of the Arms Race: Federal Policy 1978–82," in Ernie Regehr and Simon Rosenblum, eds., *Canada and the Nuclear Arms Race* (Toronto: James Lorimer & Co., 1983), 214.

18. Ernie Regehr, *Arms Canada: The Deadly Business of Military Exports* (Toronto: James Lorimer & Co., 1987), xii, 110.

19. *Ibid.*, 52.

20. Victoria Berry and Allan McChesney, "Human Rights and Foreign

Policy-Making," in Robert O. Matthews and Cranford Pratt, eds., *Human Rights in Canadian Foreign Policy* (Montreal: McGill-Queen's, 1988), 59–60.

21. Kim Richard Nossal, "Cabin'd, Cribb'd, Confin'd?: Canada's Interests in Human Rights, " in Robert O. Matthews and Cranford Pratt, eds., *Human Rights in Canadian Foreign Policy* (Montreal: McGill-Queen's, 1988), 57.

22. Department of External Affairs, "The Mulroney Government's Policy, 1985," in J. L. Granatstein, ed., *Canadian Foreign Policy: Historical Readings* (Toronto: Copp Clark, 1993), 73–85.

23. Gary B. Nash et al., *The American People: Creating a Nation and a Society: Volume Two: Since 1865*, Third Edition (New York: HarperCollins, 1994), 1075–76.

24. W. Andy Knight, "Foreign Policy: Coping with a Post-Cold War Environment," 226–30.

Chapter Fourteen

1. On the constitutional negotiations of 1981, see Kenneth McRoberts, *Quebec: Social Change and Political Crisis*, 3rd ed., (Toronto: McClelland and Stewart, 1988), 341–58; Edward McWhinney, *Canada and the Constitution, 1979–82* (Toronto: University of Toronto Press, 1982); Paul-André Linteau et al., *Quebec Since 1930* (Toronto: James Lorimer & Co., 1991), 547–52.

2. Alison Prentice et al., *Canadian Women: A History*, 2nd ed., (Toronto: Harourt Brace, 1996), 446–47.

3. Ramsay Cook, "Quebec's New Quiet Revolutionaries," in Ramsay Cook, ed., *Quebec and the Uses of Nationalism* (Toronto: McClelland and Stewart, 1986), 88.

4. *Ibid.*, 96.

5. Paul-André Linteau, René Durocher, Jean-Claude Robert, and Francois Ricard, *Histoire du Quebec contemporain: le Quebec depuis 1930* (Montreal: Boreal Express, 1986), 422.

6. Ramsay Cook, "Quebec's New Quiet Revolutionaries," 102.

7. William D. Coleman, *The Independence Movement in Quebec, 1945–1980* (Toronto: University of Toronto Press, 1984), 106.

8. Bryan D. Palmer, *Working Class Experience*, 2nd ed. (Toronto: McClelland and Stewart, 1992), 362–63.

9. Jorge Niosi, "The Rise of French-Canadian Capitalism," in Alain Gagnon, *Quebec: State and Society in Crisis* (Toronto: Methuen, 1984), 199.

10. Seymour Martin Lipset, *Continental Divide: The Values and Institutions of the United States and Canada* (New York: Routledge, 1990), 85, 87, 157–58.

11. Bryan Palmer, *Working Class Experience*, 363.

12. Ralph P. Guntzel, "Public-Sector Collective Bargaining and the Radicalization and Deradicalization of the Centrale de l'Enseignement du Quebec, 1964–1982," in Cy Gonick, Paul Phillips, and Jesse Vorst, *Labour Gains, Labour Pains: Fifty Years of PC 1003* (Winnipeg/Halifax: Society for Socialist Studies/Fernwood Publishing, 1995), 97–117; Carla Lipsig-Mumme, "Future Conditional: Wars of Position in the Quebec Labour Movement," *Studies in Political Economy*, 36 (Autumn 1991): 73–107.

13. Heather Jon Maroney, "'Who has the baby?' Nationalism, pronatalism and the construction of a 'demographic crisis' in Quebec, 1960–1988," *Studies in Political Economy*, 39 (Autumn 1992): 7–36.

14. Kenneth McRoberts, *Quebec*, 395–99.

15. Varying contemporary opinions of the Meech Lake Accord are found in Michael D. Behiels, ed., *The Meech Lake Primer: Conflicting Views of the 1987 Constitutional Accord* (Ottawa: University of Ottawa Press, 1989).

16. Events leading to the demise of the Meech Accord are traced in Andrew Cohen, *A Deal Undone: The Making and Breaking of the Meech Lake Accord* (Vancouver: Douglas and McIntyre, 1990).

17. Pierre Fortin, "How Economics Is Shaping the Constitutional Debate in Quebec," in Robert Young, ed., *Confederation in Crisis* (Toronto: James Lorimer & Co., 1991), 34–44.

18. *The Globe and Mail*, 31 October 1996.

19. *The Globe and Mail*, 31 August 1996.

20. *Le Devoir*, 30 August 1995.

21. Kenneth Munro, "Official Bilingualism in Alberta," *Prairie Forum*, Vol. 12, No. 1 (Spring 1987): 37–49.

Chapter Fifteen

1. "A Note on Political Criticism in Alberta Today," in Trevor Harrison and Gordon Laxer, eds., *The Trojan Horse: Alberta and the Future of Canada* (Montreal: Black Rose, 1995), 332–33.

2. Alison Prentice et al., *Canadian Women: A History*, 2nd ed., (Toronto: Harcourt Brace, 1996), 428.

3. *Ibid.*, 453.

4. *Ibid.*, 440–41.

5. *Ibid.*, 397; Neil Tudiver, "Building Corporate Agendas: Threat to Academic Freedom," paper presented to Society for Socialist Studies Session on The Academy on Strike, 4 June 1996.

6. Marjorie Griffin Cohen, *Free Trade and the Future of Women's Work: Manufacturing and Service Industries* (Toronto: Garamond Press, 1987).

7. Jill Vickers, "The Intellectual Origins of the Women's Movement in Canada," in Constance Backhouse and David H. Flaherty, eds., *Challenging Times: The Women's Movement in Canada and the United States* (Montreal: McGill-Queen's, 1992), 39–60; Constance Backhouse, "The Contemporary Women's Movement in Canada and the United States: An Introduction," in Backhouse and Flaherty, *Challenging Times*, 12–13; Jill Vickers, Pauline Rankin, and Christine Appelle, *Politics as if Women Mattered: A Political Analysis of the National Action Committee on the Status of Women* (Toronto: University of Toronto Press, 1993).

8. "Submission by the Canadian Advisory Council on the Status of Women to the Legislative Committee on Bill C-21, An Act to Amend the Unemployment Insurance Act," September 1989, minutes of the committee, 20.

9. Canada, House of Commons, Special Committee on Child Care, *Hearings*, St. John's, 18 March 1986.

10. Gwaganad, "Speaking for the Earth: the Haida Way," in Chad Gaffield and Pam Gaffield, *Consuming Canada: Readings in Environmental History* (Toronto: Copp Clark, 1995), 292.

11. Arthur J. Ray, *I Have Lived Here Since the World Began: An Illustrated History of Canada's Native People* (Toronto: Lester/Key Porter, 1986), 348.

12. *Ibid.*, 348–50.

13. *Ibid.*, 350–56; John Goddard, *Last Stand of the Lubicon Cree* (Vancouver: Douglas and McIntyre, 1991).

14. Michel F. Girard, "The Oka Crisis from an Environmental History Perspec-tive, 1870–1990," in Chad Gaffield and Pam Gaffield, *Consuming Canada*, 298–315; J. R. Miller, "Great White Father Knows Best: Oka and the Land Claims Process," *Native Studies Review*, 7, 1 (1991), 23–52.

15. "Beyond Oka: Dimensions of Mohawk Sovereignty—Interview with Kahn-Tineta Horn," *Studies in Political Economy*, 35 (Summer 1991): 41.

16. Arthur J. Ray, *I Have Lived Here Since the World Began*, 342.

17. *Ibid.*, 367.

18. Robin Fisher, "Judging History: Reflections on the Reasons for

Judgment in Delgamuukw v. B.C.," *B.C. Studies*, 95 (Autumn 1992): 49.

19. Arthur J. Ray, *I Have Lived Here Since the World Began*, 367.

20. Alison Prentice et al., *Canadian Women: A History*, 455–56.

21. "Interview with Kahn-Tineta Horn," 38.

22. Tania Das Gupta, "Political Economy of Gender, Race and Class: Looking at South Asian Immigrant Women in Canada," *Canadian Ethnic Studies*, 26, 1 (1994): 67.

23. Wenona Giles and Valerie Preston, "The Domestication of Women's Work: A Comparison of Chinese and Portuguese Immigrant Women Homeworkers," *Studies in Political Economy* (Fall 1996): 166.

24. Tania Das Gupta, "Anti-Black Racism in Nursing in Ontario," *Studies in Political Economy*, 51 (Fall 1996): 97–116; Himani Bannerji, *Thinking Through: Essays on Feminism, Marxism, and Anti-Racism* (Toronto: Women's Press, 1995).

25. *Edmonton Journal*, 19 January 1997.

26. Biographies of key Canadian authors who are neither of British nor French origin are found in Smaro Kamboureli, ed., *Making a Difference: Canadian Multicultural Literature* (Toronto: Oxford University Press, 1996). Bissoondath's views were expressed at length in *Selling Illusions: The Cult of Multiculturalism in Canada* (Toronto: Penguin, 1994).

27. *The Globe and Mail*, 1 May 1996.

28. Gary Kinsman, *The Regulation of Desire: Sexuality in Canada* (Montreal: Black Rose, 1987); David M. Rayside and Evert A. Lindquist, "AIDS Activism and the State in Canada," *Studies in Political Economy*, 39 (Autumn 1992): 37–76; Becki Ross, *The House That Jill Built: A Lesbian Nation in Formation* (Toronto: University of Toronto Press, 1995); Katherine Arnup, ed., *Lesbian Parenting: Living with Pride and Prejudice* (Charlottetown: Gynergy Books, 1995).

Nelson Lichtenstein and Howell John Harris write, from an American perspective: "In Canada and in most public sector workplaces, the danger of trying to organize a union is minimal; as a consequence, unionization rates are two or three times higher than in private American firms." Nelson Lichtenstein and Howell John Harris, "Epilogue: Toward a New Century," in Lichtenstein and Harris, eds., *Industrial Democracy in America: The Ambiguous Promise* (Cambridge: Cambridge University Press, 1993), 282–83.

29. Bryan Palmer, *Working Class Experience: Rethinking the History of Canadian Labour, 1800–1991* (Toronto: McClelland and Stewart, 1992), 400, 410.

30. R. Ogmundson and L. Fatels, "Are the Brits in Decline? A Note on Trends in the Ethnic Origins of the Labour and Church Elites," *Canadian Ethnic Studies*, 24, 1 (1994): 110.

31. Alison Prentice et al., *Canadian Women: A History*, 369.

32. Susan Spratt, "Interview with Cheryl Kryzaniwsky," *Canadian Dimension*, 30, 1 (February-March 1996): 41.

33. Tania Das Gupta, "South Asian Immigrant Women," 68–69.

34.Patricia Marchak, *Green Gold: The Forest Industry in British Columbia* (Vancouver: University of British Columbia Press, 1983).

35. Toby Maloney, "From Forestry to Forests: A Tale of Two Conferences," *Canadian Dimension*, 30, 6 (November-December 1996): 28–30.

36. Lori Vitale Cox, "On the Edge: Women in the Atlantic Fisheries," *Canadian Dimension*, 30, 1 (February-March 1996), 22, 24.

37. John McInnis and Ian Urquhart, "Protecting Mother Earth or Business?: Environmental Politics in Alberta," in Trevor Harrison and Gordon Laxer, eds., *The Trojan Horse*, 243–44; Larry Pratt and Ian Urquhart, *The Last Great Forest: Japanese Multinationals and Alberta's Northern Forests* (Edmonton: NeWest Press, 1994).

38. Toby Maloney, "From Forestry to Forests," 29.

Chapter Sixteen

1. Lucia Kowaluk and Steven Staples, eds., *Afghanistan and Canada: Is There an Alternative to War?* (Montreal: Black Rose, 2009); James Laxer, *Mission of Folly: Canada and Afghanistan* (Toronto: Between the Lines, 2008); Yves Engler, *The Black Book of Canadian Foreign Policy* (Vancouver: Fernwood, 2009).

2. Central Intelligence Agency, *The World Factbook, 2011*, https://www. cia.gov/library/publications/the-world-factbook/geos/us.html, accessed 22 October 2011.

3. On the underlying irrationalities of capitalist practices in the early 2000s, both American and elsewhere, as well as socialist alternatives, see Greg Albo, Sam Gindin, and Leo Panitch, *In and Out of Crisis: The Global Financial Meltdown and Left Alternatives* (Winnipeg: Fernwood, 2010).

4. Central Intelligence Agency, *The World Factbook*.

5. Intergovernmental Panel on Climate Change, *IPCC Fourth Assessment Report: Climate Change 2007*, http://www.ipcc.ch/publications_and_data/ publications_and_data_reports.shtml#1, accessed 4 February 2009.

6. Conference Board of Canada, "How Canada Performs: A Report Card

on Canada" (Ottawa: Conference Board of Canada, 2011).

7. Armine Yalnizyan, *The Rich and the Rest of Us: The Changing Face of Canada's Growing Gap* (Ottawa: Canadian Centre for Policy Alternatives, 2007), 3, 4, 28. The quotation is from page 4.

8. U.S. Energy Information Administration, "Weekly All Countries Spot Price FOB Weighted by Estimated Expert Volume (Dollars per Barrel)," http://www.eia/gov/dnow/pet/hist/Leafhandler.ashx?n=PET&=WTOTWORLD&f=W, accessed 10 October 2011; Natural Resources Canada, http://www.nrcan.gc.ca/enecne/sources/pripi/marmar-eng.php, accessed 10 October 2011.

9. Alex Koustas, Scotiabank Group, "Global Economic Research: Provincial Trends," 6 July 2011, http://www.scotiacapital.com/English/bns_econ/ptrends.pdf, accessed 10 October 2011.

10. William Marsden, *Stupid to the Last Drop: How Alberta Is Bringing Environmental Armageddon to Canada (And Doesn't Seem to Care)* (Toronto: Alfred A. Knopf, 2007); Andrew Nikiforuk, *Tar Sands: Dirty Oil and the Future of a Continent* (Vancouver: Greystone Books, 2008).

11. For the scientists' take on the oil sands/tar sands and what was necessary for them to be developed in ways that would reduce their greenhouse gas impact, see Don Woynillowicz, Chris Severson-Baker, and Marlo Reynolds, Oil Sands Fever: The Environmental Implications of Canada's Oil Sands Rush (Edmonton: Pembina Institute, 2005), http://pubs.pembina.org/reports/OilSands72.pdf, accessed 15 October 2011.

The Pembina Institute is a non-profit Alberta-based organization "to advance sustainable energy solutions through innovative research, education, consulting, and advocacy" (Pembina Institute, 2009), accessed 15 October 2011.

12. International Work Group for Indigenous Affairs, "Canada: Indigenous Leaders Reject Pipeline Equity Officer," Press Release, 16 February 2011.

13. "Canada's Tar Sands: Muck and Brass," *The Economist*, January 2011.

14. Jason Foster, "Revolution, Retrenchment, and the New Normal: The 1990s and Beyond," in Alvin Finkel, ed., *Working People in Alberta: A History* (Athabasca: Athabasca University Press, 2012).

15. *The Globe and Mail*, 12 June 2001 and 5 November 2011; Human Resources and Skills Development Canada, "Employment Insurance," 2009, http://www.hrsdc.gc.ca/egn/employment/ei/reports/eimar_2009/chapter1_1.shtm/, accessed 22 October 2011.

16. Roy J. Romanow, *Final Report: Building on Values: The Future of Health Care in Canada, Commission on the Future of Health Care in Canada* (Ottawa: Government of Canada, 2002).

17. Alvin Finkel, *Social Policy and Practice in Canada: A History* (Waterloo: Wilfrid Laurier University Press, 2006), 313–14.

18. Juha Mikkinen and Dennis Raphael, *Social Determinants of Health: The Canadian Facts* (Toronto: York University, 2010), http://www. thecanadianfacts.org/, accessed 1 March 2011; Dennis Raphael, Toba Bryant, and Marcia Rioux, eds., *Staying Alive: Critical Perspectives on Health, Illness and Health Care* (Toronto: Canadian Scholars' Press, 2010).

19. On the 2000 election, see André Blais, Elisabeth Gidengil, Richard Nadeau, and Neil Nevitte, *Anatomy of A Liberal Victory: Making Sense of the 2000 Canadian Election* (Peterborough: Broadview Press, 2002).

20. Jean Chrétien's views of his years in power are found in *My Years as Prime Minister* (Toronto: Knopf Canada, 2007). A journalistic account focusing on the prime minister's personality is Lawrence Martin, *Iron Man: The Defiant Reign of Jean Chrétien* (Toronto: Viking Canada, 2003). Focusing instead on critical analyses of government policies during the Chrétien years is Lois Harder and Steve Patten, eds., *The Chrétien Legacy: Public Policy in Canada* (Montreal and Kingston: McGill-Queen's University Press, 2006).

21. On the continuing cuts to social programs for this period, see Alvin Finkel, *Social Policy*, Chapter 12, "The Welfare State Since 1980," 283–323; Sylvia Bashevkin, *Welfare Hot Buttons: Women, Work, and Social Policy Reform* (Toronto: University of Toronto Press, 2002); and Gary Teeple, *Globalization and the Decline of Social Reform: Into the Twenty-First Century* (Toronto: Garamond, 2000). On the ravaging of unemployment/employment insurance, see Georges Campeau, *From UI to EI: Waging War on the Welfare State* (Vancouver: UBC Press, 2004).

22. Éric Bélanger and Jean-François Godbout, "Why Do Parties Merge? The Case of the Conservative Party of Canada," *Parliamentary Affairs* 63, 1 (2010): 41–65.

23. The letter can be found at http://www.cbc.ca/canadavotes2004/ leadersparties/pdf/firewall.pdf, accessed 28 October 2011.

24. On the election of 2004, see Tom Flanagan, *Harper's Team: Behind the Scenes in the Conservative Rise to Power* (Montreal and Kingston: McGill-Queen's University Press, 2009); and Elisabeth Gidengill, Patrick Fournier, Dianne Everitt, Neil Nevitte, and André Blais, "The Anatomy of a Liberal Defeat," Paper presented at annual meeting of the Canadian Political Science Association, Carleton University, Ottawa, May 2009, http:// ces-eec.org/pdf/Anatomy%20of%20a%20Liberal%20Defeat.pdf, accessed 28 October 2011.

25. "Harper Letter Dismisses Kyoto as 'Socialist Scheme,' CBC News Canada, 30 January 2007, http://www.cbc.ca./news/canada/

story/2007/01/30/harper-kyoto.html, accessed 19 October 2011.

26. On the 2006 election, see Paul Wells, *Right Side Up: The Fall of Paul Martin and the Rise of Stephen Harper's New Conservatism* (Toronto: Douglas Gibson Books, 2007); and Tom Flanagan, *Harper's Team*.

27. The early years of Conservative power are analyzed in Christian Nadeau, *Rogue in Power: Why Stephen Harper Is Remaking Canada by Stealth*, translated by Eric Hamovitch and Robert Chodos (Toronto: Lorimer, 2011); and Lawrence Martin, *Harperland: The Politics of Control* (Toronto: Penguin, 2010).

28. For the details of the Green Shift plan, see http://www.scribd.com/doc/4344304/Green-shift, accessed 1 November 2011.

29. By contrast, 88 economists produced an Open Letter that called for a bold program of stimulus, which might include a "cyclical deficit." "Open Letter from Canadian Economists on the Current Economic Crisis and the Appropriate Government Response," http://www.progressive-economics.ca/2008/10/07/open-letter/, accessed 15 January 2009.

30. Jim Stanford, "Full List of 60 Countries that Did Better than Canada," *Progressive Economics Forum*, 30 March 2011.

31. Department of Finance, Canada, "Federal Corporate Tax Reductions," August 2003, http://www.fin.gc.ca/toc/2003/taxratered_-eng.asp, accessed 3 November, 2011; Canada Revenue Agency, "Corporation Tax Rates," http://www.cra-arc.gc.ca/tx/bx/bsnss/tpcs/crptns/rts-eng.html, accessed 3 November 2011.

32. Mining Watch Canada, "Guatemala: Recuperating the Land that Belongs to Us: Rebuilding Barrio Revolucíon," 22 August 2007, http://www.miningwatch.ca/index.php?/Guatemala/Barrio_Revolucion, accessed 8 October 2010; Paul Knox, "Canada's Role in Columbia Probed," *The Globe and Mail*, 1 June 2001.

33. Derrick O'Keefe, "Three Years Later, Canada Must Be Held Accountable for Haiti Coup," *Seven Oaks Magazine*, 28 February 2007; Noam Chomsky, Paul Farmer, and Amy Goodman, *Getting Haiti Right This Time—The U.S. and the Coup* (Monroe, ME: Common Courage Press, 2004).

34. *CIA Factbook 2011*, https://www.cia.gov/library/publications/the-world-factbook/geos/ve.html, accessed 22 October 2011.

35. On Canada's role in Afghanistan, see John W. Warnock, *Creating a Failed State: The U.S. and Canada in Afghanistan* (Toronto: Fernwood, 2008); Lucia Kowaluk and Steven Staples, eds., *Afghanistan and Canada*; James Laxer, *Mission of Folly*. On the military history of the war, see Murray Brewster, *The Savage War: The Untold Battles of*

Afghanistan (Toronto: Wiley, 2011).

36. George Melnyk, ed., *Canada and the New American Empire: War and Anti-War* (Calgary: University of Calgary Press, 2004).

37. See Jack Warnock, *Creating a Failed State: The US and Canada in Afghanistan* (Toronto: Fernwood, 2008).

38. Marci McDonald, *The Armageddon Factor: The Rise of Christian Nationalism in Canada* (Toronto: Random House, 2010).

39. David Macdonald, *The Cost of 9/11: Tracking the Creation of a National Security Establishment* (Ottawa: Rideau Institute, 2011).

40. On the Guaranteed Annual Income, see Richard Pereira, "Economic Security in the Twenty-First Century—Guaranteed Annual Income: An Ecological, Democratic, Justice and Security Imperative: Positive vs. Negative," Progressive Economics Forum, 2009, http://www.progressive-economics.ca/wp-content/uploads/2010/06/pereira.pdf, accessed 15 October 2011.

41. Kevin MacKay, "Solidarity and Symbolic Protest: Lessons for Quebec Labour from the Quebec City Summit of the Americas," *Labour/Le Travail* 50 (Fall 2002): 21–72.

42. http://www.cbc.ca/news/canada/story/2007/08/23-police-montebello.htm, accessed 15 October 2011.

43. Ghada Chehade, "G20 Riots Perpetrated by Agents Provocateurs of the Police," *Global Research*, 13 July 2010, http://www.globalresearch.com/index.php?context=va&aid=20110, accessed 19 October 2011.

44. *The Globe and Mail*, 8 November 2012.

45. Richard Wilkinson and Kate Pickett, *The Spirit Level: Why More Equal Societies Almost Always Do Better* (London: Allen Lane, 2009).

Photo Credits

For reasons of space, the following abbreviations have been used to identify photo sources:

ACAM: Archives de la Chancellerie de l'Archevêché de Montréal, Montreal;
AO: Archives of Ontario, Toronto;
CWMA: Canadian Women's Movement Archives, Ottawa;
GAIA: Glenbow Alberta Institute Archives, Calgary;
INT: Intercede, Toronto;
MC: Museum of Civilization, Hull;
NAC: National Archives of Canada, Ottawa;
PAA: Provincial Archives of Alberta, Edmonton;
PAM: Provincial Archives of Manitoba, Winnipeg;
PANS: Public Archives of Nova Scotia, Halifax;
PCMA: Peterborough Centennial Museum and Archives, Peterborough;
SA: Saskatchewan Archives Board, Saskatoon and Regina;
SFUA: Simon Fraser University Archives, Vancouver;
UAA: University of Alberta Archives, Edmonton;
LBJ: Les Ballets Jazz de Montréal, Montreal.

Chapter One, Brave New World

Page 3: VE celebration in Toronto, NAC RD-885; page 4: Personnel from HMCS Prince Robert, NAC PA-116808; page 13: A Native family visits Hudson's Bay Company, NAC PA-164744; page 22: Tommy Douglas, SA R-B2895; page 25: C. D. Howe, NAC C-472; page 26: Jell-O train, PAABL-1890-3; page 28: Dr. Harold Adams Innis, NAC C-003407; page 33: Igor Gouzenko, NAC PA-129625; page 35: Canadian Seamens' Union demonstration, NAC PA-128759; page 36: Hal Banks, Montreal *Star* Collection, Gerry Davidson, photographer, NAC PA-152496.

Chapter Two, A Home Fit for Heroes

Page 41: East end cabins, Vancouver, NAC PA-154626; page 43: modern Canadian living room, NAC PA-111484; page 44: switchboard operator, Royal Victoria Hospital, Montreal, 1953, NAC PA-133210; page 48: war brides and their children, PANS, H.B. Jefferson Collection, 31.2.1, N-082; page 51: Greek and Italian immigrants, Department of Manpower and Immigration Collection, R. Beauchamp, photographer, NAC PA-127037; page 52: Westclox clock assembly, c. 1930, PCMA 79-016; page 58: Private Huron Eldon Brant, a Mohawk from Deseronto, Ontario, receives Medal of Courage from General Bernard Montgomery, NAC PA-130065; page 60:

Inuit children return to the North, NAC PA-193047; page 65: Claude Jodoin, President of the Canadian Labour Congress, and Roger Provost (seated) at the founding convention of the NDP, Ottawa, 1961, Federal Photos, NAC PA-116448; page 72: policing the asbestos strike, Montreal Star Collection, NAC PA-130356.

Chapter Three, The Regions and the Provinces

Page 81: Maurice Duplessis, NAC C-9338; page 82: Gratien Gélinas, NAC A-122724, National Film Board of Canada Collection, Ronny Jaques, photographer; page 83: Montreal slums, *Gazette* photograph, NAC P-151688; page 88: Maurice Duplessis, Trois-Rivieres, Quebec, 16 July 1952, NAC PA-115820; page 95: Joseph Robert Smallwood, NAC PA-128080, National Film Board of Canada Collection; page 97: Tommy Douglas, NAC C-36219; page 98: Keep Our Doctors Committee, SA R-B3980-1.

Chapter Four, The Politics of a "Middle Power"

Page 104: Lester B. Pearson, NAC C-70449; page 106: René Lévesque interviewing Pte. Lawrence Hall of Montreal, 14 August 1951, NAC-C79009; page 111: Ellen Fairclough in House of Commons, 9 April 1957, Duncan Cameron photographs, NAC PA-129249; page 115: progressive women working for peace in the movement to ban the atomic bomb, AO 447, courtesy of the Association of United Ukrainian Canadians.

Chapter Five, The Search for Political Identity

Page 130: party time on University of Alberta campus, UAA 79-86-4; page 133: Prime Minister Pearson lights Centennial flame, NAC C-26964; page 139: Prime Minister Pearson with Minister of Justice, Pierre Trudeau, Duncan Cameron photographs, NAC C-25001; page 140: academic quadrangle at Simon Fraser University, SFUA 87096-16, courtesy Simon Fraser University, Instructional Media Centre; page 141: A. Y. Jackson's Canadian flag proposal, Duncan Cameron photographs, NAC PA-136154; page 144: Ukrainian plaque, PAM, Boadway Collection, N 13048.

Chapter Six, English-Canadian Nationalism

Page 157: Bobby Gimby leading centennial parade, photograph by Malak, NAC C-26756; page 158: Expo '67, photo by Malak, NAC C-18536; page 162: Calgary in 1964, GAIA, *Calgary Herald* Collection, NA-2864-1539; page 173: John Grierson, NAC PA-169782; page 175: Dora Mavor Moore, Walter Curtin, photographer, NAC PA-137084.

Chapter Seven, From the Quiet Revolution to the First Sovereignty Referendum

Page 180: Cardinal Paul-Émile Léger, ACAM; page 187: mailbox bombing, Montreal *Gazette* photograph, NAC PA-157323; page 191: Charles de Gaulle, NAC PA-185519; page 193: Canadian army in Montreal, Montreal *Star* Collection, R. Banque, photographer, NAC PA-129838; page 196: Common Front demonstration, NAC PA-116453, Montreal *Star* photograph; Page 201: René Lévesque, NAC PA-115039, Duncan Cameron photographs.

Chapter Eight, The West and the East in the Period of Centralization

Page 210: "The Day of Concern," Sydney, Nova Scotia, 19 November 1967, United Steelworkers of America Collection, NAC C-98715; page 213: lobster traps, PANS, Robert Norwood Collection; page 221: University of Alberta, UAA 79-149 3A; page 223: Peter Pocklington, PAA J-5268-1.

Chapter Nine, The Women's Movement: A "Second Wave"

Page 227: Thérèse (Forget) Casgrain, Collection Thérèse F. Casgrain, NAC PA-126768; page 235: The Women's Place, CWMA, Morisset Library, University of Ottawa, Kate Williams, photographer; page 237: celebrating International Women's Day, CWMA, Morisset Library, University of Ottawa, Holly, photographer; page 241: Canadian rodeo queens, PAA, *Edmonton Journal* Collection, J-2851-1.

Chapter Ten, Canada's First People Rebel

Page 244: Preparing to hunt seal, National Film Board of Canada Collection, Bud Glunz, photographer, NAC PA-145171; page 246: Métis leader Jean Cuthand, Malcolm Norris, and Jim Brady at an anti-nuclear demonstration, GAIA PA-2218-943; page 249: Jean Chrétien, minister of Indian affairs, and prime minister Pierre Trudeau, speaking to Indian delegates concerning the Red Paper brief presented to the Canadian government in response to the White Paper, Ottawa, 1970, Duncan Cameron photographs, NAC PA-170161; page 251: Judd Buchanan, NAC PA-164787, J. Kriber photographer; page 255: Sarcee chief Gordon Crowchild opening a snowmobile area, GAIA, NA-2864-20418a; page 257: Inuit woman sewing with child, Richard Harrington, photographer, NAC PA-166823; page 259: Naskapi painted caribou skin, MC-III-B-588, S75-383.

Chapter Eleven, The Salience of Class

Page 276: Intercede, a Toronto-based advocacy group for domestic workers' rights, lobbying against proposed changes to the immigration program in 1991, photo courtesy of Intercede, Toronto.

Chapter Twelve, Neo-Conservative Times

Page 282: Parliament Hill in winter, Duncan Cameron photographs, NAC PA-168020.

Chapter Thirteen, Canada and the World in the Era of "Globalization"

Page 326: Brian Mulroney, 1983. NAC PA-146485.

Chapter Fourteen, Quebec Nationalism and Globalism

Page 333: Queen Elizabeth II and Pierre Elliot Trudeau, Canadian prime minister from 1968–79 and 1980–84, signing the Canadian constitution, Robert Cooper, photographer, NAC PA-140705; page 342: Les Ballets Jazz de Montréal, photo courtesy of Les Ballets Jazz.

Chapter Fifteen, Other Voices in a Neo-Conservative Age

Page 371: A ceremony to return medicine pipe bundles from the Provincial Museum of Alberta to the Sarcee, GAIA NA-4890-5.

Chapter Sixteen, Canada in the Twenty-First Century

Page 394: Syncrude oil facility, David Dodge, The Pembina Institute; Page 410: Stéphane Dion, The Canadian Press; Page 419: Jack Layton, Richard Lautens / GetStock.com; Page 422: Iraq War demonstration, Linda Dawn Hammond / Indyfoto.com; Page 427: police blockade; arindambanerjee / Shutterstock.com; Page 428: Occupy Montreal, John Kenney, *The Montreal Gazette.*

Index

9/11, 390, 424; attacks, 389, 421
Aberhart, William, 5, 99
Aboriginal reserves, 409
abortion, 46, 233, 236, 362, 403, 407
Action Canada Network, 315, 364
Adbusters, 427, 428
Advisory Committee on Reconstruction, 40
Afghanistan, 390; war in, 421, 423
African-Canadians, 12, 55–56, 214, 271, 341–42, 377–78
African National Congress, 122
Africville, 55–56, 214
Agricultural and Rural Development Act (ARDA), 208
AIDS, 380–81
Air Canada, 289, 382
Alberta, 5; 1993 provincial election, 297–98; and Charlottetown Agreement, 350; economy, 98–99; immigration, 49; and National Energy Program, 222, 306–8; northern region, 10; oil, 76–77, 220–22, 306–8; pension, 62; political culture, 222–23; population growth, 220; poverty, 222; as region, 215–16; social programs, 99; spinoff legislation, 382
Alberta Accord, 405
Alberta Federation of Labour, 397–98
Alberta Labour Relations Board, 261
Alberta Pacific Pulp Mill, 303, 387
Alliance for the Preservation of English Canada, 344
Alliance Quebec, 341
allophones, 201–2, 203
Anglican Church of Canada, 233
anglophones, 201–2, 203, 341, 355
Anti-Inflation Board (AIB), 147–48
anti-nuclear movement, 78
apartheid, 121–22
Arctic Waters Pollution Prevention Act, 154
Aristide, Jean-Baptiste, 420
Arnopolous, Sheila, 196–97
Artistic Woodworkers strike, 271
asbestos, 420; mines, 420

Asbestos strike, 74
Association of Commercial and Technical Employees, 239
Association des demographes du Quebec, 339
Association féminine d'éducation et D'action sociale, 183
Atlantic provinces, 10, 49, 93–96, 206–15, 350. *See also* names of specific provinces
Atomic Energy Commission (AEC), 103
Atwood, Margaret, 174, 175
automobiles, 45; industry, 89–90, 167–68
Auto Pact, 313
AVRO Arrow, 112–13

baby boomers, 127–28
Bachman-Turner Overdrive, 173
Ballets Jazz de Montréal, Les, 343
Bank of Canada, 18, 19, 20, 23, 142, 147, 149, 284, 285, 291
Banks, Hal, 35–36
bank workers, 238–39
Barrett, Dave, 224, 225
Bennett, Bill, Jr., 225, 293, 384
Bennett, R. B., 5
Bennett, W. A. C., 96, 97–98, 224–25
Berger Commission, 368
Berger, Justice Thomas, 253
Bergeron, Geneviève, 363
Bertrand, Jean-Jacques, 190, 193, 194
bilingualism, 204–5, 214–15
Bill 22, 193, 194
Bill 101, 200–1, 334, 341, 347, 417
bin Laden, Osama, 389, 421
birth control, 86, 181, 228, 240–41
Blackfoot nations, 370
Black United Front, 214
Bloc Québécois, 291, 407
Bouchard, Lucien, 351, 352, 356
Bourassa, Robert: and 1971 constitutional patriation attempt, 203–4; and aftermath of Meech Lake Accord, 349–50; government, 197–98; and Meech Lake Accord, 343–44; and sign law, 347

branch plants, 24, 27, 29, 89, 160
Britain, 24, 26, 111, 116, 118–20, 137, 283
Brazil, 389
British Columbia, 7, 13; and
 Charlottetown Agreement, 350;
 class polarization, 96–97, 224–25;
 economy, 96–98; forests, 77; hospital
 insurance program, 22; immigration,
 49; labour militancy, 70, 97; land
 claims settlements, 371–72; Liberal-
 Conservative coalition, 96; native land
 claims, 371–73; regulation of childcare,
 68–69; social programs, 225
British Columbia Treaty Commission,
 371–72
British immigrants, 48
Broadbent, Ed, 313, 314
Bush, George W., 389, 423
business: and benefits of Quiet
 Revolution, 185; and continentalism,
 163, 166, 167; "downsizing," 286; elite,
 23; francophone-owned firms, 334;
 and free trade, 310–11, 315, 316–19;
 opposition to Carter Commission on tax
 reform, 143; and social programs, 18;
 and "urban redevelopment," 55–56
Business Council on National Issues,
 310–11, 316

Cadman, Chuck, 405
Caisse de dépôts et de placements, 185,
 334
Campbell, Kim, 291–92, 363
Canada Against Poverty, 425
Canada Assistance Plan, 130, 138, 149,
 292, 301
Canada Assistance Policy, 287
Canada Council, 171, 174
Canada Development Corporation, 168, 169
Canada's Economic Action Plan, 414
Canada Health Act, 405
Canada Pension Plan, 130, 134–35, 425
Canada-U.S. Free Trade Agreement, 27
Canadian Airborne Regiment, 325
Canadian Alliance, 403. *See also* Reform
 Party
Canadian Association of Industrial,
 Mechanical and Allied Workers
 (CAIMAW), 271
Canadian Automobile Workers (CAW),
 383
Canadian Bill of Rights, 257
Canadian Brewery Workers, 269
Canadian Centre for Policy Alternatives,
 393

Canadian Chamber of Commerce, 7, 22,
 56, 75, 134, 136
Canadian Citizens Coalition, 404
Canadian Congress of Labour (CCL), 42,
 72, 73
Canadian Council of Agriculture, 15
Canadian Federation of Business and
 Professional Women's Clubs, 230, 233
Canadian Federation of Labour, 270, 383
Canadian Federation of Mayors and
 Municipalities, 42
Canadian International Development
 Agency (CIDA), 321
Canadian Labour Congress (CLC), 65,
 166, 167, 268, 269
Canadian Laws Offshore Application Act,
 322
Canadian Legion, 42
Canadian Medical Association (CMA),
 15, 21, 135, 136
Canadian Mortgage and Housing
 corporations, 42–43
Canadian Paperworkers' Union, 269
Canadian Peace Congress, 117
Canadian Seamen's Union (CSU), 35–36
Canadian Textile and Chemical Union
 (CTCU), 270, 271
Canadian Union of Postal Workers, 268
Canadian Union of Public Employees,
 238, 266, 383
Canadian Wheat Board, 419
Canadian Welfare Council, 15
CANDU reactors, 155
carbon credits, 411
carbon intensity, 395
carbon tax, 409
Carrier, Roch, 188
Carter, Kenneth, 142–43
Casgrain, Thérèse, 86, 118, 182, 226, 231
Catch 22 Harper Conservatives, 417
Catholic church, 66, 73, 74; and education
 for girls, 85; influence of, 82–84; rigid
 gender roles, 85–86; social change and,
 179–82; stand against poverty, 300; and
 Union Nationale, 83–84
CBC, 171–72, 289, 403, 409
CEGEPs, 186
Celanese, 399
censorship, 380
Chaput-Rolland, Solange, 86
Charbonneau, Archbishop Joseph, 74
Charlottetown Agreement, 350
Charter of the French Language. *See* Bill
 101
Charter of Rights and Freedoms, 328, 330

Chavez, Hugo, 421
childcare, 38, 64, 65, 68–69, 86, 92,
 138, 183, 219, 225, 232–34, 235, 236;
 national program, 406
children: adoption by gay couples, 380;
 baby bonus, 340–41; education for
 girls, 85, 182; Native, 57–58; poverty,
 300, 301–3; suburban, 47
Child Tax Credit, 152, 236, 300, 301
China, 105, 109, 129, 155, 323–24, 389
Chinese Exclusion Act, 47
Chorney, Harold, 23, 149–50
Chrétien, Jean, 292, 318-19, 399, 400,
 403, 421
Churchill Forest Industries (CFI), 217
Ciaccia, John, 374
CIA Factbook, 390
Cité Libre, 87, 139
Citizens' Housing Association, 42
civil service, 32–34, 38, 204–5
Clark, Joe, 150, 151, 285, 287, 288, 322,
 403, 404
Clarity Act, 409
class, 61, 260
coalition government, 412
Coalition of the Willing, 421, 423
Cold War, 29, 30–39, 66, 326
Combined Universities Campaign for
 Nuclear Disarmament, 118
Come by Chance refinery, 208
Committee for an Independent Canada
 (CIC), 169
Commonwealth, 118–23
commodities boom, 398
Communications Workers of Canada, 269
Communist, Communism, 70; Cold War
 witchhunt, 32–38; collapse of, 323;
 movements, 30; popular support, 7
Communist Party of Canada (CPC), 5
computers. *See* microprocessors
Confédération des syndicats nationaux.
 See Confederation of National Trade
 Unions
Confédération des travailleurs catholiques
 et canadiens (CTCC), 66, 73, 74, 87.
 See also Confederation of National
 Trade Unions
Confederation of National Trade Unions,
 74, 87, 267, 270, 339
Conference Board of Canada, 148, 392
Congress of Canadian Labour (CCL), 65,
 269, 270
Conservative party, 5, 7. *See also*
 Progressive Conservative party
constitution: 1971 attempted patriation of,

203–4; repatriation of, 328–32
Conservative Party of Canada, 404;
 campaign, 407, 414; majority, 418
Constitutional Act of 1982, 343, 358, 375
continentalism: impact of, 161–64, 367;
 reaction against, 24, 27–29
contraception. *See* birth control
Co-operative Commonwealth Federation
 (CCF), 5, 16, 42, 70, 76; 1945 election,
 17; B.C., 97–98; popular support, 7,
 15; Saskatchewan, 99–100. *See also*
 New Democratic Party (NDP)
"Cost of Living Adjustment" (COLA)
 clauses, 263
Courchene, David, 258
Cox, Lori Vitale, 386–87
Creditistes, 151, 190
Cree, of northern Quebec, 370–71
Cross, James, 194, 195
Crow, John, 290, 292
Crown corporations, 6, 25, 100, 162–63,
 210
CRTC, 172, 343
CRUISE missile, 319
Crump, N. R., 7, 8, 9
Cuba, 30, 116, 324
Cuff, R. D., 31
culture: Atlantic, 212–13; Canadian
 content rules, 173; Canadian industry,
 171–75; film industry, 173–74;
 literature, 174; Quebec, 343; recording
 industry, 172–73; theatre, 174–75; U.S.
 influence, 28-29
currency crisis, 25–26

Daishowa, 386
Day, Stockwell, 403
daycare. See childcare
DDT, 78
debt, 17, 283, 284
Decore, Laurence, 297
defence, 24, 105, 111–12
Defence Production Sharing Agreement,
 110, 112, 320
deficit, 18, 149–50, 284, 290
deforestation, 77–78
Democracy, 420
demographic changes, 128–29
Dene, 253, 254, 368
Department of Regional Economic
 Expansion (DREE), 208, 209
Departments, federal: External Affairs,
 31; Finance, 18, 19, 20, 130, 147;
 Human Resources, 292; Immigration,
 47; Indian Affairs, 57; Labour, 53, 66

Development Corporation, 208
Diefenbaker, John, 22, 34, 110, 111–17, 122–23
Diem, Ngo Dinh, 108
Dion, Celine, 343
Dion, Stéphane, 409
Dirks, Gerald, 53
displaced persons ("DP"), 48–49, 53
Distant Early Warning (DEW), 105
"distinct society," 345
divorces, 64, 127, 228
dollar, Canadian, 26, 142, 317–18, 398
Domestic Political Development, 407
"Don Messer's Jubilee," 172
Douglas, Tommy, 21, 99, 405
"downsizing," 286
Doyle, John C., 209
Drew, George, 18, 19
Duceppe, Gilles, 417, 418
Dulles, John Foster, 104, 105
Dumont, Mario, 352
Duplessis, Maurice, 5, 18, 19, 21, 73–74, 80, 83, 85, 270
Dupuis Frères strike, 73
Dutch disease, 399

École des hautes etudes commerciales (H.E.C.), 333–34
École polytechnique, 363
Economic Council of Canada, 219
economic growth, 389
economy: Alberta, 220–22, 394; Atlantic region, 93–94; Canada's in the Brave New World, 392; conditions in fifties and early sixties, 8–9; environment in late eighties, 290; industrial centre, 89; Manitoba, 216–17; popular image of post-war decades, 7–8; Quebec, 84; regional disparity, 10; Saskatchewan, 100, 218; U.S. domination, 23–29, 159–61. *See also* trade
Edmonton Council of Community Services, 68
education, 14, 63, 84–85, 182, 186–87, 363
Eisenhower, Dwight, 104, 114
Elsie Gregory MacGill, 231
employment: conditions, 271, 272–76; discrimination against women, 34, 64; ethnicity and, 90, 261; francophones, 199; white-collar jobs, 261, 261–62; women, 64, 67–68, 69, 90–91, 92, 182, 228, 239, 262, 272, 275; working day, 63-64; work week, 71–72
environment, 76–79, 154–55, 303–4, 385–88

English-language leaders' debate, 412
environment, 389
equalization payments, 206–7
Established Programs Financing, 152
European Common Market, 170
European Economic Community, 111
European Union, 395
extra-billing, 287

families, single-parent, 228, 237, 301, 361–62
family allowances, 68, 84–85, 235–36
family wage, 65, 68, 90
FBI, 33
federal election: of 1945, 7, 17; of 1957, 22; of l963, 22; of 1972, 143, 145; of 1974, 130; of 1979, 150; of 1980, 151; of 1988, 314–15; of 1993, 291–92, of 2004, 402, 405; of 2011, 416–17
Fédération des femmes du Québec, 182–83, 331, 364
federal per-vote financing, 419
Federation of Canadian Municipalities, 405
feminism, 229–32
Fennario, David, 175
Ferguson Lake (BC), 370
Filmon, Gary, 346–47
financial sector: unregulated, 390
First Nations people. *See* Native peoples
fisheries, 211, 386–87
Fishermen, Food and Allied Workers, 211
fishers, 260–61
Flemming, John, 94
food banks, 299–300
Ford: labour relations, 266; St. Thomas plant, 398; strike, 69–70, 71
Fordism, 90, 283
Foreign Investment Review Agency (FIRA), 130, 168–69, 311–12
foreign policy, 319–20, 321; under Chrétien, 324–25; and Commonwealth, 118–23; continentalism and, 164–66; foreign aid, 321; under Mulroney, 321–24; nuclear arms race, 319-20; peacekeeping, 120, 325; Third Option, 170; under Trudeau, 154–56, 319–20, 321; Vietnam War, 153–54
Forest Allies, 386
Fort McMurray, 395–97
Foulkes, General Charles, 111
francophones, 10, 85, 199, 204–5, 356–58
Fraser, Sheila, 404
free trade, 309–14; 426; agreement, 312; effect of, 316–19; election, 314–15;

opposition to, 313, 314–15, 364-65; support for, 309–11
Fregault, Guy, 88
French-language leaders' debate, 417
Friedan, Betty, 47
Friedman, Milton, 146
Front de Libération du Québec, 188–89, 194–95
"Front Page Challenge," 172
Frum, Barbara, 172
FTA. *See* US-Canada Free Trade Agreement (FTA)
Future of Health Care in Canada, 400

G7 countries, 415
G8 meetings, 426
G20 economic summit, 426–27
Gaddafi, Muammar, 423
gasoline: leaded, 303; tax, 150
Gaz Metropolitain, 334
Gaza Strip, 424
gender: idealized roles, 63–64. *See also* women, traditional roles
General Agreement on Tariffs and Trade (GATT), 26, 111
Genie awards, 174
Gini coefficient, 391, 392
Gitksan, 372–73
globalization, 282, 318. *See also* free trade; neo-conservatism
global emissions, 392
global recession, 412
global warming, 392
Godbout, Adelard, 84
Godin, Gérald, 194, 202
Gomery, Justice John H., 404
Gomery Comission, 406
Goodale, Ralph, 408
Goods and Services Tax (GST), 324
Gordon, Walter, 132, 138, 166, 167–68, 169
Gouzenko, Igor, 32
Granatstein, Jack, 31, 32
Grassy Narrows reserve, 59, 247
Great Depression, 4–5
Green Book, 19–20
Green Party, 409
Green Plan, 304
Green Shift, 409, 411
greenhouse gases, 392; emissions, 416
guaranteed annual income (GAI), 151–52
Guaranteed Income Supplement, 300
Guaranteed Income Supplement (GIS), 135
Gulf War, 322

gun registry, 419
GWG, 399

Haiti, 420
Halifax, 3, 55–56
Halifax Board of Trade, 56
Hall, Justice Emmett, 136, 137, 315
Harper, Elijah, 348
Harper, Stephen, 404, 407, 415, 416, 423; 2008 campaign, 411; government, 412, 429; stimulus plan, 414
Harris, Mike, 294, 295–97, 384, 388
Hartman, Grace, 236, 238, 383
Hawthorn Report, 250
health care, 401–02
health spending, 400
Helms-Burton bill, 324
Hogg's Hollow tunnel disaster, 51
holistic medicine, 401
home life, 45–47, 63–64
homeownership: policy of, 42; strategies, 45
homosexuals, homosexuality: discrimination against, 379–81; meeting places, 46; witchhunt against, 33–34
housing costs, 393
housing market, 391
Hong Kong immigrants, 374, 375
Horn, Kahn-Tineta, 370, 374
hospital insurance programs, 22, 136
House of Commons, 413
housing: conditions, 41, 42; social, 41–42, 43
Housing and Community planning subcommittee, 40–41, 42
Howe, C. D., 23, 25, 132
human rights, 420
Humber Environmental Action Group, 386
Hussein, Saddam, 390
Hyde Park Declaration, 24
Hydro-Québec, 184–85

Ignatieff, George, 112, 113
Ignatieff, Michael, 413, 417, 418
immigrants, immigration: Chinese exclusion, 47; Cold War policy, 34, 36–37; colour bar, 47–48; destination of, 49; in eighties, 374–75; experience of, 50–55, 375–77; families, 45; and French language issue, 192–93; Jewish, 119–20; and racism, 374–79; and Reform Party, 375–76; in sixties, 129
imperialism. See nationalism, imperialism

Imperial Tobacco Company of Canada, 134
INCO, 273, 274
income gap, 391
India, 109, 118, 155, 389
Indian Act, 58, 59, 249, 253, 256, 362
Indignados, 427
Indonesia, 30, 320–21
Industrial Enterprises Incorporated, 208
Industrial Estates Limited, 208
inflation, 9, 23, 130, 138, 140–42, 150, 151, 262–63, 284–86, 290
Innis, Harold, 27–29
Insite, 415
interest rates, 23, 285–86, 291
Intergovernmental Panel on Climate Change (IPCC), 392
international capitalism, 426
International Control Commission (ICC), 107, 108, 109–10, 153, 154
International Labour Organization, 420
International Nickel Company, 169
International Union of Mine, Mill, and Smelter Workers, 36
International Woodworkers of America, 70, 75, 383
Inuit, 60, 254
Inuit Tapirisat, 368
Inuvialuit, 368
Investment Canada, 311–12
Ipperwash Provincial Park, 370
Iran-Iraq war, 320, 322
Iraq, 421: 2003 invasion, 413; war against, 390
Israel, 424
Italian-Canadians: community, 50–51; discrimination, 50; homeownership strategies, 45; immigrant experience, 50–54; neo-fascists, 37; Québécois, 10
Italian-Canadian Soccer League, 50
Italian Immigrant Aid Society, 50

James Bay II, 370–71
James Bay and Northern Quebec Agreement, 252
Japan, 146, 155, 170, 310
Jean, Michaelle, 413
Jewett, Pauline, 320
Jews, 49, 50, 54–55
job losses, 317
jobs. *See* employment
Johnson, Daniel, 189, 190, 337
Johnson, Daniel, Junior, 351, 357
Johnson, Pierre-Marc, 337, 347
Julien, Pauline, 185, 194

Kandahar, 421
Kelowna Accord, 406, 408
Kennedy, John F., 114
Keynesianism, 20, 23, 147, 412
Keynes, John Maynard, 18
Keystone pipeline, 396
King, Mackenzie, 26, 159; and Chinese immigration, 47; and social reform, 15–21
Kinsey reports, 46
Klein, Ralph, 297–98, 337, 405
Knox United Church (Winnipeg), 232
Korean War, 105, 105–7
Kouchibouguac National Park, 213–14
Kryzaniwsky, Cheryl, 383–84
Ku Klux Klan, 37
Kyoto Accord, 406

labour: de-skilling, 239; effect of Communist witchhunt on, 35–36, 38; "essential service" legislation, 267; immigrant, 51–53, 90, 195–97, 271, 275, 376–77; militancy, 18, 51–52, 69–70, 71, 97, 141, 197–98, 264–66, 268, 338; radicalism, 264–65; shortage, 48; structure of labour force, 10; unionization, 72, 238–39, 261, 266. *See also* trade unions
language: bills, 193, 194, 200–1, 334, 341, 347; and constitutional politics, 346–48; and education of Quebec immigrants, 192–93, 201–2; French, 177; sign law, 346–47
Latin American mining, 420
Laughren, Floyd, 294
Laurin, Camille, 333
Lavell, Jeanette, 256
Layton, Jack, 405, 417, 418; cancer, 418
Lefebvre, Joseph Daniel, 77–78
Léger, Cardinal Paul-Émile, 179
Lehman Brothers, 391, 412
Lesage, Jean, 81; 1966 Quebec provincial election, 189; government, 184–88, 190
lesbians, lesbianism. *See* homosexuals, homosexuality
Letter Carriers Union, 268
Levant, Victor, 109, 110, 155
Lévesque, René, 184, 191, 200–1, 202, 306, 328, 329–31, 336, 347
Levitt, Kari, 27, 161
Lewis, David, 123, 143, 155, 405
Liberal Dominance: Last Years of, 399
liberal feminists, 230, 231
Liberal Jewish communities, 424
Liberal Party: and economic nationalism,

166; campaigns, 407; federal, 5, 7, 21, 132–34, 166; and free trade, 313, 314–15; Quebec, 80–81, 189, 190–91, 336, 351; and universal social programs, 22–23. *See also* names of Liberal prime ministers, premiers and party leaders

Libya, 390

life insurance industry, 135

Lipset, Seymour Martin, 338

living standards: Africville, 214; fifties and early sixties, 13–14; immigrants, 53–56, 271; native people, 60; Ontario, 90; workers, 271–72

logging, 385–86

Long-gun registry, 412

Lougheed, Peter, 216, 221–22, 307

Louisbourg (historic site), 212

Louiseville strike, 74

Lubicon Cree, 369

Lyon, Sterling, 219–20, 293, 330

MacEachen, Allan, 284, 372–73

MacGill, Helen Gregory, 231

MacKay, Peter. 404

Mackenzie Valley Pipeline, 253

MacMillan-Bloedel, 386

McCain, 211

McCarthyism, 37

McDonough, Alexa, 364

McKenna, Frank, 298–99, 346, 348–99

McLaughlin, Audrey, 319, 364

McLuhan, Marshall, 28–29

McNaughton, General A. G. L., 103

Macdonald Commission, 309

Macdonald, Donald, 147

Manitoba, 7; economy, 100; industrial development, 216–17; Liberal-Progressive alliance, 101; and Meech Lake Accord, 346, 348; neo-conservatism, 219; northern region, 10; politics, 216; population, 49; social programs, 218–19

Manitoba Act, 358

Manitoba Development Fund, 217

Manitoban, The, 217

Manitoba Volunteer Committee on the Status of Women, 233

Manning, Ernest, 19, 75, 99, 137, 220, 291, 380

Manning, Preston, 291, 403

maquiladoras, 316

marijuana, 415

Marois, Pauline, 417

marriage: same-sex, 403, 406, 407

Marshall Plan, 26, 35

Martin, Paul, 22, 164–65, 166, 292, 403, 406; Liberals, 413

maternity benefits, 140, 235

May, Elizabeth, 418

medical insurance, 15, 16, 20, 21–22, 133, 135, 136, 315

medicare, 135–38, 400, 405; two-tier, 400–01, 405

Meech Lake Accord, 343–48, 364

microprocessors, 239, 283

Middle East: wars, 390; policy, 424

Military payroll, 390

miners, 272–74

minorities: discrimination against, 10–13, 341–42, 375–77, 378; pay gap, 378; population, 374; women, 365. *See also* immigrants, immigration; names of specific groups

Mohawk, of Kanesatake, 369–70

monetarism, 146–50, 285–86

Montreal, 7, 89, 275, 355; immigration, 49

Morris, Joe, 148, 268

mothers' allowances, 91movements, 424

Movement Souveraineté-Association, 191

Mulroney, Brian, 291, 343–44, 348, 350; and environmental issues, 303–2; foreign policy, 321–24; and free trade, 309–15; spending cuts, 288–89; tax reforms, 289; years, 400

Mummers (drama group), 174, 212

Murdochville strike, 74–75

Muslim freedom fighters, 389

NAIRU (non-accelerating inflation rate of unemployment), 147, 286, 291

Nakogee-Davis, Mary Anne, 243–44

Nasser, Gamel Abdul, 120, 121

National Action Committee on the Status of Women, 235–37, 364–65

National Council of Welfare, 228, 229

National Council of Women of Canada, 12, 38, 42, 230, 235–37

National Energy Program (NEP), 222, 306–8, 311

National Indian Brotherhood, 249, 254

nationalism: cultural, 171–75; economic, 161–64, 166–69; imperialism, 24; Quebec, 74, 177–78, 190; *rattrapage* and, 176–78; trade union movement and, 269–71

nationalization, 6, 76, 169, 184, 218

National Liberation Front (NLF), 153

National Party, 319

National Policy, 24

National Union of Provincial Government Employees, 267

Native people: and constitutional repatriation, 331–32; discrimination against, 12–13, 56–58, 100, 245, 249, 341; environmental degradation and, 245–48; labour, 12–13, 271; land claims, 250–52, 367–73; opposition to Quebec sovereignty, 355; plays, 175; Québécois, 10; relocation policy, 59–60; schooling, 56–58, 243–45; and self-determination, 58, 252-59; self-government, 350, 367; and White Paper, 248–52; women, 234, 252–53, 256–57, 362, 374–75

NATO, 95, 103, 104, 105, 111, 113, 114, 116, 117, 155, 165, 421

Nazis, 34, 37, 376

NDP, 407; anti-war sentiment, 423; cap-and-trade system, 411; rise of, 418

Neighbourhood Services Centres (Winnipeg), 233

neo-conservatism: attack on state, 281–82; British Columbia agenda, 293; economics of, 146–47; ideology, 282–83; Manitoba agenda, 219–20, 293; Mulroney policies, 288–90; New Brunswick, 298–99; Ontario agenda, 294–97; Quebec agenda, 293–94, 334–35, 338–39; Trudeau policies, 285–86; and women's movement, 361–67. *See also* free trade

neo-liberalism, 412, 416, 419, 424: agenda, 408; global order, 426 neoliberal prescription, 390; neoliberals, 391; restructuring, 426

Netherlands, 132

New Brunswick: bilingualism, 214–15; care for elderly, 62–63; economic development, 94; federal aid, 206–8, 212; industrial development, 208; and Meech Lake Accord, 346; support for constitutional repatriation, 328; tourism, 212–13; unemployment, 212; welfare, 301–2, 302

New Democratic Party (NDP): and 1988 election, 314; Alberta, 297–98; American investors and, 169; B.C., 98, 224, 225; economic nationalists and, 169; federal, 130, 191, 200, 314, 338; and free trade, 313, 319; Manitoba, 218–19; Ontario, 294–95, 377, 380, 384; popularity, 313; Saskatchewan, 218–19; voter support, 263; Waffle

group, 169, 265, 270; and wage controls, 269. *See also* Co-operative Commonwealth Federation (CCF)

Newfoundland, 394: care for elderly, 62; Confederation, 94–95; federal aid, 206–8, 212; fisheries, 211–12; industrial development, 208, 209; labour relations, 75; and Meech Lake Accord, 347, 348; out-migration, 212; outport relocation, 96; unemployment, 212

Newfoundland and Labrador Corporation, 208

New Left, 236, 265

New Right. *See* neo-conservatism

Nishga, 250–51

NORAD, 105, 112, 116, 117, 165

Noranda Forest Inc., 316

Norstad, General Laurence, 117

North American Free Trade Agreement (NAFTA), 318–19

North Korea, 104

North West Territories Act, 358

Northern Gateway pipeline, 396

Norway: environmental sustainability, 397

"notwithstanding clause," 330, 332

Nova Scotia: care for elderly, 62; divorce laws, 64; economic development, 210; federal aid, 206-8, 212; industrial development, 208-9; lobster catches, 211; neo-conservatism, 299; oil boom, 394; racism, 12; tourism, 212–13

Nova Scotia Association for the Advancement of Coloured People, 12

nuclear arms: debate, 102–5, 113–18; deterrence, 104–5, 114–17, 155; race, 319–20

Nunavut, 254

Obama, Barack, 424: re-election, 396

Occupy movement, 428–29

Occupy Wall Street, 428

October Crisis, 194–95

Official Languages Act, 204

Official Opposition, 402, 418

offshoring, 390

oil, 76–77, 98, 100, 145, 151, 162, 220–22, 306–8, 390; exploitation of, 393; Middle East, 396; oil sands, 395; production of, 394

Oka (Quebec), 77–78, 369–70

Oldman River Dam, 303, 370

Ondaatje, Michael, 174, 379

Ontario: 1943 provincial election, 7; 1991 Rae budget, 294; affirmative action,

377; anti-discrimination legislation, 12; and Charlottetown Agreement, 350; discrimination, 12; eastern region, 10; economy, 89–90; employment, 90–91; "Golden Horseshoe" region, 10, 49; hospital insurance program, 22; northern region, 10, 89; regulation of childcare, 68; "social contract," 295, 384; social welfare, 91–93; support for constitutional repatriation, 328; welfare, 302

OPEC (Organization of Petroleum Exporting Countries), 145, 221

Operation Solidarity, 384

opting out, 188

Pakistan, 421

Paley report, 94

Parizeau, Jacques, 293, 334, 347, 351–52, 353, 354–55, 356

Parsons and Whittemore, 218, 219

Parti Action Democratique du Québec, 352

Parti Québécois: 1970 provincial election, 194; 1976 provincial election, 198–99; and 1980 sovereignty referendum, 200–3; 1981 provincial election, 328; 1994 provincial election, 351; 2011 election, 417;American investors and, 169; creation of, 192; election of new leader, 336–37; labour legislation, 332; language bill, 200–1; membership, 198, 335–36; neo-conservative agenda, 334–35, 338–39; progressive social legislation, 332–33; second term, 332–37; social democratic orientation, 200; and trade union movement, 339

patronage, 132–33

peace movement, 117–18

peak oil, 394

Pearkes, General George, 111, 112

Pearson, Lester, 31, 103, 115-16, 120–21, 129, 165, 166, 190, 208, 231

pensions, 19, 20–21, 22, 23, 62, 133, 185, 425

Permanent Joint Board on Defence, 24

Petro-Can, 130, 150, 311, 382

pharmaceutical firms, multi-national, 311

Philip, Marlene Nourbese, 379

poor houses, 62–63

postwar period, 430

potash, 100, 218

poverty: child, 300, 301–3; and education, 85; the elderly, 61–63, 300; fifties and early sixties, 9–10; immigrants,

50, 54–55, 195–96; impact of neo-conservatism, 299–303; Native people, 56–57, 100–1, 222; rates, 299; single-parent families, 228, 237, 301

Prince Edward Island: care for elderly, 62; fanning, 210–11; federal aid, 206–8, 212; industrial development, 208; tourism, 212–13; welfare, 302

Privy Council Order, 1003, 70–71, 75

Pro-Canada Network (later Action Canada Network), 315

Proclamation of 1763, 251, 372

profits, corporate, 289–90

Progressive Conservative party: Alberta, 220, 337; Manitoba, 216; name adopted, 16; Ontario, 294, 295–97; and social security, 16, 17. *See also* names of Progressive Conservative prime ministers, premiers, and party leaders

Project Democracy, 417

Protests, 429

provinces: and constitutional repatriation, 328, 329–31; and CPP, 134–35; and guaranteed annual income, 152; and medicare, 137-38; tax revenue sharing, 187-88; and universal social programs, 19–20 public ownership, 6-7

Public Service Alliance, 238, 267

Public Service Staff Relations Board, 267

Quebec, 5, 49, 408; 1966 provincial election, 189-90; 1970 provincial election, 193, 194; 1973 provincial election, 193; 1976 provincial election, 198–99; 1981 provincial election, 328; 1994 provincial election, 351; arts and culture, 343; baby bonus, 340–41; and Charlottetown Agreement, 350–51; compulsory schooling, 84–85; demographic changes, 181–82; discrimination, 10, 12, 341–42; economic backwardness, 84; economic consequences of sovereignty, 353-54; economic development, 184–85; education, 84–85, 182, 186-87; exodus of anglophones and allophones, 201–2; federalists, 178; francophone middle class, 184, 334–35; immigration, 49; intellectual movement, 87–89; labour reforms, 185; language policy, 192–93, 194, 201–2, 341; natalist policies, 339–41; nationalism, 74; northern region, 10; out-migration, 84; poverty, 195–96; public sector workers, 197–98, 333, 335, 338;

secularization, 74, 84–89, 176–77, 181–84, 186; separation of sex roles, 66; social democratic outlook, 337–38; sovereignty movement, 178–79, 348–56; "special status," 191; universities, 21; women, 86, 181–82, 339–40; women's movement, 182–84, 339, 340. *See also* Catholic church
Quebec Farm Wives' Circle, 183
Quebec Federation of Labour, 270, 355
Quebec Pension Plan, 185, 188
Quebec Provincial Police, 426
Quiet Revolution, 75, 176

racism, 10–13, 47–50, 56–58, 214, 245, 341–42, 374–79
Rae, Bob, 294–95, 384
Rafferty-Alameda dam, 303
Ralliement National, 189
Rassemblement pour l'indepéndence nationale, 189
rattrapage, 176–84
RCMP, 33–34, 36, 37, 154, 189, 194, 407
Reagan, Ronald, 283, 310, 311, 321
recession, 286, 290, 308, 398, 414
"Red Book," 304, 324
Referendum: 1980 sovereignty, 202–3; 1995 sovereignty, 352–53; Charlottetown, 350
Reform Party, 291, 375, 399, 402, 408
Regent Park, 43–44
Regina Manifesto, 5
rent controls, 41, 42, 43
Report on Social Security for Canada, 16
residential schools, 57, 59, 243–45
Retail Wholesale and Department Store Union (RWDSU), 72–73
Ringma, Bob, 379–80
Romanow, Roy, 299, 400
Royal Commission on Bilingualism and Biculturalism, 10, 204
Royal Commission on Canada's Economic Prospects, 132
Royal Commission on the Economic Union and Development Prospects for Canada. *See* Macdonald Commission
Royal Commission on National Development in the Arts, 171
Royal Commission on the Status of Women, 182–84, 231, 232–35
Royal Commission on Taxation, 142–43
Royal Proclamation of 1763, 251
Russia, 389
Ryan, Claude, 202, 327, 336

Sabia, Laura, 231, 236
Sai'kuz First Nation, 396
Saskatchewan, 21, 394; 1944 provincial election, 7; anti-discrimation legislation, 12; economy, 100; forestry development, 218; hospital closings, 299; hospital insurance program, 22, 99; labour relations, 75, 267; medical insurance program, 99; northern region, 10; out-migration, 49; politics, 216; population decline, 219; potash industry, 218; public auto insurance, 99; social programs, 218–19; uranium mining, 219
Sauvé, Jeanne, 86
Schreyer, Ed, 217, 219, 271
Seafarers' International Union, 35
Security Panel, 33, 36
self-employed, 260–61
seniors, 61–63, 288, 300
sexuality, 127, 240–41. *See also* social mores
Sharp, Mitchell, 134, 138, 168
Skye Resources, 420
Smallwood, Joey, 75
Social Credit: Alberta party, 98, 99, 215–16, 220; B.C. party, 97–98, 224, 225; movement, 5; party, 17, 18. *See also* Creditistes
socialist feminists, 230–31
Socialist International, 200
social justice, 425
social mobility, 14, 63, 64
social mores, 46, 66–67, 127, 240–41
Social Movements, in the New Millenium, 424
social statistics, 429
South Africa, 118, 121–23, 155, 323
sovereignty-association, 178, 191–92, 202–3, 349
sovereignty movement, 178-79, 188–94, 348–56
Soviet Union, 30, 31, 32, 104–5, 106, 106–7, 120, 129, 321, 323
Sponsorship Program, 404, 406
"stagflation," 145, 147
Stanfield, Robert, 142, 145, 148
Stanford, Jim, 414
Stealth fighter jets, 415
strike, 419; Air Canada, 419; Canada Post, 419
Stronach, Belinda, 404
Stronach, Frank, 404
St. Laurent, Louis, 21–22, 31
strikes, 141–42, 262–63; wildcat, 263,

265, 267. *See also* labour, militancy; names of specific strikes
Suez Crisis, 120–21
suffragettes, 229
Supreme Court, 406
Syncrude, 220–21
takeover tax, 166–68

Taliban, 421, 423
tar sands, 395–97, 416. *See also* oil sands
tariffs, 24, 27, 162; protection, 426
taxes, 18, 19, 143, 166–67, 390
T. Eaton Company strike, 72–73
television, 171–72
Telus, 399
Temagami, 388
temporary foreign workers (TFWs), 397–98
Texpack strike, 270–71
Thatcher, Margaret, 283, 319, 328, 330
Theatre Passe Muraille, 175
Third Option, 170
Third World, 30, 119, 121, 155
"This Hour Has Seven Days," 171
Toronto, 7, 43–44, 89, 274, 275, 355, 377, 380
Toronto Star, 169
Toronto Welfare Council, 91, 92
tourism, 212–13
Touzel, Bessie, 92
Towers, Graham, 23
trade: with Britain, 26; military exports, 320; reciprocity, 26; twenty-first century, 419; with U.S., 24-26, 159–160
Trades and Labour Congress (TLC), 65, 73
Trade unions, 64–66; breakway movement, 170–71, 269–70; British Columbia movement, 96–97; bureaucratic leadership, 264–65; Catholic, 73, 74; changing leadership, 383–84; collective bargaining, 70, 71; and continentalism, 166–67; impact of neo-conservatism on, 381–83; independent Canadian, 383; "international," 167, 269, 270; leaders, 426 labour relations, 70–71; and nationalism, 269–71; and Ontario NDP, 384–85; public sector, 170, 266–69; Quebec movement, 87, 184, 339; and Rand formula, 71; right to strike, 267; and tripartism, 148, 268–69; and workplace democracy, 75–76. *See also* labour; names of specific unions
Tripartism, 148, 268–69

"Triple-E Senate,' 350
Trudeau, Pierre, 129, 151, 178, 190, 197, 344; background, 139–40; and *Cité Libre*, 87; and constitutional repatriation, 203–4, 327–32; economic policies, 145–52, 284–87; federalism of, 328; foreign policy, 154–56, 319–20, 321; and Meech Lake Accord, 345–46; and National Energy Program, 151, 222, 306–8; official bilingualism, 204–5; and separatism, 203–5; and social programs, 140, 287; Third Option policy, 170; and War Measures Act, 194–95; and women's issues, 235–36
Truman, Harry, 31, 94, 107
Turner, John, 15, 288, 313, 314
twenty-first century, 389; Canada and the World, 419

unemployment, 142, 145–46, 149, 212, 262, 286, 290-91, 292–93, 313, 378, 398
Unemployment Assistance Act, 91
Unemployment Assistance Plan, 138
unemployment insurance, 16, 95, 235
Union modiale de organisations féminines catholiques, 184
Union Nationale, 5, 80, 189, 190, 198, 202
Unions. *See* trade unions
United Automobile Workers, 269, 383
United Electrical, Radio, and Machine Workers of Canada (UE), 65–66
United Farm Women of Alberta, 229
United Nations, 103, 106–7, 120
United Nations Emergency Force (UNEF), 121
United Rubber Workers, 209
United States, 48; extraterritorial laws, 163–64; and foreign competition, 310; interest equalization tax, 167; neo-conservatism, 283; and overthrow of foreign governments, 30; ownership of Canadian industry, 159–61; "right to work" legislation, 316, 382; and Suez Crisis, 120; 10 percent surcharge on existing tariffs, 170; trade with, 24–26; view of Soviet Union, 30. *See also* Cold War
unionism, 425
United States, 389
United Steelworkers of America, 74, 266, 269
United Textile Workers, 270

Université de Montréal, 363
universities, 14, 21, 38, 186–87, 363
University Women's Club, 68
uranium mining, 219
US-Canada Free Trade Agreement (FTA),
    312–13, 314–15

Valleyfield strike, 74
Vancouver, 5, 380
Vancouver Housing Association, 42
Via Rail, 289, 382
Vietnam War, 107–10, 141, 142,
    153-54, 165, 390, 421
Voice of Women, 114, 118

Waffle group, 169, 265, 270
wages, 65, 71, 90; controls, 148, 268,
    269, 285; effect of free trade on,
    316–17; family, 65, 68, 90; immigrants,
    376; miners, 272; minorities, 10–12;
    "social," 18; women, 10–11, 14, 229
wall of shame, 426
Wall Street: occupation of, 427
War Measures Act, 194, 195
wartime housing, 42, 43
Watkins, Melville, 27, 168
Welfare Liberalism, 391
welfare state, 15–23
Wells, Clyde, 347, 348
West Bank, 424
Western Canada Concept, 307, 344
West Germany, 132, 146, 155
West, the, 96-101. *See also* names of
    specific provinces
Wet'suwet'en, 372–73
wheat, 100
Wilgress, Dana, 31, 32
Wilson, Madam Justice Bertha, 362
Wilson, Michael, 289
Winnipeg, 7; manufacturing, 216; north
    end, 54–55, 57, 101
Winnipeg Free Press, 132
Winter, Robert, 133, 138
women: birth control, 86, 181, 228,
    240–41; Caribbean, 47; in civil service,
    34; and constitutional repatriation,
    331; and double work day, 226–27;
    employment, 64, 67–68, 69, 90–91,
    92, 182, 228, 239, 262, 272, 275;
    employment opportunities, 228;
    immigrant, 376–77, 384; impact of
    neo-conservatism on, 361–62, 365–66;
    Italian-Canadian, 52; movement, 226,
    229–32, 361–67; Native, 234, 362,
    374–75; political preference of, 367;

racial discrimination against, 12; and
    secularization of Quebec society, 86;
    sexuality, 240–41; social mores, 46,
    240–41; suburban life, 45–47; trade
    union movement and, 64–66, 73,
    184, 238–39, 270, 383–84; traditional
    roles, 11, 45–46, 66–67, 85–86, 226,
    229; violence against, 362–63; visible
    minorities, 365; vote, 229; wages,
    10–11, 14, 229
work, workers. *See* employment; labour
World Peace Congress, 118
World Trade Organization, 425
World Trade Towers, 389
World War II, 3–4, 24, 391

Zaccardelli, Guiliano, 407